International Money and Foreign Exchange Markets: An Introduction

International Money and Foreign Exchange Markets: An Introduction

Julian Walmsley

JOHN WILEY & SONS

Chichester · New York · Brisbane · Toronto · Singapore

Copyright © 1996, Julian Walmsley
Published by John Wiley & Sons Ltd,
Baffins Lane, Chichester,
West Sussex PO19 1UD, England

National   01243 779777
International (+44) 1243 779777

Reprinted December 1996, August 1997

Notice

Datastream is a registered trade name, trademark and service mark of
Datastream International Limited.

All data and graphs contained in this publication and which have been obtained
from the information system of Datastream International Limited ("Datastream") are
proprietary and confidential and may not be reproduced, republished, redistributed
or resold without the written permission of Datastream.

Data in Datastream's information system have been compiled by Datastream in
good faith from sources believed to be reliable, but no representation or warranty
express or implied is made as to the accuracy, completeness or correctness of the
data. Neither Datastream nor such other party who may be the owner of any
information contained in the data accepts any liability whatsoever for any direct,
indirect or consequential loss arising from any use of the data or its contents. All
data obtained from Datastream's system and contained in this publication are for
the assistance of users but are not to be relied upon as authoritative or taken in
substitution for the exercise of judgement or financial skills by users.

Library of Congress Cataloging-in-Publication Data

Walmsley, Julian.
    International money and foreign exchange markets : an introduction
  / by Julian Walmsley.
        p.   cm.
    Includes bibliographical references and index.
    ISBN 0-471-95320-2 (pbk. : alk. paper)
    1. Foreign exchange market. 2. International finance. I. Title.
HG3881.W265   1996
332′.042—dc20   95–46214
                                                        CIP

British Library Cataloguing in Publication Data

A catalogue record for this book is available from the British Library

ISBN 0-471-95320-2

Typeset in 10/12pt Times by Acorn Bookwork, Salisbury, Wiltshire
Printed and bound in Great Britain by Bookcraft (Bath) Ltd
This book is printed on acid-free paper responsibly manufactured from sustainable forestation,
for which at least two trees are planted for each one used for paper production.

Contents

List of Abbreviations   **ix**

1 Money Markets   **1**
  1.1   Introduction   1
  1.2   The US Money Market   1
  1.3   Submarkets: Federal Funds, Repos, Treasury Bills, and
        Commercial Paper   4
  1.4   Open Market Operations   7
  1.5   Other Tools of Monetary Policy   9
  1.6   The United Kingdom   12
  1.7   Germany   14
  1.8   France   15
  1.9   Japan   16
  1.10 Other Markets   18
  1.11 The ECU Market   19

2 Euromarkets and Foreign Exchange   **21**
  2.1   The Eurodollar Market   21
  2.2   Workings of the Euromarket   24
  2.3   Legal Nature of a Eurodollar   26
  2.4   The Foreign Exchange Market   27

3 The Euromarkets and Global Financial Integration   **34**
  3.1   History of the Foreign Exchange and Eurodollar Markets   34
  3.2   The Role of Offshore Centres   40
  3.3   The Market's Role in Recycling Payments Imbalances   41
  3.4   Growth of International Securitization   42

4 Links between Foreign Exchange and Money Markets   **44**
  4.1   Handling an Exposure: Foreign Exchange or Money Market   44
  4.2   Arbitrage   46
  4.3   Foreign Exchange Intervention   47
  4.4   Foreign Exchange Intervention and the Money Supply   50

5 The International Financial System   **57**
  5.1   International Monetary Fund   58

5.2   Bank for International Settlements   61
5.3   Arab Monetary Fund   63
5.4   Central Bank Swap Network   64
5.5   The Federal Reserve   65
5.6   Bank of England   67
5.7   Deutsche Bundesbank   68
5.8   Banque de France   69
5.9   Bank of Japan   71
5.10 Swiss National Bank   72
5.11 Artificial Currency Units   72
5.12 Special Drawing Rights   73
5.13 European Currency Unit   74
5.14 Green Currencies   76
5.15 Calculation of Trade-weighted Exchange Rates (Effective
      Exchange Rates)   77

6 **European Monetary Union**   **79**
6.1   Political Bankground   79
6.2   Benefits of Monetary Union   81
6.3   Costs of Monetary Union   82
6.4   Economic and Monetary Union and the Theory of
      Optimum Currency Areas   83
6.5   EMU as a Discipline   85
6.6   Technical Operation of the EMS   86
6.7   The European Monetary Institute   90
6.8   Maastricht and Convergence   91
6.9   Problems of Transition to Monetary Union   92

7 **Efficient Markets—or Chaos?**   **95**
7.1   Overview   95
      7.1.1 Efficient Markets   95
      7.1.2 Rational Expectations   97
7.2   Chaos Theory   98
      7.2.1 A Simple Nonlinear Model   99
      7.2.2 Phase Diagrams   100
      7.2.3 Strange Attractors   100
      7.2.4 The Logistic Equation   103
      7.2.5 Fractals   103
      7.2.6 Fractal Dimension   104
7.3   Neural Networks   106

8 **Forecasting the Markets**   **109**
8.1   Monetary Policy   109
8.2   Monetary Policy in Action   111
8.3   Transmission of Monetary Policy   114
8.4   Fiscal Policy   116
8.5   Balance of Payments   118

8.6	Balance of Payments Policy	121
8.7	Technical Methods of Forecasting: Charting	123
8.8	Candle Charts	125
8.9	Channels	128
8.10	Filter Rule	128
8.11	Cross-over Method	129
8.12	Momentum Models and Oscillators	131
8.13	Why Bother? The Case for Passive Management	132
8.14	Efficient Frontiers	134
8.15	Constructing a Frontier	135
8.16	Applying the Mean-Variance Optimization Approach	136
9	**Money and Foreign Exchange Mechanics**	**138**
9.1	Conventions	138
9.2	Types of Deposit	140
9.3	Yield Curve	141
9.4	Mismatch (GAP)	142
9.5	Forward Forward Rates	143
9.6	The Concept of Present Value	145
9.7	Yield Curves, Forward Rates, Zero-Coupon Curves, and Medium-term Forward Forward Rates	147
9.8	Forward Rate Agreements	148
9.9	Negative Interest Rates	150
9.10	Money Market Securities: Certificates of Deposit	150
9.11	Discount Securities	151
9.12	Foreign Exchange Calculations: Spot	152
9.13	Selling and Buying Rates	153
9.14	Cross-Rates	154
9.15	Forward Foreign Exchange Calculations: Premium and Discount	155
9.16	Hedging Costs	156
9.17	Foreign Exchange Calculations: Swaps	157
9.18	Finding Interest Rates from Swap Rates	160
9.19	Finding swap Rates from Interest Rates	162
10	**Financial Futures**	**163**
10.1	The Markets	163
10.2	Organization of the Markets	169
10.3	Eurodollar Futures	172
10.4	Treasury Bill Futures	174
10.5	Foreign Exchange Futures	175
10.6	Hedging	176
10.7	Futures and FRAs	177
10.8	Open Interest and Volume	179
11	**Interest Rate and Currency Swaps**	**180**
11.1	Origins of the Swap Market	180
11.2	Interest Rate Swaps	184

11.3   Pricing an Interest Rate Swap   186
11.4   What Determines Swap Spreads?   186
11.5   Asset Swaps   188
11.6   Currency Swaps   189
11.7   The IBM/World Bank Swap   190
11.8   Swap Credit Risk   191
11.9   Swaps Valuation and Accounting   192
11.10 Commodity Swaps   192

12 Options   **194**
12.1   The Role of Options   194
12.2   The Options Market   195
12.3   Basics of an Option Contract   198
12.4   Option Pay-off Diagrams   199
12.5   Combined Positions   202
12.6   Option Valuation   204
12.7   Volatility   207
12.8   The Binomial Model   208
12.9   Normal Distribution   212
12.10 Black–Scholes Formula   213
12.11 Measures of Option Risk and Sensitivity   216
12.12 American vs European Options   221
12.13 Currency Options   221
12.14 Garman-Kohlhagen Currency Options Model   223
12.15 Caps and Floors   224

13 Risk Issues   **229**
13.1   General Control of Risk   229
13.2   Name Risk   230
13.3   Liquidity Risk   230
13.4   Credit Risk   231
13.5   Control Risks   232
13.6   Market Risk   233
13.7   Volatility and Basis Risk   234
13.8   Control by the Authorities   235
13.9   Value at Risk   236
13.10 The European Capital Adequacy Directive   238
13.11 Interest Rate Position Risk   240
13.12 Counterparty Risk   243
13.13 Diversification and Risk Reduction   245
13.14 Netting Systems   245
13.15 Real-time Gross Settlement   246
       Appendix A   247
       Appendix B   255

Further Reading   **257**

Index   **258**

List of Abbreviations

AMEX	American Stock Exchange
AMF	Arab Monetary Fund
APT	Automated Pit Trading
BA	bankers' acceptance
BBA	British Bankers' Associaton
BECS	Bearer Eurodollar Collateralized Securities
BIS	Bank for International Settlements
BM&F	Brasiliero Mercado Futuros
BOBL	Bundesobligation
BEF	Belgian franc
CA	contract amount
CBOE	Chicago Board Options Exchange
CBOT	Chicago Board of Trade
CCFF	compensatory and Contingency Financing Facility
CD	certificate of deposit
CHIPS	Clearinghouse Interbank Payment Systems
CME	Chicago Mercantile Exchange
CP	commercial paper
CR	contract rate
DAX	Deutsche Aktin Index
DTB	Deutsche Termin Börse
ECHO	Exchange Clearing House Organization
ECP	Eurocommercial paper
EMH	efficient market hypothesis
EMI	European Monetary Institute
EMCF	European Monetary Cooperation Fund
EMS	European Monetary System
EMU	European Monetary Union
ERM	Exchange Rate Mechanism
ESAF	Enhanced Structural Adjustment Facility
ESF	Exchange Stabilization Fund
EU	European Union
EUA	European Unit of Account
EUCLID	Euroclear Interface device
FASB	Financial Accounting Standards Board
FOMC	Federal Open Market Committee
FRA	forward rate agreemnt
FRCD	floating rate certificate of deposit
FRN	floating rate note
GAB	general arrangements to borrow
GEMM	gilt-edged market-maker
GNMA	Government National Mortgage Association
IBF	International Banking Facilities
IBRD	International Bank for Reconstruction and Development
IMF	International Monetary Fund
IRR	internal rate of return
ISMA	International Securities Market Association
JGB	Japanese government bond
JOM	Japan Offshore Market
LDC	less developed country

LIBOR	London interbank offered rate	SAF	Structural Adjustment Facility
LICOM	London international commodity terms	S&L	savings & loan
		SDA	Special Drawing Account
		SDR	Special Drawing Right
LIFFE	London International Financial Futures Exchange	SEC	Securities and Exchange Commission
MATIF	Marché à terme des Instruments Financiers	SEMB	Stock Exchange money broker
MBS	mortgage-backed securities	SFTE	Société Financière pour les Télécommunications et l'Electronique
MCA	monetary compensatory amount		
MEFF	Mercato Espanol de Futuros Financieros	SIMEX	Singapore International Monetary Exchange
MTFA	Medium-Term Financial Assistance	SMI	Swiss Market Index
		SNB	Swiss National Bank
NYMEX	New York Mercantile Exchange	SOFFEX	Swiss Options and Financial Futures Exchange
OAT	Obligation Assimilable du Trésor	SR	settlement rate
		SRA	sale and repurchase agreement
OM	Optionsmaklarna		
OTC	over the counter	STMS	short-term monetary support
PIBOR	Paris interbank offered rate	TED	Treasury-Eurodollar
PRA	purchase and resale agreement	TIFFE	Tokyo International Financial Futures Exchangee
PSL2	private sector liquidity 2	VSTF	very short-term financing facility
RSI	relative strength index		

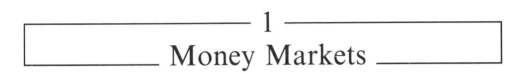

1
Money Markets

1.1 INTRODUCTION

There is much needless mystery about both domestic and foreign financial markets. But, in fact, the basics are very simple and can be summed up in two common phrases: "Time is money" and "Nothing ventured nothing gained." In jargon, the time value of money and the risk/reward balance. Net present value calculations, forward interest rate differentials, cross-currency interest rate swaps, binomial option trees—these notions sound complex, but can be boiled down to simple concepts. I have tried to avoid needless jargon when writing this book, but sometimes, for the sake of brevity, it helps to use the "correct" technical term.

1.2 THE US MONEY MARKET

Let us begin with domestic markets, in which a nation's money is traded internally. In this first discussion, we will concentrate on the United States, because the US dollar is the world's most widely traded currency. But later in the chapter, we will bring in relevant comparisons to the UK and other countries where practices differ.

To begin with, why is the money market important? A slightly high-flown answer might be that this is the market which calculates the price of time. The rate of interest set in the money market determines the time value of money, at least in the short term, and this in turn influences spending, saving and investment decisions throughout the economy. These in turn have an important influence on the level of economic activity and also on the degree of inflationary pressure in an economy. Hence the central bank, which is the guardian of the currency and which has the duty of fighting inflation, will always be closely concerned with trends in the money market. In the USA, as elsewhere, it intervenes constantly to steer the level of interest rates in what it believes to be the appropriate direction. Thus, understanding the money market is a key to understanding the operation of monetary policy.

Our next step is to define what the money market is. A simple definition might be the market in which short-term funds are lent and borrowed. In reality, the money markets in each country tend to have a slightly different structure, involving different groups of participants and different instruments. Also, other markets overlap: for example, existing bond issues, as they approach maturity, are often used for short-term investments as a substitute for money-market instruments.

The definition of short term, also, proves slippery when examined. Most money-market instruments have maturities of less than one year, and certainly by far the bulk of money-market trading activity is for less than a year. On the other hand, Eurocurrency deposits are traded for maturities as long as five years. Asset swaps—bonds coupled with an interest rate swap so that the combination appears to the investor like a money-market instrument—typically have initial maturities of four to five years.

For most practical purposes a reasonable working definition of the money-market is: that market in which funds are borrowed and lent for less than one year using instruments such as bank deposits, repurchase contracts, Treasury bills or their local equivalent, commercial paper, bills of exchange (bankers acceptances) and certificates of deposit. However, we should recognize that there may be times when this definition is unduly restrictive and a wider definition may be applicable.

Let us now put the money market in its wider context, by looking at a flow of funds table for the United States (Table 1.1). This includes the flow of funds through the whole of the US financial system, not just the money-market, because the statistics do not separate the money market alone. Here we can see that private households during this quarter were borrowers to the tune of $269.7 billion but lent marginally more and so were on balance almost in equilibrium. Nonfinancial businesses were, as a sector, net borrowers, raising $152.5 billion and on-lending $35.3. Mortgage pools were in balance because their activity consists of buying loans that are financed with matching bonds. In this quarter the main net supplier of credit to the system was the private financial sector.

An important channel through which money-market flows are influenced is the foreign exchange market. This is less apparent in the United States, where the domestic money market is large in relation to the international market. But it can clearly be seen in the case of a country such as Switzerland. Inflows from abroad

Table 1.1 Direct and Indirect Sources of Funds to US Credit Markets, 1994/Q2

	Borrowing	Lending
US Government and FRB	122.9	−8.2
Foreign	−4.6	54.2
State and local government	−53.8	−70.5
Households	269.7	270.2
Nonfinancial business	152.5	35.3
Mortgage pools	88.6	88.6
Private financial firms	241.3	447
	816.6	816.6

Source: Adapted from *Federal Reserve Bulletin*, January, 1995.

into a small country can swamp the domestic money market with excess liquidity. During the late 1970s, for example, foreign demand for Swiss francs was very strong because of the weakness of the dollar. The flow of money into Swiss francs pushed the Euro-Swiss franc deposit market into negative interest rates. One had to pay a Swiss bank for the privilege of placing money with it. Subsequently, the Swiss government imposed a 10% per quarter term commission tax, so that foreigners were receiving minus 40% p.a. on Swiss franc deposits. Yet because the Swiss franc appreciated by 50% during one year, such an operation was still worthwhile.

Conversely, if a currency is seen to be under pressure, funds will flow out of that currency into others that are perceived to be stronger. The authorities will often then raise interest rates to defend the currency. A classic example was the ERM crisis of 1992, when overnight French franc rates hit 150% p.a. In those currencies where exchange controls are in place, the effects can be spectacular. It was reported[1] that overnight Irish punt rates reached 48,000% during the crisis. During an earlier crisis, the author was present on one occasion when Euro-French francs were lent at 5000%.

A related effect arises when the central bank intervenes to support, or alternatively to lower, the value of its currency. If the central bank intervenes in support of its currency, it buys the domestic currency, and sells foreign exchange. Thus, the amount of domestic currency in circulation declines, which tends to push up domestic interest rates. Conversely, if it intervenes to lower the value of its currency, it supplies domestic currency to the market. Thus the supply of domestic currency in the hands of the market rises, tending to push down interest rates. Because the US dollar is the most widely traded currency in the world (largely because professional foreign exchange traders usually trade the US dollar as one side of their deal), the net effect on the US money markets is that there is a constant swirl of funds into and out of the Federal Reserve (Fed) and the dollar holdings of other central banks, resulting from the ebb and flow of foreign exchange transactions. (The technical effects of these transactions are analyzed in more detail in Chapter 4.)

Another set of effects on money-market rates can be the flow into and out of the accounts of other non-money-market participants. The Treasury has already been mentioned, but another example could be a major stock market issue. Again, this is less relevant to the United States. But in the UK, for example, large privatization issues such as British Telecom have led to significant money market effects on occasion. Investors subscribing to the issue wrote cheques that then flowed though the clearing system to produce substantial short-term distortions in the marketplace. Likewise, there are seasonal effects on the money-market for holidays such as Christmas, or Easter, when the public generally withdraws cash in the form of notes and coin from the banking system. This tends to drain funds from the money market, which then return after the holiday. Also, any interruption in the process of clearing cheques for settlement can have money-market effects. If the planes flying from Chicago to New York with cheques for clearance are held up by fog, then the amount of float in the US financial system briefly expands, until the cheques are finally cleared. This tends to push interest rates down, in the absence of countervailing intervention by the Fed.

1.3 SUBMARKETS: FEDERAL FUNDS, REPOS, TREASURY BILLS, AND COMMERCIAL PAPER

So far, we have talked of the money market as if it were a single entity. This is not, in fact, the case. In most countries, the money market consists of a series of interconnected pools of money.

The most important submarket in the United States is that for Federal funds (Fed funds). By definition, Federal funds are balances held at the Federal Reserve. A bank that holds such a balance can settle a claim on it by another bank through same day transfer. It can arrange for that other bank's account to be credited with immediately available funds. Therefore, Fed funds play a central role in the US money market. They are the final means by which banks settle debits and credits with each other.

Another reason why Fed funds are so important is that banks are required by the Fed to hold a minimum average balance in their reserve account at the Fed over the week—Wednesday to Wednesday. The minimum average balance is based on the total deposits held by the bank or depositary institution during the current settlement week.

Most Fed fund transactions are for overnight maturity. This is done mainly because the amount of excess funds that a given lending bank holds varies daily in an unpredictable way. Transactions for longer periods also occur, although more rarely. Fed funds traded for periods other than overnight are referred to as term Fed funds.

Because of their central role in the financial system, the interest rate payable on Fed funds is a key indicator of US financial policy. The market watches the Fed funds rate like a hawk, to see if there has been any change in official policy. A change in the Fed funds rate is generally regarded as signaling a change in Fed monetary policy (unless it is caused by technical factors beyond the Fed's control, such as unpredicted changes in bank reserves).

Another important submarket is the market for repurchases (or "repos). This arises primarily from the financing requirements of bank and nonbank dealers who are trading in government bonds, certificates of deposit, and bankers' acceptances. Much of their trading activity is financed by borrowing. The borrowings are secured by the assets purchased with the borrowed funds. The normal technique is as follows. The dealer finds a corporation, money-market fund or other investor who has funds to invest overnight. The dealer sells them, say, $5 million of securities for roughly $5 million, which is paid in Fed funds to his or her bank by the investor's bank against delivery of the securities sold. At the same time, the dealer agrees to repurchase these securities the next day at a slightly higher price. Thus, the buyer of the securities is in effect making the dealer a one-day loan secured by the obligations sold to him. The difference between the purchase and sales prices on the repo transaction is the interest the investor earns on his loan. Alternatively, the purchase and sale prices in a repo transaction may be identical; in that case, the dealer pays the investor some explicit rate of interest.

The Fed is heavily involved in the repo market as part of its open market operations (discussed in the next section). The Fed buys Treasury bonds from the key market-makers—called primary dealers. The purchase is coupled with a commitment

by the primary dealer to buy the bonds back tomorrow at a slightly higher price—
the difference being effectively overnight interest. The repo is in fact a loan by the
Fed to the primary dealer, but it is a loan secured on the Treasury bond. Thus it is
considered a very safe investment, and the Fed arranges repos not only for itself but
also for its "customers," which are other central banks whose currency reserves are
held in US dollars. (The use of repos as a tool of monetary policy is discussed in the
next section.)

The Fed and the primary dealers are by no means the only players in the market,
which is huge. Municipalities, banks, insurance companies, and companies all use the
market for short-term liquid investments. Current estimates of the aggregate size of
the US repo market are in excess of $2 trillion (million million).[2] The Fed funds and
repo markets are essentially for overnight money: longer-term Fed funds (term Feds)
and repos (term repos) do exist but are much less common. For longer periods,
investors use other instruments.

The primary market consists of trading in newly issued instruments, and the secondary market consists of trading in the instruments after the primary market is
ended. The distinction is more important in the bond market, but applies also to
short-term money markets. The volume of secondary market activity varies from
instrument to instrument. An indication of the level of trading in different instruments is given in Table 1.2. It is confined to statistics reported by primary dealers,
but gives a good overall indication of activity in the market as a whole.

As Table 1.2 shows, Treasury bills—bills issued by the US government with a
maturity of up to one year—are a very important part of the market. The very high
quality of this "paper" (the general term for any tradeable debt) means that the
market for it is very large and liquid: that is, large amounts can be traded in a single
trade without difficulty. Blocks of $50–100 million in a single transaction present no

Table 1.2 US Primary Dealers: Transactions (US$ m. Daily Average)

	1991	1992	1993
Immediate transactions			
US Treasury bills	34,161	44,360	43,022
US Treasury bonds	102,288	114,550	124,445
Federal agencies debt	5 804	6 756	11,114
Federal agencies MBS	15,419	19,085	23,777
Future and forward transactions			
US Treasury bills	3 369	3 132	2 310
US Treasury bonds	12,547	15,108	18,021
Federal agencies debt	191	203	182
Federal agencies MBS	13,104	16,427	25,461
Option transactions			
US Treasury bills	0	0	0
US Treasury bonds	4 552	4 123	4 828
Federal agencies debt	0	0	0
Federal agencies MBS	449	327	792

Average of Oct./Nov./Dec. for each year.
Source: *Federal Reserve Bulletin*, various issues.

problem. There is also a market for trading Treasury bills before they are actually issued—the when issued or WI market. The WI market trades bills once they have been auctioned but before settlement takes place. It is also possible to trade bills before the auction, sometimes called the WIWI market.

Treasury bonds and notes are issued for longer maturities—up to 30 years—and although they are closely linked to the money markets are really a separate market. Federal agency securities are bonds issued by agencies of the US government such as the Government National Mortgage Association (GNMA) and again are part of the wider capital markets rather than the money markets as such.

A key part of the US money market, which has grown enormously during the 1980s (partly because of the troubles of the American banking system) is commercial paper (CP). The CP market is now larger than that for Treasury bills in terms of outstanding volumes though, as Table 1.2 shows, trading in the secondary market is negligible (the paper is normally held to maturity). Commercial paper consists of a short-term promissory note, usually maturing in 30 days or less, issued by a large company. Because of its short maturity, CP is widely regarded as a very safe invest-ment for short-term funds. Commercial paper is generally issued on demand in response to the needs of investors, on a continuous basis. To sell CP, a company must agree to be "rated" by a rating agency such as Moody's or Standard & Poor's who assess the credit quality and rate the CP accordingly.

This is an expensive and time-consuming process and for smaller sums of money many firms use the bankers' acceptance (BA) market. A firm shipping goods, say from the United States to Germany, might agree to take payment in the form of a bill drawn on the German importer. Once it has received the bill, it takes it to its US banker who, in exchange for a commission, agrees to "accept" it: if the German firm does not pay, the bank will. Once the bill has been accepted by the bank, it becomes a high-quality instrument (assuming the bank's name is of high quality). The bill can be sold to investors. The BA is now backed by the German firm, the accepting bank, and in the last resort by the goods being shipped. Thus it is a very safe investment and BA's usually trade at interest rates below CP, which is backed only by the promise to pay of the issuing firm. However, the BA market has stagnated while the CP market has grown.

An important short-term market is that for certificates of deposit (CDs). Certifi-cates of deposit are issued by banks and are available in maturities ranging from as short as 14 days to as long as 5 or even 7 years. The bulk of the market is usually under 6 months in maturity. In recent years, in the domestic US market, the CD has been overtaken by the deposit note, an instrument resembling a corporate bond with a minimum maturity of 18 months (thus avoiding a reserve requirement) and usually paying a fixed rate. (If the bank wants to pay a floating rate, it will issue a floating rate deposit note, or it will do an interest rate swap. It commits itself to paying a floating rate to someone in exchange for that party paying it a fixed rate. The fixed rate income on the swap covers the fixed cost on the deposit note, leaving the bank paying a floating rate on the combined package of note and swap. Swaps are explained in detail in Chapter 11.) A related instrument to the deposit note is the medium-term note, which is really an extension of the CP market to longer maturities.

While so far we have talked about trading assets and liabilities that will appear somewhere on a bank's or company's balance sheet, there is an important set of influences on trading in the money market that comes from trading in off-balance-sheet instruments, commonly known as derivatives (discussed in Chapters 10–12). As well as interest rate swaps, these include financial futures and interest rate options. Trading in the financial futures markets, in particular, is of such volume that sometimes it will drive the "cash" or on-balance sheet markets. US trading in money-market-related futures is concentrated on the Chicago Mercantile Exchange, which has contracts based on Treasury bills and on Eurodollar deposits.

The interest rate swap market (see Chapter 11) is closely linked both with the cash money market and the futures markets. When the range of Eurodollar futures contracts was extended out to three years from two years, the Exchange stated that this was partly at the request of the interest-rate-swap trading community. The market for forward rate agreements (see Chapter 9) is less important in the United States than in London but is another area linking the money markets to off-balance-sheet trading.

1.4 OPEN MARKET OPERATIONS

For many reasons, central banks sometimes want to adjust either the supply of money or the level of interest rates. They have available to them a number of techniques to do this. Different methods are used in different markets. We will begin by describing those commonly used in the United States, and then talk about some of the techniques used elsewhere.

The simplest operation consists of a purchase of Treasury bills or government bonds from the banks. The banks' holdings of cash will rise, while their holdings of securities will fall. There is a permanent injection of reserves into the financial system. This might not always be desirable: the system may be only temporarily short of reserves. In that case, the Fed will use repurchase agreements (repos); and, in fact, repos are the main operating tool of the Fed.

The Fed intervenes on the "open market" to supply funds to the market, or to drain funds from the market. The primary technique by which this is done is the daily "go-around," at around 11.30 a.m. The Fed decides whether it wants to supply funds to the market or to drain funds from the market. Having made this decision, it will do either a repurchase operation, in order to supply funds, or a reverse purchase, in order to drain.

The effect of these operations will depend on the reserve ratios on banks' liabilities. To see why this is so, consider an imaginary country called Home. Its currency is Home currency (HC). Assume that there is only one bank, call it Barclays, and the only other means of payment is cash. Suppose the government prints HC 1 million and pays it to Home Machine Company in exchange for machinery. HMC pays the cash into Barclays, whose balance sheet now becomes (assuming nil balances to start with):

	Liabilities	Assets
HMC deposit	HC 1 million	HC 1 million cash

Suppose that the government requires Barclays to hold 10% of its assets in cash. Then Barclays can lend the other HC 900, to General Motors Company (GM). They proceed to mark a credit limit for GM who draw this down, by taking out cash. Barclays' balance sheet is now:

Liabilities	Assets
HMC deposit HC 1 million	HC 100, cash
	HC 900, GM loan

GM hands the cash over to Shell in exchange for oil. Shell deposits the cash with Barclays:

Liabilities	Assets
HMC deposit HC 1 million	HC 1 million cash
Shell deposit HC 0.9 million	HC 0.9 million GM loan

Barclays can now lend 90% of HC 0.9 million, that is, HC 0.81 million to ICI. They will pay the money to Ford, who will deposit it with Barclays, and so on.

In fact, the system keeps expanding until the original HC 1 million in cash represents 10% of Barclays' total assets, which will total HC 10 million. At this point, Barclays will not lend any more money. If it did, the ratio of cash to assets would fall below 10%, and the government would object. In other words, the 10% ratio means that an extra HC 1 million of cash can support deposits of HC 10 million. The deposits created are 10 times the original cash. If the reserve ratio is R, the multiplier is $1/R$. In our example, $1/0.1$ equals 10.

It follows that if we lower the reserve ratio to 5%, the multiplier rises from 10 to 20. The smaller the reserve ratio, the bigger the multiplier. Equally, a draining of reserves from the system will force it to shrink by the same ratio. So, open market operations can be a very powerful force by which the central bank can influence the level of the banking system's activity.

There is one important point about reserve requirements: their effect on banking systems depends critically on how they are structured. The US system has traditionally been to require 3% reserves to be held on transaction and time deposits (though this was relaxed in 1990 to help the US banking system recover from its difficulties), which must be placed in an account with the Fed that pays no interest. This factor led to the growth of the huge Eurodollar market, which is exempt from reserve requirements.

An example may show the effects. Consider a bank with the alternative of taking a deposit in the United States or of booking the deposit through its London branch in the form of a Eurodollar deposit (see Chapter 2). Suppose that the domestic deposit attracts a 3% reserve requirement; suppose that the reserves must be held in the form of noninterest-bearing deposits at the Fed.

Assume the deposit is for $100. If the deposit is taken in the United States, only $97 is available for on-lending: the other $3 must be placed with the Fed, earning no interest. Suppose the bank pays 10% on the deposit. The $97 must be lent out at

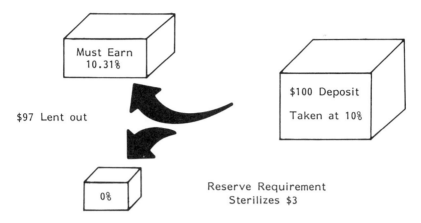

Figure 1.1 Impact of reserve requirements

10/0.97 = 10.31% to cover the extra costs of the sterilized reserve balance of $3: that is, if rates are at 10%, the reserves cost 0.31%. A bank that does not have to hold reserves can afford to bid, say, 1/8% better and lend 1/8% cheaper, beating the US bank by 0.25%, and still have a profit margin of 0.06%. (See Figure 1.1.) This fact has spawned a multitrillion dollar market, the Euromarket, discussed in Chapter 2.

Open market operations, then, depend on reserve requirements for their effectiveness. But the interaction of reserve ratios and other controls can sometimes have unpredictable results because of the complexity and sophistication of today's financial markets. Accordingly, open market operations are not always as simple, nor as powerful, as the pure theoretical model would indicate.

Still, they do give a flexible and effective way of steering the markets. Each day, the Fed enters the market to undertake these daily smoothing operations. Hence the common cry in the dealing room at 11.30 a.m. New York time or thereabouts, "Fed does repo" or "Fed does reverses." (A further refinement is that the Fed can operate in the market on behalf of its customers, or on behalf of the Fed System. The two are referred to as customer repo and system repo, respectively. The latter is thought to have policy significance whereas the former, which is an operation by the Fed on behalf of other central banks who want to invest their reserves in dollars, is not thought to have policy significance.)

1.5 OTHER TOOLS OF MONETARY POLICY

If the Fed wants to make a more permanent adjustment to the level of bank reserves, it can do so in one of two ways. It can offer to buy or sell Treasury bonds on an outright basis, rather than on a repurchase or resale basis where the operation will unwind; alternatively, and much more rarely, it may move to alter the level of its reserve requirements. The former operation is more common: usually, the Fed will signal to the market that it is willing to buy certain amounts of government bonds. (Often referred to in the market as a "coupon pass," meaning that the Fed is making a pass though the market to buy coupon-bearing government bonds. A similar operation on Treasury bills is referred to as a bills pass.)

Altering reserve requirements is a much more fundamental step, which the Fed takes only rarely. In 1980, for example, the Fed raised its "marginal reserve requirements" by 3%. Rises in bank borrowing were penalized by this method, which was an attempt to squeeze the domestic credit growth rate. Since that time, changes in reserve requirements have rarely been used as a element of monetary policy, since they have widespread and often distorting effects. In December 1990, however, the Fed released its reserve requirements on time deposits to encourage banks to lend.

Another means by which the Fed supplies funds to the banking system is through its so-called discount window. This is the facility whereby the Fed, as lender of last resort, stands ready to supply funds to any member of the Federal Reserve System who needs them. A bank which is experiencing temporary financing difficulties, such as Continental Illinois in May 1984, may apply to the Fed for short-term assistance. Technically, the assistance is provided by a loan from the Fed against security of instruments that are eligible for rediscount at the Fed, such as eligible BAs, Treasury bills, or other high-quality short-term monetary instruments. The discount window does not, however, form part of the normal routine monetary policy tools. This is because it is kept only for specific crisis requirements, and to a lesser extent for specific seasonal needs of certain agricultural or other banks.

In general, the senior management of most US banks display a universal reluctance to borrow from the Fed unless they absolutely have to. They prefer to keep a good record with the Fed, so that in time of trouble there will be no question of their being able to get help if they need it. Since borrowing at the discount window is a very cheap source of finance, there is some temptation to use the discount window as a cheap borrowing method: but the Fed regulates this strictly, and is not slow to indicate its displeasure if it feels that a bank is abusing the facility. In consequence, senior management are very wary of using the facility unless there is a very good reason.

Other central banks use similar tools to the Fed, but the balance of usage varies. (See the discussion of monetary policy in certain countries that follows.) The repurchase agreement is widely used, but nowhere is it so widely used as in the United States. Most central banks use repos on a longer-term basis than daily. For example, since 1985 the Deutsche Bundesbank has regularly used repo agreements for 28- or 29-day periods. More recently it has also used two-week repos on a regular basis. In 1993 the Bundesbank concluded 52 sets of open market repo operations, of which 19 were "double-decker (i.e. consisting of two tranches of differing maturities).

Such agreements are normally offered weekly; two-month repurchase tenders are sometimes executed also. To supplement repos, the Bundesbank also uses other open market techniques. One is the sale of very short-term Treasury bills at rates between its discount rate and the repo rate in order to prevent an excessive fall in day-to-day rates.

The Bank of Canada continuously uses repos with money-market jobbers (the group of investment dealers authorized to enter into such agreements); they are called purchase and resale agreements (PRAs). If the Bank wishes to offset unwarranted short-term pressure on rates, it may initiate special PRAs in amounts and at rates of its choosing. If the Bank wants to drain funds, it will do sale and repurchase agreements (SRAs).

The Bank of England, by contrast, tends not to use repurchases that often. It normally manages the money market by short-term operations though specialist firms (the "discount houses" and certain others) trading in short-term money-market instruments to whom it will lend funds overnight, or to whom it sells Treasury bills to drain funds. Repurchase agreements are occasionally used on a medium-term basis for a month or more, if there is expected to be a unusual seasonal drain on liquidity, or some other special situation. In April 1994 the Bank moved to put these arrangements on a more permanent footing, introducing a master agreement to govern its repo transactions with the market.[3] In the 1994 Budget, however, it was announced that during 1995 the Bank would move towards an "open gilt repo market—previously bond-borrowing privileges were restricted to gilt-edged market-makers—and it seems likely that repos will become a more important part of its policy armoury from 1996 onwards.

Open market operations in Japan tend to focus on purchases of bills by the Bank of Japan: for example on January 28, 1991, the Bank of Japan injected JPY 1.10 trillion into the market by buying a total of JPY 1.1 trillion of bills and recalling JPY 90 billion of outstanding loans. It offered to buy JPY 150 billion in Treasury bills under repurchase agreements starting January 30 and maturing March 6.

Activity in the Australian money market is similar to that in the UK, with a group called "authorized dealers" who function as the main conduit for the Reserve Bank of Australia's money-market operations. The authorized dealers absorb the ebbs and flows of the banking system's fund needs. In turn they deal with the Reserve Bank in Treasury securities, or borrow money directly under the "lender of last resort" facility. The Reserve Bank of Australia and the Reserve Bank of New Zealand also use repurchases fairly regularly.

Repurchase agreements are widely used elsewhere, for example in Italy, Sweden, and Spain. In Italy the Banca d'Italia introduced foreign currency repos at the end of 1992 (following the ERM crisis) to mitigate a temporary scarcity of securities and rebuild official reserves.

Repurchase agreements depend for their functioning on banks holding sufficient quantities of eligible bonds. In Norway, for example, changes in reserve requirements in late 1986 meant that banks shed their holdings of Treasury bills and were compelled to hold certain volumes of government paper. As a result, repurchase agreements have not been used as an instrument as liquidity control since 1987, their place being taken by fixed-rate loans by the central bank (F-loans), which are distributed by auction. In addition, liquidity is also managed by central bank purchases of CDs, foreign exchange swaps, and overnight loans (D-loans).

Foreign exchange swaps are an important means of liquidity management in a number of countries, particularly those where the foreign exchange market is large in relation to domestic money markets, such as Switzerland and the Netherlands, but also in larger countries such as Germany. During 1993, for example, the Bundesbank conducted seven foreign exchange swap transactions equivalent to DEM 40 billion with domestic banks in order to manage domestic liquidity. The mechanics are laid out in Chapter 4.

Following this brief survey of central bank monetary policy tools, we turn to a short comparative survey of major money markets outside the United States.

1.6 THE UNITED KINGDOM

The chief money-market assets in the UK can be divided into the "prime liquidity" category which covers eligible bills of exchange (£21 billion as of mid-1994), Treasury bills (£6.5 billion), Corporation bills (very small outstandings—similar to Treasury bills but issued by municipalities), and secured bank deposits (£8 billion) with one of the eight discount houses, eight Stock Exchange money brokers (SEMBs) or 20 Gilt-Edged market-makers (GEMMs). The second category includes bank CDs (£55 billion outstanding), building society CDs (£10 billion outstanding), and wholesale deposits by nonbanks (£70 billion) and by banks (£80 billion). In addition there is a sterling CP market, although the secondary market is extremely limited.

Traditionally, the core of the UK money market was the "discount market." This consisted of a group of discount houses, who were the only counterparties with whom the Bank of England would deal in its domestic money-market operations. The Bank would buy and sell Treasury bills, eligible bills issued by UK local authorities, and eligible bank bills with these firms. In turn, the discount houses absorbed the ebb and flow of commercial banks' funding needs. If they had surplus funds, the commercial banks could use them to increase their deposits with discount houses (usually "at call"), or buy money-market instruments from them. Likewise, where banks were short of funds, they could recall their call money loans from the discount houses, or sell paper to the houses. In exchange for their standing continuously ready to make markets in these instruments, the discount houses benefited from the privilege of access to the Bank as "lender of last resort."

After the "Big Bang" that reformed the London financial markets in 1986, the Bank of England in 1988 widened the discount market to include those commercial banks or other financial institutions who wished to take part in the market. Institutions accepted by the Bank as dealing counterparties were offered a direct dealing relationship with the Bank in eligible bills (bills eligible for rediscount at the Bank); borrowing facilities at the Bank; and facilities to borrow and lend gilt-edged stock. In exchange for these privileges, these firms undertook to offer callable deposit facilities and bids and offers of eligible bills to the market continuously, as well as to take part in the weekly underwriting of the Treasury bill tender.

The primary instruments of the Bank of England's money-market policy are open market operations, conducted on a daily basis. The normal daily procedure is for the Bank to make a forecast of the money market's overall position, that is, whether it expects to have to inject or drain reserves—about 9.45 a.m. The estimate is published on the news screens, for example, Reuters Monitor page RTCA—with a breakdown of the main contributory factors. If a very large shortage is forecast, the Bank may call for an early round of offers of eligible bills from the discount market and other institutions with which the Bank has agreed dealing facilities.

By noon, the Bank is generally in a position to know the maximum probable shortage. A fresh forecast is made, and published if it is significantly different. At this point, the Bank will—if there is a shortage—normally call for offers of eligible bills. If there is a surplus, then, unless it is very large, the Bank waits until around 2.00 p.m. when it will invite bids for Treasury bills of appropriate maturities. If, after this, a discount house finds itself short of funds, it may borrow on a secured basis at 2.45 p.m. direct from the Bank. Interbank dealing continues until 3.00 p.m. when the Town Clearing begins. If the Bank forces the discount houses to borrow for a minimum period rather than overnight, it is usually taken as a signal that it wishes to keep interest rates high.

The Bank has recently moved to make permanent the temporary gilt "repo" facility. This was arranged following the huge official foreign exchange intervention-induced shortages that were created at the time of sterling's exit from the ERM in September 1992. The gilt repo facility is now available to all banks and building societies, the discount houses and the GEMMs, and conducted every two weeks.

In the November 1994 Budget it was announced that the UK would move to follow practice in the US and France, among other countries, by operating an "open" market for gilt repurchases ("repos"). Previously the Bank of England had restricted access to this market. Only GEMMs were allowed to borrow gilts through the repo market. Thus only GEMMS could sell gilts short. Unfortunately this meant that banks running sterling interest rate swap positions which they wished to hedge by selling gilts short could not do so (unless they were GEMMs). Restricting the repo market also restricted the Bank's flexibility in money-market operations.

These changes should help to smooth the excessive volatility of money-market rates which arose from two regulatory changes: first, in April 1985 it was announced that eligible banks no longer had an obligation to maintain deposits with the discount market; second, in 1988 the implementation of the Basle Concordat allowed foreign banks in the UK to maintain their liquidity in foreign currency. As a result, the clearing banks were able to build up large portfolios of commercial bills and effectively control the money market by using discount houses as booking offices, rather than true intermediaries.

There is a wide range of other participants in the London money market, particularly from overseas. The domestic sterling money market is in fact considerably smaller than the main money market in London, the Euromarket (see Chapter 2); thus the domestic market is very closely integrated into the international ebbs and flows of the currency markets, particularly since the abolition of exchange controls in 1979, and even more so since the entry of the UK into the exchange rate mechanism of the European Monetary System (see Chapter 6). The level of UK interest rates is therefore very strongly influenced by the strength or otherwise of sterling.

Finally, another important set of influences on the domestic UK money market is the market for derivatives such as financial futures (see Chapter 10). Financial futures contracts based on three-month sterling deposits were introduced in London in 1982; outside the ambit of the money market but closely linked there is also significant trading in a futures contract based on British government bonds (gilt-edged bonds). The growth of these derivative instruments has contributed to a relative decline in the secondary market in CDs, especially those longer than three months. While the total outstanding has continued to increase with inflation, they have lost their role as the principal traded vehicle in the London money market.

1.7 GERMANY

In relation to the size of the economy, the German money market is fairly small and underdeveloped. It is predominantly an interbank market in which financial institutions trade central bank balances in a manner similar to the US Fed funds market. Three main types of money-market paper are available in Germany: Treasury bills (*Schatzwechsel*), discount Treasury paper (*Unverzinsliche Schatzanweisungen—U-Schätze*), and prime acceptances. It was only in 1986 that the Bundesbank permitted the issuance of CDs by banks. The Bundesbank is directly involved as a counterparty in the vast majority of money-market transactions and thus directly controls rates on money-market paper.

The Bundesbank has kept tight control of the domestic financial situation, even after the 1985–86 liberalization: it made CDs and short-term bank bonds subject to reserve requirements, and objected to the introduction of money-market mutual funds. Another inhibiting factor in the market was the turnover tax that stifled the growth in short-term money-market paper: this was lifted at the start of 1991, along with the legal restrictions inhibiting the development of CP.

The major instruments in the German market include:

1. Treasury bills and Treasury discount paper (*Unverzinsliche Schatzanweisungen*, commonly referred to as *U-Schätze*); total outstandings at mid-1994 were about DEM 25 billion.
2. Securities repurchase agreements ("repos). These instruments are the chief source of short-term borrowing by German banks, totaling about DEM 131 billion at mid-1994. However, they are conducted very largely with the Bundesbank. Repos conducted with commercial customers are treated as bank deposits and attract a minimum reserve requirement.
3. Short-term Treasury bills (usually a three-day maturity). These are used by the Bundesbank to drain liquidity. Amounts in issue vary rapidly.
4. Commercial paper. Since liberalization in 1991 a small market for deutsche mark CP has emerged, with about DEM 12 billion outstanding in mid-1994.
5. Floating rate notes (FRNs). While strictly a class of bond, the FRN is often bought by investors as a substitute for money-market assets. About DEM 180 billion of FRNs were estimated to be in circulation in the German financial markets in mid-1994.

It should be noted that the market for CDs plays no significant role in Germany. Also it should be added that the Bundesbank actively discourages the development of money-market instruments which might weaken its control—thus for example in 1994 it withdrew "Bulis (short-term paper issued by the Bundesbank to soak up excess money-market liquidity), depriving money-market investors of a suitable investment instrument.

The market for derivatives is also relatively limited, in that the Deutsche Terminbörse (the German financial futures market, DTB) only began operations in 1990. The relatively conservative nature of German financial circles, and the late start of the DTB, have held up development. However, most major banks are now active in derivative markets on a substantial scale and the market is now developing rapidly.

The Bundesbank, which is legally independent of the German government and not obliged to follow the latter's instructions, has a very wide range of policy instruments with which to control domestic money markets. These include minimum reserve requirements, rediscount quotas, Lombard credit, open market securities operations and foreign exchange transactions. In addition, it can fix the level of discount and Lombard rates and repurchase rates.

Minimum reserve requirements are set by the Bundesbank on a long-term basis, that is, they are rarely changed. However, in March 1993, and again in March 1994, the Bundesbank cut required reserves with the twin purposes of streamlining the minimum reserve system and reducing the competitive disadvantage of the domestic financial system *vis-à-vis* the Euromarkets.[4] Rediscount quotas are also set on a long-term basis; they are the quotas fixing the amount of paper which the Bundesbank will rediscount for each individual bank. The global total is changed only rarely and usually in line with the perceived growth of the financial system as a whole; however, changes in the rediscount quota can sometimes signal a fundamental change in the Bundesbank's monetary policy.

Lombard credit represents loans granted by the Bundesbank to banks to overcome temporary liquidity squeezes. Technically it takes the form of a loan against specified collateral, as distinct from the rediscount facility where the Bundesbank buys paper from the bank. From time to time, the Bundesbank shuts off supply of credit via the Lombard facility or restricts access; it has also provided "special" Lombard credit (notably in 1973–74 and 1981) where loans are made on restrictive terms. Normally, however, Lombard credit is not limited as to quantity, unlike the discount facility, which is restricted by rediscount quotas.

The Lombard rate tends to represent an effective ceiling for day-to-day rates, and the discount rate an effective floor, but as we said earlier in the chapter, repurchase agreements form the Bundesbank's main technique for day-to-day liquidity management. They are in two forms: fixed rate (volume tender) and variable rate. In a fixed rate tender, the Bundesbank fixes the interest rate in advance and invites bids from banks. The banks say how much paper they want to sell to the Bundesbank at that rate.

The variable rate form comes in two types. Under the first approach, the Bundesbank specified a minimum acceptable rate. Banks then bid the amounts they would sell at various rates. The highest rate bids were filled first, down to a cut-off point: the "allotment rate." Successful bids were filled, not at the rate bid, but at the weighted average rate of accepted bids. This gave banks an incentive to bid aggressively, knowing they would not actually pay the rate they bid but something lower. Thus in 1988 the Bundesbank amended its approach: no minimum rate is set, and banks have actually to pay the rate they bid. The fixed-rate tender is sometimes used by the Bundesbank in fixed amounts at times of interest rate uncertainty to calm the market's nerves. Otherwise the variable rate tender is more common.

1.8 FRANCE

The money market in France was for many years heavily circumscribed by official controls. However, French financial markets generally were greatly liberalized during the 1980s and the money market has benefited in parallel. For example, until

January 1986, only financial institutions and a small number of nonfinancial firms were allowed to hold French Treasury bills and notes in current accounts; there was a secondary market but its role was very limited. In January 1986, the authorities began issuing Treasury bills available to all investors; there is a weekly auction along the lines of the US system.

Similarly, a group of firms resembling the US primary dealer system (Spécialistes en Valeurs du Trésor) was set up to help ensure liquidity in the market for government securities including Treasury bills. Settlements are through the SATURNE system, set up in September 1988. Secondary market liquidity in Treasury bills is still limited but improving. There is good liquidity in the "when-issued" market (marché de calé) whose trading volume is quite large relative to the normal secondary Treasury bill market—about 30% or so.

The volume of other money-market paper, including CDs and CP, has begun to grow rapidly (totaling FRF 700 billion compared with just under FRF 500 billion of Treasury bills) but the secondary market remains small. The CD market remains oriented to tailor-made issuance intended to be held to maturity rather than traded, and most money-market paper is very short—under 90 days to maturity at the time of issue, which does not encourage secondary market trading. However, in 1993 a law defining the status of repos (pension livrée) was passed, and the growth of the French repo market has been very substantial.

One area in which Paris has developed rapidly is in financial futures, where the MATIF (Marché à terme des Instruments Financiers) has proved a strong challenger to London International Financial Futures Exchange (LIFFE) as the centre for European derivatives trading. In the first nine months of 1990, 1,497,463 contracts were traded on PIBOR (Paris interbank offered rate) for a total nominal value of FRF 7500 billion or about US$1500 billion, compared with a nominal value of about $6000 billion for its sterling counterpart and $26,000 billion for the Chicago Eurodollar contract.

In line with the liberalization of the markets, the tools of monetary policy in France have moved to a pattern more similar to that of the United States and UK. Where previously there was a fairly all-embracing system of credit controls that limited the growth of bank lending there is now a much more flexible set of policy tools which are primarily market-oriented. The Banque de France's open market operations on a day-to-day basis are reflected in its intervention rate, which determines the conditions on which it supplies funds to the market.

Official repurchase operations (opérations sur appel d'offre) are the primary money-market intervention tool. On Mondays and Thursdays the Banque de France invites primary dealers to submit bids specifying the amount of securities and the interest rate at which they are willing to trade. A second tool is pensions de 5 à 10 jours, a lending facility available to credit institutions at their discretion; when in need of funds, they can borrow at the official facility rate which is generally 75–100 basis points above the intervention rate.

1.9 JAPAN

The Japanese money market was historically divided into two parts—the interbank market, restricted to financial institutions and in which the Bank of Japan executed

Table 1.3 Key Japanese Financial Changes

1979	First yen CD issue permitted
	First *gen-saki* (bond sale/repurchase) with foreigners allowed
1980	Exchange control liberalized. Previously, what was not permitted was forbidden; now, what is not forbidden is permitted
1981	Banks allowed to sell government bonds
1985	Euro-yen FRNs, zero coupons, dual currency and warrant bonds permitted. Creation of yen-denominated BA market. Money-market rate certificates permitted. Government bond futures market starts
1986	Any borrower rated A or better permitted to tap Euro-yen bond market. Foreign commercial banks permitted to make Euro-yen issues. Japanese banks allowed to deal in yen-denominated foreign loans. Stock Exchange commissions reduced. Japan Offshore Market opened
1987	Yen CP permitted
1988	Bank of Japan shortens term of its bill operations to allow more flexibility; BoJ allows more flexibility in interbank rates particularly for unsecured call money
1989	JGB bond borrowing market permitted
	TIFFE futures on Euro-yen created
1991	"Window guidance" (individually negotiated quarterly ceilings on commercial bank lending growth) abolished

policy, and the open market. The call money market, the US dollar call market, and the bills market were part of the restricted interbank market, while others were open. The financial system in Japan has been steadily liberalized over the last 15 years and is now almost wholly free of institutional rigidities although this does not mean it is independent of official guidance. Table 1.3 shows some key developments in recent years.

The results of this liberalization have been that the bond repurchase market (*gen-saki*), which was originally almost the only unregulated short-term money market, has stagnated while other markets have developed, notably the call money market that has now been greatly liberalized, and the market for CDs. The unsecured overnight call money rate is now a key money-market rate. Traditionally, the call money market was divided into morning loans, which are settled before the bill clearing at 1.00 p.m., afternoon loans which are settled by the close of business, and unconditional call money which are settled the next day and are automatically extended from day to day unless called back. Until 1985, all unconditional call money was collateralized but in that year, unsecured call money was permitted; unsecured call money is normally overnight rather than extendable as in the case of secured unconditional call money.

Although liberalization took time to come through, the development of the Japan Offshore Market (JOM) since 1986 was an important safety valve for the banks since it let them do much of the interbank trading that was restricted onshore; by August

1988, the JOM's volume had hit $395 billion (compared with $160 billion in New York's International Banking Facilities, created in 1981). The JOM has proved a reliable source of interbank funds when the domestic bill market dried up and thus gave the banks valuable flexibility.

1.10 OTHER MARKETS

The domestic Swiss money market is fairly restricted, despite the international importance of the Swiss franc in the foreign exchanges and the Euromarket. Historically the domestic market has been almost exclusively a primary interbank market, because of a transfer tax which effectively eliminated secondary market trading activity. The effect of this was substantially reduced in 1994, but still active participants in the domestic market number fewer than 40 banking institutions. The main operating instrument is foreign exchange swaps, conducted daily at 9.00 a.m. Apart from swaps, the Swiss National Bank introduced repos in September 1992 to manage the short-term liquidity needs of the banking system.

The Canadian money market is heavily influenced by its southern neighbour. There is a very large volume of "northbound" and "southbound" foreign exchange swaps (see Chapters 2 and 4 for influences on the market); but there are a number of institutional differences. One interesting feature of Canadian policy is the use of an official interest rate swap program (see Chapter 11) by the government of Canada: by end-1989, CAD 3 billion were outstanding, for terms ranging up to just under 15 years. The 1989 Bank of Canada Annual Report stated that "If the average spread between three-month bankers' acceptances and three-month Treasury bills continues to be just under 15 basis points . . . the government's effective floating rate cost of funds on its swaps will translate into about 72 basis points below the three-month Treasury bill rate." The main day-to-day technique for influencing market liquidity and interest rates is the adjustment of deposit balances that the chartered banks and other direct clearing members of the Canadian Payments Association hold at the Bank of Canada. The most common operation is the purchase and resale agreement (PRA). Occasionally special purchase and resale agreements (SPRAs) will be used to inject larger or longer-term amounts of liquidity, or Sale and Repurchase Agreements (SRAs) may be used to drain funds. During 1992, for example, the Bank of Canada offered SRAs on 26 days, PRAs on 111 days, and SPRAs on 24 days.

The Australian money market was considerably liberalized during the 1980s, as Table 1.4 shows. Though the liberalization ended in tears insofar as it encouraged the rapid growth of bank lending to entrepreneurs whose firms later proved to be unsound, it also laid the groundwork for a much more flexible and innovative financial system. Current money-market arrangements are that at 9.30 a.m. each morning the Reserve Bank of Australia (RBA) announces the liquidity position of the banking system and announces its dealing intentions for the day. The RBA deals in collateralized short-dated repurchase agreements with banks and official discount companies; it also operates from time to time in foreign exchange swaps to smooth the operation of the domestic money market.

Table 1.4 Australian Money Market Liberalization

1979	Sydney Futures Exchange begins trading interest rate futures
1980	Bank deposit interest rate ceilings lifted
1981	Restrictions on overseas investment liberalized
1982	Quantitative controls on bank lending lifted
1983	Foreign banks allowed to set up in Australia
	Exchange controls abolished
1984	Reserve Bank introduces repos on government securities with authorized dealers; a group of "reporting bond dealers" is created
1985	Restrictions on foreign investment in Australian securities lifted
	Formation of new trading banks permitted

1.11   THE ECU MARKET

Finally, a new transnational money market is developing: that for the ECU. At present, there is still a relative shortage of money-market instruments, but the currency's importance as the centrepiece of the European Monetary System (EMS) is such that the market will almost certainly develop further despite the setbacks of 1992/93. It is presently a pure Eurocurrency market (see Chapter 2) but it is included for comparison with other markets. The ECU itself is explained in detail in Chapter 6. Briefly, it is (at present) an artificial currency used in a number of European countries.

There is no domestic ECU market, since there is no country whose currency is the ECU. (As a result, there is no ECU lender of last resort, which at the moment poses potential problems to the ECU clearing system, which is described in Chapter 6.) There are two distinct ECUs, the private ECU and the official ECU. Their composition is identical; but private ECUs can be created by bundling together the appropriate amounts of currencies into a basket. Official ECUs can only be held by official institutions and are created as a result of swap arrangements between the European Monetary Cooperation Fund and members of the EMS. Private and official ECUs are not exchangeable (or fungible, to use the technical term).

Private ECUs are traded like any other currency. Major commercial banks provide continuous quotes for the ECU (normally they have computer systems for calculating the ECU value from the currency rates held in their systems) and these can be seen on the appropriate Reuters/Telerate screens. An ECU clearing system is operated by the Bank for International Settlements (BIS) in conjunction with the ECU Banking Association that has about 85 members worldwide; all ECU transactions are cleared daily through this system. Primarily because of political problems, there is no "lender of last resort" for the private ECU clearing system, and until there is further progress at the political level the development of the private ECU seems likely to be relatively slow: after rapid growth in the 1980s, the crisis of 1992/93 slowed activity considerably.

Until recently, one problem with trading private ECUs was that the Deutsche Bundesbank defined the ECU as an index-linked unit of account, the use of which is banned in Germany (because of past inflationary excesses in the 1930s): the restrictions were revoked only in June 1987.

The EEC Commission is keen to develop the role of the ECU as a step towards creating a single monetary area in Europe; the first steps, therefore, have been for an exchange market, a clearing system, and bank deposits in the currency to develop. The next step has been to encourage the development of other financial markets. The first moves here were in the bond market: in April 1981, the Société Financière pour les Télécommunications et l'Electronique (SFTE) issued the first ECU bond. ECU bonds have now been issued by a wide range of issuers, and in particular the governments of Italy, France and the UK have substantial bond issues outstanding that are quite liquid.

At the money-market end of the yield curve, there are good deposit markets but other instruments are a bit limited. The British government issues one-, three- and six-months discount Treasury bills.

The main method of payment for and delivery of the bills is through the Euroclear and Cedel clearance systems. Other governments also issue "domestic" ECU paper: the Italian government's CTE issues, usually for five years, have played an important part in generating ECU swaps (see Chapter 11) because of tax considerations. It has also issued shorter term Treasury bills (BTE). The Spanish and French governments have ECU bonds outstanding: the French (OATs) are fairly liquid. In March 1991, the UK government issued a 10-year ECU Eurobond for ECU 2.5 billion which provided a liquid benchmark for the market but as mentioned the general market activity fell sharply as a result of the crisis of 1992/93.

NOTES

1. *Risk* magazine, October 1992
2. Throughout this book, 1 billion means 1000 million and 1 trillion means 1 million million.
3. See "Money market operations since September 1992, *Bank of England Quarterly Bulletin*, February 1995, p. 12.
4. On this and the current framework of German monetary policy, see "Money market management by the Deutsche Bundesbank," *Deutsche Bundesbank Monthly Report*, May 1994.

2
Euromarkets and Foreign Exchange

In Chapter 1, we discussed domestic money markets. In this chapter, we begin by discussing the Euromarket, which is a transnational money market, and then move on to its twin sister, the foreign exchange market.

2.1 THE EURODOLLAR MARKET

What is a Eurodollar? Briefly, it is a dollar deposit that is traded outside the United States. If Citibank in London places a US dollar deposit with Barclays Bank in London, that is a Eurodollar deposit transaction. The key feature of this operation is that it is not subject to Fed requirements. The Fed imposed a reserve requirement of 3% on deposits taken by US banks until 1990. Therefore, for every US$100 deposited, only $97 could be lent out. If interest rates were 10%, the bank had to charge 10.31% to cover the cost of reserves. Therefore, a bank taking a US dollar deposit in London could profitably undercut its domestic US competitor.

This efficiency in reserve costs is the key reason for the spectacular growth of the Eurodollar deposit market, from its origins in the late 1950s to the multitrillion dollar market that it is today. Legend has it that the origin of the markets, however, was not because of this reserve efficiency, but political. During the 1950s, the Soviet Union was concerned that if it were to invest the dollars that it was earning from the sale of its oil abroad in the United States, it would face the possibility of a political decision to freeze its assets, since the cold war was then at its height. (Jacques Attali, in his biography of Siegmund Warburg, states that the origins of the market go back even earlier, to the time of the Korean War, when the Chinese placed some deposits with Banque Commerciale pour l'Europe du Nord in the name of the National Bank of Hungary.)

In 1958, pressure on sterling led the Bank of England to ask British merchant banks to switch the financing of their third-country trade into US dollars. British merchant bank demand met Russian supply, and the Eurodollar market was born. During the late 1960s, market growth was fueled by restrictions placed on it by

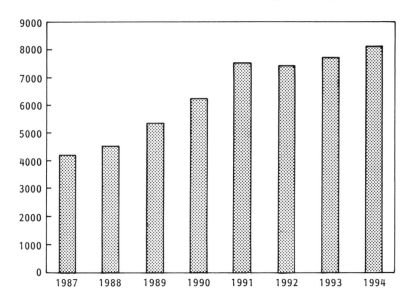

Figure 2.1 Total Euromarket Assets ($bn). Source: BIS

President Johnson, as the Vietnam War placed a strain on the American balance of payment. A further kick to growth was given in the 1970s by the two successive oil crises, when Eurobanks were deeply involved in attempts to recycle the OPEC dollar earnings in the form of loans to less developed countries. Figure 2.1 shows the growth of the market over the years. It highlights how in recent years the pre-eminence of London has been challenged by the development of the International Banking Facilities in New York and the Japan Offshore Market in Tokyo.

Figure 2.2 shows the distribution of lending activity between the main centres— the UK remains market leader at $894 billion at end-1989 but is challenged by Japan's $830 billion and the $570 billion booked out of the United States. The high Luxembourg figure is misleading in that it should really be largely added to the German figure. Bundesbank reserve requirements (unlike those of the Bank of England) take no account of currency, so German Euromarket activity is largely conducted from Luxembourg.

A significant difference between Euromarket and many domestic deposit markets is that the Euromarket is almost exclusively concerned with matched deposit dealing. That is, each deposit (liability) of an international bank will tend to be matched by an asset (usually a deposit in another bank) of the same currency and of similar maturity. Deliberate mismatches might be incurred with a view to making a profit, but the book of each bank as a whole will be matched within certain periods. Hence loans are typically made for a specified period and funded by a deposit of a similar period. This is very different from a domestic market, where typically large amounts of lending are done on the basis of a prime (or base) rate, with these loans being funded day to day in the domestic overnight or short-date money-market, or from retail deposits.

The key role of the Euromarket is twofold:

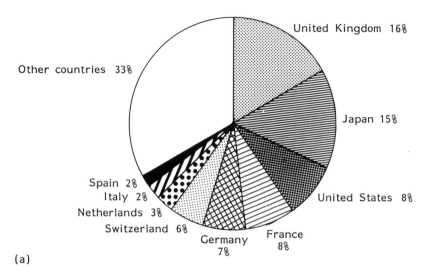

(a)

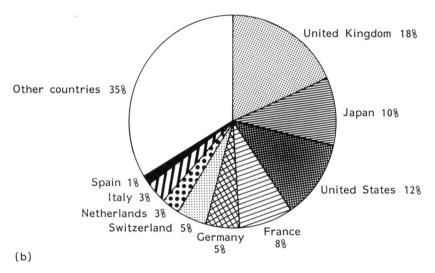

(b)

Figure 2.2 (a) Cross-border Assets. March 1994; (b) Cross-border Liabilities. March 1994. Source: BIS.

1. It provides the links between different forward foreign exchange markets. As we shall see later, forward foreign exchange rates are determined by relative interest differentials between Eurocurrency deposits in the currency in question.
2. It provides a mechanism for the taking and placing of deposits free of domestic central bank restrictions. This has spawned a free-wheeling and innovative international banking system, where commercial banking and investment banking have blurred to produce a range of instruments from Eurocommercial paper (ECP), though syndicated Eurocredits to Eurobonds and even Euroequities.

The market is incidentally linked with a range of other markets, including those for interest rate and currency swaps, interest rate and currency options, financial futures, gold, and oil and other commodities. These will be discussed later.

2.2 WORKINGS OF THE EUROMARKET

By its nature a professional, wholesale market, the Euromarket has a wide range of participants. The objectives of the Euromarket dealing operation vary from bank to bank. There are at least four central objectives usually present: to fund the bank's Eurocurrency loan book; to provide a service to depositing customers; to make profits from deliberate position taking; and to ensure that the bank is seen in the marketplace both as a taker and placer of funds, so that its name is kept in the market and is favorably received when it is necessary to raise funds.

By far the bulk of Euromarket's activity is concentrated in the time deposit market, that is, in the taking and placing of unsecured funds, without involving the purchase or sale of paper. This is different from the US practice, where apart from the Fed funds market, banks typically lend to each other by means of repurchase agreements (involving, at least nominally, the repurchase and sale of securities), or by means of CDs. The great bulk of the market is of rather short maturity. A proportion of these deposits is on call, meaning they can be withdrawn without prior notice. However, since payment is normally effected by means of transfers in the currency's home country, the minimum practical period for delivery is usually two days. This payment convention corresponds to that in foreign exchange—two working days are required for delivery.

The great bulk of Eurodollar deposits carry a fixed maturity. Normally, the deposit will be effective two business days after the contract is put into effect, and mature, for example, 90 days later. However, it is also possible to deal "value today" or "value tomorrow," depending on time zone considerations.

Although the majority of Eurodollar deposits are time deposits, CDs also play an important part. By far the largest market is for Eurodollar negotiable CDs. These are large-denomination time-deposit liabilities evidenced by a written instrument or certificate. The certificate specifies the amount of the deposit, the maturity date, the rate of interest, and the terms under which the interest is calculated. While banks are free to offer their customers CDs in any size, the minimum denomination acceptable for secondary market trading—the buying and selling of previously issued securities—is usually $1 million. The term to maturity of newly issued CDs is based on negotiation between the bank and its customer, the individual instrument usually being tailored to fit the liquidity requirements of the purchaser.

The operation of the market is best understood by following a deal. For instance, a major company such as Exxon has a placement of $10 million in funds to make for three months. Exxon calls various banks and, on the basis of the rates quoted, decides to place the deposit with Barclays Bank. An interest rate of 10% is agreed on the 3-month deal (which actually runs for 91 days). The interest due is calculated as US$252,777.78:

$$\frac{10}{100} \times \frac{91}{360} \times \$10m. = \$252,777.78$$

An acceptance ticket is written, containing the basic facts of the deal. This ticket is then passed to the backup operation of the bank, and a separate confirmation is sent out by the backup office. On the start date of the deposit—the spot date—a CHIPS payment (i.e. a payment through the New York clearing house) is made by Exxon from, for example, Citibank to Barclays, for account of Barclays' Nassau branch. The funds never leave New York. They are simply credited to Barclays Nassau on a memorandum account at Barclays in New York. At maturity, Exxon decides that it wishes to roll the deposit over for a further three months. On checking the rates, it finds that Bank of America now pays a better rate than Barclays. Accordingly it instructs Barclays to transfer the principal and interest due by means of a CHIPS payment to Bank of America's London branch. Again the funds do not leave New York.

Eurocommercial paper existed in its own right before the arrival of underwritten facilities. Attempts were made in the early 1970s to develop an ECP market, which reached a peak of $2 billion in outstandings. But in 1974 the lifting of US balance of payments controls cut back the market, as US companies found it cheaper to fund domestically. The growth of today's market began with underwritten facilities.

Underwritten note facilities began in 1978, with an issue by the New Zealand Shipping Corporation. But the instrument attracted little attention. None were issued in 1979, and the 1978 to 1983 period saw only a total of 86 facilities representing US$9 billion. The market began then to change its shape: during the early development of the market, the emphasis was mainly on underwritten facilities, but then the emphasis began to shift towards issues that are not underwritten—true ECP.

The market has now clearly matured into an important short-term source of funds for global borrowers. The early rapid pace of growth dropped back in view of the higher level shorter-term rates in 1989–90 and growing liberalization of domestic CP markets in countries such as Japan but has picked up again recently (see Table 2.1).

Table 2.1 Euronotes (in Billions of US Dollars) by Type and Currency

Type/Currency	Amounts Outstanding			
	Dec. 1992	Dec. 1993	March 1994	June 1994
Total Euronotes	186.8	255.8	290	330.9
Eurocommercial paper	78.7	79.6	81.2	86.4
Banks	21.9	18.2	18.4	35.9
Nonbanks	56.9	61.4	62.8	50.5
US dollar	65.3	65.4	65.2	68.3
Other currencies	13.5	14.3	16	18.1
Other short-term Euronotes	37	29.6	30.8	28
Medium-term notes	71	146.6	177.9	216.5
Banks	25.2	48.4	60.3	82.8
Nonbanks	45.9	98.2	117.6	133.6
US dollar	32.8	63.9	74.6	86.1
Other currencies	38.3	82.7	103.3	130.4

Source: BIS.

2.3 LEGAL NATURE OF A EURODOLLAR

Finally, it is worth touching on an issue which was raised very briefly earlier. What is a Eurodollar? We said then that it was a dollar deposit which was traded outside the United States. Similarly, a Euro-deutsche mark is a deutsche mark deposit traded outside Germany. We do need to make some refinements to this definition, however. For example, the International Banking Facilities (IBF) in New York, and the Japan Offshore Market, allow effectively for the onshore trading of Eurocurrencies. A dollar deposit placed with an IBF in New York is in fact a Eurodollar, because it is not subject to Fed requirements. By contrast, a dollar deposit placed in Frankfurt is not a Eurodollar, because it is actually subject to Bundesbank reserve requirements. (Bundesbank reserve requirements do not operate by currency, but by the location of the deposit-taker.) Thus, the key determining factor in whether a currency deposit is or is not a Eurocurrency deposit is whether or not it is exempt from domestic reserve requirements.

A related issue is the legal question of jurisdiction over the Euromarkets. Traditionally, the Bank of England had jurisdiction over the Eurodollar and Eurocurrency activities of banks operating in London. It is the supervisory authority for these banks, and in London its word is (for practical purposes) law. But the taking and placing of US dollar deposits (as was explained earlier) actually involve a transfer of US dollar funds across the books of a bank in New York. Thus, Eurodollar activities are potentially subject to interference from the US authorities.

This apparently arcane point has been a vital issue on several occasions, notably the freeze imposed on Iranian assets by President Carter, the dispute between the United States and Libya which led to the freezing of Libyan assets, and the multinational freeze on Iraqi assets after the Iraqi invasion of Kuwait. The whole issue hinges on the sensitive question of the extraterritorial application of one country's law (in this case, the United States) in the domestic activity of another country (in this case, the UK). There have been a number of legal cases that have shed light on related issues. They go back to the seizure of assets in Palestine in 1947 (*Barclays Bank* v *Arab Bank*), the case against Chase Manhattan regarding deposits in its branch in Saigon, the numerous cases arising out of the Iranian freeze, and perhaps most interesting the case of *Libyan Arab Foreign Bank* v. *Bankers Trust*.

The salient facts of the case are as follows. In 1973 Libyan Arab Foreign Bank (LAFB) opened a call deposit account at the London branch of Bankers Trust (BT). In 1980 a demand current account was opened in New York to give easy access to the New York clearing system (CHIPS). It was agreed between LAFB and BT that all day-to-day payments would be made out of LAFB's New York account but that any balance of over US$500,000 would be transferred to its London account in tranches of US$100,000, or the other way if there was a shortfall in New York, at the end of each day. It was further agreed that the New York account would be checked twice daily at 2.00 p.m. and 4.30 p.m. to check whether transfers should be made. President Reagan's freeze regulations came into effect at 4.10 p.m. Eastern Standard Time and within minutes the US Treasury had informed US banks of its effect. As a consequence, LAFB found its accounts in both New York and London frozen.

In the case, BT contended that Eurodollar denominated accounts were not repayable on demand in cash anywhere outside the United States, since they had to clear through the CHIPS system in New York. In September 1987, the High Court in London came to the view that the deposits were in London, subject to English law. The Presidential freeze of Libyan assets could affect the usual transfers via New York clearing, but this was not the only possible way to repay the money to the Libyans. Bankers Trust was obliged to use all methods open to it to discharge its obligation. It could pay cash (that is, banknotes) in dollars or in sterling, and it was obliged to pay not only the $131 million on the London deposit account but also an addition $161 million which should have been (but was not) transferred from the New York account to the London deposit account.

The issue of whether the home office of a Eurobank will be held liable for Euro-currency deposits at its foreign branches was addressed in the United States in *Wells Fargo Asia Ltd.* v. *Citibank*. Wells Fargo had deposits with Citibank in Manila. The authorities in the Philippines imposed a freeze on foreign payments in 1983. Wells Fargo sued in New York for repayment in New York. The court held that under the law of the Philippines, the branch was not a separate legal entity, and therefore Citibank was obliged to repay with assets from anywhere, as long as such assets were not from the Philippines branch. After a series of cases, judgment was ultimately given in favour of Wells Fargo. This decision has been criticized and indeed seems illogical.[1]

Clearly, each case will depend entirely on its circumstances. What the LAFB case does suggest, however, is that in general at least the British courts will tend to uphold the freedom of the Euromarkets from interference by other governments, unless the UK government also chooses to support this interference by making the actions of governments subject to legal enforcement in London. Naturally, the legal status of Eurocurrency deposits in other centres depends on the local legal arrangements.

2.4 THE FOREIGN EXCHANGE MARKET

What is the foreign exchange market? What is its role? It is the arena in which currencies of one country are exchanged for another, it is where settlement is made for international purchases and sales. Just as the domestic money market is the place where financial flows through a single economy are managed, so the foreign exchange market is where financial flows between countries are settled. Payments for imports and exports flow through the foreign exchange market; as do payments for international purchases and sales of assets. A Japanese investor buying IBM shares will go through the foreign exchange market to buy the US dollars to pay the broker who has sold him the shares. In recent years, these international investment flows have played an increasingly important part in the foreign exchange market as securities markets have become more global. The foreign exchange market is also an arena for trading activities on a global scale by a range of participants. Their activities can drive currencies up and down depending on short-term views about the directions of important factors such as relevant interest rates, relevant inflation rates, and so on. (See Chapter 8.)

The foreign exchange market, therefore, is a turntable for the international flow of funds. Funds move into a country when its economic policies are seen as attractive or when firms within it are seen as being dynamic and well-managed, so that the stock market is attractive. Funds will flow out if there is political uncertainty, if interest rates are perceived as too low in relation to inflation, or if the country is perceived as running a chronic deficit on its balance of trade or payments, with no action forthcoming to rectify the problem. (These issues are discussed in more detail in Chapter 8.)

From time immemorial, governments and their central bankers have tried to influence the foreign exchange market. Typically, this has been done in two main ways: exchange controls and intervention. Exchange control regulations prevent the citizens of a country from doing certain things (such as sending money abroad) which are felt by the central bank to have a negative effect on the exchange rate. Intervention can take two forms: either changing the level of interest rates on the currency so as to make it more or less attractive to foreigners, or else buying or selling the currency so as to raise or lower its market value. Sometimes a central bank can get away with merely looking as though it will do something: dealers will cry "the Bank of Japan is checking levels in the dollar," and that in itself may be enough to trigger a move in the dollar/yen rate. At other times, the central bank has to put its money where its mouth is, sometimes in ever larger and more desperate quantities. The Bank of England, for example, during the 1960s and 1970s often had to spend large amounts of money to support sterling. Those sums had to be borrowed from elsewhere— either from the Bank for International Settlements (BIS) or the International Monetary Fund (IMF) (see Chapter 5).

Although statistics have improved, nobody knows how big the world market for foreign exchange really is. All we do know is that it is huge. A recent estimate by the BIS (Tables 2.2 and 2.3) put the average daily turnover in the world market at $880 billion in April 1992 (net of double counting), which compares with an average daily turnover on the New York Stock Exchange of $9.5 billion for 1993. It also compares with the total foreign exchange reserves of all countries as reported by the IMF at the end of 1993 of SDR 709 billion (equivalent to $1050 billion). In other words, the entire reserves of all countries, if committed to foreign exchange intervention, could be swallowed up in two days' normal trading volume of the market. Turnover in the spot market alone, at an estimated $400 billion, is equivalent to 40% of world reserves. Of course, exchange rates are determined by the net demand for currencies

Table 2.2 Growth in Foreign Exchange Turnover 1989–93 (%)

	Total Turnover
UK	53
United States	39
Japan	8
Singapore	38

Source: *Central Bank Survey of Foreign Exchange Market Activity*, BIS, March 1993.

Table 2.3 Foreign Exchange Market Activity in April 1992 ($bn)

UK	300
United States	192
Japan	126
Singapore	76
Switzerland	68
Hong Kong	61
Germany	57
France	36
Australia	30
All other countries	208
Total	1131

Source: *Central Bank Survey of Foreign Exchange Market Activity*, BIS, March 1993.

rather than gross turnover, and also central bank intervention can have psychological effects. But the BIS concludes: "exchange market intervention on its own is bound to be of only limited significance over a longer period."

Figure 2.3 shows the growth of world foreign exchange reserves since the early 1960s and also shows the percentage change on an annual basis. Although the absolute figures have grown very rapidly during the 1980s, the speed of growth has never again attained the explosive 60% growth seen in 1971 when the pressure on the US dollar was at its height and all major governments were aggressively intervening to try and maintain the US dollar's link with gold. The BIS survey, whose coverage has been gradually expanding since the first survey in 1983, showed a total growth in turnover 1989–92 of 42%; turnover in the four countries which reported also in 1986 doubled between that date and 1989, so that it looks as if growth slowed significantly in the world foreign exchange market in 1989–92.

Other key features of the most recent survey are the strong rise in the share of the deutsche mark in world foreign exchange trading, partly reflecting of course the impact of reunification. The share of London in world turnover actually grew significantly during this latest three-year period, from 25% of the world total to 30% in April 1992. The BIS commented: "a larger share of trading in both US dollars (26%) and DEM (27%) takes place in the UK than in either the US (18%) or Germany (10%) respectively. In addition, over 40% of all reported deals involving the ECU have one counterparty located in the UK."

The share of Japan fell by three percentage points, while Singapore overtook Switzerland. Another noticeable feature was the rising proportion of forward transactions, largely because of the growth of derivatives activity.

Participants in the market consist of five main groups: central banks, commercial banks, other financial institutions, corporate customers, and brokers. By far the largest volume of trading is conducted by commercial banks, but the role of other financial institutions has grown considerably with the growth of global investment and also the growth of the derivatives markets in which the investment banks play an important role. In the corporate sector, the two largest trading groups have

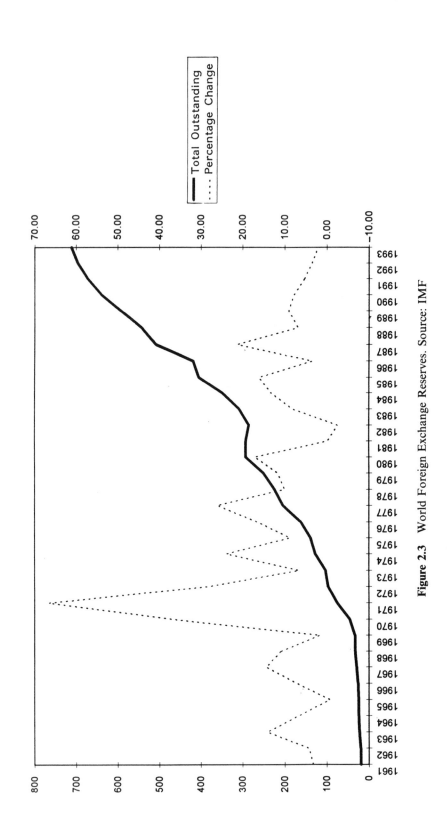

Figure 2.3 World Foreign Exchange Reserves. Source: IMF

traditionally been the oil companies and commodity companies. This is because commodity markets generally trade on an international basis in a single currency (usually the dollar, but also sterling for certain commodities), but have sales denominated in the local market currency. The role of the central banks is generally passive, responding to events. But occasionally their policies can take on tremendous significance for the market players. Their role is discussed more fully next.

Of the counterparties involved in the London market, 6.9% of turnover was done direct with customers. This compares with 15% in 1989. (However the earlier figure included a category of "other financial institutions" which is now shown separately, accounting for 15.2%.) The remaining 92.1% was interbank business, of which 34% was traded through the intermediation of a foreign exchange broker (see below) and 24% through an automated dealing system.

Though the customer turnover percentage may seem low, a single customer transaction can give rise to three or four interbank transactions in the normal course of events. The reasons are explained later, but as an example, a forward sterling/deutsche mark transaction by a British bank in London with a British customer could give rise to a spot dollar sterling and a spot dollar/mark transaction, together with a dollar sterling swap (spot versus forward) and a dollar/mark swap.

The vast majority of foreign exchange dealing is very short term: the BIS survey showed that 64.3% of trading in 1992 was for seven days' maturity or less; 34.5% was for up to one year and only 1.2% for over one year.

The workings of the foreign exchange market differ a little in detail from centre to centre. In some countries, for example, particularly continental Europe, it is traditional for there to be a daily "fixing." In Germany, for example, it is customary for the banks to group together customer orders of a smaller amount and to present them as bids or offers at the daily fixing with the Bundesbank. The rate is moved until the balance of orders on either side is sufficient to clear the market, if necessary with some supplementary sales or purchases by the Bundesbank, and the daily "fixing rate" is then announced. The fixing rate is applied to certain routine transactions by the banks for their customers.

More and more, though, a worldwide pattern of foreign exchange trading is emerging that is common between the different centres. The major participants are the central banks, commercial banks, companies, and foreign exchange brokers. Banks typically trade directly with other banks on the international markets, although sometimes they will trade through a broker if this is more convenient. In domestic markets, they will often also trade directly with one another but tend (perhaps more than internationally) also to use the services of a broker. Each of the two methods has its own advantages. In dealing directly, a bank can normally be sure of getting a price at which it can deal. The convention is that a bank which receives a call from another bank asking for a quotation will quote a "2-way" price at which it is prepared to buy or sell the currency. But this price may not be the best available in the market at the time, or it may only be good for a limited amount. On the other hand, it is the job of the broker to find his customer the best possible price in the market, by using his large communications network with many other banks in the market. Accordingly, on some occasions, a better price may be obtained through the broker: this, however, incurs a brokerage fee. At the same time, a bank contacted by a broker need not necessarily make a "2-way" price, so that the broker may not always be able to find the right side of the deal.

In some centres, brokers are allowed to service companies in the foreign exchange market. It is quite common to see this in domestic money markets, but still unusual in the foreign exchange market. Banks dislike the practice, generally, because of the possible credit risk problem and the possible risk to customer relationships. In other centres, the practice is forbidden. Another restriction can be a ban on dealing with banks outside the country. When operating tight exchange controls, a central bank will often require all commercial deals to be done with an authorized bank in that country (since otherwise the controls are very hard to police).

Exchange controls are the earthworks that prevent the foreign exchange tide from flowing freely round the world. But the liberalization and globalization of the markets during the 1980s now mean that most important countries have relatively free markets. As an example of what that has meant for previously restricted markets, the Deputy Governor of the Reserve Bank of Australia said in 1989 that before the 1983 liberalization of the Australian market, foreign exchange turnover was estimated at A$1 billion daily; six years later, it was A$35 billion daily.

Now all major countries are effectively free from exchange controls, and the world's communication networks are now so good that we can talk of a single world market for foreign exchange. It starts in New Zealand around 9.00 a.m., just in time to catch the tail end of the previous night's US market. Two or three hours later, Tokyo opens, followed an hour later by Hong Kong and Manila and then half an hour later by Singapore. By now, with the Far East market in full swing, the focus moves to the Near and Middle East. Bombay opens two hours after Singapore, followed after an hour and a half by Abu Dhabi, with Jedda an hour behind, and Athens and Beirut an hour behind still. By this stage, trading in the Far and Middle East is usually thin and perhaps nervous as dealers wait to see how Europe will trade. Paris and Frankfurt open an hour ahead of London, and by this time Tokyo is starting to close down, so the European market can judge how the Japanese market has been trading by the way they deal to close out positions. By lunch-time in London, New York is starting to open up, and as Europe closes down, so positions can be passed westward. During the afternoon in New York, trading tends to be quiet. The problem is there is nowhere to pass the position to. The San Francisco market, three hours behind, is effectively a satellite of the New York market. Positions can be passed on to New Zealand banks, but the market there is relatively limited. Increasingly, there has been a tendency for banks to open two or three shifts so as to run 24-hour dealing rooms, but the vast majority of the market still tends to work in daylight hours.

Like its trading, the influences on the foreign exchange market are worldwide. Not only domestic and international money markets, but a range of other markets also influence trading activity. Flows of funds into and out of the major stock markets, and the major bond markets, can have a significant impact. So, too, can sharp movements in either gold, oil, or some of the other major commodities. Activities in the futures markets can have an impact, as can flows arising out of the markets for interest rate or currency swaps, currency options, or other financial options markets. We will look at all of these markets in more detail. But before we do that, it may be useful to look at the history of these markets. While the details of past history may not seem relevant as we try to make sense of the maelstrom of information being pumped at us by the Reuters and Telerate screens and the newspapers, it is as well to remember Santayana: "Those who do not remember history are condemned to relive it." The forces that shaped the past may still be relevant to understanding the events of today.

NOTE

1. See E.M.A. Kwaw, *Grey Areas in Eurocurrency Deposits and Placements*, Dartmouth Publications, Aldershot, UK, and Brookfield, USA, 1994.

3
The Euromarkets and Global Financial Integration

In this chapter, we consider the role which has been played by the Eurodollar and foreign exchange markets in helping the process of global financial integration. We begin by considering the historical development of the markets, and move on to look at the process of financial integration which began to accelerate in the 1980s.

3.1 HISTORY OF THE FOREIGN EXCHANGE AND EURODOLLAR MARKETS

The history of foreign exchange markets goes back a very long way: they were old when the Bible reports money changers being chased out of the Temple by Jesus Christ. The global market itself began to develop during the nineteenth century, as the term "cable" for sterling will attest. It derives from the rate for the cable transfer between London and New York.

By the 1920s, the markets were developed enough for Maynard Keynes to form a syndicate to speculate on the deutsche mark. But the economic chaos resulting from the Depression of the 1930s led to the so-called "beggar thy neighbour" policies of competitive depreciation whereby one country, in order to try to boost the level of its exports, would depreciate its currency aggressively, only to be overtaken by another country intent on doing the same. This led to a reaction.

In 1944, the Allies met at Bretton Woods to lay down a post-war foundation for stable exchange rates. This took shape in the form of the International Monetary Fund (IMF) (see Chapter 5). The object was to provide a system whereby exchange rates would be held stable and, if necessary, countries could be supplied with the finance to ensure that this took place.

The IMF's Articles of Agreement permitted adjustment of the currency's par value only if the country's balance of payments was in "fundamental disequilibrium". This was an imprecise concept, but it came to mean that exchange rates would be adjusted only as a last resort and only in conjunction with other policies to redress the disequilibrium.

The system worked well to begin with, since in the immediate postwar world financial flows were very tightly regulated by exchange controls in a number of countries. In 1958, however, the international convertibility of most major currencies was restored, and the international financial system began to experience regular exchange rate crises.

Early pressure on the US dollar led, in 1963, to the introduction of the interest equalization tax. This was a tax on bond issues made in the United States by foreigners. It led to the growth of the Eurobond market and thus helped the growth of the Eurodollar market, which was also helped by the existence of the US Regulation Q. This was a Fed regulation restricting the rate of interest that could be paid by US banks on deposits to 5.25%. As US interest rates rose with inflation, so much US dollar deposit activity shifted to the Euromarket.

Once the pressure on the dollar eased, the next flash point was the pound sterling, which was widely perceived as overvalued given the UK's relatively high exchange rate, poor labour practices, and low productivity growth. The US dollar, however, also began to come under increasing pressure for similar reasons, exacerbated after 1965 by the impact of the Vietnam War on the US balance of payments.

Sterling was the first to crack, in 1967, partly as a result of the Seven-day War between Israel and Egypt, which triggered concern about sterling balances. These were balances held in sterling by foreign central banks and international investors as a result of the then key role played by sterling in the international financial system. The devaluation of sterling by 14.6% in November 1967 temporarily calmed the situation, but only briefly. The US dollar now stood exposed to the full force of international speculation, with sterling removed from the firing line.

In 1969, the fall of General de Gaulle resulted in strong upward pressure on the deutsche mark. The French franc was devalued by 11%, and the deutsche mark revalued by 9.3%. During 1970, the situation calmed down somewhat, but in 1971 the downward pressure on the dollar and the upward pressure on the deutsche mark were strongly renewed.

On May 28, 1971, US Secretary of the Treasury John Connally announced that "we are not going to devalue. We are not going to change the price of gold." On August 15, President Nixon suspended convertibility of dollars into gold, and announced a domestic wage price freeze. In December, a meeting at the Smithsonian Institution in Washington agreed a realignment of currencies included a devaluation of the dollar.

Figure 2.3 puts in perspective the pressure on the international financial system during this period. As governments intervened to support the US dollar in ever larger amounts, world foreign exchange reserves exploded, growing by over 60% in 1971. (To see how intervention increases reserves, see Chapter 4.)

The Smithsonian agreement marked the beginning of the end for the gold–dollar link. The US Treasury had sold, net, more than US$10 billion worth of gold between December 1958 and August 1971, cutting its gold stock in half. Sales to France and in the London gold market to stabilize the market price around the official price accounted for much of this total. In an effort to create an alternative international reserve asset, the United States pressed for the creation of a reserve asset whose supply could be systematically increased as the world economy expanded. This approach eventually resulted in an agreement to create special drawing rights (SDRs) of the IMF in 1968; the first allocation of SDRs was made in January 1970. None of these efforts, however, were sufficient to offset the underlying economic weakness of the dollar at a time when the economies of other countries were expanding after the devastation of World War II.

In March 1972 the European Economic Community (EEC) decided to fix narrow margins of 2.25% between member currencies, in order to form a "snake" in the Smithsonian "tunnel." This became the seed which later grew into the European Monetary System (EMS). During May, the UK, Denmark, Ireland, and Norway joined the snake; in June, the UK and Ireland left the snake, together with Denmark (which rejoined in October). The pressure on the US dollar continued, and the German government adopted exchange control measures designed to prevent the inflows from abroad; at about the same time, the Swiss introduced negative interest rates, with the same objective.

In February 1973 the pressure on the US dollar became intense, and the United States announced a 10% devaluation. This triggered the announcement by Japan, followed by Italy and Switzerland, that their exchange rates would float; in March, the EEC ministers announced the joint float of snake currencies against the US dollar. The era of floating exchange rates had begun, although at the time, the situation seemed purely temporary.

The adoption of floating exchange rates turned out to be a very useful device in view of the imminent economic chaos caused by the Yom Kippur War in the autumn 1973, which resulted in the imposition by OPEC of an oil embargo. Initially, the US dollar benefited as the oil producers redeposited their reserves in US dollars and sterling. The banks involved then proceeded to recycle the OPEC deposits by on-lending them to developing countries to help them finance their balance of payments problems. Such recycling was actively encouraged by major governments. But when the developing countries were unable to repay their borrowings, official support for the banks involved was hard to find, and the less developed countries (LDC) debt crisis of the early 1980s began.

In both the United States and the UK, the failure of economic policy to produce the required reduction in balance of payments deficit led to severe pressure on the currency. Sterling experienced the crisis first, falling through $2.00 in March 1976; in June, the UK was forced to borrow US$5.3 billion under an international standby facility. In January 1977 the IMF approval of a loan to the UK, together with a further standby loan from the BIS allowed sterling to begin to recover, which in turn exposed the position of the US dollar to international attention.

The US dollar came under intense pressure during the summer and autumn, with other countries having to make desperate efforts to prevent outflows from the United States into their currency. In November, Japan imposed a 50% marginal reserve requirement on "free yen" balances, and in December the Bundesbank increased marginal reserve requirements on nonresident deposits to 100%. Negative interest rates in Switzerland reached −40% per annum.

In July 1979, Paul Volcker was appointed Chairman of the Federal Reserve, and in September and October he raised the US discount rate from 10 to 12% imposing an 8% marginal reserve requirement, and announcing a "new monetary policy" that would focus henceforth on levels of bank reserves, rather than interest rates. Although this had the effect of temporarily stabilizing the situation, a further round of pressure began to develop in December 1979, when OPEC raised the oil price another 30% and the Soviet Union invaded Afghanistan. The price of gold moved from just under $400 per ounce at the end of September to $512 per ounce at the end of December, and $850 per ounce on January 25th.

In December 1981, the United States introduced International Banking Facilities (IBFs) which effectively allowed Euromarket activity in New York. IBFs are subject to restrictions aimed at stopping any leakage between IBFs and domestic banking. This was emulated in 1986 by the Japan Offshore Market.

Also in 1981, the new Reagan administration decided to move away from what it judged to have been the heavy levels of foreign exchange intervention inherited from the previous administration. This reflected an ideological view that exchange rates were the product of economic policies, and that the "supply side" policies of the new administration would be sufficient to produce satisfactory market conditions. In reality, what happened was that a combination of short-sighted tax cuts, aggressive increases in defense spending, and a lack of administrative control produced a very rapid rise in the US budget deficit, which was offset by very tight Fed monetary policy. This pushed the US dollar up sharply.

This in turn produced other repercussions, particularly for the LDCs, which had borrowed US dollars in order to finance the balance of payments deficit caused by previous oil price rises. The strength of the dollar and high dollar interest rates made their position increasingly difficult, and in August 1982 Mexico triggered the beginnings of an international LDC debt crisis by announcing that it could not meet its obligations. Partly as a response, and partly because US inflation was showing signs of coming under control as a result of the strength of the dollar and the relative slow-down of domestic demand, the Fed began to ease interest rates. This in turn triggered a strong bull market in US dollar bonds and subsequently in US equities.

By the summer of 1985, it was apparent that the ideologically based US policy of "benign neglect" of the US dollar appreciation (based in part on the simplistic view of President Reagan that "a strong dollar shows that the United States is strong") had led to massive distortions of international payments in balances. The US external deficit was beginning to explode, as the United States was becoming increasingly uncompetitive: this in turn was leading to domestic US demands for protection from foreign competition.

On September 22, at the Plaza Hotel in New York, the finance ministers of the Group of Five (United States, Japan, Germany, UK, France) met to try to deal with the situation. Behind the scenes, delicate negotiations on intervention strategy took place. A statement of intervention policy, dubbed the "nonpaper" because of its sensitivity, was prepared but never made public. The nonpaper looked for a 10–12% fall in the dollar, and intervention shares assigned as follows: United States, 25%; Germany, 25%; Japan, 25%; UK, 12.5%; France, 12.5%. The Europeans, however, objected feeling that the United States and Japan should share more of the burden. The United States offered a compromize; United States, 30%; Germany, 25%; Japan, 30%; UK, 5%; France, 10%.

The nonpaper did not discuss interest rates and monetary policy, nor did the central bank governors attending the Plaza meeting discuss monetary policy or interest rates at the meeting. They considered the topic too sensitive to be discussed in the presence of politicians.

By January 1986, the United States was pressing other members of the Group of Five for a coordinated cut in interest rates, citing lower US growth estimates for 1986 and also the collapse in oil prices as a justification. The Treasury secretary, James Baker, warned that unless other countries cooperated, the dollar would fall further. The central bankers, however, resisted this pressure. It was against this background that in February 1987 officials of the Group of Seven met at the Louvre in Paris. They expressed concern that "further substantial exchange rate shifts could damage growth and adjustment prospects in their countries". Therefore, they agreed to "cooperate closely to foster stability of exchange rates around current levels".

In fact, the commitments were much more precise: two specified mid-point rates were agreed: DEM 1.8250 to the dollar and JPY 153.50 to the dollar. Plus or minus 2.5% was determined as a first line of defense for mutual intervention on a voluntary basis, while at 5% consultation on policy adjustment was to be obligatory. Between these limits of 2.5 and 5%, intervention efforts were expected to intensify. Agreement was also reached on a total amount of US$4 billion of "war chest" for intervention purposes, with intervention totals assigned as roughly one-third to the United States, one-third to Japan, and one-third to European countries.

However, the failure to follow through in terms of fiscal coordination undermined the success of the Louvre Accord. Tensions grew between the United States and other partners, particularly Germany. Veiled threats by the United States to force a further dollar depreciation unless Germany expanded its economy more rapidly unsettled the markets, triggering the crash of October 19th in the US stock market. This, in turn, so terrified the US administration that US interest rates were pushed artificially low for too long. By the end of the year, the dollar's value had fallen 21% against the yen and 14% against the deutsche mark from its levels at the time of the Louvre Accord in February. In these circumstances, the Group of Seven officials held a telephone conference in late December and in conjunction with the central banks operated a "bear trap" against dollar speculators. The US dollar was forced up sharply at the start of January 1988.

By early 1989, the dollar was again rising strongly, until in early April the Group of Seven announced strong opposition to a further dollar rise, coupled with official dollar sales by the Bank of Japan (the first such intervention since late 1985). During 1989, the US dollar continued its ascent: it benefited from the withholding tax fiasco in Germany, repeated government crises in Japan, and also the massacre in Tienanmen Square in China in June of 1989. In the latter quarter of the year, the dollar eased back, partly in response to the Group of Seven meeting on September 23, 1989 when the finance ministers and central bank governors publicly criticized the rise in the dollar as being inappropriate. Over the course of the year as a whole, net sales of dollars by 19 countries participating in the "consultation" of policy amounted to no less than $75 billion, with the United States and Japan contributing $40 billion, and the Bundesbank $4 billion.

Events in the international financial markets during 1990 could not help but be overshadowed by the dramatic developments on the geopolitical scene: the collapse of the Berlin Wall in November 1989 and the subsequent rapid move toward German reunification transformed the prospects of the deutsche mark. A country with a strong external surplus, low inflation, and low interest rates was transformed into a much weaker economy with enormous capital requirements to refinance the crumbling infrastructure left by the failed Communist regime. Long-term bond rates in Germany rose sharply over the course of the year, underpinning also a rise in Japanese interest rates, which over the course of the year triggered a collapse in the Japanese stock market. Stock markets around the world were further severely damaged by the invasion of Kuwait by Iraq in August 1990. This triggered a sharp rise in the price of oil from $18 to over US$40 at one point.

As the Kuwaiti crisis built towards war, the dollar began to weaken. In February 1991, just before the launching of the final attack on Iraqi forces, the authorities intervened to support the dollar and turned the tide. The subsequent rise of the dollar was particularly strong against the deutsche mark, as the German difficulties with the absorption of the former East Germany became apparent. In July, intervention was required to stop the dollar rising too rapidly.

In November 1991 the Finnish exchange rate crisis showed the scale of the pressures which can now be brought to bear on small currencies. The Bank of Finland later revealed that in 1991 as a whole gross official sales of foreign currency had amounted to the equivalent of 17% of GDP, or nearly 80% of annual exports.

During the latter part of 1991 negotiations within Europe proceeded over European Monetary Union (EMU) and in December 1991 the terms of EMU were broadly agreed in the Maastricht treaty of December 1991. However, in the autumn of 1992 a serious crisis forced sterling and the Italian lira outside the EMS on September 16 ("Black Wednesday"), when the Spanish peseta also devalued, but remained within the EMS. The Swedish and Norwegian currencies also came under very heavy pressure, with Sweden raising its marginal lending rate to 500%. The proximate cause of the crisis was the continuing German insistence on raising interest rates to curb the inflationary pressures generated by the absorption of the new *Länder*.

The Bank of England later published an estimate of the volume of official intervention which had taken placed over the four months to end-September: the figure was over $160 billion; the Bank of Italy estimated its intervention during September at over $100 billion. Nevertheless, exchange market pressures persisted. In mid-November the peseta and the escudo were forced to devalue and the Swedish krona was forced to float, while the BIS reported subsequently that Norwegian intervention in two days of this crisis amounted to 46% of Norway's nongold reserves. In January 1993 the Irish pound was devalued by 10%. In May the peseta and escudo were forced to devalue again.

The upward pressure on German rates caused a further EMS crisis in the summer of 1993. Intense speculation against the Danish kroner and the French and Belgian francs during July led at the start of August to the decision to widen the EMS fluctuation margins to 15 from 2.25%—an admission of defeat by the European Union in the face of large international capital flows. (The EMS is discussed in detail in Chapter 6.)

In its review of developments, the BIS commented:

"as one currency after another fell, so did the competitive position of others worsen, thus increasing the risk that one or other of them would become the object of the next speculative attack.

As to intervention itself, the question necessarily arises as to whether it was, in some sense, insufficient. Or was it simply ineffective in the new globalized financial world?

Technology, innovation, free capital mobility and investors' desire for international portfolio diversification have by now all combined to increase vastly the potential for
shifting large amounts of financial capital around the world, and across currencies, at
great speed . . . it is probably no exaggeration to say that the period from late 1991 to
early 1993 witnessed the most serious and widespread foreign exchange market crisis
since the breakdown of the Bretton Woods system twenty years ago."[1]

The BIS also commented that the failure of policy responses to achieve the desired
objective of pacifying the markets meant that policy became almost completely
"boxed in": the only conceivable way out was a realignment. But the ERM had
become for many politicians both the cornerstone of their drive towards European
unity and of their counter-inflation policy:

"the result of all this was that, when the crisis broke, it proved impossible to address, at
the beginning, the issue of a general realignment . . . this piecemeal approach to crisis
management opened the way for official positions to be misunderstood or misrepre-
sented."[2]

The subsequent easing of EMS tensions allowed German and French rates to be
lowered and this, together with falling US rates, led to spectacular worldwide bull
runs in bond and equity markets during 1993 which were brought to an abrupt end
in February 1994 when the Fed began to tighten interest rates. Heavy losses were
incurred by a number of financial institutions, notably the so-called "hedge funds";
but the six successive increases in US rates failed to lift the US dollar which drifted
down during most of 1994, and reached historic lows against the Japanese yen,
breaking the psychologically important JPY 100 level, after which it plunged rapidly
to JPY 84.

During the first half of 1995 the strength of the yen was coupled with severe
pressure on Japanese financial institutions, as the extent to which the country's
much-vaunted superiority had been based on a financial bubble, became clear.
Another problem which hit the international financial system was the backwash of
the Mexican crisis (the so-called "Tequila effect"). Many Latin American countries,
and indeed other emerging markets, suffered severe short-term capital outflows after
the bungled devaluation of the Mexican peso in December 1994 led to a reappraisal
by investors of the prospects for emerging markets.

Alongside these developments, significant changes had been taking place in the
Eurocurrency markets. After a period of rapid growth (12% p.a. from 1983 to 1990)
international interbank credit shrank by 4.4% in 1991 and thereafter recovered only
slowly. The major factor behind this was the retrenchment of Japanese banks, whose
share in total interbank claims dropped from 36% at the end of 1990 to 29% by
September 1994. The slack was taken up by banks from the European Union, whose
share grew from 35 to 44% over the period, with French francs, Italian lira, deutsche
marks and pesetas being the main growth sectors. Growth in these sectors was at
least in part attributable to the parallel crisis in the EMS.

3.2 THE ROLE OF OFFSHORE CENTRES

The role of offshore centres in international finance is often not well understood. At
the level of the private individual, these centres are most commonly associated with

tax havens such as the Bahamas or the Cayman Islands. However, the importance of such centres in wholesale international finance is quite limited, apart from serving as the booking location for some transactions which need to be tax-transparent (e.g. the Cayman Islands are a common location for the "shell companies" set up for asset swap transactions—see Chapter 11). The main offshore centres with which we shall be concerned are locations like London, Singapore or Bahrain. These are locations which specialized in handling transactions in the currencies of other countries: Euro-transactions. Primarily, they provide a location which is exempt from domestic reserve requirements. This exemption does not mean that the market is unsupervised; London, as one of the first offshore centres in the form of the Eurodollar market, has always been supervised by the Bank of England.

Following the successful development of London and other offshore centres, both the United States and Japan moved to create what might paradoxically be called an onshore offshore facility for banks to operate Eurocurrency business from the home country, provided that these centres did not do business in the domestic market. The American version was called the International Banking Facility; the Japanese the Japan Offshore Market. In an IBF, a US bank in New York could take Eurodollar deposits, provided that it refrained from lending them to an American resident. Similarly, a Japanese bank could take Euro-yen deposits in Tokyo in the JOM, provided these were not then lent to a domestic Japanese resident. The purpose of these entities was to allow American and Japanese banks to operate in the Euro-markets without incurring the operating costs of setting up overseas. However, in order to prevent the domestic monetary policy framework from being undermined, it was necessary to "ring fence" these operations by preventing them from lending to domestic residents.

The net result is that "offshore" operations are quite often carried out onshore. The reason for the creation of the IBFs and the JOM is that the national authorities concerned recognized the competitive advantages of offshore centres and wished to ensure that the national banking system was able to enjoy these advantages, while retaining the traditional framework for domestic monetary policy operations.

3.3 THE MARKET'S ROLE IN RECYCLING PAYMENTS IMBALANCES

In the early days of the Euromarkets, they tended to be seen as an arena for speculative operations. The coincidence of their growth with the growth in internationally footloose money was widely commented on, likewise their role in financing the speculative attacks on the dollar which led to the abandonment of the fixed exchange rate regime. However, the quadrupling of oil prices between October 1973 and January 1974 precipitated an unprecedented transfer of wealth from consumers to oil producers and confronted the international monetary system with the twin problems of accommodating this transfer and financing the resulting payments deficits. Among the more notable countries resorting to the Eurodollar market for balance of payments financing purposes were France, Japan, the UK and Italy. Subsequently, a number of LDCs came to the Eurodollar market for financing.

The very rapid expansion of financing activity through the Euromarkets began to put banks' capital ratios under strain. Because of the general financial gloom at the time (best encapsulated in a headline in the *Evening Standard* at the time of the second oil price rise: "The End of Civilization as we Know it") it was difficult for banks to raise new equity capital. In addition, banks were funding short term (usually with three- or six month deposits) but were making three- or five-year loans to the borrowing countries. Thus the international banking system came under severe pressure. The collapse of the US National Bank of San Diego, and the losses sustained by the United California Bank in Basle, the Union Bank of Switzerland and Westdeutsche Landesbank were followed by the collapse of Franklin National Bank and finally by that of Herstatt Bank. The mishandling of this last by the Bundesbank, which closed the bank during working hours, resulting in settlement losses—of which the most notable was $10 million by Hill Samuel—triggered fears of a "domino-style" banking collapse in which a chain of defaults could occur. This led to a shrinkage in the market.

In the event, the feared collapse did not occur, and the market did play the central role in recycling the surplus dollar deposits from the oil producers to the countries requiring balance of payments finance. In the light of this experience, the commercial banks began to widen their horizons and to search out borrowers from around the world. Many of these were developing countries with high ambitions but low standards of public conduct: much of the money lent ended up in the pockets of corrupt politicians or bureaucrats. The announcement in August 1982 by Mexico that it was unable to repay its borrowings on time was the first in a series of defaults by Argentina, Brazil and a number of other countries. Bankers who had been encouraged by politicians to "support the emerging nations" during the oil crisis were now surprised to be told that it was their irresponsibility in lending these countries too much money which was the root of the problem.

3.4 GROWTH OF INTERNATIONAL SECURITIZATION

The problem which banks had experienced with capital ratios earlier was now compounded by the impact of these losses. The result was pressure to find alternative financing routes whereby borrowers could be financed through the securities market rather than the banking system. At the same time the authorities were seeking to find methods to stabilize the position of the LDC borrowers. In 1989 the Brady plan was announced: in essence this provided borrowers with finance on the basis that the borrower issued bonds whose repayment at maturity was guaranteed by the purchase of zero-coupon US Treasury bonds. Investors took the risk that the interest would be paid on the bonds.

During this period, also, were seen the beginnings of a market for trading in loans to LDCs. Banks began to sell their loans at a discount—in hopeless cases such as North Korea, debt was sold sometimes at 15% of par. By 1993 the market had evolved to the point where the Emerging Markets Trading Association could estimate annual turnover at $3000 billion, and the bonds of Mexico, Brazil and Argentina were rivalling those of major European countries in turnover terms. The market was severely affected by the "tequila effect"—the backwash of the Mexican devaluation in December 1994—but the volume of trading of countries' distressed debt remained large and likely to expand further.

This trend was but one part of a wider international trend towards the securitization of bank assets. Pressures on bank balance sheets from the increased demand by regulators for higher capital, combined with heavy losses from lending to LDCs in the early 1980s, and on property loans in the middle to late 1980s, meant that banks had to charge an increasingly large spread to recover their costs. As a result, the securities markets offered efficient alternatives to the banking system. The trend began first in the United States, where securitization of the mortgage market was very successful, with total outstandings exceeding US$1 000 000 by the late 1980s. Internationally, the trend was seen first at the short end of the market, with the development of Euronotes. These began in underwritten form in 1985, and developed rapidly. The capital implications of underwriting meant that as the Basle ratios began to bite the market began to switch to non-underwritten issuance in the form of Eurocommercial paper (ECP). By the early 1990s the ECP market was a significant source of funding for international firms and a key investment arena for short-term investors, thus contributing further to the process of global integration of short-term money markets.

NOTES

1. *Annual Report 1994*, pp. 196, 200.
2. *Ibid*, pp. 198–199.

4
Links between Foreign Exchange and Money Markets

This chapter explores the links between foreign exchange and money markets. We start by seeing how the two link up at the level of a trader's position. Then we look at what this means for arbitrage. Then we look at how central banks intervene in the foreign exchange market, and in the domestic money market; and finally we discuss the effects that foreign exchange intervention can have in the domestic money market.

4.1 HANDLING AN EXPOSURE: FOREIGN EXCHANGE OR MONEY MARKET

We start with the point of view of a firm with foreign exchange exposure in a currency. As long as a currency has effective spot and forward exchange markets and money markets, and as long as exchange controls permit, an exposure can always be hedged in either market.

Suppose the treasurer of a British subsidiary of a US company has a deutsche mark payment coming due in 90 days. He needs the funds now to send to the United States. He can borrow deutsche marks against his receivable and convert them into US dollars now. Alternatively, he can sell the deutsche marks forward against US dollar and borrow US dollars against the foreign exchange. The choice between the two will depend on the rates involved (see Table 4.1).

A dealer in a bank has the option of handling positions in the same way. If a CHF deposit is received for 90 days, and sterling lent for 90 days, these will be the option of choosing the money market or the foreign exchange route. The dealer can on-lend the Swiss francs or do a foreign exchange deal. The dealer would buy sterling to on-lend and sell the sterling forward against CHF to repay the CHF deposit at maturity. Table 4.2 shows how the T-accounts would look.

Table 4.1 Financing a DEM Receivable: Money Market Route versus Foreign Exchange

	Money Market Route		Foreign Exchange Route	
Day	Cash In	Cash Out	Cash In	Cash Out
DEM				
Day 1	DEM loan proceeds			Convert to US$
Day 90	Receivable	Repayment of DEM loan	Receivable	Pay to bank to settle forward FX deal
US$				
Day 1	DEM loan proceeds	Remit to HQ	US$ loan proceeds against FX	Remit to HQ
Day 90				Repay US$ loan with proceeds of forward

Money market route	Foreign Exchange Market route
Step 1 Borrow DEM	Step 1 Sell DEM forward against US$
Step 2 Buy US$ and pay US parent	Step 2 Borrow US$ and pay United States
Step 3 Receive DEM and repay loan	Step 3 Receive DEM and settle forward deal
	Step 4 Use proceeds of forward to repay loan.

Table 4.2 Matching a Swiss Franc Liability and a Sterling Asset

	Money Market Route			Foreign Exchange Route	
Day	Cash In	Cash Out	Day	Cash In	Cash Out
CHF					
Day 1	CHF deposit	On-lent to market	Day 1	Receive deposit	Sell CHF for £STG
Day 90	Repay CHF	Market repays	Day 90	Receive CHF	Repay CHF deposit from forward
£STG					
Day 1	Borrow from market	Make £STG loan to customer	Day 1	Proceeds of CHF spot sale	Lend to customer
Day 90	Repay market	Customer repays	Day 90	Customer repays	Pay for forward CHF purchase

Step 1 Take CHF deposit; on-lend to market	Step 1 Take CHF deposit; swap it for £STG
Step 2 Lend £STG to customer, funding in market	Step 2 Lend £STG to customer
Step 3 Receive CHF repayment from market Repay customer deposit	Step 3 Receive £STG repayment from customer
Step 4 Receive £STG repayment from customer Repay market	Settle forward CHF purchase

4.2   ARBITRAGE

It follows from Tables 4.1 and 4.2 that there is a very close connection between the interest rate and the forward exchange rate. For example, suppose the Swiss franc is at a premium forward against sterling. In other words, the Swiss franc is more expensive in the future than it is now. The dealer who is selling Swiss francs spot and buying them forward at a more expensive price in order to lend sterling will need to make more on sterling lending than he would on Swiss franc lending. Otherwise, it would not be worthwhile switching the funds into sterling. From this, we can derive some general rules. (The exact calculations are set out in Chapter 9.)

First, *the currency with the lower interest rate will sell at a premium in the forward market against the currency with the higher interest rate.* Suppose US dollar three-month deposits yield 20% and deutsche mark three-month deposits yield 10%. Then the deutsche mark must sell at a premium in the three-month forward market. Suppose it did not; suppose it sold at a discount. That means, conversely, that the dollar is at a premium against the deutsche mark. So a German investor could buy dollars spot and sell them forward at a profit. In addition, 10% interest differential is picked up. In a free market, this situation could never last. Investors would buy US dollars spot and sell them forward until the weight of forward selling had driven the US dollar to a discount. That is, the forward deutsche mark would show a premium.

The second rule is that *this premium (on an annualized basis) will tend to equal the interest difference.* Suppose, in our example again, it did not, and that it were only 5% p.a. Then it would cost a German investor only 5% p.a. to buy spot dollars and sell them forward. Yet he would receive a 10% interest improvement, so there is still a net profit of 5%. Again, in a free market, this situation would not last. Funds would move out of deutsche marks into dollars until there were no net profit in doing so; that is, until the forward margin (premium or discount) in annual terms equaled the interest differential.

Third, *it follows from the equality of interest differentials and forward margins that if one changes for any reason, the other will move to offset it.* In practice, the interest differential tends to be the dominant factor, because the vast bulk of activity in the forward exchange market is conducted interbank on a swap basis. This relationship can be summed up as: if the interest differential moves in a currency's favour, the forward margin moves against it.

To continue our example, suppose German interest rates rise from 10 to 15% while the US dollar rate remains at 20%. Interest rates have moved in the deutsche mark's favor. So the forward premium on deutsche mark will fall from 10 to 5% p.a. so that it equals the new interest differential of 5%. Conversely, suppose now that US dollar rates also fall to 15%. The interest differential has moved against the US dollar, so the forward margins move in favor of the US dollar: the premium on deutsche marks (that is, discount on US$ against DEM) disappears entirely because both interest rates are now at 15% and the differential is zero.

It should be stressed that "interest differential" is very crude. To be strictly accurate, one should use something like "net accessible interest differential". In other words, the interest rate should apply to borrowing and lending that are accessible to the international market-unaffected by exchange controls. To take a classic case, during the period of heavy upward pressure on the Swiss franc in 1977–79, interest rates on the domestic Swiss money market were running at around 2–3% p.a. But those interest rates were not available to nonresident holders of the Swiss francs. They were, on the contrary, charged a negative interest rate of—at its peak—10% per quarter, or rather more than minus 40% p.a. Domestic Swiss rates were not "accessible" to the market.

Secondly, the interest rate should be "net". It should be adjusted for any reserve requirement factors, interest withholding taxes, or other adjustments applicable to nonresidents. For example, before the introduction of International Banking Facilities (IBF) in New York, a US bank was able to pay a better interest rate on a dollar deposit with its branch in London, compared with the rate it could pay for a deposit with its head office in New York, because the latter was subject to the full range of Fed System reserve requirements.

Equally, if nonresidents were placing funds in a centre where an interest withholding tax is levied on nonresidents, they would need to allow for this tax before comparing an interest rate on a deposit in another currency that does not attract withholding tax. It is possible that the withholding tax could be reclaimed under a double tax treaty between the depositor's country and the country in which the deposit is made. But against this must be set the extra cost and inconvenience of processing the claim, and so forth. Also, many of the countries that are Euromarket centres have a rather limited network of double tax treaties.

Finally, it should be mentioned that the relationship between the net interest differential and the swap market permits a bank's dealer to "create" a forward market if a deposit market is available. For example, if a dealer is asked to quote a forward price for a small amount of five-year Thai bahts, there is a problem. The forward Thai baht market does not stretch that far forward and there is no real Euro-baht deposit market. But if deposit quotes can be obtained for five years in the domestic Thai market, and if it is felt safe to assume that these are in line with what would prevail in the Euro-baht market if there were one, a swap price can be manufactured using the approach used in Chapter 9. Naturally, this is a very rough and ready procedure. It would only be safe to do it for a small-sized deal and then only if adequate margin were taken.

In fact what happens is that if the dealer has to sell forward Thai bahts, spot Thai bahts are bought now and placed on deposit, funding with borrowed dollars. The forward sale absorbs the dealer's foreign currency liquidity at maturity. Likewise, a forward purchase creates forward liquidity in the foreign currency (see Figure 4.1).

4.3   FOREIGN EXCHANGE INTERVENTION

Intervention by central banks in foreign exchange markets, in its "pure" form, consists of purchases/sales of foreign currency against domestic currency in the spot or forward markets. Other forms of intervention are indirect, such as money-market operations, charges in reserve requirements, and so on (see Chapter 1). In its "pure" form, then, intervention can be divided into spot, swap, and outright forward operations.

A study by the BIS (*Exchange Market Intervention and Monetary Policy*, Basle, 1988) found that official intervention took place mainly in the spot market. However

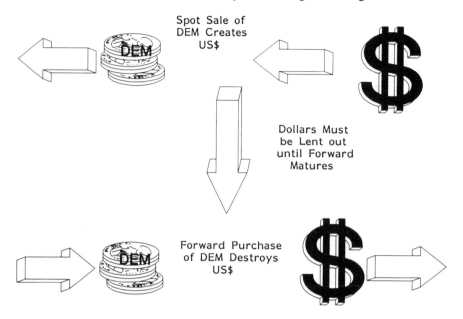

Figure 4.1   Creating US$ by Selling and Buying DEM

Switzerland, Germany, the Netherlands and Austria used foreign exchange swap operations regularly to influence money market rates.

A spot purchase or sale of foreign currency against domestic currency tends to have an immediate effect on the spot exchange rate. If the deutsche mark is rising, and the Bundesbank appears in the market to sell deutsche marks and buy US dollars, this will tend to depress the deutsche mark spot rate. It will also increase the Bundesbank's foreign exchange reserves by the amount of US dollars bought. It may affect the German money supply, depending on who buys the deutsche mark and whether they invest the deutsche mark in bank deposits or government bonds or are forced (as in 1970) to place the deutsche mark in a special deposit with the Bundesbank. In the last two cases, the inflow is "sterilized" but in the first case it feeds through into the money supply. (See a discussion of this problem later in the chapter.)

An outright forward purchase or sale of foreign currency against domestic currency tends to have an immediate effect on the margin between the spot and forward rate. The effect on reserves does not show up until maturity, when it is the same as outlined in the last paragraph. The Bank of England intervened in this way during 1964–67. The aim was to support the forward sterling rate and so reduce the discount on forward sterling. This would cut the cost of forward cover on sterling assets and so encourage investment in sterling assets. At the same time, operating on an outright rather than a swap basis meant the Bank did not have to supply spot sterling to the market. But the devaluation of 1967 meant that these forward operations cost the Bank £350 million, and they were then abandoned.

A swap operation also alters the margin between the spot and the forward rate. But it has an immediate impact on the spot market as well. The counterparties receive funds on their accounts now. If the Bank of England had intervened in the swap instead of the outright market, it would have been selling sterling spot and buying it back forward. The counterparties would have been long of spot sterling, which they would probably have sold off. That was why the Bank dealt outright forward. But swaps have been used by some central banks to affect the cost of forward cover: a notable example is the Bundesbank which had amounts outstanding of up to $2.7 billion in 1958–69 and 1971. However, experience tended to show that these swap interventions were misused by the combination of interest rate arbitrage and Bundesbank swap transactions to carry on "round-trip trades" that made it possible to obtain interest rate profits without using additional funds. The Bundesbank still deals in the swap market (Table 4.3). The aim of these swaps was not to cut the cost of forward cover, but liquidity management. This type of operation is common also in the Netherlands and Switzerland.

Figures 4.2–4.5 show how the Central Bank of an imaginary country called Home provides liquidity via a swap that runs over the domestic money-market reporting date.

Another example of the link between the foreign exchange and domestic money

Table 4.3 Bundesbank Use of Swaps to Influence Money Markets (DEM bn)

Year	DEM bn
1984	3.3
1985	5.0
1986	24.0
1987	10.9
1988	3.0
1989	2.2

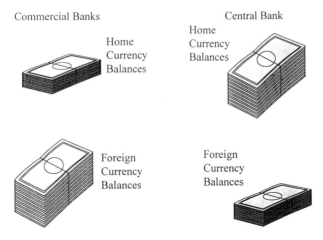

Figure 4.2 Domestic Liquidity Shortage

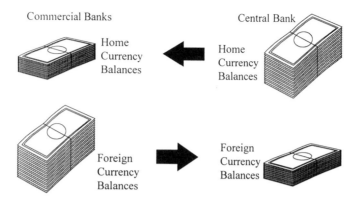

Figure 4.3 First Leg of Swap: Central bank provides Home Balances in Exchange for Foreign Currency Balances

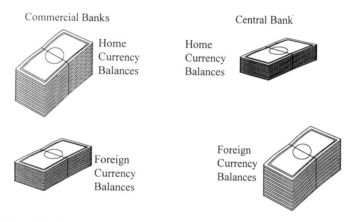

Figure 4.4 Reporting Date: Home Currency Balances of Commercial Banks Increased by Swap

markets can be seen if we look at a drawing by the Federal Reserve Bank of New York on its swap network (see Chapter 5) to finance sales of foreign currencies and stabilize the dollar. The drawing normally leads to two opposite and offsetting effects on bank reserves. First, the sale of a foreign currency for dollars by the Fed in the exchange market causes a fall in US bank reserves. The US bank receives foreign currency, paying over dollars to the Fed. This cuts its dollar reserves. Second, the reserves work their way back into the system (see Figure 4.6).

The way in which this happens will vary. It depends on the course of action taken by the securities trading desk at the Fed. Consider a swap with the Bundesbank. To start with, the swap drawing results in a credit of deutsche marks to the Fed's account at the Bundesbank. It also results in a credit of US dollars to the account of the Bundesbank at the Fed. The latter account is then debited with these dollars that are invested in a special US Treasury certificate of indebtedness. As a result, Treasury cash balances at the Reserve Bank increase. Under normal circumstances,

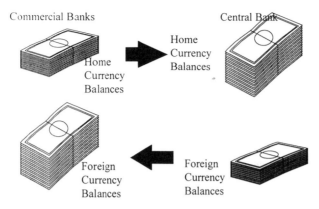

Figure 4.5 The Swap Unwinds: Commercial Banks' Home Balances Fall back to Original Level

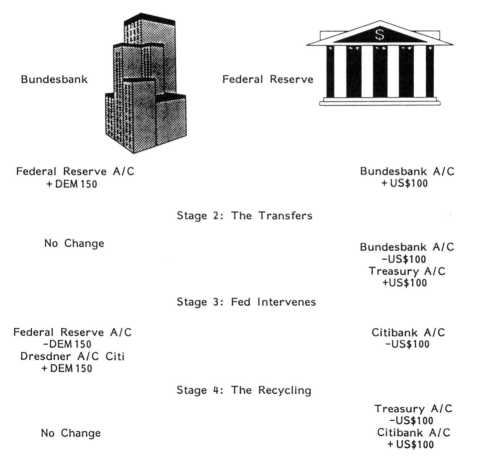

Stage 1: The Drawing (US$1 = DEM 1.50)

Bundesbank   Federal Reserve

Federal Reserve A/C
+ DEM 150

Bundesbank A/C
+ US$100

Stage 2: The Transfers

No Change

Bundesbank A/C
−US$100
Treasury A/C
+US$100

Stage 3: Fed Intervenes

Federal Reserve A/C
−DEM 150
Dresdner A/C Citi
+ DEM 150

Citibank A/C
−US$100

Stage 4: The Recycling

No Change

Treasury A/C
−US$100
Citibank A/C
+ US$100

Figure 4.6 Federal Reserve Swap Drawn on Bundesbank

US$1 = DEM 2

	DEM	US$
Federal Reserve A/C −200		−100 Citibank A/C
Dresdner Bank		
A/C Citibank +200		

Figure 4.7 Intervention Financed by Federal Reserve Balances

the US Treasury will then spend these dollars in the course of its operations, putting reserves back into the system, so the original reserve draining is offset. By comparison a direct intervention by the Fed in the foreign exchange markets to sell an existing balance of deutsche marks, that is, its own holding rather than the proceeds of a swap-drawing will have an immediately draining effect on bank reserves, unless offset by other action (see Figure 4.7).

4.4 FOREIGN EXCHANGE INTERVENTION AND THE MONEY SUPPLY

At various points in this chapter we have touched on the links between foreign exchange and money markets and how these are used by participants in the market, particularly by central banks when intervening. It is important to understand the wider effects of these links, because they affect the way in which central banks and governments operate their policies. For instance, a central bank that is committed to intervening in defense of a fixed exchange rate cannot control its money supply. If it does want to control money supply, it cannot intervene in unlimited amounts. To see why, we need to look at some examples of what happens when intervention takes place. The exact effects can be complex. They depend on our definitions of the money supply and the assumptions we make about how flows involved are financed. Very roughly, things work like this. If the authorities refuse to intervene in the foreign exchange market, an inflow of foreign currency will not change the country's foreign exchange reserves. Hence the inflow need not necessarily change the domestic money supply. But if the authorities intervene to buy the foreign currency, there will be an effect on the reserves. All other things being equal, this will affect the domestic money supply.

Perhaps the country which has had greatest experience of foreign currency inflows, and where these inflows have made most impact, is Switzerland. Because of Swiss support for a weakening dollar, Switzerland's reserves rose in December 1978 to 150% of average exports. That figure compares with 50% for the previous month. The change for the United States and for the UK during this period was negligible. As a result, the Swiss money supply, which had grown by less than 1% on average during 1977, grew by 19.8% during 1978.

It became clear to the Swiss authorities that this process could not be continued indefinitely. During 1979, the degree of dollar support was sharply reduced. That allowed a much more restrictive monetary policy. The money supply was actually reduced during 1979 by 1.2%. This was achieved at the price of a firm exchange rate.

From an average of US$ 1 = CHF 2.4035 during 1977, the Swiss franc strengthened to average 1.7880 during 1978 and 1.6627 during 1979. But a price was paid for this policy. The effects of the very rapid growth of money supply during 1978 and the subsequent weakening of the exchange rate during 1980 and 1981, were seen later in the consumer price index. This had risen by 0.8% on average during 1978, but rose 3.7% during 1979, 4.0% during 1980, and by March 1981 had risen by 6.4% compared with the same month of the previous year.

The detailed interrelationships are perhaps best understood by taking another case study. An interesting example occurred in the UK during 1977. The pound sterling was extremely firm during most of 1977. Sterling benefited from the arrangement of a medium-term standby facility for the Bank of England by the BIS in January 1977 and the decision by the Wilson government to raise medium-term external finance from the IMF. Until October of 1977, the Bank of England sold sterling to stop the pound from rising. As a result, the UK's external reserves rose. This tended to boost the money supply. To understand what actually went on, we will look again at our country called Home.

We start by making certain assumptions. First, all payments to Home residents from abroad are made in Home currency (HC). Second, the banks do not themselves hold foreign currency, nor do they lend HC abroad. Third, the public sector has no foreign currency transactions. Finally, we assume that nonresidents' HC deposits are excluded from the definition of the money supply.

We start with the way in which foreign exchange is taken into or paid out of the official reserves. The reserves are held by the Exchange Stabilization Fund (ESF). The ESF's working balances in HC are held in Treasury bills. When the ESF buys foreign currency it sells these Treasury bills back to the government. In exchange, it receives HC with which it can then pay the seller of foreign currency. In order to finance the payment to the ESF, the government is forced to borrow elsewhere. In effect, government securities are switched from the ESF to other holders.

Consider the case of a Home exporter who is owed HC 100 for an export delivery. Assume the overseas customer does not already hold HC. Then this customer will have to sell foreign currency for HC and pay the proceeds to the HC account of the exporter. Under our assumptions, the bank receiving the foreign currency will sell the currency immediately to the ESF. In order to buy the foreign currency from the bank, the ESF sells its Treasury bills to the government. This forces the latter to borrow elsewhere. In the absence of any other buyer, the government borrows from the banks. In effect, HC claims on the government are switched from the ESF to the banks. As there is a rise in the Home exporter's HC deposits, the money supply increases. The transactions associated with this change, as they affect the balance sheets of the banks and the ESF and the balance of payments, are shown in Table 4.4.

An inflow may also take the form of a rise in HC bank deposits held by overseas residents. This will not affect the money supply. In this case, the overseas resident sells foreign currency to a Home bank and places the proceeds in an HC account. The bank again immediately sells the foreign currency to the ESF. The ESF sells Treasury bills back to the government, which borrows HC from the bank. So the bank has effectively taken an HC deposit from a nonresident in order to on-lend it immediately to the government. However, this time there is no increase in the money

Table 4.4 Effects of a Home Current Account Surplus

Sector	Liabilities	Assets
Home banks		
Private sector HC deposits	+ 100	
HC claims on Treasury		+ 100
ESF		
Official reserves		+ 100
HC claims on Treasury		− 100
Balance of payments		
Current account: exports		+ 100
Capital account		
Change in reserves (increase, −)		− 100

Table 4.5 Effects of a Home Capital Account Surplus

Sector	Liabilities	Assets
Home banks		
Nonresidents' HC deposits	+ 100	
HC claims on Treasury		+ 100
ESF		
Official reserves		+ 100
HC claims on Treasury		− 100
Balance of payments		
Current account: exports		+ 100
Capital account		
Change in reserves (increase, −)		− 100

supply, as nonresidents' HC deposits are not included in the definition. The transactions are set out in Table 4.5. All of this has worked on the assumption that the ESF buys all foreign currency that is offered to it. Assume the ESF never intervenes, and assume still that neither Home banks nor the Home private sector hold foreign currency. Then it is clear that any foreign currency sold to Home residents is immediately sold back to nonresidents, because we have assumed that Home people never hold foreign currency. The exchange rate must move until nonresidents are willing to buy back the HC. It is the exchange rate which now takes the strain. The reserves do not change.

Let us now allow for residents' foreign currency holdings. They only affect the Home money supply when Home residents switch foreign currency into HC. To prove this, assume a Home current account surplus of HC 150 (see Table 4.6). Suppose that HC 50 of this is actually paid to the Home private sector in foreign currency. Suppose this foreign currency is deposited with the banks (who on-lend it to nonresidents). A further HC 60 worth is paid to Home residents in foreign

Table 4.6 Effects of Home Current Account Surplus when Intervention Takes Place

Sector	Liabilities	Assets
HC deposits of private sector	+ 100	
HC deposits of nonresidents	− 30	
HC claims on public sector		+ 70
Foreign currency deposits of private sector	+ 50	
Foreign currency loans to nonresidents		+ 50
Balance of payments		
Private sector current account surplus		
which is used to finance:		+ 150
Foreign currency lending by Home banks (increase, −)		−50
Overseas HC deposits with Home banks (increase, +)		−30
Overseas lending to Home public sector (increase, +)		−10
Change in reserves (increase, −)		−60

currency and immediately sold for HC. The ESF finances its purchases of foreign currency by selling Treasury bills that are bought by the bank. The rest is financed by a fall in foreigners' HC bank deposits of HC 30 and a fall of HC 10 in overseas holdings of public sector HC debt. We assume this is sold to the banks. So bank lending to the government rises by the HC 10 of public sector debt, and HC 60 which the banks lend to the government to finance the increase in reserves. That makes a total of HC 70. This feeds straight through into Home money supply. So does the HC 30 fall in foreigners' HC bank deposits which are paid to UK residents. So there is a net rise in Home's money supply of HC 100. This is equal to the private sector current and capital account surplus on the balance of payments less the increase in Home private sector foreign currency holdings. In other words, the HC 50 paid to Home residents in foreign currency, which was not switched into HC, had no effect on Home's money supply.

Now let us boil this down to what matters. Foreign currency inflows and outflows can affect a country's money supply. That can happen only if the ESF, in our example, is intervening in the foreign exchange market on a net basis. That is, the ESF must not just buy and sell in the market to smooth exchange rate movements, but must be supplying foreign currency to the market or absorbing currency from the market. If intervention is taking place, the effect on the money supply need not be the same as the amount of intervention. As we saw, if the inflow produces a rise in nonresidents' deposits, the money supply need not be affected. Equally, the effect on the money supply depends on how the ESF finances its interventions. In our example, if the ESF's Treasury bill holdings could be refinanced from overseas, the effect on money supply would be offset. In other words, foreign currency flows will tend in general to affect the money supply—but not always; it depends on what else is happening. But, as a rule of thumb: if Home central bank supports HC, it drains funds from Home money; if it supports another currency, it adds funds to the Home market.

A useful, detailed discussion of these issues may be found in *Does Foreign Exchange Intervention Work?* (D.M. Dominguez and J.S. Frankel, Institute for International Economics, 1993). This studied daily intervention data for the USA,

Germany and Switzerland. Their conclusion was that intervention, by influencing market expectations, can be effective irrespective of whether or not the intervention is sterilized. This was not, in general, the view taken in the Jurgenson Report (*Report of the Working Group on Exchange Market Intervention*, US Treasury, Washington, 1983) which suggested that sterilized intervention had, at best, transitory effects.

5

The International
Financial System

Now that we have looked at some of the major markets, it is time to see how they fit together. In this chapter, we see how individual domestic markets and the market for foreign exchange and international deposit markets mesh to form part of the international monetary systems. We look at some of the problems and ideas that have influenced the development of the system and we describe its components.

If one had to pick out three strands that weave the story together, they would probably be international liquidity, adjustment, and choice of reserve asset. We will look at each briefly. The word 'liquidity' means having enough cash to meet day-to-day needs. For an individual, that means having enough cash in the bank, or readily saleable assets such as government bonds, to meet his or her regular monthly bills. For a country, it means having enough foreign currency to pay its monthly bills: the balance of imports, exports, and other cash flows, into and out of the country. It has to be in foreign currency because (with certain exceptions, such as US dollars) other countries prefer to be paid in their own currency.

Liquidity and adjustment are in a sense opposites. If I do not have enough liquidity to meet my monthly bills, I have to cut my spending (or borrow). In other words, I have to adjust my behaviour. It is the same for a country that is continually spending more abroad than it earns from abroad. In the end, it usually has to adjust its policies. The more liquidity it has, the less hurry there is about adjusting. The less liquidity it has, the more rapidly it must act. So liquidity and adjustment are a kind of trade-off. Very often, countries have tried to put off adjusting their economies by using up liquidity, or by trying to get liquidity by borrowing. In most cases, they end up having to make adjustments—either to devalue their currency (to make their exports more competitive internationally and help the country earn more abroad) or cut back on spending on imports, often by painful domestic tax increases or interest rate rises. Over and over again the UK, Italy, Brazil, Mexico, and other countries have had to make the forced choice between adjustment and international liquidity. Much of the Western world faced the same choice during the oil shocks of 1973/75 and 1979/80.

The third strand is choice of reserve asset. International liquidity consists of reserves of foreign currency, or gold, which is generally saleable for currencies, and certain other items. After the war, in 1945, international liquidity was held almost entirely in gold, US dollars, and sterling. As confidence weakened in these two currencies, liquidity was switched into other currencies or gold. And the shock waves from these shifts of liquidity were seen in repeated currency crises (as we saw in Chapter 4), which ended in sterling's 1967 devaluation and the 1971/73 devaluation of the US dollar. Still today, as confidence in a currency fades or grows, international liquidity ebbs away from or flows into that currency.

5.1   INTERNATIONAL MONETARY FUND

The origins of today's international monetary system go back to 1944 when the Bretton Woods conference was held. At this conference, the International Monetary Fund (IMF) and the International Bank for Reconstruction and Development (IBRD, more commonly known as the World Bank) were established. The latter is mainly involved with development finance—a topic not covered here. The IMF aims to see that its members run their exchange rate and balance of payments policies in an orderly way. If need be, it helps them do so by lending them money. The funds to do this come from members' subscriptions (quotas), the IMF's borrowings, and other sources.

Under the original Articles of Agreement of the IMF, members agreed to make their currencies convertible; that is, not to restrict exchange of their currencies for others. They also agreed to fix par values for their currencies in terms of gold. This meant fixed exchange rates among currencies. It also meant (in theory) convertibility from currencies into gold. To help members meet these aims, the IMF would lend to them in proportion to their quotas.

The structure of the IMF is defined in its Articles of Agreement. It has a Board of Governors, which is its highest authority and meets once a year. But its day-to-day running is controlled by an Executive Board and the managing director. There are 21 executive directors. Of these, six are appointed by the countries with the largest quotas: United States, UK, Germany, France, Japan, and Saudi Arabia. The others are elected by the remaining members of the Fund. The Executive Board selects the managing director, who is also Chairman of the Executive Board.

The subscription, or quota, of a country depends on its national income, foreign currency reserves, and other factors. Quotas are normally reviewed at least every five years. The size of the quota decides two important things: how much a country can borrow from the IMF, and how much voting power it has. A country can borrow up to 100% of its quota, plus certain special facilities.

The borrowings are made in a series of slices or "tranches". The more a country borrows, the more closely the IMF supervises its policies. For the first borrowing (the first credit tranche), the IMF requires a borrowing country to "make reasonable efforts" to overcome its problems. For second and higher tranches, the Fund usually only lends on a standby basis. This means: (1) there are performance targets that the borrower must meet; (2) successive instalments of the borrowing are only allowed if the targets are met.

The mechanics of the borrowing (drawing) are that a country uses its own

Table 5.1 The United Kingdom Borrows DEM from the IMF General Account (£1 = DEM 3.00)

	UK Account with IMF (in £)	German Account with IMF (in DEM)
I. Before drawing		
SDR holdings	100	100
Reserve tranche	0	0
Borrowings under		
First credit tranche	0	0
Second credit tranche	0	0
Third credit tranche	0	0
Fourth credit tranche	0	0
General account holdings	£100 (UK original quota)	DEM 300 (German original quota)
II. UK borrows DEM 300 and pays in £100		
SDR holdings	100	100
Reserve tranche	0	300
Borrowings under		
First credit tranche	100	0
Second credit tranche	0	0
Third credit tranche	0	0
Fourth credit tranche	0	0
General account holdings	£200	0

currency to buy the currencies of other countries (or SDRs which are explained later). So a drawing on the IMF by a country raises the Fund's holdings of the country's currency, but reduces its holdings of the other currencies. The makeup of the Fund's resources changes, but not the total. An example is shown in Table 5.1. The account of the IMF that holds these currencies is called the general account (as distinct from the SDR account).

Borrowings are made in tranches. The first of these is the reserve tranche: it is equivalent to drawing down a credit balance. For the reserve tranche, the country is lending its currency to the IMF. Suppose the UK needs to borrow deutsche marks. The UK buys deutsche marks from the Fund and pays sterling. The Fund's deutsche mark holdings are now less than the amount Germany originally paid in: it is as if Germany had lent the Fund deutsche marks to buy the UK's sterling. The difference between Germany's original quota and the Fund's present deutsche mark holdings is credited to Germany as its reserve tranche. A country has automatic access to the reserve tranche (since, after all, it lent the money to the Fund). After that, it can borrow four subsequent tranches, each equal to 25% of its quota, and, as we saw, subject to tighter and tighter control by the IMF.

In addition to its general balance of payments assistance, the Fund has a number of special facilities designed to address needs arising from specific factors. The first of these, established in 1963, was the compensatory financing facility, designed to help stabilize the earnings of countries exporting primary commodities. Countries experiencing balance of payments difficulties for reasons beyond their control, because of temporary shortfalls in export earnings, could borrow under this facility, if they cooperated with the Fund to find solutions to their problems. In 1988, the facility was broadened to become the compensatory and contingency financing facility (CCFF). This facility supersedes the compensatory financing facility, but keeps its essential features. It adds a mechanism for contingency financing of member countries that have entered into adjustment programs supported by the Fund. The compensatory financing facility's feature has been retained, but to it has been added a contingency mechanism, activated only in conjunction with Fund-supported programs of adjustment.

A second special facility, designed to smooth out fluctuations in the prices of primary commodities and so reduce variations in the export earnings of participating countries, is the buffer stock financing facility, which was established in June 1969. Through this facility, the Fund can finance members' contributions to international schemes aimed at stabilizing commodity prices by building up a buffer stock.

During the 1970s, the IMF provided an oil facility. From 1974 to 1976, the Fund lent SDR 6.9 billion to 55 countries to help them overcome the impact of the oil price of 1973 and 1974. In 1986, the structural adjustment facility (SAF) was set up to provide low-cost financial assistance to low-income members facing serious balance of payment problems and needing to undertake programs of structural adjustment. In December 1987, the enhanced structural adjustment facility (ESAF) was set up to provide additional assistance to these countries. Countries eligible for SAF loans may borrow under the ESAF, but access under ESAF is considerably larger; it is normally expected to average about 150% of quota over a three-year program period, with provision for up to 350% in exceptional circumstances, compared with 70% under the SAF.

The most recent facility created by the IMF is the so-called systemic transformation facility, a temporary facility created in response to the needs of Russia and the other economies in transition. It provides financial assistance to eligible members experiencing balance of payments needs resulting from severe disruptions in traditional trade and payments arrangements. It was created in April 1993 to expire at the end of 1994.

All this lending has to be financed. The main source of funds is the quotas subscribed to the IMF by member countries. Extra facilities have had to be arranged when the quotas were not enough. The first of these arrangements was known as the general arrangements to borrow (GAB). The GAB were set up in January 1962 in case the Fund had to make a large loan to the United States or the UK, the main reserve currency countries at the time. It was a four-year arrangement with 10 industrialized countries (the Group of Ten). Switzerland later took part as an associate (not directly, because Switzerland is not a member of the IMF). The GAB continue in force, standing in 1989 at SDR 17 billion. As well as from the GAB, the IMF has borrowed direct from certain countries in other ways. For example, in March 1981, the IMF borrowed two annual tranches of SDR 4 billion from the Saudi Arabian monetary authority. Other facilities have been arranged from time to time with other countries and through the Bank of International Settlements (BIS). All of the Fund's lending and borrowing activities we have discussed so far are channeled through its general resources account. There is another account called the special drawing rights

(SDR) account. SDR was created in July 1969 under the First Amendment to the IMF Articles of Agreement.

During the late 1960s, there were discussions of a possible shortage of international liquidity. It was feared that this might slow the growth of world trade. One way of increasing liquidity would have been an increase in the official price of gold. Legally this was tantamount to a devaluation of the dollar. The United States firmly opposed it. An alternative was to create a new form of international reserve asset through the IMF. The special drawing right was called by this name to emphasize that it was a kind of borrowing, rather than a new currency. This was done to pacify France, who had argued for a revaluation of gold.

Members of the IMF can use SDRs to make international payments between themselves just as they could use US dollars. When it was originally created, the possible uses of the SDR were very restricted. Over the years, they have been widened so that central banks can buy or sell SDRs among themselves, use SDRs to make loans or as security for loans, and deal in SDR swaps or forward SDRs.

In January 1981, the valuation of the SDR was very much simplified (see the section on currency units below). It is now a basket of five major currencies, whose weights are revised every five years. In practical terms, the SDR is now equivalent to any other currency, with one major difference: private individuals cannot own it. SDRs can only be owned by member countries of the IMF and by 16 "prescribed holders" including the BIS, the Swiss National Bank, and various regional central banks (such as the Eastern Caribbean Central Bank) and development banks.

5.2   BANK FOR INTERNATIONAL SETTLEMENTS

The BIS is the central bankers' central bank (Table 5.2). It is very discreet, and very influential. It was founded in 1930 to act as a trustee for the loans associated with the Young Plan for German reparations. The first members of the bank were the central banks of Belgium, France, Germany, Italy, Japan, and the UK, together with three private US banks. The Federal Reserve Bank subsequently became a member along with all the major European central banks (although, curiously, the Fed never took up its directorship of the BIS until September 1994, for various reasons concerned with the presence on the Board of certain Communist countries and the importance of gold in BIS activities).

The Board of Directors is composed of the governors of the central banks of Belgium, France, Germany, Italy, and the UK, together with co-opted directors from among the governors of those member central banks that do not have an ex officio representative on the Board. There are also five representatives of finance, industry, or commerce appointed by the governors of the permanent member central banks.

The BIS has three main functions. It acts as a bank, primarily as a central bankers' bank; it acts as a gathering place for central bankers, and a vehicle for international monetary cooperation; and it acts as trustee for various international loans. The BIS's role as an intermediary provides a number of advantages to other central banks. The first is anonymity: sometimes it is not convenient for a central bank to be seen to withdraw its funds from the market. The second is risk spreading: a deposit with the BIS is very safe since the bank is highly liquid. (Typically, three-

Table 5.2 Member Central Banks of the Bank for International Settlements

Country	Central Bank
Australia	Reserve Bank of Australia
Austria	Austrian National Bank
Belgium	National Bank of Belgium
Bulgaria	Bulgarian National Bank
Canada	Bank of Canada
Czech Republic	Czech National Bank
Denmark	National Bank of Denmark
Estonia	Bank of Estonia
Finland	Bank of Finland
France	Bank of France
Germany	German Bundesbank
Greece	Bank of Greece
Hungary	National Bank of Hungary
Iceland	Central Bank of Iceland
Ireland	Central Bank of Ireland
Italy	Bank of Italy
Japan	Bank of Japan
Latvia	Bank of Latvia
Lithuania	Bank of Lithuania
Netherland	The Netherlands Bank
Norway	Central Bank of Norway
Poland	National Bank of Poland
Portugal	Bank of Portugal
Romania	National Bank of Romania
Slovakia	National Bank of Slovakia
South Africa	South African Reserve Bank
Spain	Bank of Spain
Sweden	Bank of Sweden
Switzerland	Swiss National Bank
Turkey	Central Bank of the Republic of Turkey
United Kingdom	Bank of England
United States	Federal Reserve System
Yugoslavia[1]	National Bank of Yugoslavia

Source: *Federal Reserve Bulletin*, October 1994.

quarters of the BIS's assets have maturities of under three months.) Finally, deposits placed with the BIS can usually be withdrawn at very short notice. The BIS uses the funds received from central banks primarily for lending to other central banks. Its lendings may be swaps against gold, covered credits secured by a pledge of gold or marketable short-term securities, unsecured credits, standby credits, and the like. It places the balance of its funds in short-term deposits with international banks.

The banking activities of the BIS are probably less vital than its role as a vehicle for international monetary cooperation. The most important part of this role is the least obtrusive: the monthly meetings of the BIS's board in Basle. Before the foundation of the BIS, meetings of governors of central banks were usually attended with a blaze of publicity and speculation concerning a crisis. Routine meetings on a

monthly basis have contributed much toward closer international monetary under-
standings. As a result, the BIS has been closely involved in almost every major international financial crisis since World War II. The gold pool from 1961 to 1968
operated on the basis of directives issued in Basle by the governors of the central
banks of the Group of Ten. Successive packages launched in defense of sterling were
usually arrange at Basle. The network of swap arrangements maintained by the
Federal Reserve Bank of New York developed originally from the swap arrangements undertaken at the first Basle Agreement.

The BIS also played, until 1994, a central role in the technical operations of the
European Monetary System (EMS). Because of its original responsibility as a coordi-
nator for international settlements in Europe, it has been closely involved in European
payment arrangements since World War II. During its lifetime, it has managed the
Agreement on Multilateral Monetary Compensation set up in 1947 to handle postwar
European clearing arrangements, the 1948 Intra-European Payments Agreement, the
European Payments Union of 1950, its successor, the European Monetary Agreement
of 1958, and most recently the European Monetary Cooperation Fund (EMCF)
established in 1973, and the private interbank ECU clearing system.

The BIS also acted as agent for the European Monetary Fund, the successor to
the EMCF, set up in 1979. That is, it handled the settlement of balances on behalf of
the countries in the EMS. It also ran the EEC's system of short-term monetary
support and manages the financial aspects of EEC borrowings from overseas, and
the private interbank ECU clearing system. These activities were handed over to the
fledgling European Monetary Institute in January 1994.

Finally, the BIS has an important research and coordination role in the Euromarkets. Its Annual Report and Quarterly Statistics are widely regarded as the most
authoritative sources of information on developments on the Euromarkets. And the
BIS also provides the secretariat for the Committee on Banking Regulations and
Supervisory Practices set up in December 1974 by the central bank governors to
coordinate bank supervision after the Herstatt crisis (when Bankhaus ID Herstatt
failed after unwise foreign exchange speculation).

5.3 ARAB MONETARY FUND

There is a regional Arab equivalent to the IMF, the Arab Monetary Fund (AMF),
although it is neither large nor active. The AMF was set up by the Articles of
Agreement of the Arab Monetary Fund concluded in April 1976 at Rabat in
Morocco. The AMF was modeled closely on the IMF, and includes 20 Arab coun-
tries: Algeria, Bahrain, Egypt, Iraq, Jordan, Kuwait, Lebanon, Libya, Mauritania,
Morocco, Oman, Qatar, Saudi Arabia, Somalia, Sudan, Syria, Tunisia, UAE, Yemen
Arab Republic, and People's Democratic Republic of Yemen together with Palestine.
Egypt's membership was suspended in April 1979. In the same month the AMF's
paid-up capital was increased to 124 million Arab accounting dinars (AAD
1 = SDR 3).

The major shareholders of the AMF are Saudi Arabia and Algeria. Its headquarters are in Abu Dhabi, and its primary work is to help member states with their
balance of payments problems through short-term and medium-term loans (not

exceeding seven years). It also gives guarantees designed to ease member borrowings from other sources. The AMF tries, too, to coordinate the monetary policies of member states and to extend technical assistance to their banking and monetary institutions.

Before the creation of the AMF, there were several Arab institutions which provided project finance, but none of them offered balance of payments support. This assistance was usually arranged on an *ad hoc*, bilateral basis through high-level political discussions with the leadership of the states concerned. The AMF represents an attempt to rationalize and institutionalize this function. On the other hand, with paid-in capital of only approximately US$400 million, it was a rather modest beginning. Furthermore, its development was held back by alleged embezzlement of large sums by a senior official.

5.4 CENTRAL BANK SWAP NETWORK

A foreign exchange swap is a spot purchase of a currency coupled with a forward sale. The calculations involved are discussed later. The effects on the timing of a bank's exposure, and how swaps are used by central banks to intervene in foreign exchange and money markets, are discussed in Chapter 4. This section discusses a rather special use of the swap by central banks: to borrow/lend foreign currency in exchange for domestic currency as a secured credit. The purpose is to lend the borrower foreign currency with which to intervene in the market.

The technique was first developed systematically by the US Federal Reserve in the early 1960s. The first agreement was made by the Fed with the Banque de France in 1962. Between 1962 and 1967 the Fed negotiated agreements with other central banks and the BIS. Table 5.3 shows how the Fed swap network looked as of June 1994. Other countries have also put together swap arrangements, notably the UK in defense of sterling; and the Bank of Japan, for example, has a swap arrangement with the Swiss National Bank for JPY 200 billion. The European Monetary Fund depends entirely on swaps for its resources.

We will look at the Fed network in detail since it is the most important. It consists of a set of standby credit agreements between the United States and other countries. Each arrangement provides for an exchange of currencies between the two countries with a commitment to reverse it in three months. At first, these swaps gave a full exchange risk guarantee to both central banks. After July 1973, the exchange risk on drawings by the Fed was shared evenly with the foreign central bank from which it was borrowing. Other central banks borrowing from the Fed had to take the full risk. Then in 1981, it was agreed that the earlier system would be restored.

To see how the swap network actually works, let us suppose the Fed wants to sell deutsche marks to support the US dollar. Suppose it needs DEM 220 million (equivalent, say, to US$100 million) from the Bundesbank. What actually happens is that it sells the Bundesbank US$100 million in exchange for DEM 220 million, with an agreed reversal in three months' time at a fixed rate. The Bundesbank's reserves of foreign exchange rise by US$100 million and those of the Fed rise by DEM 220 million. In other words, the swap has increased both central banks' reserves. This apparent magic is caused by the fact that central banks report their reserves as the

Table 5.3 Federal Reserve Swap Agreements as of June 30, 1994 (in Millions of US$)

Institution	Amount
Austrian National Bank	250
National Bank of Belgium	1 000
Bank of Canada	2 000
National Bank of Denmark	250
Bank of England	3 000
Bank of France	2 000
Deutsche Bundesbank	6 000
Bank of Italy	3 000
Bank of Japan	5 000
Bank of Mexico	3 000
Netherlands Bank	500
Bank of Norway	250
Bank of Sweden	300
Swiss National Bank	4 000
Bank for International Settlements	
Dollars against Swiss francs	600
Dollars against other authorized European currencies	1 250
Total	**32 400**

Source: *Federal Reserve Bulletin*, September 1994.

total of the assets in foreign exchange, without deducting the contingent liability on any forward exchange deals.

Central bank swaps, like any other swaps, can have an effect on the domestic money market. We saw how this works in Chapter 4. But in general the main reason central banks use them is to lay hands on foreign currency with which to defend their own currency. The Fed for many years did not hold foreign exchange reserves; hence its interest in developing the swap technique in the early 1960s. Once the network was in place, the Bank of England became an active user in the 1960s to defend sterling; the Banque de France around the time of "the events of May" in 1968—and on other occasions—also used the system, as have many other central banks. During the period of "benign neglect" of the dollar, the swap network was used only to give support to the Banco de Mexico; since the reversal of that policy, the authorities would certainly use the swap network if they needed to but in practice have not felt the requirement. During 1989, for example, the only use made of the network was a short-term drawing by Mexico.

5.5 THE FEDERAL RESERVE

In addition to the multinational institutions that we have described, there is a second set of key players in the international monetary system; the central banks of individual countries. Of these, the most important are the Fed, the Bank of Japan, the Bundesbank, the Bank of England, and the Banque de France.

Of the central banks we shall look at, the Fed is unique not only because of the central world role of the dollar but also because it is not one bank but 12. It is a system rather than a bank. It was set up by Act of Congress much later than most other central banks—1913. The Federal Reserve Act divided the United States into 12 districts. It provided for the creation within each of a District Federal Reserve Bank. The system as a whole is controlled by the Fed's Board of Governors in Washington. The Board has seven members appointed by the President and confirmed by the Senate. Members of the Board are appointed for 14-year terms, which limits the political control exercised by the President over the Board. The Chairman of the Board, who is named by the President, serves in that capacity for only four years but can be reappointed. But the Chairman's term does not start when the President's does, so an incoming President may have to wait until well into the term before appointing a new Chairman. Also, the Fed's independence is bolstered by the fact that it is a legally independent institution. The President and executive arm of the US government can exercise no direct control over it.

The Fed is subject to US law, and so in the end comes under the authority of Congress. The relevant law is the Full Employment Balanced Growth (Humphrey-Hawkins) Act of 1978. The Act requires the Fed to present each year a report on monetary policy to Congress by February 20 and July 20. In the first of these, the Fed is required to set annual monetary policy targets. These have to be reviewed in the second report which also provisionally sets the next year's.

The way in which the Fed handles monetary policy is as follows. Although it is in principle a group of 12 banks, in practice the Fed works through two major bodies. The New York Fed handles the system's intervention in money and foreign exchange markets. Policy decisions on intervention are mainly controlled by the Federal Open Market Committee (FOMC). Members of the FOMC include all 7 governors of the system, together with the President of the New York Reserve Bank, and the presidents of 4 of the other 11 district banks. Every member of the FOMC has one vote, but the Chairman of the Board of Governors has a decisive part in setting policy. He acts as chief spokesman for the system. It would be very unusual for a major policy action to be decided on by the FOMC if the Chairman of the Board of Governors had voted against: indeed, the news of a 4 to 3 vote against Paul Volcker in February 1986 was a major shock to the markets, even though the vote was subsequently reversed.

The FOMC normally meets about once a month. It reviews economic conditions, its goals, and current policy guidelines. At the end of the meeting, the FOMC issues a directive to the manager of the open market account in New York. (The open market account is the system's portfolio of US Treasury and Federal Agency securities, and bankers' acceptances, acquired in open market operations.) The directive sets a short-term target which the FOMC thinks is needed to meet its annual target. And it usually sets a limit on the movement in the Fed funds interest rate. For example, the key parts of the October 1994 directive were:

"The Federal Open Market committee . . . reaffirmed at this meeting the ranges it had established in February for growth of M2 and M3 of 1 to 5 percent and 0 to 4 percent respectively, measured from the fourth quarter of 1993 to the fourth quarter of 1994. The Committee . . . seeks to maintain the existing degree of pressure on reserve positions . . . slightly greater reserve restraint would or slightly lesser reserve restraint might be acceptable in the intermeeting period."

Note the difference of emphasis: tightening "would" be acceptable while easing "might" be. This directive was fairly evenly balanced; on other occasions, of course, the direction would be much more clear-cut.

The control of America's gold and foreign exchange reserves ultimately rests, not with the Fed, but with the US Treasury. The Secretary of the Treasury is legally responsible for stabilizing the exchange value of the dollar, through the Exchange Stabilization Fund (ESF) which is owned by the Treasury and which controls US gold and foreign exchange reserves. The swap network was a way for the Fed to get hold of foreign exchange to use for intervention. But that is only temporary: it has to be repaid. The ESF owns the US gold reserves and foreign exchange acquired from SDR sales and IMF drawings.

Policy on foreign exchange is controlled by the Treasury, whether the Fed likes it or not. Unfortunately, the Treasury is by its nature controlled by a politician. Thus, policy has swung back and forth over the years in line with changes in political complexion of the cabinet. During the 1960s, the Fed, with Treasury support, became very involved in international efforts to prop up fixed exchange rates. It developed a currency swap network; the Treasury issued Roosa bonds (US Treasury bonds in foreign currency). By 1971, the US Treasury Under Secretary John Connally had come to an "America first" view, which led to the dollar devaluation and the breaking of the gold–dollar link. For a few years, there was little intervention; "benign neglect" of the dollar was the policy. By 1977, this had led to unsustainable pressure on the dollar, and the swap network was reactivated. In 1981, under President Reagan, the pendulum swung back to another kind of benign neglect, based on the idea that intervention was wrong in principle. By 1985, this had led to unsupportable upward pressure on the dollar and was abandoned at the Plaza Agreement.

5.6   BANK OF ENGLAND

The Bank of England is the second oldest central bank (after the Sveriges Riksbank) in the world, and was founded in 1694. Until 1946, when it was nationalized, its shareholders remained private. So its evolution into the role of a central bank has been very gradual, in comparison with that of the Fed which was born as a full-fledged central bank. The Chancellor of the Exchequer controls the Bank, under the Bank of England Act of 1946. The Treasury has open-ended power to give directives to the Bank on any subject except the affairs of a particular bank customer. Thus, unlike the Fed, the Bank of England is legally completely subordinate to the executive arm of the government. However, the Bank has traditionally exercised an independent influence of its own, largely because of its excellent working contacts with the City of London, from which the Treasury has traditionally been rather remote, and its network of overseas contacts with other central banks.

The Bank is controlled by its Court of Directors, which consists of the Governor, Deputy Governor, and 16 directors, all appointed by the Crown. The term of office of the Governor and the Deputy Governor is five years, that of the directors is four years. Four of the directors retire each year; they are eligible for reappointment.

The Bank of England is, with the Department of Trade to a minor degree, solely responsible for controlling what UK banks do. This centralization of control, together with the Bank's close working contacts with the banking system, has generally meant that its attitude toward regulation of city activities has been pragmatic and informal, in contrast to the bias toward regulation that we saw in the US markets. This flexibility and informality helped the rapid development of the City of London's international financial activities during the 1960s and 1970s despite the weakness of sterling.

However, the UK's entry into the EEC forced the Bank to harmonize its attitudes with the more legalistic approach of its counterparts in Europe. For example, the Bank had to introduce, for the first time, a legal definition of a bank and banking activity, in the Banking Act of 1979. For the first time, also, this Act introduced a requirement that a bank should be recognized as such by the Bank of England in order to operate.

A more legalistic approach was also forced on the Bank as a result of the Financial Services Act of 1986, and the wider involvement of banks in the securities industry through the so-called "Big Bang" of around that time, under which the stock market was reformed and banks became heavily involved in the securities industry. Although the Bank of England had always been closely involved in the UK securities industry by virtue of its deep involvement in the City, the effects of "Big Bang" were to tie it even more closely into the securities markets. The Bank's role is thus wider, yet less clearly defined than that of the Fed.

As in the United States, the Treasury controls the UK's gold and foreign exchange reserves. But their day-to-day management is entrusted to the Bank of England, which was responsible for the country's reserves long before the Treasury was. Indeed, the low gold content of UK reserves can be traced back to the Bank's private sector origins. During the nineteenth century, its attitude was "maximum banking profits consistent with convertibility of sterling"; this meant low holdings of noninterest-bearing gold. More recent gold outflows were caused by the defense of sterling during the 1960s and 1970s. Since July 1979, 20% of the UK's reserves are on deposit, in exchange for ECUs with the EMF.

During 1993 the British government took two small, but significant, steps toward granting greater independence to the Bank of England. The minutes of the meetings between the Chancellor of the Exchequer and the Governor of the Bank are now published, about six weeks after the event. In addition, the Bank now publishes an "Inflation Report" setting out in some detail its views on the prospects for inflation. These two steps should help to bolster the Bank's position *vis-à-vis* the government when the time comes for difficult decisions to be made.

5.7 DEUTSCHE BUNDESBANK

Unlike the Bank of England, the Bundesbank is legally independent of its government. Unlike the Fed's, that independence is not fettered by any equivalent of the Humphrey-Hawkins Act. Of the world's major central banks, the Bundesbank is probably the strongest: it has benefited from the German people's horror of inflation after their experiences of the 1930s. The Deutsche Bundesbank law of 1957 lays down in Article 12 that the Bundesbank "shall not be subject to instructions from the Federal Government." Of course, the Bundesbank must support government policy as far as it can without compromising its primary duty, the safety of the currency. And during the headlong rush to German monetary unification in 1989/90, the wishes of the Bundesbank were overridden by the political masters in Bonn, who were determined to achieve monetary unification on terms that would be acceptable in East Germany, even though the Bundesbank did not approve the details of the rate of exchange between the deutsche mark and the old ostmark.

The Bundesbank is controlled by a Central Bank Council, which usually meets every two weeks on a Thursday. (Sometimes these meetings are followed by a press conference, sometimes not. If it is announced that no press conference will be held, the market usually assumes there will be no change in policy.) The Council's members are appointed by the President of the Federal Republic, on the government's recommendation (which must follow consultation with the Council). The members' terms are usually eight years. The Bundesbank controls 11 provincial central banks, each of which handles official business in its *Land* (province).

Unlike the United States, the UK, or France, but like Switzerland, Germany does not have any equivalent to the ESF. The Bundesbank owns the country's reserves. Every change in the level of reserves alters the size of the Bundesbank's balance sheet and so the level of domestic currency (compare Chapter 4). The Bundesbank also owns Germany's gold reserves, which have remained fairly stable since 1971. Most of the gold holdings were acquired during 1951–61, when the German "miracle" was taking place. In fact, in 1967, under US pressure—exerted in the form of military leverage—Germany made a formal commitment that it would not try to convert its dollars into gold (compare other central banks' holdings, discussed next).

5.8   BANQUE DE FRANCE

The Banque de France dates back to Napoleon (it was founded in 1800) and, like Napoleon, has always been a strong believer in tight central control. More than any of the other central banks, it has traditionally had influence everywhere in its banking system. It has branches around the country, helping it to keep in close contact with credit conditions in each area. Its knowledge reaches down to the most minute details. For example, every bank, when approached to open a new account for a customer, had to contact the Banque. It must check whether or not any problems have ever been reported with this customer (and must report any problems as they occur). This gives the Banque credit information on every individual and company in the country.

Until 1946, the Banque de France, like the Bank of England, operated as a private company. Under the nationalization law, a reform of the Banque's statutes was provided for, but it did not in fact take place until 1973. The new statutes gave the Banque a much freer hand and laid down a new structure. Control of the Banque rests with the Governor, two Deputy Governors, and the General Council. The Governor and his deputies are appointed for an unlimited term by the President of the Republic. The Council consists of 10 members, of whom one is elected by the staff of the Banque, and the rest are appointed by the government. Counsellors serve for six years. The Council normally meets once a week.

As part of the process of adapting the French financial system toward European monetary union, a new law was passed in 1993. This requires the Banque to operate "without seeking, or accepting, instructions from the government or any other person." Responsibility for defining monetary policy is given to a new Council for Monetary Policy whose members are appointed for nine years by the National Assembly, the Senate and the Council of State. This enshrines the independence of the Banque—a radical departure from its historic role as an institution of government.

In any event, the role of the Banque had already considerably altered, with the liberalization of the French financial markets during the 1980s. In particular, in 1985/86 the Banque abandoned its system of credit control. From December 1986, monetary policy has essentially been put into action by the Banque's fixing of its intervention rate on the interbank money market. At the same time, to offset the weakening of its direct control over credit, the Banque laid greater emphasis on reserve requirements. It widened the range of institutions subject to the reserve requirements, to include savings banks, municipal savings banks, and the major centralized savings institutions. Reserve requirements on sight deposits were lifted from 3 to 5%, raised to 5.5% in October 1989. Over the same period, other increases were made on term deposits, CDs and the like. The French financial system has been greatly liberalized compared with the tight controls imposed during the 1970s. The fundamental change has been the effective abolition of exchange control. This has opened the French financial system to external influences for the first time for 50 years. At the same time, however, strict internal fiscal discipline and the conquest of inflation by determined monetary policy have meant that the French franc has been able to become much more closely linked to the deutsche mark in the EMS (see Chapter 6).

France's gold and foreign exchange reserves are owned by the Fonds de Stabilization des Changes (Exchange Stabilization Fund) that is controlled by the Treasury but managed on a day-to-day basis by the Banque de France. For many years, France favored the role of gold as an international monetary asset. This emphasis flowed primarily from a political insistence that the financing of international trade and the source of international liquidity should not depend on any single national currency. Specifically, it should not depend on the dollar. The classic statement of this position was by General de Gaulle in 1965: "We hold as necessary that international exchange be established . . . on an indisputable monetary base that does not carry the mark of any particular country. What base? In truth, one does not see how in this respect it can have any criteria, any standard, other than gold . . . which does not have any nationality, which is held eternally and universally. . . ."

From 1970 to 1980, whatever the original political reasons, this policy was extremely profitable for France, as gold went from US\$35 per ounce to US\$850. From 1980 to 1990, as gold moved from US\$850 to US\$390, however, that policy has been less attractive. In 1960, France held 446.89 million ounces of gold; in 1970, 100.91 (down from the peak of 449.54 in 1967: the "events of 1968" caused some drain). By 1980, the figure was 81.85 million ounces (but this total will have been affected by the swap made by all EMS members with the European Monetary Coop-

Table 5.4 Holdings of gold in millions of ounces

	1970	1980	1990	1994
USA	316	264	262	262
Germany	114	95	95	95
Switzerland	78	83	83	83
France	101	82	82	82
Italy	83	67	67	67
Netherlands	51	44	44	35
Belgium	42	34	30	25
Japan	15	24	24	24
Austria	20	21	20	18
UK	39	19	19	18
Canada	23	21	15	4

eration Fund, under which 20% of reserves were deposited in the exchange for ECUS). This figure held constant throughout the 1980s, as the price of gold collapsed in the early part of the decade, and remained low for the rest of the period.

A comparison of central bank gold holdings at this point may be of interest (Table 5.4). It will be seen that while almost all central banks (apart from Switzerland, Austria and Japan) cut their holdings considerably in the 1970s, most have held their gold holdings frozen at the same level for the last 15 years. Canada is the obvious exception, along with the Netherlands and Belgium.

5.9 BANK OF JAPAN

Of the central banks we are considering, the Bank of Japan and the Swiss National Bank are the only ones still with private shareholders. Legally the bank is a special corporation under the Bank of Japan Law of 1942 (although it traces its origin to 1882) which is held 45% by the public and 55% by the government. In practice, the private shareholders have no say in running it. The Minister of Finance can give general directives to the bank, and can dismiss its officers. The usual Japanese "consensus" system, though, means that formal instructions almost never have to be given to the bank, but this does not mean that there are not often strong arguments between the two regarding policy.

The highest decision-making body of the bank is its Policy Board, which is composed of the Governor, two representatives of the government (one representative each from the Ministry of Finance and the Economic Planning Agency), and four appointed representatives (one from the city banks, the regional banks, commerce and industry, and agriculture). Of these seven, the government representatives do not have voting power, so that decisions are taken by majority vote of the Governor and the appointed members. The appointed members are selected by the cabinet and approved by both houses of Diet for terms of four years, with reappointment possible. The Policy Board's decisions on discount rates and open market operations are independently made. However, discount rate changes would normally be subject to consultation with the Ministry of Finance. In the end, the Bank of Japan will normally have its way, but this may be preceded by a lengthy period of arguments with the Ministry.

Japan, like the United States, the UK, and France, has a separate foreign exchange fund. In fact it has a Foreign Exchange Funds Special Account and a Precious Metals Special Account for the gold reserves. The Foreign Exchange Funds Special Account raises its finance by borrowing from the Bank of Japan, by issuing short-term bills (Foreign Exchange Fund bills), and by selling surplus foreign currency balances to the Bank of Japan.

5.10   SWISS NATIONAL BANK

The Swiss National Bank (SNB), founded in 1905, has two headquarters. The legal and administrative headquarters are at Berne, but the bank's Directorate is at Zurich. It is a private corporation, but most of its shares have been held since the beginning by the Cantons and Cantonal banks. The SNB is controlled by a Bank Council consisting of 40 members. Detailed control of the Bank is handled by a bank committee, chosen by the Council. But for practical purposes, the body which matters is the Directorate, which fixes the discount rate and decides on monetary policy. It consists of the Governor and two Deputy Governors, appointed by the Federal government for six years. It also has deputy members, are also appointed by the government for six years, and section directors, elected by the bank committee.

The SNB's international relationships are different from those of the other central banks we have looked at, because Switzerland has a strict policy of international neutrality. This has caused it to refuse to join the IMF and the World Bank. But the SNB works in parallel with other central banks, for instance in lending money to the IMF under the GAB and other IMF financings. The SNB is a shareholder in the BIS—not surprising, since the latter's headquarters is in Basle.

Like the Bundesbank, the SNB owns the country's reserves, and they form part of its balance sheet. So any currency inflow immediately inflates the SNB's balance sheet. The bulk of the reserves are held in gold. The high level of gold holdings is partly due to the traditional legal requirement that 40% of the Swiss note circulation be backed by gold.

5.11   ARTIFICIAL CURRENCY UNITS

In this section we explain what an artificial currency unit is. We look at the two most important, the SDR and the ECU. Then we look at the EEC's green currencies, and at the concept of a trade-weighted exchange rate.

Artificial currency units can be split into three main types. These are standardized units used in international monetary cooperation; units of account used in multinational agreements; and "currency cocktails" consisting of units created out of a number of national currencies.

Standardized units with the aim of helping international transfers have included the gold franc of the Latin Monetary Union which nominally existed among

Belgium, France, Greece, Italy, and Switzerland between 1865 and 1921, and the CFA franc of the Communauté Financière Africaine. However, they have been rare.

Units of account have been widely adopted for the purpose of international agreements. Examples include the accounts of the BIS which have been kept in "Swiss gold francs" since 1930; the Telecommunication Convention of 1932 (which adopted the gold franc of the Latin Union as its unit of account); the Convention for the Unification of Certain Rules Regarding Air Transport, 1929 (which adopted the so-called Poincaré gold franc); and the EEC unit of account (which was defined as equal to the then gold equivalent of one US dollar). The EEC unit has now been phased out in favour of the ECU (see below). The chief aim of the artificial currency has been to help the bookkeeping of a multinational organization such as the BIS or EEC or (as in the case of the air transport convention) to lay down international standards of value for payments.

Currency cocktails have had a slightly different purpose, namely to protect borrowers or lenders from the effects of currency fluctuations. Hence, they are primarily a post-1945 phenomenon. The first such cocktail was the European Unit of Account (EUA) which was launched in 1961 with a bond issue for SACOR of Portugal. However, this original version of the EUA was essentially a currency option; the investor had the option of taking payment in one of the 17 currencies of members of the European Payments Union.

Currency baskets consist of an average of a number of currencies. The first basket was the Eurco, but the concept was effectively launched by the (IMF) when in June 1974 it revalued its SDRs by setting one SDR equal to the sum of specified amounts of selected currencies. As these currencies fluctuated, so the value of the SDR fluctuated. In 1975, the EEC followed suit by setting up a new European Unit of Account, which in 1979 was superseded by the European Currency Unit.

5.12 SPECIAL DRAWING RIGHTS

The nature of the SDR is twofold: it constitutes an international reserve asset and also an international unit of account. The SDR was created by the First Amendment to the IMF's Articles of Agreement. This created a special drawing account (SDA) at the IMF. Member states were issued with SDRs, permitting them to obtain convertible currencies from the SDA under certain circumstances. Only member states, and certain designated official institutions, may at present legally hold SDRs. During 1970, the first tranche of SDR allocations was made, in three annual installments, totaling SDR 9500 million approximately; allocations were made according to member states' quotas at the IMF. The valuation of the SDR at this time was defined in terms of the gold value of one US dollar.

However, in 1971 the US dollar was devalued. The SDR did not devalue, and its value was set at SDR 1 = US$1.08571. Following the second dollar devaluation of February 1973, its value was set at SDR 1 = US$ 1.20835. The IMF recognized the arrival of a floating exchange rate system and on July 1, 1974 introduced a new SDR, consisting of 16 units of currency, whose values were added together to produce the value of one SDR. This was the so-called standard basket. (See Appendix 1 for a discussion of the mathematics of currency baskets.) The amounts were chosen to reflect the relative importance in world trade of the currencies involved, and were set so that the value on July 1, 1974 of the new and the old SDR was US$1.20835. The method used was to determine the percentage share of the basket to be held by each currency. These percentages are converted into units of currency on the base date. These then constitute the basket.

The composition of the SDR basket was revised effective July 1, 1978. It was announced that this basket would be revised at five-year intervals. However, effective January 1,1981 the IMF announced a new, simplified basket for the SDR consisting of five major currencies, which is now revised every five years. The most recent revision (as of January 1, 1991) resulted in the following basket:

Currency	Amount
US$	0.572
DEM	0.453
£stg	0.0812
FRF	0.800
JPY	31.8

To find the exchange rate for the SDR we calculate the total dollar value of the "bits" of national currency in the basket. To find the interest rate we would take a weighted average of interest rates, weighting them according to the weight of the currency in the SDR.

As we said earlier, private institutions may not legally hold SDRs, although they may deal in instruments linked to the value of the SDR. IMF member states, and certain designated official institutions, including the BIS, the SNB, the World Bank, the International Development Association, the Andean Reserve Fund, the AMF, the East Caribbean Currency Authority, the International Fund for Agricultural Development, and the Nordic Investment Bank are allowed to hold SDRs.

In recent years private institutions have become more involved in the SDR market (although in point of fact, this should be referred to as "the market for currency instruments index-linked to the SDR" since the banks cannot legally own SDRs). For example, since 1975, and particularly since the introduction of the simplified basket in 1981, a market in deposits linked to the SDR has existed. However, the SDR market has never grown to the extent that its main artificial-currency competitor, the ECU market, has. This is probably because the US dollar is a significant component of the SDR: if you wish to diversify out of dollars, it makes little sense to switch into the SDR when you can switch into the ECU which has no dollar component.

5.13 EUROPEAN CURRENCY UNIT

The European Currency Unit (ECU) has its origin in the EEC Unit of Account, which was created under the Treaty of Rome for the purpose of providing a unit of account for EEC institutions. It was then defined as equal to 0.88867,088 grams of 0.9 fine gold, the official par value of the US dollar. Following successive devaluations of the US dollar the emergence of floating currencies, and the creation of the

SDR basket concept, the EEC decided to introduce a basket unit of account for its own accounting. This was known as the European Unit of Account (EUA) (not to be confused with the earlier, private European Unit of Account). It was defined as equal to the sum of the following amounts:

FBC 3.66 + LuxFr 0.14 + HFL 0.286 + DKK 0.217 + DEM 0.828 + ITL 109 + FFR 1.15 + :GBP 0.0885 + IEP 0.00759.

The EUA was introduced first in 1975 in respect of the Lomé Convention on development aid, and the European Investment Bank's balance sheet. It was subsequently introduced in respect of the European Coal and Steel Community's operational budget (1976), the General Budget of the European Communities (1978), and customs matters (1979).

The ECU was created in 1979 with a value identical to that of the European Unit of Account, and an identical composition (but with a revision clause permitting changes, unlike the EUA). It took over all the existing functions of the EUA and was also introduced as the unit of account for the EMS (see Chapter 6), where it took over from the European Monetary Unit of Account, a slightly different unit of account used for the bookkeeping of the European Monetary Cooperation Fund previously. Under the EMS, EEC members' currencies are linked to a central rate defined in terms of the ECU. (See Appendix 1 on the mathematics of currency basket parities.)

The ECU as an official currency was born on December 18, 1978, as part of the setting up of the EMS of linked exchange rates by members of the EEC. The EEC regulation which created it defines the ECU as a "basket of members' currencies," that is the sum of fixed amounts of each of the members' currency. The first definition of the amounts fixed the makeup of the ECU from its beginnings to the first revision, which took place on September 17, 1984, when the Greek drachma was included, Greece having joined the EEC in the interim. In September 1989, the basket was revised again to accommodate two new members, Spain and Portugal.

The value of the ECU in US dollars is found by taking the dollar value of DEM 0.1828, adding to it the value of £0.0885 sterling, and so on. The EEC provides an official value each day using central-bank-provided exchange rates at 2.30 p.m.; the result is quoted on Reuters Monitor page FXEZ. As well as being the official unit of account for all EEC transactions, the ECU also plays a key role in the EMS, since EMS members' exchange rates are defined in terms of a "central rate" fixing their currency in terms of the ECU.

Official ECUs can only be held by the central banks of the EEC and other central banks who have been given permission. Private ECUs are traded like any other currency; in the Bank of England's 1986 foreign exchange survey, ECU trading was reported at around $900 million daily. Major commercial banks provide continuous quotes for the ECU (normally they have computer systems for calculating the ECU value from the currency rates held in their systems) and these can be seen on the appropriate Reuters/Telerate screens. ECU lending by banks in the BIS reporting area grew from ECU 14 billion in 1983 to ECU 90 billion in 1988. ECU certificates of deposit have also been issued and there is an active and important ECU bond market. The British government, for example, issued ECU 2 billion of gilts (gilt-edged bonds, so-called because of their high quality) in February 1991 and the

French government also issues regularly in the ECU market as does Italy. The role of the ECU in the EMS is discussed more fully in Chapter 6.

5.14 GREEN CURRENCIES

Reference is occasionally made to "green" currencies. These are the notional rates of exchange used by the EEC in the management of its Common Agricultural Policy. As such, they cannot be dealt in directly. However, they do impinge on the foreign exchange operations of corporations involved in EEC agriculture.

In 1962, the EEC issued its Regulation 129/62 setting up a unit of account for agricultural purposes. Its value was declared equal to 0.88867 088 grams of fine gold-equivalent to US$1 at the time. This gave rates of exchange (green rates) of u.a.1 = DEM 4.0 = FFR 4.93706, for example. Hence, when the EEC set a price of unit of account 212.30 per tonne for white sugar, this was equivalent to DEM 849.20 and FFR 1048.14.

However, in 1969, the French franc devalued, changing its parity against gold so that its value against the unit of account moved to FFR 5.55419. This would have resulted in a rise in the price of white sugar to 212.30 × 5.55419 = 1179.15, a rise of 12.6% which would have been paralleled in all other agricultural commodities. The inflationary effects of this were unacceptable to the French government, which arranged to postpone the devaluation of the green rate.

This meant, however, that white sugar sold in France still for FFR 1048.14: if exported to Germany, the French exporter would receive DEM 849.20, for which his bank would give him FFR 1179.15. It was necessary to prevent cheap French exports from swamping the German market. The EEC decided to place a tax on French exports to the rest of the EEC, and to subsidize French imports from the EEC. These taxes and subsidies were referred to as monetary compensatory amounts, or MCAs.

The move to floating exchange rates during 1971–73 forced the EEC to move toward a corresponding system of floating MCAs to offset exchange rate movements. This came in a series of regulations of which the most notable were 974/71, providing for variable MCAs, and 509/73, providing for a weekly variation in MCAs to cope with the floating of sterling. By this stage, telegrams from the EEC Commission to member states, setting out new MCAs, averaged 40–50 feet (12–15 m) in length.

In order to simplify matters, a new system was devised in June 1973 (Regulation 1463/74). The unit of account on which the system depended was no longer linked to the US dollar but to the central rates of the "joint float" currencies of the EEC. This meant that for member currencies, MCAs were fixed provided central rates were unchanged, even if the joint float varied against the dollar. For nonmember currencies, such as sterling, variable MCAs continued in force.

Following the entry into force of the EMS (see Chapter 4) on March 12, 1979, the unit of account laid down for calculating agricultural prices was the ECU. The EEC wanted to maintain the common level of prices. So it was decided that the price levels in old units of account would be multiplied by an adjustment coefficient. This factor came to 1.208953. Summing up simply, we can say that

$$\text{Green rate of exchange} + \text{MCA} = \text{Market rate of exchange}$$

Over the years the Commission has tinkered many times with the system of green currencies in a despairing attempt to arrive at a system which was workable but which coped with the fact of a single market for agricultural produce and multiple markets for exchange rates. The most recent reform (February 1995) means that in effect the green rates adjust to market rates quite quickly—if there is a devaluation. If there is a revaluation (i.e. farmers in the country affected will lose income) the system provides for a 50-day period to assess the impact of the revaluation. In effect the system is biassed in favour of devaluations and against revaluations, just as its predecessor was. The previous system resulted in a divergence of 20% between green rates and market rates cumulatively over a decade—i.e. a hidden 20% increase in farm subsidies which was borne indirectly by European consumers.

5.15 CALCULATION OF TRADE-WEIGHTED EXCHANGE RATES (EFFECTIVE EXCHANGE RATES)

While not strictly an artificial currency unit, the calculation of a trade-weighted index for a currency is related to the concept and so is included here. Before the advent of floating rates, a devaluation or revaluation of a currency occurred against all other currencies simultaneously. A 5% revaluation of the deutsche mark against the US dollar implied a 5% revaluation against the French franc, and so on. With the advent of floating rates, however, the impact of a 5% revaluation against the US dollar coupled with a $2\frac{1}{2}$% devaluation against the Swiss franc is not clear-cut. Hence attempts were made to take account of the average change of a currency against all others.

A 20% depreciation of the Argentine peso against the deutsche mark is less important to Germany than a 10% depreciation of the French franc, since France is a much more important trading partner for Germany than Argentina. So the various currencies' changes need to be weighted by taking account of the share of a country's trade held by a partner currency.

Such a trade-weighted index may be called a "simple average" trade-weighted index. Suppose we have four countries, A, B, C, and D. Suppose we are constructing a trade-weighted index for A and that A's exports and imports are conducted with B, C, and D in the following proportions: B, 50%; C, 30%; D, 20%. Suppose in Period 1 we have the following exchange rates for one unit of A's currency against the others:

$$A1 = B2 = C2.5 = D3.$$

Suppose in Period 2 A revalues against B by 10%, devalues against C by 20%, and revalues against D by 15%. Then we can weight the percentage changes and add them:

$$+10\% \times 0.5 - 20\% \times 0.3 + 15\% \times 0.2.$$

The weighted change is 2%: so if we express the index for Period 1 as 100, that for Period 2 is 102.

However, this simple index takes no account of the effects of the exchange rate on changes in third-country trade. Thus, because A has devalued against C by 20%, it is now able to encroach on C's trade with B, and so on. To take full account of these effects requires a matrix of cross-elasticities in international trade, and this is the approach adopted by the IMF in its multilateral exchange rate model and by the Bank of England in its index for sterling.[2]

The exact method of calculation is complex and varies from country to country. A widely used index is that calculated by Morgan Guaranty Trust Co. of New York which is a geometric index of exchange rates weighted by proportions of trade. Morgan also calculates a "real" effective exchange rate. This makes an adjustment to take account of inflation to attain the "real" effective exchange rate. Suppose that taking 1977 as a base, the US dollar has appreciated in effective terms from 100 to 107.5. Suppose that inflation over this period has been 22.5%: the "inflation-adjusted" or "real" effective index will total 130. The Japanese yen may have appreciated in effective terms over the same period by 12%, but if inflation in Japan over that period has been only 15%, the real effective exchange rate index will have risen only to 127. A difficulty in interpretation here is the choice of correct index to apply: export prices, domestic retail prices, or wholesale prices, for example. The inflation-adjusted index produced by Morgan Guaranty uses wholesale prices of nonfood manufacturers.

NOTES

1. The membership of the Central Bank of Yugoslavia is currently suspended pending a final determination of the legal status of the Yugoslav issue of the BIS's capital.
2. The most recent revision of the Bank's index is descsribed in the February 1995 edition of the *Bank of England Quarterly Bulletin*. No conceptual changes were made but the trade weights were updated to 1989–91 values and the index was rebased to 1990 = 100.

6

European Monetary Union

-

6.1 POLITICAL BACKGROUND

The question of European Monetary Union (EMU) merits a separate chapter for several reasons. Firstly, in its own right, of course, the European Union (EU) represents a significant international economic force. Any major policy decisions taken by that entity will have large international repercussions. In the context of this book, however, another reason for devoting a separate chapter to the subject is the fact that it raises a number of interesting technical questions for the foreign exchange and money markets. The process of unifying currencies raises several technical points.

This is a book about foreign exchange and money markets, rather than politics. But, inevitably, the EMU has very significant political implications. Because these political implications are so important, and in order to try and put the discussion in a reasonably neutral framework, it may be appropriate to begin by stating my personal opinions, so that readers may adjust for them if they wish. My own belief is that a single European currency is not necessarily a bad thing. Nor is it necessarily a particularly good thing. What is unambiguously bad is to seek to frame the discussion of EMU in terms which seek to hide the crucial issues. The European Commission has been as guilty of this offence as the most ardent Eurosceptics. The central point is that a single monetary union is entirely unworkable without a single fiscal union. There must be a centralized European budget and a centralized European taxation system if the EMU is to work in practice. A single budget and a single taxation framework necessarily imply a unified central government. Since the most basic definition of a government is "an entity which is capable of militarily defending its borders and of enforcing its taxation decrees internally," that probably also implies a unified European force. Unless and until the political implications of EMU are thought through and accepted by all parties it will be very difficult to make it work.

It is perhaps worth making the point that although currency union has political implications it need not, despite the claims of British Eurosceptics, imply abandonment of the nation state. Belgium and Luxembourg have operated a monetary union for years; and until 1979 Ireland and the UK had a monetary union. That did not mean a political union—as the IRA and the Ulster Unionists made violently clear.

Historically—to telescope complex events into a few sentences—the origins of the EU go back to the vision of Jean Monnet. He perceived that by creating an apparently minor technical entity, the European Coal and Steel Community, it would be possible to create unobtrusively a framework which could then begin to be used for other forms of European cooperation, which could then again unobtrusively be used to develop into a European framework for economic cooperation, which became formalized in the Treaty of Rome. The technique of the founding fathers, if one may so refer to them, was to create Europe by stealth. This is not meant as a criticism; it was probably the only practical way to do it, and the results have in many respects been thoroughly desirable.

The primary driving force behind the original concept was so to bind France together with Germany that another European war would become impossible. Even the most ardent defender of the concept of a nation state would probably concede that another European war would be undesirable; and most would probably concede that the prospect of a major war between France, Germany and other major European nations is now almost unthinkable. With the example of Yugoslavia nearby, they would probably concede that to that extent the achievements of the EU have been unambiguously good.

The central point of the Eurosceptic case concerns the loss of sovereignty implicit in the creation of a single currency. The attachment of such Eurosceptics and believers in the nation state to the concept of "economic sovereignty" is difficult to understand. A general theme throughout this book has been the enormous difficulty in today's financial markets, where huge sums of money move globally at almost the speed of light, in managing an economy independently of the global financial markets. Short of a full-scale retreat into autarchy, such as was attempted in Communist Romania, the notion of independent economic sovereignty today is difficult to sustain. Indeed, given the inextricable linkages between national economies today, it is not obvious why anybody (apart from some politicians seeking the personal gratification of a sense of power) would necessarily wish for economic sovereignty.

So far as the UK is concerned, it is certainly not clear that UK economic policy has been better conducted on an independent basis than might conceivably be done as part of a European Union. Some of the more irresponsible excesses of both parties might in fact have been avoided.

In summary, then, I believe that a single European currency and EMU would probably not be a bad thing. However, the costs of the transition (see below) have almost certainly been grossly understated, as have the degree of disruption and the extent of the operational changes in national financial systems which will need to be made. The typical proponent of EMU, on the evidence of the material which I have read, has very little interest in, and possibly understanding of, the actual functioning mechanics of financial systems. As a result, the cost/benefit analysis is by no means clear-cut.

The only argument in favour of EMU which is unassailable (in its own terms) is the political one. If you believe that Europe should be unified politically, then EMU is unambiguously a good thing; it is also a necessary condition. I am not personally convinced that the political benefits are so overwhelming; the idea that a political entity is necessarily better because it is bigger is not particularly convincing.

For many, of course, the unspoken agenda behind monetary union was the notion that the power of a resurgent and reunited Germany could be contained within a larger unit. It is not evident that achieving a single European polity is the only solution to this "problem." An equally effective approach might be to build coalitions on specific issues with a view to outvoting a German government, if it were felt that the German government had a wrong notion on a particular issue. After all, it might be that the cure were worse than the disease: the idea of a single European currency, dominated by German policy, is not particularly appealing either. In financial markets, for example, the notion that European financial markets should be reduced to the relatively primitive level which the Bundesbank would clearly—in an ideal world—like to see (i.e. no money-market funds, a restricted short-term money market, and a high level of minimum reserve requirements) would be profoundly unattractive in London. It would, incidentally, have the effect of driving the entire Euromarket outside the EU (perhaps to Zurich?).

This discussion has focused more on the political issues than is customary in a book of this nature; the reason is that the entire debate is intensely political by its very nature, and to ignore the underlying political issues is to distort the discussion. But having, as it were, put my cards on the table, so that the reader may adjust for any bias, we will now seek to set out some of the key analytical issues.

6.2 BENEFITS OF MONETARY UNION

The European Commission[1], estimated the savings from having a single currency which would eliminate the present cost associated with converting one EU currency into another. They estimated the resulting savings at approximately ECU 15 billion p.a., or about 0.4% of EU GDP. This is based in part on a confidential survey on the foreign exchange related revenues of banks in the Community. That survey estimated that a little less than 5% of aggregate bank revenues came from foreign exchange activities between EU currencies, and given that the banking sector accounts for about 6% of the GDP of the Union, the net bank revenue impact was estimated at about 0.3–4% of EU GDP. This estimate has been widely reported and relied upon elsewhere.

This is a very disreputable statistical exercise. Quite evidently this "saving" is not a saving at all. It simply represents a transfer from one sector of the European Union to another: from the banks, to the users of financial services. There will be an off-setting reduction in the profits of the banks, which will correspondingly reduce the Union GDP. The net benefit to the EC as a whole, therefore, will be considerably less: only to the extent that some of the foreign exchange revenues are earned by non-union banks will there be a net benefit to the EU. Presumably some of that benefit will be offset by higher social security payments to redundant foreign exchange dealers!

By contrast, a second component of foreign exchange transactions costs identified by the Commission is undoubtedly important: there will be efficiency gains in speeding up the process of funds transfer between countries within the EU. On the other hand, in a world where funds can be moved globally at the speed of light, it continues to take three days to clear a cheque drawn on a London bank and present it at another London bank; so the speed with which the banking system in fact handles money movements across the Union may not indeed increase at the pace hoped for by the Commission. Banks are strangely reluctant to give up the profits they make from "playing the float."

In summary, while there will undoubtedly be transactions cost savings and efficiency improvements from the adoption of a single currency, the financial impact in terms of contribution to EU GDP is likely to be at best marginal.

One major benefit will be the removal of exchange rate uncertainty for intra-Community business. The EU, with more than 300 million consumers, represents a very substantial market. Businesses wishing to sell throughout the European Union will clearly benefit from economies of scale, but currently face exchange risk on sales from, say, France to Germany. In theory, risk-averse agents will reduce their activity in an area such as trade and investment for export, if the risk, i.e. the variability on the return they can obtain from this activity, increases. Eliminating this risk should result in higher volumes of cross-border trade and investment, which should in turn produce a more efficient allocation of resources within the Union.

In practice, the empirical evidence on exchange rate variability is not conclusive. A number of studies have found no convincing effect and a major study undertaken by the IMF[2] concluded that it had not been able to find a systematic link between short-term exchange rate volatility and the volume of international trade. Some individual studies[3] have found a significant effect of exchange rate variability on international trade. However, these studies generally refer to the major floating currencies. The variability between EC currencies is much less than, for example, the variability of sterling against the US dollar. Thus, studies concentrating specifically on European currencies and intra-EC trade appear to have found only very small effects.

On the other hand, the evidence of surveys of business opinion strongly suggests that many firms find exchange risk an inhibiting factor. Furthermore, exchange risk is clearly a much bigger problem for the small-sized firm, since for multinationals with large cash flows, the transactions costs of managing foreign exchange hedging are extremely small. By contrast, a small exporter with a sale totaling perhaps £5000 would find that the cost of forward exchange hedging would be a significant factor. By liberating small firms from the cost of exchange risk, the move towards a single currency would clearly be strongly beneficial.

6.3 COSTS OF MONETARY UNION

The process of unifying the deutsche mark and the Ostmark was referred to earlier. This example shows that currency unification is perfectly feasible, even for two radically different economies. However, one of the factors which made it workable was the fact that at the same time the entire East German legal and economic structure was being absorbed into that of the former West Germany. It seems improbable that this will take place on a Europe-wide scale. Therefore, existing national systems—e.g., national company law, corporate accounting and computing systems, existing legal contracts—will all have to be converted, rather than simply being scrapped. In many respects this will be more difficult than the German unification process, where much of the old regime was simply swept away.

Even if the enabling legislation for a transition to the new currency in the UK for example, simply specifies that "all existing legal documents shall be re-interpreted to refer to the ECU instead of sterling and all existing obligations are to be converted at a rate of x per pound," there will be substantial transition costs. To take a simple example, it will be necessary for all existing quoted companies' reports and accounts to be converted into the new currency for at least five years back, purely for investors to be able to arrive at a reasonable historical perspective on the company. The costs of restating balance sheets and profit and loss statements to a new currency will, in a number of cases, be nontrivial.

Other nontrivial technical costs will include the retooling of all existing automated teller machines (ATMs), where the new ECU banknotes are of different size from those currently in use; replacement of all automatic vending machines and other machines using coin or banknote recognition (such as railway and underground ticket machines); the cost of rewriting computer software to handle bond market calculations in those countries whose interest convention differs from that finally adopted for the ECU (for example, British government bonds pay semi-annual interest on a 365-day year; German government bonds pay annual interest on a 30/360-day year). There will also be the cost of adapting financial markets to the single monetary framework which will be an inevitable corollary of a single currency. For example, either the German banking system will have to adopt the British monetary control regime under which reserves requirements are imposed in eligible liabilities in sterling but not foreign currencies, or the British markets will have to adapt to the German system of imposing reserve requirements on all currencies, at a significantly higher level than that prevailing in the UK. Very significant adaptation costs will arise as one money market shifts over to the procedure operating in the other. Even more significant adaptation costs will arise if neither side can agree on a suitable procedure, and that prevailing in some third country such as France is adopted.

These considerations are reinforced by the *Survey on the Introduction of the Single Currency: A First Contribution on the Practical Aspects* published by the European Banking Federation in Brussels in March 1995, which estimated that banks would need to spend three to four years preparing for the single currency with costs of ECU 8–10 billion (£6–8 billion). To these costs must, of course, also be added the costs of the banks' customers, which might well be as much again. The propaganda from the European Commission has remarkably little to say on all of these matters, while waxing eloquent on the merits of a single currency and the savings in transactions costs which would accrue.

6.4   ECONOMIC AND MONETARY UNION AND THE THEORY OF OPTIMUM CURRENCY AREAS

One argument which has been put forward for EMU is based on the argument that the EU will be an optimum currency area. The theory of optimum currency areas was developed in the 1960s to determine what should be the appropriate domain within which exchange rates are fixed.[4] Mundell pointed out that exchange rate flexibility is of no use between the USA and Canada if, due to a shock to the industrial structure, both countries are hurt by a shift in the relative economic of their eastern and western parts. Instead, what is needed is a change in the relative prices of eastern and western products. Therefore, the right criterion for designing a currency area should be the degree of factor mobility within the region, since a high degree of factor mobility would provide the adjustment channel which is lost in a fixed exchange rate regime.

For these reasons, Mundell concluded that the optimal zone for a single currency was determined by the area within which labour was willing and able to move freely. Clearly, labour mobility in the EC is relatively low. There are a number of reasons, but the primary one is obviously the linguistic problem of working in a country where the language is not one's mother tongue. On these grounds, currency zones ought to be small. Thus, using the Mundell criterion, the EMU would certainly not be an optimal currency zone.

In addition, Mundell argued that a fixed-exchange rate system tends to have an inherent deflationary bias, while common currency areas have a built-in inflationary bias. Suppose that the UK and Germany are linked by a fixed exchange rate, and German exporters succeed in winning business from British exporters. The UK balance of payments will weaken, the German balance will strengthen. The UK authorities will tend to raise domestic interest rates and tighten credit to strengthen the balance of payments. This will tend to reduce British demand for German exports, transmitting a deflationary impact to the German economy. By contrast, Mundell argued, if the two form part of a common currency area, then the authorities will be rather more preoccupied with preventing unemployment in the UK. Hence, they will tend, in response to the same initial shift of demand for the countries' exports, to loosen monetary conditions in the currency zone as a whole, thereby giving an inflationary boost to both countries.

This analysis rests on a number of assumptions, some of which may well not be justified; however, it is worth making the point that the reunification of Germany in 1990 is a classic illustration of the argument. In an effort to ease the pain of restructuring the German economy, the German authorities tolerated a substantially higher degree of domestic inflation with a view to sustaining employment in the East. As a result, monetary policy was tightened, and through the fixed exchange rate links of the ERM deflation was imposed on the unwilling members of the ERM.

The Mundell approach assumes that the optimal currency zone policy-makers can manage the exchange rate in such a manner as to maintain full employment, by devaluing the currency if necessary to improve competitiveness. For this to work, real wages must fall in the optimal currency zone which will only occur if workers experience "money illusion" and fail to increase their wage demands sufficiently to offset the loss of purchasing power caused by the devaluation.

As McKinnon argued in reply to Mundell, other things being equal (that is, given the other features of the labour market), there will be one overriding factor determining how far workers passively accept a fall in their real wage as a result of devaluation: the degree of openness of the economy. In a very small economy, almost all consumption is likely to consist of imports or tradable goods. The effect of, say, a 10% devaluation is therefore likely to be a nearly 10% rise in the cost-of-living index. Workers are likely to press for compensation for the effects of such an increase. On the other hand, in a large economy, where imports may well be only a small proportion of the typical consumption basket, the impact of even a 10%

devaluation will be small. For example, if imports account for only 5% of consumption, the direct effect will only be a 0.5% (that is 10% of 5%). Hence, McKinnon argues, in large economies, devaluation is unlikely to provoke a significant response on the part of wage earners. In general, therefore, McKinnon puts forward the case for very large currency areas. The larger the zone, the more closed the economy of the region it covers. Hence, the smaller the weight of traded goods in the consumption baskets of its workforce, and the easier it will be to effect a reduction in the real wage without workers realizing or bothering to respond. On this argument, the EU might meet the optimum currency area criterion—and on this argument, the larger the better.

6.5 EMU AS A DISCIPLINE

There is an extensive literature on the operation of the ERM.[5] The literature supporting the view that the ERM has exerted a strong and independent influence upon members' counter-inflationary stance typically emphasizes the disciplining role played by Germany *vis-à-vis* other ERM members; in particular the "reputational" benefits that can result if high inflation countries tie their nominal exchange rate to that of the country with the highest anti-inflation credibility. Analytical models of this hypothesis have usually been cast in a game-theoretic framework, often in the spirit of Barro and Gordon[6]. For example, Sargent[7] contains an interesting description of a game of "chicken" between a central bank and a finance ministry. This struggle for dominance between the monetary and fiscal authorities represents a situation of Stackelberg warfare. The central bank asserts that, come what may, it will not engage in inflationary monetization, in the hope of forcing the fiscal authorities to take steps to reduce the deficit. In the British context, Buiter and Miller[8] have identified a similar game of chicken in the 1970s between the trade unions on the one hand and the monetary and fiscal authorities on the other. Unions submitted inflationary wage demands in the expectation that demand management would be accommodating.

This line of thinking was clearly applied by some countries in the ERM. As pointed out by Buiter and Kletzer:[9]

> "One way to increase the likelihood that the Central Bank will win the game of chicken with the fiscal authorities is by convincing the latter that the Central Bank is implacably, irrevocably and unalterably opposed to any and all inflation . . . it is not wise for anyone to play a game of chicken with an adversary who may be slightly insane. Believing it is dealing with an anti-inflationary fanatic of doubtful rationality, the Treasury may prefer to give in rather than test the resolve of the Central Bank."

The possible rationality of choosing an agent who does not exactly share one's objectives (or who may even be irrational) is explained very clearly in Schelling.[10] This line of thinking, which traces back to the game theory analysis of nuclear warfare, has clearly been applied by a number of countries—including the UK—as part of a strategy to borrow the anti-inflationary credibility of the Bundesbank. Under this approach, the Bundesbank plays the role of the madman with the finger on the nuclear trigger who can be used to terrify domestic unions into noninflationary demands.

6.6 TECHNICAL OPERATION OF THE EMS

The process of creating the European Monetary System (EMS) was begun in 1972 by the creation of the "snake in the tunnel," a system where certain European currencies were fixed against each other but fluctuating within a "tunnel" against the US dollar. The move in 1973 to floating exchange rates derailed this and the system was relaunched in 1979 as the European Monetary System.

The EMS consists of three components: the Exchange Rate Mechanism (ERM), the European Monetary Cooperation Fund (EMCF), and the European Currency Unit (ECU). The ECU is explained in detail in Chapter 5. Briefly, it consists of an artificial currency unit that is made up from small amounts of the currencies of EMS members. The dollar equivalent of those currencies is added together to provide the value of the ECU.

The ERM is a system under which those EMS members that take part are committed to keeping their currencies fixed against each other within certain bands. This is done by declaring a parity or central rate for each currency against the ECU. This implies a parity grid. The current parity grid, which was set up in March 1995 when the Spanish peseta and Portuguese escudo devalued is shown in Table 6.1.

At the time of writing, the intervention bands within the EMS have been set at 15%. The original bands were 2.25%; the wider bands were set as a result of the 1993 EMS crisis. (Presumably at some point the EU will seek to return to the narrower bands.) When a currency reaches the permitted limit it is said to be at the intervention point. When any two currencies reach their compulsory intervention rates against each other, the two central banks concerned are obliged to meet all bids/offers made to them at the relevant rate. This obligation is only binding, however, between the hours of 0800 and 1500 GMT. In some cases, this might mean a central bank selling a currency not held in its foreign exchange reserves or in an amount that exceeds its current holdings. Operationally this does not cause a problem, because the intervening central bank has the right to draw upon the very short-term financing facility (VSTF) of the EMCF, which is explained below. At the intervention point, access to the facility is automatic and the amount of credit available is unlimited. Since November 1987, however, the VSTF has also been available, in certain circumstances and in limited amounts, to finance intervention before a currency reaches a compulsory intervention point. However, such intervention may not be undertaken without the prior consent of a central bank whose currency is being used in the intervention.

There is an early warning system called the divergence indicator that measures the percentage of permitted fluctuation a currency has reached. When the divergence indicator is at 75% of the permitted maximum fluctuation, there is a presumption that the relevant central bank will intervene. But because the interactions of the parity grid are complex (see Appendix 1), in practice it is quite common for currencies to reach their compulsory intervention points before reaching or crossing their divergence threshold.

The EMCF is important because of its short-term lending to EMS central banks when they are intervening in the foreign exchange markets. (It is often referred to as FECOM—Fonds Européen de Coopération Monétaire.) It runs the settlement and lending operations of the EMS. But it is itself run by the European Monetary Institute (EMI); it is not like the IMF in having a large independent staff. It evolved from the EMCF. The EMCF was set up by the Council of Ministers of the EEC in April 1973. They wanted it to aim at "(1) the progressive narrowing of the margins of fluctuation of the Community currencies against each other; (2) interventions in Community currencies on the exchange markets; and (3) settlements between central banks leading to a concerted policy on reserves."

The EMCF has helped partially to achieve (1), and also partially (3), through the workings of the EMS. Progress on (2) has been limited, because a great deal of the time intervention has been caused by EEC currencies' movements against the US dollar rather than among themselves. But a good deal of Community intervention is now carried on in other EMS currencies.

The EMCF's main job is to run the VSTF which finances intervention in EMS currencies. The VSTF allows unlimited credit among central banks involved in the EMS. The central bank that borrows from the EMCF (say it is the Banca d'Italia) can extend the term of its borrowing by using the short-term monetary support facility (STMS). Otherwise it must repay within 45 days of the end of the month when it borrowed the money. (The maximum the Banca d'Italia can borrow under VSTF is 75 days.)

When it repays, the Banca d'Italia, in our example, must first use its holdings of the lender's currency. If it has borrowed from the Bundesbank it must repay as much as it can in deutsche marks. But usually EMS central banks only hold working balances in other EMS members' currencies, so most of the debt has to be repaid in other currencies. Up to 50% of the remaining debt can be settled in ECUs. After that, the Banca d'Italia can only use ECUs for repayment if the Bundesbank agrees. In the light of the complaints made in the Bundesbank's Annual Report for 1992 that agreement might well not be forthcoming:

> "[denomination of intervention support in ECUs] leads to heavy losses on the part of the creditor central bank if exchange rates are ultimately changed despite everything . . . [Also] . . . currencies not participating in the ERM have a share of over one-fifth in the ECU basket. If the market value of the ECU falls . . . the creditor central bank suffers corresponding losses . . . such an outcome can be accepted only with difficulty over the long term."[11]

Otherwise, settlement must be made in proportion to the currencies in the borrower's reserves. Say 30% of Italy's reserves were in US dollars: then 30% of its repayment would have to be in US dollars.

If it did not want to repay immediately, the Banca d'Italia would turn to the STMS. The STMS lends to EMS central banks to finance temporary balance of payments deficits. Each country has a debtor quota, this amount being the maximum it is allowed to borrow, and a creditor quota, the amount it is committed to lend. On top of that there is the rallonge, which is a safety margin for the system as a whole. So a country can be asked to lend its creditor quota plus the total of the rallonge. Equally, it can borrow its debtor quota plus half of the rallonge. Take Germany as an example. The total it could borrow is ECU 1740 million debtor quota plus ECU 4400 million, half of the rallonge, for a total sum of ECU 6140 million. It must lend, if asked to, ECU 3480 million, its creditor quota, plus ECU 8800 million, the rallonge, for a total of ECU 12,280 million. The lending amounts are twice the borrowing amounts. This gives a safety margin for the system as a whole. If a country

Table 6.1 Bilateral Central Rates and Selling and Buying Rates in the EMS Exchange Rate Mechanism from 9 January 1995

		BEF LUF 100 =	DKK 100 =	FFR 100 =	DEM 100 =	IEP1 =	NLG 100 =	PTE100 =	ESP100 =	ATS 100 =
Belgium/ Luxembourg	S		627.88	714.03	2395.2	57.7445	2125.6	23.365	28.1525	340.42
	C		540.723	614.977	2062.55	49.7289	1830.54	20.1214	24.2447	293.163
	B		465.665	529.66	1776.2	42.826	1576.45	17.3285	20.8795	252.47
Denmark	S	21.4747		132.066	442.968	10.6792	393.105	4.32100	5.20640	62.9561
	C	18.4938		113.732	381.443	9.19676	338.537	3.72119	4.48376	54.217
	B	15.9266		97.943	328.461	7.92014	291.544	3.20460	3.86140	46.691
France	S	18.88	102.1		389.48	9.3895	345.65	3.79920	4.55780	55.3545
	C	16.2608	87.9257		335.386	8.08631	297.661	3.27188	3.94237	47.6706
	B	14.005	75.72		288.81	6.964	256.35	2.81770	3.39510	41.0533
Germany	S	5.63	30.445	34.625		2.8	(103.058)*	1.13280	1.36500	16.505
	C	4.84837	26.2162	29.8164		2.41105	88.7526	0.975561	1.17548	14.2136
	B	4.175	22.575	25.675		2.076	(76.4326)*	0.840140	1.01230	12.241
Ireland	S	2.33503	12.6261	14.3599	48.1696		42.7439	0.49841	0.566120	6.84544
	C	2.0109	10.8734	12.3666	41.4757		36.8105	0.404620	0.487537	5.89521
	B	1.73176	9.36403	10.65	35.7143		31.7007	0.348453	0.419859	5.07688

Netherlands	S	6.3434	34.3002	39.0091	(130.834)*	3.1545		1.27637	1.93793	18.5963
	C	5.46286	29.5389	33.5953	112.673	2.71662		1.09920	1.32445	16.0149
	B	4.70454	25.4385	28.9381	(93.0325)*	2.33952		0.946611	1.14060	13.7918
Portugal	S	577.090	3120.50	3549.00	11903.30	286.983	10564.0		139.920	1691.80
	C	496.984	2687.31	3056.35	10250.50	247.145	9097.55		120.493	1456.97
	B	428.000	2314.30	2632.10	8827.70	212.838	7834.70		103.770	1254.70
Spain	S	438.944	2589.80	2945.40	9878.50	238.175	8767.30	96.3670		1404.10
	C	412.461	2230.27	2536.54	8507.18	205.113	7550.30	82.9927		1209.10
	B	355.206	1920.70	2184.40	7326.00	176.641	6502.20	71.4690		1041.30
Austria	S	39.6809	214.174	243.586	816.927	19.6971	725.065	7.97000	9.60338	
	C	34.1107	184.444	209.773	703.55	16.9629	624.417	6.86356	8.27008	
	B	29.3757	158.841	180.654	605.877	14.6082	537.74	5.91086	7.12200	

S = Exchange rate at which the central bank of the country in the left-hand column will sell the currency identified in the row at the top of the table.

C = Bilateral central rate.

B = Exchange rate at which the central bank of the country in the left-hand column will buy the currency identified in the row at the top of the table.

* These buying and selling rates will not be operational. Reflecting a bilateral agreement between the German and Dutch monetary authorities, the following rates will continue to apply:

Netherlands (100DM: selling 115.2350, buying 110.1675)

Germany (100FL: selling 90.7700, buying 86.78)

needs to borrow, and all other countries in the system are also in deficit but one, the larger lending quotas plus the rallonge mean that the whole of the burden can be shifted to the country running a surplus.

The STMS can be used for a total of nine months. A country wanting to borrow for a longer period would apply to the EMCF for medium-term financial assistance (MTFA). As a matter of fact, no one ever has, so the MTFA need not concern us much. We should note that lendings, if made, would be for two to five years and subject to economic policy conditions laid down by the EEC Council of Ministers. (This is probably why no one uses it: politically it is easier to be seen obeying the IMF, which is an impartial world body, than obeying other EEC members.)

As with all lendings, the EMCF's credits have to be financed. The resources are provided by member central banks. They have each deposited 20% of their gold and dollar reserves with the EMCF. Technically what happens is that they swap the gold and dollars for ECUs issued by the EMCF. The swap is for three months. As each swap matures it is rolled over, but the amount involved is adjusted in line with the market value of gold and the dollar. The EMCF's control over these reserves is very limited, though, since the central banks actually retain the dollars and gold involved, and they receive the interest earned on the dollars. However, the arrangement does represent a step toward the pooling of EEC reserves.

6.7 THE EUROPEAN MONETARY INSTITUTE

The Treaty on European Union (usually referred to as the Maastricht Treaty) was signed in February 1992. After a difficult ratification process, it came into effect on November 1, 1993. As a result, on January 1, 1994, the regulations on the second stage of European economic and monetary union (EMU) came into effect. Stage one, which began after the recommendations of the Delors Committee were accepted at the Madrid summit in June of 1989, comprised closer economic and monetary cooperation between member states within the existing institutional framework, aiming at greater convergence of economic performance. It also involved the completion of the Single Market and the strengthening of Community competition policy.

The key feature of stage two is the creation of the European Monetary Institute. The EMI has, among its other key functions, taken over the administration of the EMCF and the accompanying financing mechanisms. It will monitor the running of the EMS, facilitate the use of the private ECU and oversee the development of the ECU clearing system, be consulted by the national authorities on monetary policy (although during stage two, monetary policy in individual countries remains firmly in the province of the national central bank) and report annually to the European Council on the preparation of technical procedures for stage three. However, the EMI will not intervene in foreign exchange markets on its own account, and members will not be obliged to hold reserves with it.

All EU central bank governors will be members of the EMI, but there is also a full-time president who will not be simultaneously a governor. It was agreed in the protocol to the Maastricht Treaty that in exercising their responsibilities under the EMI statute, governors should be independent, but that national central banks themselves need not be independent in stage two.

The EMI is recognized under EU law as an EU body. Internal organizational matters are largely left to the EMI's management, with a few exceptions such as the appointment of the president. The senior decision-making body of the EMI is the EMI Council. This comprises the president of the EMI and the governors of the national central banks. Its independence from the influence of member states or other Community organizations is guaranteed in article 8 of the EMI statute. The president of the EMI is chosen by a political process. A candidate is recommended by the EMI Council and confirmed by the European Council; the European Parliament is also consulted. (The first president of the EMI is Alexandre Lamfalussy, previously General Manager of the BIS. The first vice-president is Maurice Doyle, Governor of the Central Bank of Ireland.) The EMI is funded by the national central banks, rather than member states. Funding is determined according to article 16.2 of the EMI's statute and the secondary legislation on the EMI Key. The EMI Key is determined on the basis of two factors, equally weighted. These are 1992 population and GDP and market prices averaged over the five years up to and including 1991. On this basis, for example, the UK's share would be around one-sixth, a little less than those of Germany, France and Italy.

6.8 MAASTRICHT AND CONVERGENCE

The other key feature of stage two is that it is designed to achieve a process of economic convergence which will facilitate the creation of a single monetary zone. The protocol on convergence criteria annexed to the treaty, lays down four key criteria which will determine whether or not a particular economy has converged sufficiently closely to the norm to be eligible to join stage three. These are:

1. The achievement of a high degree of price stability—this will be a rate of inflation which is close to that of, at most, the three best performing member states.
2. A government financial position where the government deficit is at or less than 3% of GDP at market prices, and the ratio of government debt to GDP is 60% or less.
3. The observance of the normal fluctuation margins provided for by the exchange rate mechanism of the EMS for at least two years.
4. Durability of convergence being reflected in long-term interest rate levels. In particular, over a period of one year beforehand the member must have an average nominal long-term interest rate that does not exceed that of at most the three best performing member states in terms of price stability by more than two percentage points.

At the time of writing very few—perhaps three or four—EU members meet these criteria. They were strictly drawn, primarily to overcome the Bundesbank's fears that Germany might be dragged into monetary union with states running irresponsible fiscal policies which would corrupt the German anti-inflation stance. Ironically, the cost of reunifying Germany meant that soon after the Maastricht Treaty was ratified Germany itself failed to meet the criteria. In addition, the ERM crises of September

1992 and July 1993 meant that progress toward (3)—and by implication (4)—was severely set back.

A little-noticed provision of the treaty which became operative with the beginning of the second stage is the exclusion of liability by the Community and the other member states for the debts of individual countries within the Union. This rule is intended to underscore the responsibility borne by each country for its own public finances and to make sure that everything is done to avoid excessive deficits. If we are totally convinced that the process to EMU will be smooth, this is not a major question. On the other hand, if we have doubts as to whether or not that will happen, the explicit exclusion of "joint and several liability"—to use the legal jargon—means that countries such as Greece must be evaluated strictly on their own merits in terms of government creditworthiness.

Finally, with the entry into force of the Maastricht Treaty, the composition of the ECU currency basket has been permanently fixed. Previously, there had been a provision requiring a five-yearly review of the makeup of the ECU basket. As a result of the treaty, one ECU is now defined as the sum of the following currency amounts:

DEM 0.6242, FFR 1.332, GBP 0.08784, ITL 151.8, NLG 0.2198, BEF 3.301, LUF 0.130, ESP 6.885, DKK 0.1976, IEP 0.008552, GRD 1.440, PTE 1.393.

6.9 PROBLEMS OF TRANSITION TO MONETARY UNION

By way of historical sidelight, it may be worth mentioning that the first repercussion of the original EMS was the paradoxical one of splitting two currencies which had previously been unified: the pound sterling and the Irish punt.[12] The Irish punt entered the EMS, but sterling did not. This illustrates one of the difficulties of transition: the difficulty of securing simultaneous agreement from the various governments involved. As is well known, the British government at Maastricht secured an "opt-out" permitting it to choose not to take part in the single European currency when it is introduced. Even for those governments which do choose to take part, however, there will be difficult technical problems.

But the primary problem is that to some extent the introduction of EMU reflects the technique of Jean Monnet referred to earlier—of seeking the larger political objective by introducing an apparently technical reform. This is difficult to achieve in the monetary framework not merely because of governments' attachment to sovereignty. A transition which can be achieved in, say, the coal and steel market, is much more difficult when there is a very large, and very well-informed, worldwide audience who have a financial stake in the outcome, and the ability to influence that outcome.

Collectively, participants in the international financial markets have very large sums of money riding on bets about the relationship between individual currencies. These participants are accustomed to monitoring carefully the gap between political rhetoric and economic reality. The process of creating the EMS is a fragile one, and inherently vulnerable to disruption by large-scale financial flows if at any point the markets perceive that the rhetoric of the system and the economic realities do not coincide. It was this gap between rhetoric and reality in September 1992 which led sterling and the Italian lira to be driven from the ERM. The markets perceived that certainly the UK, and probably the Italian governments would not be able to support the economic pain of continuing to keep the level of domestic interest rates high enough to keep them in line with German interest rates.

The difficulty for the EU, therefore, is that the technical process of achieving a single currency by gradually moving towards irrevocably fixed exchange rates is inherently vulnerable to the market. If the market comes to the conclusion that the current exchange rate relationships between EU members is unsustainable, then—as was vividly demonstrated in September 1992 and again in July 1993—the volumes of flows through the foreign exchanges are more than sufficient to dominate the resources of the EU central banks. Plainly, therefore, it will be difficult to achieve a gradual transition to EMU. At any point in the process, if the markets become convinced that there is a disequilibrium, another speculative storm is liable to blow the ship off course.

An alternative approach which has been suggested in some quarters is the so-called "Big Bang." That is, an arrangement whereby existing national currencies are abolished overnight and replaced with the new single European currency (presumably the ECU). This transition would be irrevocable. It would resemble, in fact, the abolition of the ostmark, and its replacement by the deutsche mark in the process of German reunification. As that example shows, such an approach is perfectly feasible. But, as was mentioned earlier in the section on the costs of monetary union, the move to EMU will imply operational changes in a whole range of areas. It has even been estimated that the printing of the requisite banknotes will take several years to accomplish, given the existing printing capacity available. Hence the practicality of the "Big Bang" approach is just as much in doubt as is that of the gradual transition.

None of these considerations rule out a move to monetary union, given sufficient political will on all sides. However, some doubt must remain for the moment whether all parties—not just the British government—are fully prepared to accept some of the practical consequences of monetary union; nor, it would appear, are they willing to take the necessary practical steps to achieve it. (An example is the complete absence of political commitment to the process of achieving a satisfactory ECU clearing system for the private sector).[13]

NOTES

1. *One Market, One Money*, Oxford University Press, 1992, p. 640.
2. *Exchange Rate Variability and World Trade*, Occasional paper No. 28, 1984.
3. R.D. Grauwe, "International trade and economic growth in the European Monetary System", *European Economic Review*, 1987.
4. See e.g. R.A. Mundell, "A theory of optimum currency areas", *American Economic Review*, 1961; R.I. McKinnon, "Optimum currency areas", *American Economic Review*, 1963; P.B. Kenen, "The theory of optimum currency areas: an eclectic view" in R.A. Mundell and A.K. Swoboda (eds), *Monetary Problems of the International Economy*, University of Chicago Press, 1969; Y. Ishiyama, *The Theory of Optimum Currency Areas*: a Survey IMF staff papers, 1975.
5. Some of which is reviewed in the "Exchange rate mechanism of the European Monetary System: a review of the literature", *Bank of England Quarterly Bulletin*, February 1991.
6. R.J. Barro, and D. Gordon, "Rules, discretion and reputation in a model of monetary policy", *Journal of Monetary Economics*, 1983.

7. T.J. Sargent, *Rational Expectations and Inflation*, Harper and Row, New York, 1986.
8. "The theory of optimum deficits and debt" in Federal Reserve Bank of Boston, Conference Series No. 27, *The Economics of Large Government Deficits*, 1983.
9. "Reflections on the fiscal implications of a common currency", in A. Giovannini and C. Mayer, *European Financial Integration*, Cambridge University Press, 1991.
10. *The Strategy of Conflict*, Harvard University Press, 1969.
11. *Annual Report*, 1992, p. 84 of the English version.
12. In the context of the perennial discussion of whether forward foreign exchange rates are determined by relative interest rates or by expectations of future rate movements, it may be worth mentioning that the author was present in the Barclays Bank dealing room when the Irish punt forward rates were being established for the first time. The procedure adopted was to take the domestic Irish rates of interest and the domestic UK rates of interest and derive the implied forward foreign exchange rates from them in accordance with the formulas set out in Chapter 9. This is, perhaps, the nearest we will get to a controlled experiment on this subject.
13. See, for example, the discussion in *Towards a Single European Securities Trading Market*, ISMA Centre, ISMA, Zurich 1993; *Derivatives in the Context of a Single European Securities Market*, ISMA, Zurich, 1994.

7

Efficient Markets—or Chaos?

7.1 OVERVIEW

In this chapter we focus on some of the theoretical issues regarding models which have been developed for the analysis of foreign exchange markets. There are a very wide range of theoretical models, too wide to be covered here: the interested reader is referred to the texts listed in the "Further Reading" section. In particular Copeland[1] provides a useful outline of the Mundell–Fleming model, the Dornbusch model, and a number of others. Here, we focus firstly on the "efficient markets" hypothesis, and then on some of the more recent work on nonlinear dynamics of foreign exchange markets.

7.1.1 Efficient markets

In 1953 Maurice Kendall[2] found to his surprise that he could identify no predictable patterns in equity prices. Prices seem to evolve randomly. They were as likely to go up as they were to go down on any particular day, regardless of past performance. Further studies, such as those by Cootner,[3] confirmed that it was extraordinarily difficult to find any predictable patterns in the market. The concept of the efficient market hypothesis (EMH) was developed as a result of these researches. In essence, the EMH states that an efficient market is one which already reflects all available information. It is customary to refer to three forms of the hypothesis: the weak-form hypothesis simply requires that the market already reflects all information implied in past prices; the semi-strong form requires that the market reflect all publicly available information; and the strong-form hypothesis requires that the market reflect all public and privately available information. In both stock markets and foreign exchange markets there has been a long-running debate between academics and practitioners.

On the whole, practitioners reject the efficient markets theory. From their viewpoint, there is one overwhelmingly good reason for doing so, namely that if it were true, there would no point in their being paid high salaries to trade the markets. Secondly, at any given time, it is generally possible to point to one or more individuals who can demonstrate an outstanding track record in the markets. Over the years, various "stars" have risen and fallen; while they are rising, they are often used as counter-examples to reject the theory.

On the other hand, even if trading results were randomly distributed, if we were using a 5% significance test, we would expect to find that one trader in 20 would have "stellar" results in any given period. Similarly, in the context of the equity markets, it has been pointed out, for example, that if a fund manager succeeds in outperforming the market by 2% p.a. with a 6% standard deviation of returns, which would not be untypical, it will take 36 years before we can be reasonably certain that such a outperformance is not the result of a statistical fluke. The trading career of the average foreign exchange dealer is undoubtedly a good deal shorter than 36 years.

Still, in regard to the foreign exchange markets there is in fact a good deal of empirical evidence that mechanical trading rules (such as "filter trading rules") can generate excess profits, which is not consistent with the EMH. A recent study by Levich and Thomas[4] reviews the evidence of this area in the 1970s. Studies, for example, by Dooley and Shafer[5] reported the results of studies of various filter rules. We can define an $x\%$ filter rule as one which leads to the following strategy for speculating in the market, say, for sterling against the US dollar: whenever sterling rises $x\%$ above its most recent trough (a buy signal), borrow dollars and convert into a long position in sterling; whenever sterling falls $x\%$ below its most recent peak (a sell signal), sell any long sterling position and take a short sterling position by borrowing sterling and converting the proceeds into dollars at the spot exchange rate.

The Dooley and Shafer calculations were adjusted to reflect the interest expense and interest income of this exercise and they reported results for 1, 3 and 5% filter rules. The earlier study found that "for the whole sample the 1, 3 and 5% filters are remarkably profitable." In one case, for example, the 1% filter rule for the French franc would have yielded an annual rate of return of 16% over the two and a half year sample period. The later study found that these strategies remained profitable over a longer time period. For three currencies (yen, guilder and sterling) every filter was profitable in every subperiod. On the other hand, each filter would have generated losses in at least one other currency during at least one subperiod studied.

In the study by Levich and Thomas referred to earlier, the profits that could be earned by applying filter rules to the actual market prices from January 9, 1976 to December 1990 are compared with the profits that might have been generated by applying similar rules to a series of randomly generated simulated patterns. In 15 out of 30 cases, the profits of the actual series ranked in the top 1% of all the simulated series. In 10 further cases, the rank is in the top 5%. Thus in 25 of the 30 cases, Levich and Thomas rejected the hypothesis that there was no information in the original market series that could be exploited for profit in the filter rules. Similar results were reported by Surajaras and Sweeney, albeit from a simulation again.[6]

When we consider that the academic evidence on efficient markets with respect to equity markets has generally been fairly convincing, and when we consider that the foreign exchange markets—by virtue of their size and far greater liquidity—should be far more efficient than equity markets, these results are surprising. They help to explain why "technical analysis" has become more popular over the years in the foreign exchange markets.

As evidence of this latter point, Frankel[7] points out that the magazine *Euromoney* runs a yearly August review of between 10 and 27 foreign exchange forecasting services. In 1978, 18 forecasting firms described themselves as relying exclusively on economic fundamentals and only 2 on technical analysis. By 1985, the positions had been reversed: only one firm reported relying exclusively on fundamentals, and 12 on technical analysis. In general the use of the economic fundamentals to forecast exchange rates (see Chapter 8) has been rather unsuccessful. Hence the popularity of technical analysis as a substitute.

7.1.2 Rational expectations

If the markets were efficient, no profits could be made either from following filter rules, or by following the various types of technical analysis offered by technical analysis firms. Yet, as we have seen, there is some evidence to suggest that filter rules and other mechanical trading rules can produce sustained profits over time; and certainly, there are many traders in the marketplace who swear by technical analysis. One possible explanation might be that the process by which expectations are formed in the marketplace does not conform with that predicted by theory. Most of the modern theory of finance and macroeconomics assumes the existence of a representative agent whose decision is an aggregate of those of market participants. Such an economic agent is said to hold a fully rational expectation with respect to a variable if that agent's subjective expectation is the same as the variable's mathematical expected value, conditional on an information set containing all publicly available information. For the market to be truly efficient, it is therefore necessary that market participants efficiently use all the information available to them, and process it in an unbiassed and rational manner.

Participants in the market will be well aware that the market does not always process information in a rational manner. In practice, the market is driven by a combination of fear, greed, and rumours. This in itself would not destroy the rational expectations hypothesis, so long as the aggregate of all participants produced a collective expectation which behaved similarly to that required by the theory. A good deal of work has been done on exchange rate expectations. Dominguez,[8] Frankel and Froot,[9] and Takagi[10] all report various work in this area. Different biases of different types have been reported: for example, Ito[11] reported the results of surveys of Japanese market participants. Participants tended to have "wishful expectations": exporters expected a depreciation of the yen, and importers expected an appreciation of the yen. Market participants tended to forecast a short-run "bandwagon" effect, but a longer-run "mean-reverting" effect. In summary "we can conclude that we have strong evidence against rational expectation formation in the Tokyo foreign exchange market." Another recent study[12] analyzed the reports of a monthly survey of exchange rate expectations reported in *Business International Corporation*; this paper corroborates the finding that exchange rate forecasts are not rational and that agents do not use all available information in an efficient manner.

One possible means of rescuing the EMU is to appeal to the possibility that the risk premium required by the market is unstable. Clearly, if the risk premium varies over time (i.e. the possible divergence between the expected rate and the current forward exchange rate widens or shrinks because the market is more or less willing to undertake arbitrage and speculative transactions that would narrow the gap, because of changing perceptions of the risk of being in the market) then it becomes difficult to assert whether or not expectations are rational (in the sense defined above). Undoubtedly there are times when market perceptions of risk change significantly. For example, during the Gulf War crisis of 1990, there were clearly much greater risks of taking forward foreign exchange positions, given the high degree of uncertainty that prevailed until the ground war began. Similarly, at the time of the Plaza Agreement in 1985, extreme volatility in the US dollar might well have discouraged a number of participants from taking forward positions. It is not clear, however, why the risk premium should constantly be varying over time, in the absence of major crises of this type.

A gradual realization of the difficulties implicit in the EMH has coincided with the development of radically different ways of modeling the complexities of the real world. As the power of personal computers has grown exponentially in recent years so it has become more feasible to consider more complex analytical tools, specifically the analysis of nonlinear dynamics, discussed below.

7.2 CHAOS THEORY

Until recently, most analytical work in economics and finance theory has been conducted in terms of two types of model: deterministic and stochastic. Deterministic models consist of sets of equations which contain no random terms. Such models are typically forecastable and any inaccuracy in the forecast must be attributed to computational error. Stochastic models, by contrast, contain elements which have random components. In this case, the best that can be achieved is a forecast represented by the conditional mathematical expectation, which will have an inaccuracy equivalent to the stochastic component.

Most of these economic and econometric models are "linear" in structure. Economic entities are assumed to react in a "linear" fashion to events. In attempting to predict the growth of consumers' expenditure we might write

$$CE = 11\,554 + 0.778 \times Income$$

In this deterministic model, consumers' expenditure rises linearly with income. A comparable stochastic model would add a random error term, while retaining the linear framework. The widespread use of such models has generally been because linear models are analytically much more tractable. Once the possibility exists of nonlinear responses—e.g. over a certain income threshold, consumers' expenditure begins to decline—we are into more difficult mathematical territory.

More recently, research has shown that a third type of model, deterministic but nonlinear, can be formulated. The most significant feature of these new models for our purposes is that, although they involve no random component and therefore are deterministic, they are even in principle unforecastable, and in practice can only be approximately forecast over a very short horizon.

Nonlinear systems are much more difficult to model than linear systems. But in physics and other sciences, scientists have had to wrestle with nonlinear systems when considering fluid hydrodynamics, meteorology, population growth, and a whole range of other areas. There is no reason why economists and econometricians should get off more lightly. In recent years, however, much work has been done in the field of nonlinear dynamics. This work, carried on in a number of scientific fields, has been collectively christened "chaos theory."

Understanding these nonlinear systems is not always easy because they entail dynamic feedbacks. Hence typically nonlinear systems depend critically on initial conditions. This phenomenon is sometimes referred to as the butterfly effect: "The weather in Moscow changes if a butterfly claps its wings in Brazil." In other words, a small change in initial conditions can produce far-flung and unexpected effects. These considerations mean that analyzing nonlinear systems is sometimes most easily done by visual inspection.

7.2.1   A simple nonlinear model

Let us begin our discussion by considering a simple nonlinear model of exchange rate determination.[13] We will consider changes in the logarithmic price of foreign currency, which we will denote by S_t for time t. We assume that S_t has a long-run equilibrium level, which we will denote by $\overline{S}$. This is taken as determined by such factors as relative money supply, output capacity and so on, and is assumed constant. We assume that the change in the log price of foreign currency is proportional to the gap between the level in the last period and the long-run equilibrium level. That is

$$\Delta S_t = \theta(\overline{S} - S_{t-1})$$

Let us assume that the parameter θ, which measures the speed with which we return to equilibrium, is itself related to S_t. Let us assume that:

$$\theta = \alpha S_t \quad \alpha > 0$$

In other words, the higher S_t—that is, the more expensive foreign currency becomes and the more our domestic currency is devalued—the more quickly we return to equilibrium. It should be stressed that the model we are presenting here is not intended as an explanation of foreign exchange dynamics, but to examine the implications of nonlinear behaviour. We can rewrite these two equations in the form

$$\Delta S_{t+1} = \alpha S_t(\overline{S} - S_t)$$

Alternatively, we can rewrite this equation as:

$$S_{t+1} = (1 + \alpha\overline{S})S_t - \alpha S_t^2$$

By assumption, we have said that $\overline{S}$ is a constant. It is convenient, therefore, to specify a simplifying value for it. If we now write

$$\overline{S} = -(1 - \alpha)/\alpha$$

then we can rewrite our equation as

$$S_{t+1} = \alpha S_t - \alpha S_t^2 = \alpha S_t(1 - S_t)$$

This equation is not as simple as it seems. Mathematicians refer to it as the logistic equation. Before discussing it in more detail, it may be helpful to introduce the concept of a phase diagram and the related concept of an attractor.

7.2.2 Phase diagrams

If we have a system with two variables, x and y, we can plot each variable against the other at a given point in time on a standard xy graph. This is called the "phase portrait" of the system, and it is plotted in phase space. The dimensionality of the phase space depends on the number of variables in the system.

As an example, suppose we set a pendulum swinging, and plot its speed against its position (Figure 7.1). When the pendulum is given initial energy, it swings back and forth, but each swing becomes shorter and slower, from the effects of gravity, until the pendulum stops. If the phase space of the system is plotted as position versus velocity, we get a spiraling line that ends at the origin, where the pendulum has stopped. We can say that the pendulum is attracted to the origin.

7.2.3 Strange attractors

In our previous example, the pendulum is attracted back to its origin. The origin is stable. This need not always be the case. For example, if every so often we pushed the pendulum sideways and threw it out of orbit, the pendulum would continually tend to return toward the origin still, but not from the same angle and it would rather tend to seek a region around the origin. Many apparently "chaotic" systems have an infinite number of solutions contained in a finite space. The system is attracted to a region in space. These systems, where the object is attracted back to places which vary over time, have "chaotic" or "strange" attractors.

A well-known example is the so-called Henon attractor. Henon was a French astronomer who was plotting the orbits of heavenly bodies. The model which he adopted for the orbits in question ended up by describing the series as:

$$x_{(t+1)} = 1 + y_t - ax_t^2$$
$$y_{(t+1)} = bx_t$$

When presented as a time series (Figure 7.2), the results plotted out in a seemingly random way. When presented as a phase space (Figure 7.3), the presence of a strange attractor is immediately evident.

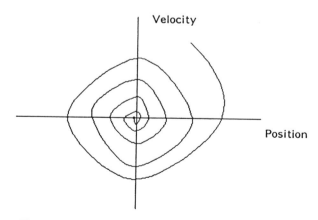

Figure 7.1 Phase Portrait of Point Attractor: Pendulum

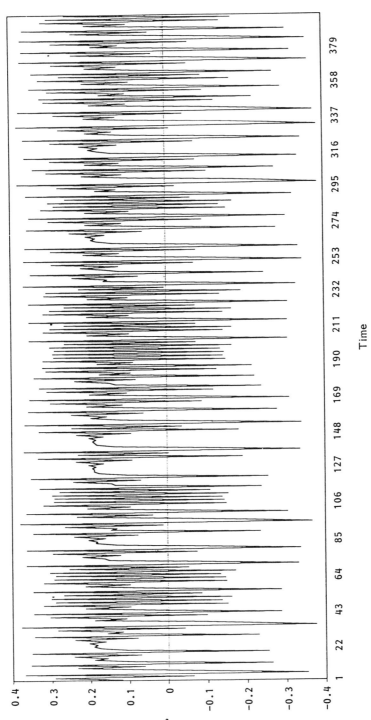

Figure 7.2 The Henon Attractor Plotted as Time Series

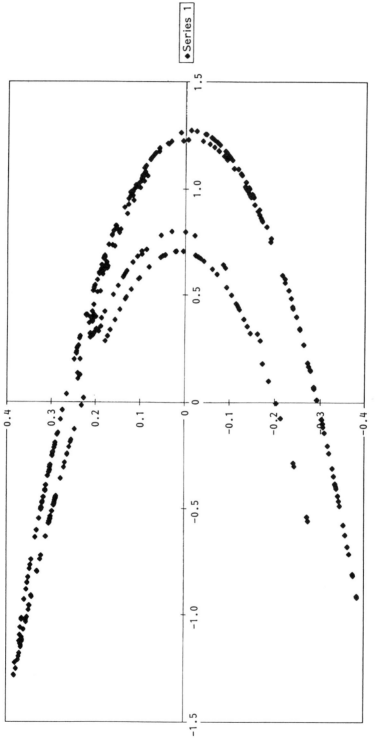

● Series 1

Figure 7.3 The Henon Attractor in Phase Space

For the economist or foreign exchange analyst, the concept of strange attractors and their depiction in phase space creates an interesting alternative method of looking at time series. Just as looking at the Henon data in the form of a phase space is immediately enlightening, so the application of the phase space technique may throw an interesting light on economic time series.

7.2.4 The logistic equation

Let us now return to the logistic equation. The attached charts (see Figure 7.4) show how the equation behaves for different values of α. For values of α between 0 and unity, the equation will always converge to zero. For values of α between 1 and 3 the steady state solution will be $1 - 1/\alpha$. For values of α between 3 and about 3.45 the equation cycles between two solutions. For larger values of α this double cycle becomes unstable and we observe the development of 4-cycle, 8-cycle and 16-cycle solutions. For values of α above 3.57 this cascade of period-doubling bifurcations evolves into an infinite number of possible solutions.

The reason for introducing the logistic equation is not to pretend that it has any real-life application to the foreign exchange market. The purpose is simply to show that a very simple equation, apparently deterministic, can in fact produce complex, unpredictable and chaotic results. This subject is discussed in much more depth in de Grauwe et al.[14] who show that under reasonable assumptions about the way speculators process information, chaotic behaviour is possible. On this argument, our analysis of exchange rate dynamics should focus on seeking to detect whether chaotic patterns exist.

Chaos theory presents an interesting new way of looking at foreign exchange and other markets. By looking at them from a different perspective, we may perhaps gain new insights. Another example of this is the application of fractals.

7.2.5 Fractals

Another of the concepts which has emerged with the growth of interest in chaos theory in recent years has been the concept of a fractal. The concept of a fractal was introduced by the well-known French mathematician and scientist, Benoit Mandelbrot. The technical definition of a fractal is not intuitive ("A fractal is a set for which the Hausdorff Besicovitch dimension strictly exceeds the topological dimension").[15] It is not easy to give a simple definition: but we can say that a fractal is an object in which the parts are in some way related to the whole. Fractals are self-similar.

A simple example would be a tree. Trees branch according to a fractal scale. Each branch, with its smaller branches, resembles in some way the tree as a whole. When we look at time series—e.g. the returns on the S&P 500, or interest rate levels—different parts of the chart tend to resemble each other (as technical analysts argue when looking for "head and shoulders", etc.). So time series often have a fractal quality.

Fractals are in very widespread use in a number of areas: because of their self-similar quality, they have proved useful for example in image compression. Video signals can be compressed by using fractal techniques. Another use which I cannot resist mentioning is as generators of interestingly complex images. A shareware

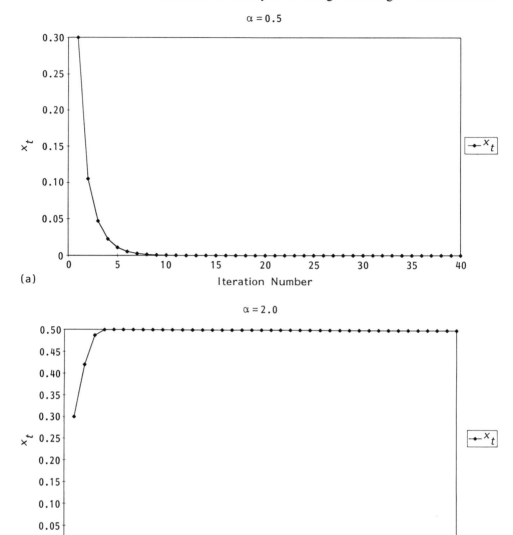

Figure 7.4 Lambda = (a) 0.5; (b) 2.0; (c) 3.2; (d) 4.0

computer program called FRACTINT is widely available which can be used to explore the behavior of different fractals.

7.2.6 Fractal dimension

The important thing about a fractal, for our purposes, is its dimension. We are brought up to think of two or three dimensions. A diagram on a piece of paper is

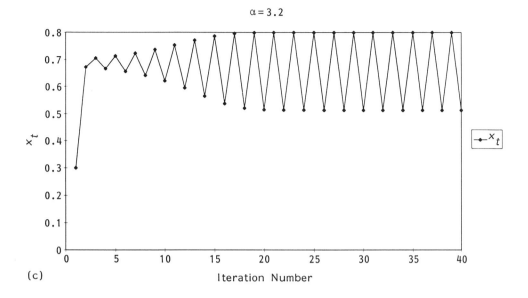

(c)

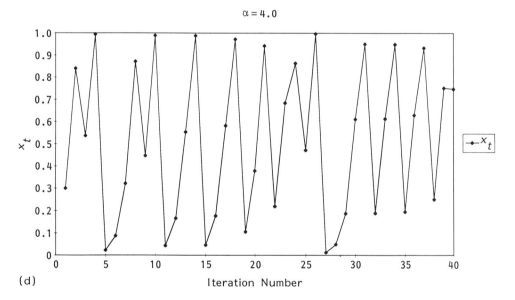

(d)

drawn in two dimensions. A physical object is seen in three dimensions. Fractals, however, have partial dimensions.

This is not an obviously intuitive concept. One way to approach it is to ask: how long is the coastline of the UK? We can measure the coastline by running a measuring device around the coastline on a very accurate Ordnance Survey map. Alternatively, we can measure it by walking the coastline. Then again, we can measure it by running a device in and out of each nook and cranny in the rocks along the coastline. In each case, we will reach different answers. The finer our measuring instrument, the longer the coastline!

Mandelbrot argued that the appropriate measure of a complex line like this is its fractal dimension. Coastlines are jagged lines, so their fractal dimension is greater than one (their Euclidean dimension). The more jagged they are, the more their fractal dimension approaches 2 (the Euclidean dimension of a plane).

How do we measure the fractal dimension of such a coastline? One possible approach is to count the circles of a certain diameter that are needed to cover the coastline. Then we increase the diameter, and again count the number of circles. If we continue to do this, we will find that the number of circles has an exponential relationship to the radius of the circles:

$$N(2r)^D = 1$$

where N = number of circles, r = radius, and D = fractal dimension. We can rewrite:

$$D = \log N/\log(1/2r)$$

Using this method we find, for example, that the coastline of Norway has a fractal dimension of 1.52; that of Britain, 1.30. Norway's fjords make its coastline more jagged than the UK.

For our purposes this measure of jaggedness is interesting. The fractal dimension can be used as the measure of jaggedness, or volatility, of a time series. As with the use of phase space, so with the fractal dimension: it is possible that by using a different analysis of the time series, we may be able to attain a more powerful insight. Other applications of fractal analysis are discussed in various books by Peters,[16] while a more theoretical approach may be found for example in Pesaran and Potter.[17]

7.3 NEURAL NETWORKS

To conclude this chapter, it may be worth mentioning briefly another approach to the analysis of complex time series. This is the neural network approach, which has evolved from artificial intelligence work. To analyze complex situations, artificial intelligence teams have developed two approaches: expert systems and neural networks. Expert systems require us to lay down a set of rules (as they would be applied by an expert in the field). But this can be laborious and complex. Neural networks are computer systems that are "trained" to learn. Sejnowski and Rosenberg[18] created a neural network called NETtalk that learned the correct pronunciation of words from ASCII characters even though it began with no linguistic rule. It taught itself *overnight* to the level of a six-year-old child by listening to correct pronunciation of speech from text. By contrast, the computer firm DEC designed an expert system (DECtalk) that took 20 *years* to devise the necessary knowledge base. So intuitively, neural nets look the more promising approach to handle complex tasks like stock market analysis.

What is a neural net? It is a system which contains a large number of interconnected nodes (sometimes called neurons, by analogy with the human brain). The output state of each node is determined by the inputs from each of its neighbours. A network is "taught" by presenting it with a set of sample data as "inputs" and varying the weighting factors applied to each connection between nodes until it achieves appropriate answers. Then we let it loose on real data and hope for the best.

This approach has one limitation: it is difficult to trace the step-by-step logic the system uses to arrive at the outputs from the inputs provided. A system-user must generally rely on the output as a gauge of the system's consistency and reliability. On the other hand, one could say this of a foreign exchange trader. It is not always clear how traders arrive at decisions. We depend on their performance to assess whether in fact they are any good. So the fact that we do not understand the system—it is a "black box"—is not necessarily a reason for completely rejecting it.

On the other hand we do need to be sure that the system is capable of continuing to learn, as conditions change. This means designing it to "teach" itself each time new data becomes available. Many firms are currently working on neural network technology—for example BZW announced a neural net system for stock picking in 1993. Since these systems are proprietary, it is difficult to tell how successful they are. But White[19] built a neural system and gave it daily returns for IBM shares over 500 days in the mid-1970s: the system could find only random fluctuations. His conclusion was that: "it won't be easy to uncover predictable stock market fluctuations with neural nets, and if you succeed, you'll probably want to keep it secret." In a similar trial Kryzanowski et al.[20] took data on 120 companies for 1984–89. The results were a 66% accuracy in predicting whether a share's overall return next year will be positive or negative. However the results for 1989 were 49% accurate—which is disturbing as this was the most recent year, so that the system was becoming less successful rather than more so.

NOTES

1. L.S. Copeland, *Exchange Rates and International Finance*, 2nd edn, Addison-Wesley, UK, 1994.
2. "The analysis of economic time series, part I: prices", *Journal of the Royal Statistical Society*, 1953.
3. *The Random Character of Stock Market Prices*, MIT Press, 1964. For an entertaining discussion of this and related issues see also B. Malkiel, "*A Random Walk Down Wall Street*", 4th edn, WW Norton & Co., New York, 1985.
4. "The significance of technical trading-rule profits in the foreign exchange market: a bootstrap approach", *Journal of International Money and Finance*, 1993.
5. *Analysis of Short-run Exchange Rate Behaviour March 1973–September 1975*, International Finance Discussion Papers No. 76, Federal Reserve System, Washington, 1976; M.P. Dooley and J.R. Shafer "Analysis of short-run exchange rate behaviour: March 1973 to November 1981", in (Eds) D. Bigman and T. Taya, *Exchange Rate and Trade Instability*, Ballinger, Cambridge, USA, 1983.
6. P. Surajaras and R.J. Sweeney, *Profit-making Speculation in Foreign Exchange Markets*, Westview Press, Colorado USA/Oxford UK, 1992.
7. J.A. Frankel, "International financial integration: relations between interest rates and exchange rates", in D.K. Das (Ed.), *International Finance: Contemporary Issues*, Routledge, London, 1993.
8. K.M. Dominguez, "Are foreign exchange forecasts rational? New evidence from survey data", *Economics Letters*, May 1986.
9. J.A. Frankel and K.A. Froot, "Using survey data to test propositions regarding exchange rate expectations", *American Economic Review*, March 1987; "Short-term and long-term expectations of the yen–dollar exchange rate: evidence from survey data", *Journal of the*

Japanese and International Economies, March 1987; *Exchange Rate Forecasting Techniques: Survey Data, and Implications for the Foreign Exchange Market*, IMF working paper No. 90/43, IMF, May 1990.

10. S. Takagi, *Exchange Rate Expectations: a Survey of Survey Studies*, IMF staff papers, June 1991.

11. T. Ito, "Foreign exchange rate expectations: micro-survey data", *American Economic Review*, June 1990.

12. S. Cavaglia, W.F.C. Verschoor, and C.P. Wolff, "Further evidence on exchange rate expectations", *Journal of International Money and Finance*, 1993.

13. This section draws on the treatment in L.S. Copeland, op. cit.

14. P. de Grauwe, H. Dewachter, and M. Embrechts, *Exchange Rate Theory: Chaotic Models of Foreign Exchange*, Blackwell, Oxford, UK, 1993.

15. B. Mandelbrot, *The Fractal Geometry of Nature*, 1983.

16. E. Peters, *Chaos and Order in the Capital Markets*, John Wiley & Sons, 1991; *Fractal Market Analysis*, John Wiley & Sons, 1994.

17. M.H. Pesaran and S.M. Potter (eds), *Nonlinear Dynamics, Chaos and Econometrics*, John Wiley & Sons, 1993.

18. Johns Hopkins Technical Report No. 1, Johns Hopkins University, USA, 1986.

19. *AI Expert*, December 1989.

20. *Financial Analysts Journal*, August 1993.

8

Forecasting the Markets

This chapter provides a brief account of how market participants seek to forecast interest and exchange rates. For more detail, there are many excellent books on the subject, some of which are listed in the list of Further Reading. The purpose is not to recommend any single method since there is never a single best method. It will vary with the state of the market. Sometimes market psychology focuses on a particular factor, either because it is seen as critical in itself or because it is thought that the central bank or government of the country concerned thinks it is critical. At other times, news regarding that particular factor will be totally ignored. Sometimes, a particular technical theory (charting, oscillators, or some other technical measure) seems to perform particularly well, and gains adherents. Then its failure causes it to go out of fashion.

There are as many different ways of exchange rate forecasting as there are points of view. Broadly, though, one can class them into two kinds: fundamental and technical. We will start with fundamental methods and then move on to technical methods.

The fundamental approach to interest and exchange rate forecasting focuses on the basic factors that shape the performance of an economy and hence the interest rates and exchange rate of the country concerned. Political or social factors vary widely and we will not attempt to describe them in this book. The economic factors that are relevant can be broadly classified into monetary, fiscal, and external policy.

8.1 MONETARY POLICY

During the late 1970s and early 1980s, there was a phase when "Monetarism" became a key component of economic policy in a number of countries, including the United States, the UK, and several others. The most notable experiment was by Paul Volcker in the United States, whose 1979 New Economic Policy was a form of strict monetarism that produced very sharp swings in interest rates. In recent years, an element of pragmatism has come back into most countries' monetary policy, as the realization has dawned that pure monetarism has many inherent problems. Nobody doubts that monetary policy means something; the question is exactly how much.

It would probably be fair to say that monetary policy only became a practical option when exchange rates were allowed to float in 1973. As we saw in Chapter 4, you cannot have a completely fixed exchange rate and complete control of the money supply at the same time, unless you are very lucky. The intervention needed to stabilize the exchange rate will usually show up somewhere in the money supply. It was this factor that determined Mrs Thatcher's resistance to the UK's entry into the Exchange Rate Mechanism (ERM) of the European Monetary System (EMS). She argued that entry into the ERM meant that the UK would lose its monetary policy independence.

In late 1974, Germany became the first country to announce a formal money supply target for the year ahead. In early 1975, the United States followed, along with Switzerland and Canada. In 1976, France and the UK announced targets. In many cases, these countries later adopted stricter versions, but then gradually came to relax the purity of their commitment to money supply targets.

By way of example, the history of broad money targets in the UK since 1980 can be summarized as follows:

1980/81	Target ranges set for sterling M3 (£M3) for four years
1982/83–83/84	Common target ranges set for £M3, M1, and PSL2
1984/85–85/86	Separate target ranges set for M0 and £M3
1986/87	£M3 target range set for 1986/87 only. Illustrative ranges for future years set only for M0
1987/88–92/93	No target ranges set for broad money aggregates. Illustrative ranges set for M0
1993/4–95/96	Medium-term monitoring ranges set for M4 and M0[1]

The original ideas behind monetarism came from the quantity theory of money. This starts with a truism: the total money stock in a country circulates at a certain speed to finance the country's economic activity. To see what this means, imagine we are on an island with $500 in bills. The only product on the island is loaves of bread. Say 2000 loaves are produced, and paid for at 50 cents each. The annual value of production is $2000 \times \$0.50 = \$1000$. The turnover of the economy (its annual production value) equals the quantity of production (call it q) multiplied by its price (call it p).

Every year the stock of money, $500, must turn over twice to pay for the turnover of the economy (Figure 8.1). If the islanders' children burn $250, there is only $250 in bills on the island. The money stock would have to circulate twice as fast (four times a year) to pay for the turnover. The number of times that money circulates in an economy is called its velocity. When the stock of money was $500, the annual velocity was two. Now it has had to rise to four.

The idea behind quantity theory was that velocity is usually fairly stable over time. A change in the quantity of money will show up in the price or quantity of output. Suppose our island prints another $250. The money stock is now $500 again. But suppose velocity now stays stable at four. Then our $500, turning over four times a year, is enough to finance annual turnover of $2000 but production of loaves is only 2000 (assume it cannot be increased). Then the extra supply of money can only end by bidding up prices until each loaf costs $1. When we assumed constant velocity, we assumed people are just as inclined to spend money as before. If they get twice as

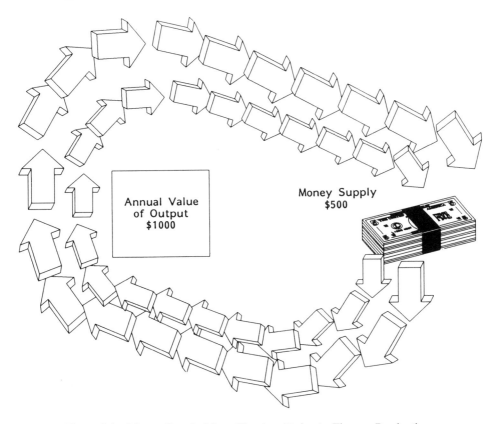

Figure 8.1 Money Supply Must Circulate Twice to Finance Production

much money, they will spend twice as much. If there is only the same number of loaves, the producers of loaves will be able to raise their prices.

The complications to this theory in real life mean it does not really work in this way. However, many traders, and many central banks, believe that controlling the money supply is important in controlling inflation. If the markets see that a central bank has the money supply under control, that makes the market more confident about that currency. As a result, monetary policy is important for a trader to understand.

8.2 MONETARY POLICY IN ACTION

The first complication arises from deciding which money supply. Most countries have a range of financial instruments that could be considered money: notes and coin, demand deposits, balances on time deposit that can be used to make payments, certificates of deposit, and so on. Variations in the holdings between these can produce variations in money supply without any overall change in holdings of financial assets in the economy. In recent years, the pace of financial innovation in the major Western economies has been such that it has been extraordinarily difficult for central banks to decide what exactly was the money supply.

Another set of problems comes from the fact that the central bank faces a dilemma between the money it supplies and the price at which it supplies the money—the interest rate. We saw in Chapter 4 that there was a similar dilemma with fixed exchange rates. If a central bank held the exchange rate rigidly fixed, it had to be ready to intervene in unlimited quantities. If it did not intervene, it had to let the rate move free. There is a similar problem in the domestic market. The central bank cannot fix the interest rate at which it will supply money, and also the amount of money it supplies. It must choose one or the other. Normally, central banks have tended to focus on the level of interest rate. But to do this, they also often manipulate the quantity of money available in the banking system by controlling banking reserves. The classic example of the extreme version of this policy was in the United States under Paul Volcker. In October 1979, the Fed decided to aim at very strict control of reserves in the banking system, regardless of the effect on interest rates. The effects can be seen in Figure 8.2.

Once a central bank has decided on its target, it must decide how it wants to implement it. To see what is involved, let us go back to our island. Now that the islanders have understood the link between money supply and inflation, they decide to appoint a central bank to deal with the problem. The central bank decides that for the year ahead that it can realistically expect production of loaves can grow by 10%, from 2000 to 2200. But because of the recent inflation, the bakers' workmen have been getting restless and are demanding an increase in wages. So it seems likely that the island will probably have inflation of, say, 5%.

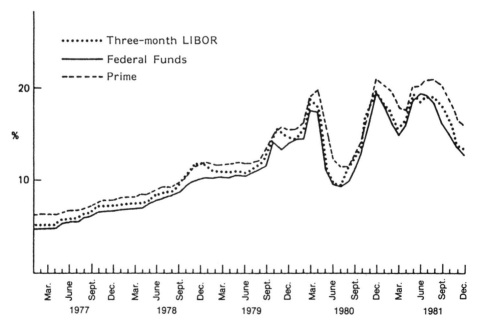

Figure 8.2 Prime, Federal Funds and Three-month LIBOR 1977–81 (Monthly Averages in %). Source: Data Resources Inc.

The central bank decides that velocity will probably remain stable, at four. It assumes that the price of a loaf will be 5% higher, namely $1.05. It assumes that production will be 2200. So it expects that the value of turnover on the island (gross national product) will be $2310 = 2200 × $1.05. So it knows the money supply, circulating four times a year, must be enough to finance annual turnover of $2310. In other words, it concludes that the money supplied must equal $577.50, since if this amount turns over four times during the year, it equals $2310. In fact, the money supply must expand by just over 15%, to finance the 10% rise in production and 5% inflation.

Suppose, now, that the central bank decides that this is too high. It does not want inflation to be as high as 5%. Suppose it aims for 2.5%. Then it will expect the price of a loaf at the end of the year to be $1.025. It expects the growth in production in loaves to be unchanged, at 10%. This inflation figure implies a value of GNP = 2200 × $1.025 = $2255. If the velocity of circulation is still expected to be four, this means a supply of money of $563.75 will be sufficient. That is, the money supply must grow by just over 12.5%, financing a rise of 10% production and 2.5% inflation (see Figure 8.3)

When it decided to squeeze inflation by squeezing the money supply, the central bank made two big assumptions. First, it assumed that inflation could be cut from 5 to 2.5% without affecting production. But it might be that the bakers' workmen who

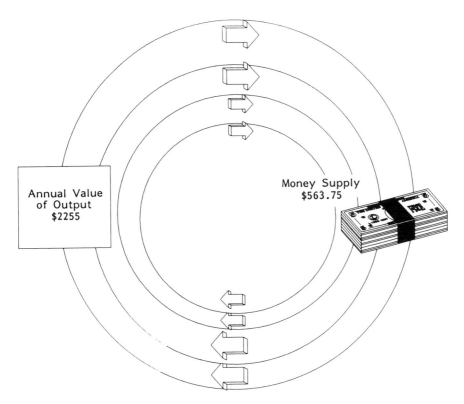

Figure 8.3 Now Money Supply Must Turn over Four Times to Finance Production

we said were restless, might not be prepared to produce 10% more loaves without getting a larger increase in wages. They might go on strike, or they might not work as hard. In any event, production might not rise as fast as the central bank expects. In that case, its money supply target would be pitched too high, and inflation would rise higher than its intended 2.5%, while production would fall below target.

The second big assumption that the central bank made was that velocity would stay stable at four. But suppose, for some reason, velocity fell to three. Then the projected money supply of $563.75 would only be enough to finance a GNP of $1691.25. If prices rose to $1.025, production would have to fall to 1650 loaves per annum. Conversely, for production to remain steady at 2200, the price per loaf would have to fall to 76.875 cents.

What has happened has been a collapse in demand. As we said earlier, if you assume a stable velocity, that means you assume people are as likely to spend money as they did in the past. If velocity falls, that means people are no longer spending the money as quickly as they did. So when the central bank makes its forecast for the year ahead, it has to forecast not only inflation and production, but also how it thinks people's spending and saving habits are likely to move during the coming year. All this makes the process of fixing a monetary target quite complicated, and the process of achieving it even more complex.

Coming back from our island to reality, let us look at how some central banks look at these problems. In December 1989, the Bundesbank forecast a growth of real production potential in 1990 of 2.5%. The price level was assumed to rise at an average annual rate of 2%. In addition, $\frac{1}{2}$% was allowed to take account of the slowdown in trend of the velocity of circulation of money. This yielded a growth rate of about 5% for the money stock M3. Because there was some uncertainty about the underlying calculations, the target was formulated in terms of a corridor of 4–6%.

Other central banks follow a rather similar process, but often much less formally than in Germany. The major complications in this approach arise from the instability of velocity of circulation of money. The approach of the Bank of England was well summarized by Mervyn King, its Chief Economist, in a recent article:[2]

> "Money is not a mechanical indicator to be taken solely at face value. That is why it is sensible to set 'monitoring ranges' for the growth of one or more monetary aggregates, rather than precise target ranges. . . . This is also why we see our task as understanding as much as we can about velocity, and explaining in the *Inflation Report* the behaviour of each of the monetary aggregates . . ."

In the same article Mr. King points out that changes in velocity have affected the predictive power of broad money in both the United States and Germany since 1980 and quotes Alan Greenspan from his Humphrey Hawkins testimony in July 1993:

> "the historical relationships between money and income and money and the price level have largely broken down, depriving the aggregates of much of their usefulness as guides to policy."

8.3 TRANSMISSION OF MONETARY POLICY

Once a central bank has decided on its monetary policy, we need to understand how a change in policy is transmitted through the financial system and affects money supply. There are two main ways of looking at this process. One side looks at the liabilities of the banking system, and the other looks at the assets.

Monetarists tend to look at the liability side. The view that focuses on the asset side has been described as the "European (and IMF) view of money creation." Both views must be true. The liabilities of the nation's banking system must always equal its assets. It is a question of which is primary. Just as some banks are inherent lenders, needing deposits with which to fund themselves, and other banks inherently deposit-takers, needing places to lend, one side or other of the national balance sheet can be seen as the driving force. And on your view of which side is primary, depends your view of the effectiveness of the individual policy tools involved.

Monetarists generally accept that interest rates are not very effective as a means of controlling the money supply. They therefore tend to argue for direct control on the liability side of the balance sheet. One way to do this is to control the supply of reserves available to the banking system. As we saw in Chapter 4, a change in the reserves of the banking system changes its liabilities in proportion to a multiplier. So by controlling total reserves, the central bank can control total bank deposits.

Others would argue that when the authorities attempt to control any monetary total, the activities of the financial system in creating substitutes will change the demand for it. So its behaviour will not reflect conditions accurately. This, again, fits in with the view referred to earlier as the European view of money creation. On this argument, controlling the supply of reserves to the banking system to stop it granting credit will mean that borrowers will look elsewhere (through the security markets for example). This is often called "disintermediation." Unless the central bank is always widening the network of its controls over lending, its money supply targets will became less and less useful. During the 1960s when the Bank of England tried to run direct controls on bank lending, all that happened was that nonbanks took up the slack demand for credit.

From the point of view of the market, it is my opinion that nobody really cares which targets are chosen, or which policy is adopted, as long as the markets are convinced that the authorities are really determined to keep the situation under control in the medium term. A classic example is the case of Switzerland, which was forced by inflows of foreign currency to abandon money supply targets entirely in 1979, without in any way affecting the market's belief in the long-term determination of the Swiss National Bank to hold down inflation.

The effects of the German reunification problem across the rest of Europe led to a widespread interest in the monetary policy transmission mechanism. There was concern that the higher German interest rates which were imposed as a result of the fiscal difficulties associated with German reunification forced, via the ERM, the rest of Europe to raise interest rates and to accept slower rates of real economic growth. The Annual Report of the BIS in 1994 contains an interesting discussion of the transmission of monetary policy. It points out that monetary policy affects macroeconomic developments in several ways. By influencing real interest rates, it has a direct impact on the saving/investment choices of firms and households. It also operates through a cash-flow channel by affecting the disposable income of the private sector. The operation of the cash-flow channel is affected both by the level of outstanding indebtedness and its structure—specifically, its distribution between fixed and variable rate debt. In Germany and France a substantial proportion of lending is at predominantly fixed rates. In contrast, variable rate lending is predominant in the UK, the United States, Canada, and Japan. The BIS presents evidence to suggest that the pass-through of changes in official interest rates to the cash flow of both firms and households in the UK is both rapid and large. By comparison, in France the pass-through is smaller and more delayed. In the UK, interest payments increase in the same quarter as the official interest rate change, and reach a new plateau after approximately two quarters. In contrast, in France the change in the interest rate induces little immediate response, with the effect reaching its maximum after six quarters. Moreover, it is much smaller than in the UK. Similarly, the BIS estimates that the effect of a 1% rise in interest rates reduces GDP in the UK by 0.5% after four quarters, but in France the response is again smaller and more delayed.

8.4 FISCAL POLICY

We turn now to the other major area of policy which interacts with monetary policy: fiscal policy. This can be crudely defined as the government's tax and spending policy. Two aspects of fiscal policy are relevant: first, its impact on the economy as a whole, and second, its effect on flows of tax payments through the markets.

The second effect is much simpler to understand than the first. As we said in Chapter 1, when money is withdrawn from bank accounts to pay taxes, liquidity flows from the private sector to the public sector. That is, tax payments tend to drain the money markets of liquidity. This is why the money markets became very tight over important tax payment dates, for example, April 15 every year in the United States. In the UK, January and February are traditionally tight months, because corporation tax becomes due and payable then.

The impact of fiscal policy on the economy as a whole is more complex. Many people think of fiscal policy as being government deficit spending, and therefore almost automatically inflationary. To show why this need not be true, we must look at why governments started using fiscal policy to manage their economies after the World War II. During the worldwide slump of the 1930s, most people felt that fiscal policy was not a good way of boosting an economy out of a slump. Keynes showed that they were wrong. He argued that if the government spent an amount equal to the shortage of demand in an economy, it would create the extra demand without causing excess demand.

As long as the government did not spend more than the amount of the "deflationary gap," this need not cause inflation. On the contrary. The government was simply making use of slack sources in the economy. For some years after the war, this approach worked quite well in several countries. But the real world is very complex, and peoples' expectations tend to rise over time. So if the government is always seen to be supporting the economy like this, political pressure tends to build up to provide too much support, which tends to produce inflation.

More recently, people have argued that to add government spending to private spending is misleading. Private spending, they said, tends to be "crowded out" by government spending. So extra government spending does not change the volume of demand in an economy—only its composition. All these issues are still controversial and unresolved. For our purposes, we need to look at how the effects of fiscal policy are transmitted to the economy.

Suppose we have the following: the US banking system in total has liabilities of $10 000 million and assets of cash $800 million; Treasury bills, $1000 million; and loans, $8200 million. Suppose in the next quarter the government runs a deficit of $280 million. That $280 million is paid to people who deposit it with the banks. Suppose that all of the deficit is financed by issuing Treasury bills. Suppose that the banks are the only buyers of Treasury bills. Then the $280 million extra in deposits that the banks receive is entirely invested in Treasury bills. So at the end of the quarter, we have a new balance sheet for the banking system of liabilities $10 280 million, and assets of cash $800 million; Treasury bills, $1280 million; and loans, $8200 million (Figure 8.4). It looks as if nothing has changed, except that the balance sheet of the banking system has grown by $280 million on both sides. It is almost like a conjuring trick. What happens is that the government has spent more, the proceeds have come into the private sector's hands, which has lent the money to the banks, who have lent it back to the government. It is a more or less instant recycling. The key link is the fact that the government's "promise to pay" is regarded by the banks as being a completely safe investment. The circle can only be completed if the banks have confidence in the government's promise and invest all their extra deposits in Treasury bills.

Though it seems that nothing has changed, three things have in fact happened. First, the incomes of companies or individuals have risen by $280 million. So, other things being equal, their spending will tend to go up. This will push up someone else's income, and so on. Second, the public is now more liquid. It holds $280 million more bank deposits than it used to. If it has a planned ratio of bank deposits

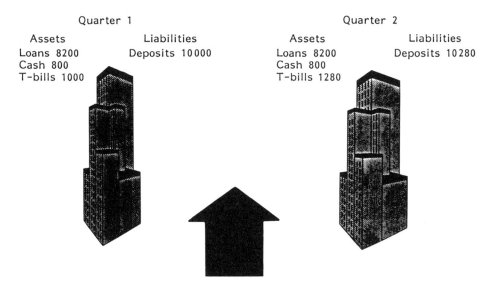

Quarter 1		Quarter 2	
Assets	Liabilities	Assets	Liabilities
Loans 8200	Deposits 10000	Loans 8200	Deposits 10280
Cash 800		Cash 800	
T-bills 1000		T-bills 1280	

Government Injects $280 Million of Liquidity

Figure 8.4   Impact of Injection of Liquidity

to total assets, the actual ratio will now be higher than planned. The public will start to shift assets out of bank deposits into other assets. Third, the banks hold more Treasury bills. If they have a planned ratio of Treasury bills to total lending, they will want to expand their lending.

So a rise in the government's deficit tends to expand the public's income, expand the public's holdings of bank deposits, and allow the banks to lend more. The effect of these changes on the rest of the economy depends on several things. If there is a great deal of unemployment, the effect will be different than if the economy is already fully stretched. Another question is the effect of the deficit on individuals' expectations about the future. If all other things are equal, though, we can say in general that a rise in the government's deficit tends to increase both economic activity and inflation.

8.5 BALANCE OF PAYMENTS

The balance of payments can be described as a record of a country's international economic accounts. That is, it records the goods and services that the economy has sold to and bought from the rest of the world, and the changes in the country's claims on and liabilities to the rest of the world. Because the balance of payments consists of double-entry bookkeeping, its components must necessarily balance, just like the accounts of a company. It is meaningless to say that a balance of payments is not in balance, just as it is meaningless to say that the accounts of a company do not balance.

When concern is expressed over a country's balance of payments, what is usually meant is that part of the balance—for example, the current account—is behaving in a way that puts strain on other parts of the balance that are needed to finance it. Hence the foreign exchange markets usually look at the behavior of the trade account or current account of a country to assess the likely pressure on a currency arising from the need to finance any deficit. But in theory, the behavior of any part of the balance of payments is irrelevant. Some other component in the balance will move to offset it.

For the sake of comparability, we shall concentrate on the presentation used by the IMF in its *Balance of Payments Manual*. The balance of payments breaks down into two main components: the current account, referring to goods, services, income, and transfers; and the capital account, covering financial assets and liabilities.

The current account itself can be broken down into the trade balance and other current items. The trade balance is the difference between exports and imports of goods. The other items in the current account include earnings from shipping and the like, spending on travel, income from investment (in the form of interest and dividends, or reinvested earnings which are left invested in the country where they were earned), and other goods and services. They also include transfers which can be either migrants' transfers or other transfers including official spending. The capital account can be split into four main sections:

1. direct investment: purchases of factories overseas and the like;
2. portfolio investment in shares or bonds;

Table 8.1 Home Country Balance of Payments

Exports	190
Imports	165
Trade balance	+25
Interest and dividends	− 15
Transfers	+40
Shipping, etc.	− 10
Current account	+40
Capital account	
Direct investment	+200
Net lending	− 100
Portfolio investment	−30
Change in reserves (–rise)	−110

3. other capital movements: borrowing and lending, changes in the credit terms given or taken by firms in international trade;
4. movements in the country's official reserves.

These ideas can best be understood by looking at a specific case. Table 8.1 shows a simplified balance of payments for our old friend, Home Country. Home has earned a surplus on its trade accounts, because its exports at 190 were larger than its imports, at 165. So its trade balance shows a surplus of +25. It has had to pay interest and dividends to companies overseas that have invested in it, so there is a transfer on current account outwards, that is, –15. Quite a few workers from Home have gone abroad to work at better paying jobs, and they are sending money back to their families. So transfers from abroad back to Home show up a surplus of +40 in the balance of payments. Goods coming into Home tend to be shipped in foreign ships, so Home has to pay away 10 on its shipping and transport account.

When we add these three items to the trade balance, we find that Home has a current account surplus of +40. In a sense, that represents an inflow of cash. To show what happens to this cash, we look at the capital accounts. We see that firms from overseas are buying factories in Home, so that there is an inflow on direct investment account of 200. Home's banks have tended to prefer to lend abroad, so on net lending there is an outflow of 100, and similarly Home's investors tend to buy foreign stocks. So there is an outflow on portfolio investment of 30. If we add up what we have so far—current account +40, direct investment +200, net lending –100, portfolio –30—we come to a total of +110.

The current account and the balance of capital accounts so far have meant a cash inflow of 110. The Home government adds these to its foreign currency reserves. To make the double-entry system balance, a rise in reserves has to be negative. (Any government's foreign exchange reserves are held, by definition, in foreign currency. Usually, these foreign currency reserves are held in Treasury bills or similar instruments overseas. In effect, the Home government is lending money to other governments by placing its reserves in these countries. So a rise in reserves has to be treated just the same as a net lending by Home's banks abroad.)

With the simple example in mind, we will look briefly at a more complicated case. We will look at the US balance of payments for 1992/93 (Table 8.2). We can see that

Table 8.2 US Balance of Payments, 1992–93 (in billion of US$)

	1992	1993
Exports	440.4	456.9
Imports	−536.5	−589.4
Trade balance	−96.1	−132.5
Military transactions	−3.0	−0.8
Investment income	4.5	3.9
Other services	58.7	57.6
Remittances, etc.	−32.0	−32.1
Current account	−67.9	−103.9
Net private capital flows	41.9	12.8
Net official asset flows	43.1	70.0
Errors	−17.1	21.1

the trade deficit grew strongly in 1993, because imports grew faster than exports, as the strengthening recovery pulled in imports, while the continuing recession elsewhere in the world held back US exports. Therefore, the trade deficit worsened from $96 to $133 billion. Investment income made a small positive contribution, up from the negative levels of the late 1980s. Other service income (e.g. insurance earnings, travel), however, helped to reduce the current account for 1993 to $103.9 billion. This deficit was financed via the capital account: private US entities borrowed $12.8 billion, and the government borrowed $70 billion (helped in large part by the fact that 1993 was a wonderful year for US bondholders, so foreigners were happy to buy US Treasury bonds). Finally there was a substantial unrecorded inflow through the errors and omissions account.

The capital account is complex. First, there is a very large error element in the US balance of payments accounts. Part of this comes from errors and omissions in the reporting of current account transactions. But people think that most of the error is from unrecorded flows of private capital. In 1993, this unrecorded inflow was very large. And it swung by $38 billion from the 1992 level. Other components of the capital account—short-term bank loans and portfolio investment, in particular—are very unstable, moving in response to perceived swings in confidence, interest rate levels, or corporate earnings prospects (in the case of equities).

Another very important source of capital flows can be changes in the terms of credit granted by firms in international trade. But the important point to realize is that the balance of payments consists of a whole new set of interconnected flows. As we said earlier, these must always balance just like any set of accounts; the critical question is whether or not the balance is achieved without strain.

If we think of the balance of payments as being a company's accounts, we can see there is a cash flow element—the current account—and there are the changes in balance sheet items that show up as capital flows. We can see that it is not necessarily a good or bad thing to be running a surplus or deficit on current account. A current account surplus is equivalent to a positive cash flow, and a deficit equivalent to a negative cash flow. A company (country) can be having a negative cash flow for many reasons, some good, some bad. It may have a negative cash flow because it is buying inventory so as to produce goods from inventory to sell later. Or it may be buying investment equipment from abroad, again with a view to building up production.

But, just like a company, a country cannot run a negative cash flow forever. It can only do it as long as other people are willing to lend to it. Hence, the foreign exchange market's concern about the current and trade accounts. These give a quick and easy indication of how the country's cash flow is doing. But it is also important to look at the balance sheet side, the capital flows.

8.6   BALANCE OF PAYMENTS POLICY

We now look at those government policies that affect the balance of payments. The most important of these are policy on the exchange rate, policy on borrowing from abroad, and trade policy. Exchange rate policy will be affected by many factors. But to put them in context, let us look at a simple case. Once again, we look at our Home Country. Home's exports per year are running at 100 widgets, while it is importing 200 widgets. The balance of widget trade, therefore, is in heavy deficit. Home's dictator is getting worried, so he orders a devaluation of the currency. In the past, Home's currency (HC) was set at HC 2 = US$1. The dictator announces that henceforth the parity will be HC 3 = US$1.

Since all Home's widget exports are priced in HC, buyers of Home's widgets find that they are cheaper. Suppose that in the past the widget was priced at HC 2.0, so that the price to the foreign buyer was US$1. Suppose that Home's widget exporters keep their widget prices fixed in HC. Then, the foreign buyer finds that he or she has only to pay US$0.67 per widget that he buys from Home instead of US$1 as in the past. Home's exports are now one-third cheaper, and hence more competitive in international terms. Foreign buyers will buy more Home widgets, and less from elsewhere, so that Home's exports will rise.

Now let us look at Home's imports of widgets. Suppose that foreign sellers of widgets to Home priced their widgets in dollars. Suppose that they priced each widget at US$1. Then each widget was costing the Home importer HC 2 to buy. But after the HC devaluation, assuming that foreign sellers of widget keep their prices fixed at US$1, the Home importer finds that each widget now costs him HC 3. Clearly, he is going to tend to prefer to buy his widget domestically, rather than from the world market. So Home's imports should also fall.

The net result of all these changes should be an improvement in Home's trade balance. This is the classical argument for devaluation of a currency. Conversely, the classical argument for a revaluation is when the trade surplus is excessive. Revaluing the currency makes exports from the country more expensive, and imports into it cheaper, so it tends to reduce the trade surplus.

The real world is not so simple. The first point is that a devaluation of a currency usually increases domestic inflation. To see why, let us look again at Home's imports from abroad. We saw that the effect of the devaluation made imports more expensive. We assumed that this meant that Home people would cut back their imports of widgets. But part of Home's imports probably consist of essential raw materials, like oil or metals, which are used in the production of widgets. So the effect of the devaluation will be to increase the costs of these essential imports and push up domestic widget production costs. The devaluation will also push up the price of imports of food and other consumption goods. That will probably lead Home's trade unions to ask for more wages. So a devaluation tends to be inflationary. In some countries where there is a very high level of essential imports from abroad, such as the UK, it has been suggested that the effect of a devaluation is washed out after a couple of years by the domestic inflation that results from it.

We should also notice the effect on domestic production. We saw that a devaluation of the HC made Home's exports more competitive in the world markets. We said this would lead to an increase in Home's exports of widgets. But if Home's producers of widgets were already working flat out at full capacity, they would not produce more for exports. To be fully effective, a devaluation is best made when there is surplus domestic production capacity that is available to meet the extra world demand for exports that the devaluation creates.

Another complication is that very often exporters work on the basis of orders for some months or years ahead. So the effects of a devaluation or revaluation will not show up immediately in export or import volumes. What would happen to Home's balance of payment if the volumes of exports and imports did not change? Clearly, widget exports of 100 units now earn less in foreign currency, because their US dollar price has fallen from $1 to $0.67. So instead of earning $100 from abroad, Home only earns $67. Conversely, the import price of a widget is still fixed at US$1, so Home is still spending $200 a year to buy widgets from abroad. The first effect of a devaluation is perverse. It worsens the trade deficit. Earnings from exports fall; imports cost the same in dollar terms as they did before. This is often called the J-curve effect. The reason is that the trade balance looks like a J: to start with, it goes down the first part of the curve of the J, and then it goes up again later.

As to how long each stage lasts, economists and econometricians have been spending a long time trying to find out. The answer is, of course, that it varies a great deal among countries and over time. It depends on the average contract period for exports and imports; and it depends on the currency in which trade is invoiced.

Another complication in real life is that if an exporter is invoicing in foreign currency when his own currency is devalued, he has two choices: he can either cut his foreign currency price, in which his exports become more competitive and he sells more; or he can keep his price the same and sell the same volume but make more profit. If he keeps his foreign currency price unchanged, the effect of the devaluation simply feeds through to corporate profits. It does not produce any immediate improvement in the balance of payments (although, of course, because exporting is now more profitable, it will probably tend to increase the number of exporters over time).

Another area of balance of payments policy is trade policy. A government can discourage imports by tariffs, or by nontariff barriers. These latter are especially important in certain countries, such as Japan. Another way in which a country can try to reduce imports is by import deposits. These have often been used, for example, in Italy when the government wants to bring the balance of payments under control. An importer has to put down, say 50% of the value of the goods to be imported. The money has to be deposited, interest free, at the central bank.

After this basic outline of some of the fundamental factors that affect exchange rates, we turn now to technical methods for forecasting.

8.7 TECHNICAL METHODS OF FORECASTING: CHARTING

For many years, some people active in markets such as the stock market and foreign exchange markets have argued that the best way to forecast future movements in rates is to analyze the patterns that can been seen in past movements. Collectively, the approaches that are used are often referred to as technical or chartist. The former, being the broader term, is the one that I shall use here.

The technical approach was first used in the equity and commodity markets. When exchange rates began floating, though, certain traders decided that they should look at a currency as just another commodity. The technical approach began to be applied to currencies. Chartists or technicians say that history repeats itself. They are more interested in the fact that a currency or interest rate breaks its historical support level than the reason for it. They look for unusual volumes of trading and breakouts, rather than the fundamental factors behind the market. In essence, technicians or chartists say that a price reflects the consensus of everyone in the market. They look at the movement of the herd, and believe in its statistical regularity. The chartist approach is the most widely known of the technical approaches, but there are others. They include the use of moving averages (and their more sophisticated variants, Box–Jenkins techniques), filters, price–volatility relationships, price momentum indices, and other techniques.

A very interesting analysis of the importance of these technical methods can be found in the *Bank of England Quarterly Bulletin* for November 1989, which reported a survey of chief foreign exchange dealers in the London market. The survey had a wide coverage, including over 200 responses. It assessed the way in which these dealers used technical methods. The survey found that about 90% of respondents used these methods for very short-term forecasting (intra-day to one week), with 60% judging them to be at least as important as fundamentals. At longer forecast horizons, of one to three months or six months to one year, the weight given to fundamentals increased and for one year or over, 85% judged fundamentals to be more important than charts, with nearly 30% relying on pure fundamentals. Therefore, even if you do not yourself believe in technical methods, it is important to understand how they work, because they clearly influence other people and how they behave in the short term, if not the medium term.

One approach, which can been seen either as simplistic or very sophisticated, is simply to argue that the forward exchange rate in the date in question is the best available forecast of the exchange rate. At the simplest level, it is a convenient expression of the market's views. The more sophisticated theorists would argue that the forward rate, because markets have efficiently priced all available information, represents the best possible forecast at any given time. Using the forward rate as a forecast has the major advantage that it is quick and cheap.

Empirical results on this were presented by C. Dunis and M. Feeny.[3] In general, while the dollar was rising (January 1980–February 1985), the mean forward premium was positive while the mean exchange rate change was negative, which resulted in significant forward rate prediction errors for the deutsche mark, Swiss franc, Dutch guilder, and four other currencies. In the weak-dollar period covering March 1985 to December 1988, the bias in the forward premium tended to have the opposite sign. Over the entire nine-year period, the average forward rate forecasting errors appear small and not significantly different from zero. Thus over the whole period, the forward could be viewed as an unbiassed predictor. But for periods of years on end, following the forward rate would have meant consistently getting it wrong in one direction or another.

The same book reports a series of studies on whether it is possible to outperform the forward rate. In some cases, technical strategies seemed to produce profits. However, there are two risks here. First, as more and more people follow the technical strategies, it will become more and more difficult to make money from them. Second, there is a selection problem: which technical strategy?

Let us look at the possible technical methods in more detail. We begin with charting techniques. One of the most popular charting techniques is the bar chart (Figure 8.5). Generally, a bar chart records a price or rate daily, with a vertical line representing the daily price trading range. A small horizontal bar is often used to identify the closing price on a particular day. One studies the trend of these movements in an effort to find patterns. If a price repeatedly reaches a level without being able to break through it, that becomes the resistance area. If, later, the resistance area is penetrated upward, a significant price rise is expected. The signal is especially strong if the breakout happens when trading is active. Similarly, if a price seems to bounce off a floor price level. It is considered a sell signal if the price later falls through this level.

A second pattern which analysts look for is a trend line. By definition, a trend line requires a number of observations before it can be established. It is identified by successive daily levels which are continually higher or lower than the previous day's level. For example, a clear uptrend occurs when each day's low is reached at a higher level. When those are connected for an extended time, they form a trend line.

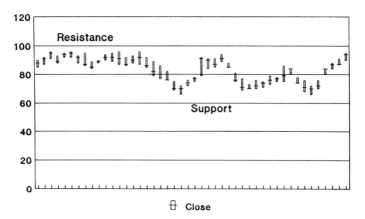

Figure 8.5 Basic Bar Chart Formation (Adapted from E.W. Schwartz, *How to Use Interest Rate Futures*, Dow-Jones Irwin, Homewood, Ill., 1979, p. 86)

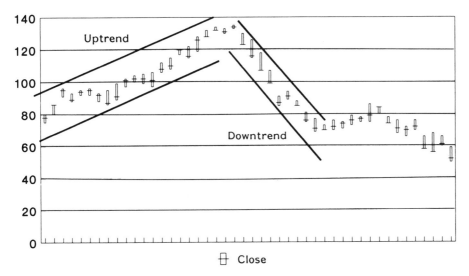

Figure 8.6 Channels (Adapted from E.W. Schwartz, *How to Use Interest Rate Futures*, Dow-Jones Irwin, Homewood, Ill., 1979, p. 86)

Closing prices may occur at random above the line, but none should occur below the trend line. Equally, a downward trend is seen from successive daily highs that are lower than previous ones. If the lines connecting the daily lows and those connecting the daily highs are parallel, this implies that the volatility of the market is not changing and a channel has been created. A breakout from a channel is considered a strong technical signal for a major uptrend or downtrend (Figure 8.6).

Another important pattern is the head and shoulders formation (Figure 8.7). Essentially it consists of four distinct periods: the left shoulder, the head, the right shoulder, and an abrupt penetration through the level of the neck. If the neck level is not broken through, the formation is normally considered meaningless.

Another important formation is the double top. (Figure 8.8) This usually signals the end of a rally. Often, the second top is sustained for a shorter period than the first one. Both the head and the double top formation may be reversed, in which case they are referred to as the inverted head and shoulders and the double bottom. In both cases, of course, the formations signal the reversal of a previous downward movement.

8.8 CANDLE CHARTS

Candle charts are a Japanese invention. They developed in their present form in the Meiji period, based on early ideas of rice merchants. Generally, candle charts are produced in colour, with price falls shown in black and rises in red. The chart is drawn just like any bar chart that shows the day's opening and closing prices. The difference lies in the portrayal of the space between open and close. In a candle chart, this space is drawn with a thicker line, red in colour if the close was higher

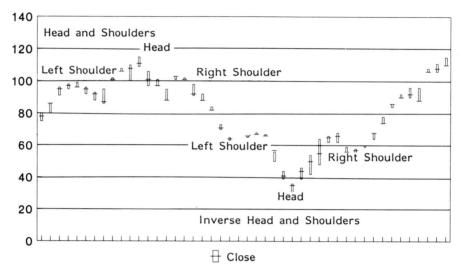

Figure 8.7 Head and Shoulders Formations (Adapted from E.W. Schwartz, *How to Use Interest Rate Futures*, Dow-Jones Irwin, Homewood, Ill., 1979, p. 86)

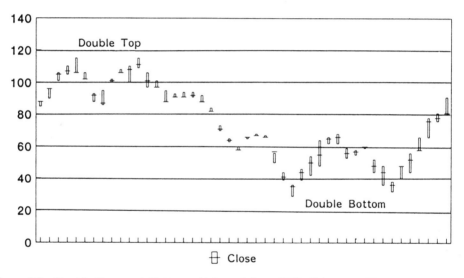

Figure 8.8 Double Tops and Bottoms (Adapted from E.W. Schwartz, *How to Use Interest Rate Futures*, Dow-Jones Irwin, Homewood, Ill., 1979, p. 86)

than the open, black if lower. Intra-day moves outside this range will show as a thin black line protruding above or below the body, giving the appearance of a candle and its wick (Figure 8.9).

The Nippon Technical Analysts Association have produced a full treatment of the interpretation of candle charts (Y. Abe *et al.*, *Analysis of Stock Prices in Japan*). The analysis covers a wide range of patterns, of which a sample is shown in Figure 8.10. The basic patterns are:

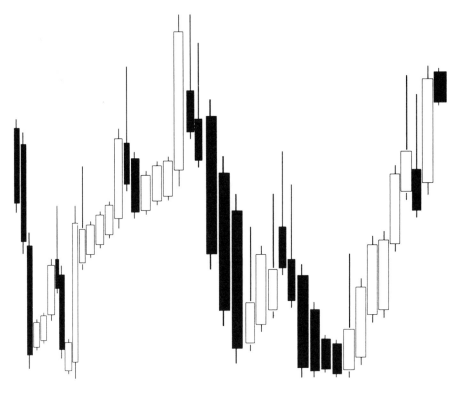

Figure 8.9 Sample Candle Chart

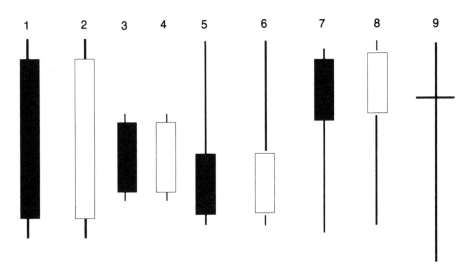

Figure 8.10 Typical Candle Patterns

1. Major yin: Market closes near the low. Strongly bearish.
2. Major yang: Market closes near the high. Strongly bullish.
3. Minor yin: Market turning down.
4. Minor yang: Market turning up.
5. Yin with upper shadow: Market moved up from the opening, but could not hold the gain and closed below the opening. Rather bearish.
6. Yang with upper shadow: Rather bullish.
7. Yin with lower shadow: Bearish.
8. Yang with lower shadow: Bullish.
9. *Jujisei* (cross): Market closes at same price as it opened: A reversal is possible.

8.9 CHANNELS

Several chartist concepts are used in another form by technical analysts who do not rely primarily on charts, but purely on the price series itself. For example, the channel concept can be used as part of a computer model.

We can define the ideas formally in this way. The highest and lowest closing price of the last N days are found. We get a sell signal if a price on day $(N + 1)$ is lower than the lowest close of the N days. Stop orders are used to take action when the signals are given. Only one position can be signaled per day. We always have a position, be it long or short. We are never "square." When we get a new buy or sell signal, the old position is cut out at the same time. This method takes away any element of judgment. If the high and low of the day are equal, then we assume that the market is locked limit. Nothing is done on that day. The trade will be done at the opening on the first day the market is not locked. This set of rules defines an intra-day closing price channel. A parallel definition can be made for an inter-day closing price channel. In this case, we only get a buy signal if the close on day $(N + 1)$ exceeds the highest close of the last N days. We then deal at the next day's opening.

8.10 FILTER RULE

Another technical method of analysis is the filter rule. This is independent of charting concepts. Investors following an $x\%$ filter rule take a long position in a currency that has risen $x\%$ from its most recent low point. They hold the position until the currency falls by $x\%$ from the highest level reached since the position was opened. Suppose we use a 2% rule. When a currency rise 2% from its recent low, we buy. When it falls 2%, we sell. The signal to sell is also a signal to go short. The short position is then until it is closed out on the next buy signal. Several studies have suggested it is possible to profit from filters. But one needs to allow for transactions and timing costs.

This point applies to all theoretical models. An interesting study in the equity market[4] showed how difficult it is to translate a wonderful model into real profits. The classic case is the Value Line Fund in the United States. Its actual 1965–86 outperformance over the market was 2.5% p.a.; the paper portfolio based on the Value

Line rankings with weekly rebalancing has outperformed by almost 20% p.a. The difference is execution costs (higher in equities), lags in being able to implement, and failure to have orders executed at the theoretical price.

8.11 CROSS-OVER METHOD

Another technical method, more popular than the filter, is the crossover method, sometimes called the moving average method. This also is completely independent of charting concepts. We work out two moving averages from the price. One is a short-term average, and one a long-term. If the short-term average is above the long-term average, one should be long, and if the short-term average is below the long-term average, one should be short. Actually this theory boils down to the "bandwagon" technique: go long if the market has gone up, short if it has fallen.

The method works like this. The average of p days' closes and n days' closes are calculated where p is less than n. The p index, then, is the short-term index, and n the long-term. People often use 5, 10, 15, 20, or 200 days for the averages, for instance, a 5-day and a 15-day or a 10-day and 20-day average. The averages include today's close and use only business days. If the average of series p (the short-term) is above the average of series n, a buy order is placed on the opening the next day. Conversely, if below, a sell order is placed on the opening the next day. As before, the aim is always to hold a position, be it long or short. When we get a new buy or sell signal, the old position is cut out at the same time. If the high and low of the next day are equal, then, again we assume that the market is locked limit, and a trade cannot be made on that day. The trade will be done on the first day that the market is not locked.

Moving averages can be refined by using weights, so that the most recent data is given more importance. We can define the simple moving averages as follows:

$$\text{Ma}_t = \frac{1}{n}(S_t + S_{t-1} + \dots + S_{t-n+1})$$

where S_t = exchange rate on day t and n = number of periods in average. Using the same notation and calling a_i the series of decreasing weights we can write:

$$\text{Ma}_t = \frac{a_1 S_t + a_2 S_{t-1} \dots + a_n S_{t-n+1}}{a_1 + a_2 + \dots a_n}$$

A particularly interesting and useful sort of weighted moving average is the exponential moving average. We can replace the weights we just used by a geometric progression $1, a, a^2 \dots a^{n-1}$ and write:

$$\text{Ma}_t = \frac{S_t + aS_{t-1} + a^2 S_{t-2} + \dots a^{n-1}S_{t-n+1}}{1 + a + a^2 + \dots + a^{n-1}}$$

The exponential moving average is widely used in currency trading systems, because it is simple to update and decreasing weight is given to older data. It can be shown that we can write:

$$\text{Ma}_{t+1} = (1 - a)S_{t+1} + a\text{Ma}_t$$

and in particular if $a = 1/n$ where n is the number of periods in the moving average, we can write

$$\text{Ma}_{t+1} = \frac{(n-1)S_{t+1} + \text{Ma}_t}{n}$$

As a result, it is very simple to update an exponential moving average. Only the latest price and the previous period moving average need to be known. By comparison, to update a simple moving average requires deleting the oldest data in the previous period's moving average.

In practice, the above equation is often used with a reversal of the coefficient, in order to avoid giving too much weight to the last data:

$$\text{Ma}_{t+1} = \frac{(n-1)\text{Ma}_t + S_{t+1}}{n}$$

This formula is often used in updating several technical indicators, particularly the relative strength index (RSI).

When we are using a moving average model, we may well want to know the next crossover point. (The treatment below follows that of Dunis and Feeny.) Finding in advance a possible crossover implies predicting the exchange rate that would make both moving averages equal, just before the short-term average crosses above or below the long one. This can be done as follows. Using our earlier notation and assuming n is greater than p, we can write that crossovers occur when:

$$\frac{1}{p}\left(\sum_{j=1}^{p-1} S_{t-j+1} + S_{t+1}^*\right) = \frac{1}{n}\left(\sum_{j=1}^{n-1} S_{t-j+1} + S_{t+1}^*\right)$$

where $S_{t+1}^* = $ the rate that would trigger the stop. After rearrangement, this can be written

$$S_{t+1}^* = \frac{np}{n-p}\left(\frac{\sum_{j=1}^{n-1} S_{t-i+1}}{n} - \left[\frac{p-1}{p}\right]\frac{\sum_{j=1}^{p-1} S_{t-j+1}}{p-1}\right)$$

We can substitute out the two moving averages prevailing at time T by rearranging the equation above

$$S_{t+1}^* = \left[\frac{np}{n-p}\right]\left\{\left[\frac{n-1}{n}\right]\frac{\sum_{j=1}^{n-1} S_{t-i+1}}{n} - \left[\frac{p-1}{p}\right]\frac{\sum_{j=1}^{p-1} S_{t-j+1}}{p-1}\right\}$$

If we call STMA_t the short-term moving average prevailing at time t and LTMA_t the long-term moving average at the same period, the crossover level that would reverse the model in the following period is therefore

$$S_{t+1}^* = \left[\frac{np}{n-p}\right]\left\{\left(\frac{n-1}{p}\right)\text{LTMA}_t - \left(\frac{p-1}{p}\right)\text{STMA}_t\right\}$$

The necessary information is readily available at time t, so here it is quite easy to place a timely stop order with a bank if one wishes to.

8.12 MOMENTUM MODELS AND OSCILLATORS

Probably the best known variation on moving average crossover strategies are the momentum models. Although they operate exactly the same as crossover models, their decision rule is based on either the difference between the faster and the slower moving average or on their ratio. With momentum models based on differences in moving averages, the momentum index will be positive in a rising market, when the faster moving average lies above the slower one. Conversely, it will be negative in a declining market, when the faster moving average lies below the slower one. The decision rule is to buy the currency whenever the momentum index crosses above the zero line into positive territory and to sell it when the momentum index crosses back below the zero line into negative territory (Figure 8.11).

Provided one uses the same pair of moving averages, the signals will be the same for this type of momentum model as for the double moving average crossover when constantly in the market. The same applies to the ratio momentum index, where the index will stand above one in a rising market when the faster moving average lies above the slow one. Conversely, it will be below one in a declining market. The decision rule is to buy when the index crosses above the one level and to sell when it moves back below.

What, then, is the point of momentum models rather than straight crossover models? If we use the ratio form of the momentum model, to get rid of scale effects that might arise from a long-term trend in the currency, we can define levels beyond which the momentum index series very seldom varies. If we manage to identify these levels, we can then define them as overbought or oversold levels for a given exchange rate. One could use the reversal of the momentum index in the overbought or oversold area only as a signal to close out an existing position, rather than buying a

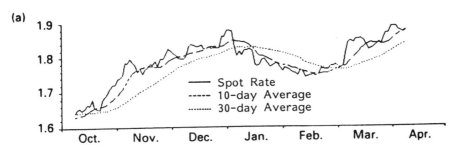

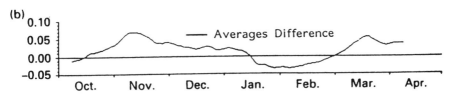

Figure 8.11 (a) GBP/USD Rate from 8 October 1987 to 8 April 1988; (b) Momentum Index Showing the Difference in the Averages. Source: Datastream. Reproduced from C. Dunis and M. Feeney. *Exchange Rate Forecasting*, Macmillan Press, London, 1989

new one. A new position will then be triggered only when the momentum index crosses back over the crossover line. This would lead to the model not being constantly in the market and may sometimes be more profitable. If used in the ratio form so that they are free of scale effects, momentum models can help select from several exchange rates the one that is diverging most. Thus, momentum models allow comparisons between currencies.

Probably the most widely known oscillator is the relative strength index (RSI). It measures the velocity of currency moves by dividing the average of up variations by the average of down variations over N events. The mathematical formula is such that the index is normalized between zero and 100. This has the advantage of making it comparable across different currencies so that we can identify those which are most strongly overbought or oversold. The general formula for an N-event RSI is

$$RSI_t^n = 100 - \frac{100}{1 + RSI_t^n}$$

where

$$RSI_t^n = \frac{1/n \sum_{i=1}^{n} a_{it}}{1/n \sum_{i=1}^{n} b_{it}}$$

and

$$a_{it} = S_{t-i+1} - S_{t-i} \quad \text{if } S_{t-i+1} > S_{t-i}$$
$$b_{it} = |S_{t-i+1} - S_{t-i}| \quad \text{if } S_{t-i+1} < S_{t-i}$$

Commonly used signals for overbought and oversold are 70 and 30, respectively.

A word of caution is merited: overbought and oversold indicators seem to work better for closing out existing positions than for opening new ones. When a currency breaks out of its most recent range, the oscillator will rapidly move into the overbought or oversold area. A consolidation of the move may then occur, which will translate into what might prove only a temporary reversal of the oscillator. If one followed the oscillator to open a new position, one might open a new position that is contrary to the currency trend, which has been established by the new breakout. In that sense, it may be better to use momentum indicators as a further decision rule in addition to the traditional crossover.

8.13 WHY BOTHER? THE CASE FOR PASSIVE MANAGEMENT

There is a wide range of trading theories from which to choose, both fundamental and technical. How do we find the best method? If I knew for certain I would not bother to write this book: I would have retired on the proceeds. But let us try to find a sensible way to operate. First, we have to set criteria for choosing the best theory. We need to know which theory is going to anticipate the future more accurately than the market will.

This raises the question of what the market's anticipation is, since the forward cannot strictly be taken as the market's anticipation, being dominated by interest differentials. However, there is no other clear-cut measure of expectations, short of conducting a regular sample poll. Also, the forward rate is relevant for the corporate treasurer or the investor, in that he or she has to decide whether or not to hedge a position. The current forward rate represents the alternative to taking an open position. So the forward rate is about the best option. But using the forward rate as a benchmark is only applicable if a method produces explicit forecasts. If, like most technical services, it simply produces a buy or a sell signal, another test is to work out the total return that would have been earned by slavishly following the service's signals.

The potential user should be clearly aware that track record itself is no guarantee of future performance. A second qualification which I would make from a personal point of view is that in committing oneself to a technical service, one must not be prepared merely to accept possibly long strings of losses but one must also be prepared to accept as an act of faith the technical method being used in the belief that is the best of all possible methods at this point in time. It is essential, therefore, that the trader or speculator who is following these services be prepared to accept a substantial commitment of capital even if there is a long series of losses, in the hope that the tide will turn eventually. Against this, however, it must be said of the fundamental services that the market's view of fundamentals changes unpredictably. A fundamentalist betting against the US dollar from 1982 to 1985 would have been right, but would have lost money for three years.

It is by no means impossible to beat the forward rate. However, the profits from this are not risk free, so that the person aiming to beat the forward rate has to be prepared to assess the return on capital. Given the rapid reversals in exchange rates and the volatility in the market, it is not obvious that the specific profits are high relative to the risk involved: that is, equal or better returns might be obtained by employing the capital elsewhere.

This line of thinking has led many to consider another approach: the passive management of foreign exchange risk (some people call it "mean-variance optimization" or something similar). This approach is particularly applicable to longer-term investors or borrowers. The most basic argument is "it'll all come out in the wash." That is, over a long period of time, currencies tend to swing back and forth and there is no a priori reason for knowing where in the cycle we are at any given time. The US dollar swung from DEM 1.67 in 1978 to DEM 3.46 in 1985 and to DEM 1.80 in 1989. If the investor is investing in a spread of international assets for the purpose of diversifying risks, and has a long-term time horizon, then the impact of foreign exchange is itself a diversifying influence.

This argument is based on two contentions. First, that in the long run you cannot time the market consistently so as to make profits from foreign exchange (see Chapter 7). Secondly, in the long run, hedged and unhedged international investments should offer the same returns. Suppose they did not. That would imply that foreign exchange markets continuously over- or underpriced the cost of hedging a given currency. The cost was always above or below the actual change in value that took place. For any given period, that might be true, since the hedging cost is technically driven by interest differentials. But in the very long run, there is no reason to believe this would happen. If it did, it would imply that an investor in one country would be consistently rewarded for taking foreign exchange risk and an investor in another would be consistently penalized. That seems contradictory.

If we accept the argument for passive management, then the next question is how to implement it, specifically the choice of neutral position. There are two possibilities: always hedged or never hedged. The benchmark in the former case would be an unhedged index, and a hedged one in the latter instance. The choice between the two depends on the investor's philosophy. One possible approach, used by many investors in managing their domestic portfolios, is that suggested by modern portfolio theory, that is, we opt for the choice that offers us least risk for the same return. Putting it another way, we look to choose a position on the efficient frontier.

8.14 EFFICIENT FRONTIERS

Suppose you think that neither you nor anyone else has the gift of permanently timing the market right. Then the modern portfolio theorist argues that you should focus on setting up an "efficient" portfolio. You start by deciding how much risk you want to take. Risk is defined as variability of return. It is measured by the standard deviation of returns from an asset over time.

Suppose you are a US investor considering whether to invest overseas. The Salomon Brothers High Grade Corporate Bond Index returned an annual 10.53% in the 10 years prior to 1988. Its annualized standard deviation was 15.4%. Over the same period, the Salomon Brothers Non-US Bond Index returned 12.29% in US dollar terms. Its annualized standard deviation was 16.34%. The non-US bond index gave higher returns, at the price of higher risk.

The point of modern portfolio theory is that risk falls as you include different types of assets, as long as their returns are not perfectly correlated. Diversification pays. Say you hold both equities and bonds. They will not normally both perform badly in the same year. So the weak performance of one will be offset by the other. The portfolio as a whole will be more stable than either asset individually. Diversifying reduces your risk.

Let us look at a practical example. Suppose you think, after studying history and making your forecasts, that the following asset classes will produce a certain pattern of risks and returns. Let us say, over the next five years, you expect:

	US bonds	Non-US bonds
Return	8%	9.5%
Risk	9%	12%

And let us suppose you think the returns will have a correlation of 0.4, that is, US bond returns will vary in line with non-US bond returns 40% of the time. To work out the risk of the combined portfolio, we need the covariance between the two assets, that is, the standard deviation of each asset (or pair of assets, if there were more than two) multiplied together and weighted by the correlation between the assets. So the covariance is $0.09 \times 0.12 \times 0.4 = 0.00432$. We'll also need the variances of the two assets, which is the square of the standard deviation (0.0081 and 0.0144, respectively).

8.15 CONSTRUCTING A FRONTIER

Now we can find the risk and return of a portfolio combining these elements. Suppose we start by holding everything in US bonds. Then we gradually push up the share of non-US bonds to 100%. Finding the return is an easy calculation: a weighted average. The risk is a little more tricky.

Let us take the risk when we have 30% in non-US bonds. The calculation is

$$0.0081 \times 0.49 + 0.0144 \times 0.09 + 2 \times 0.7 \times 0.3 \times 0.00432 = 0.007\,0794$$

In other words:

US bonds' variance × square of 70% weight + non-US bonds' variance × square of 30% weight + 2 × 70% US weight × 30% non-US weight × covariance

That is the variance of the combined portfolio: to find the standard deviation we take the square root, which comes out at 0.084 139 or 8.41%. Now we do the sums for all the different weights and we get:

As you push up the share of non-US bonds, the risk of the combined portfolio falls from 9.00 to 8.41% when you have 30% in non-US bonds. While the risk is falling, though, the return is rising. You can get 30 basis points more return for less risk, if you push the share of non-US bonds from 0 to 30%. The chart shows the same thing visually. If you are happy to take more risk in exchange for more return, you can push the non-US bonds up to 50% or even beyond (Figure 8.12).

We can apply this approach to constructing a solution of our problem. Suppose we are a company with a given pattern of borrowing needs over say the next five years. We can say, well, we have no real idea of what the exchange rates will do over

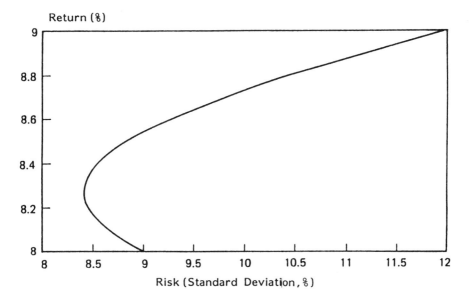

Figure 8.12 Risk and Return: Effect of Higher Share of Non-dollar Bonds

the next five years. But we would like to set up our borrowings in a manner that gets us close to the efficient frontier. That is, we want the pattern of our liabilities to get us the lowest cost for the least risk. This is the mirror image of the investor's problem, who wants the highest return for the least risk. Suppose we want our borrowings to be five-year borrowings. Then we could take historical data and from it construct a frontier from the interest costs and exchange rate movements of the currencies in which we can borrow. We would set up our borrowing program in accordance with that efficient frontier. (In practice, things could get more complex: one might be looking at a three-dimensional version of the frontier to allow for different maturities.)

There are several caveats. First, what we have done is said: "We cannot forecast exchange rates. Instead, we will forecast that past returns, past variances, and past correlations can be projected into the future." It is by no means clear that this is right. Second, there are a good many practical issues, to which we now turn.

8.16 APPLYING THE MEAN-VARIANCE OPTIMIZATION APPROACH

Suppose we have constructed an efficient frontier which tells us as an investor (or as a borrower) what the possible combinations of risk and return are. Let us look at it from the point of view of an investor this time. An investor considering hedging foreign currency risk has three possible choices: forward foreign exchange, financial futures, or currency options (or, indeed, some of the so-called third-generation hedging products that combine forward exchange and options). Let us suppose that we decide to keep things simple and stick to forward exchange.

The normal route, then, would be to sell forward currency against your equities or bonds, in the forward exchange market. Suppose you are a US$-based investor and you hold 150 million JPY worth of 10-year Japanese government bonds, because you believe Japanese interest rates are about to fall. However, for the same reason, you expect a weakening in the yen. Then you would sell forward JPY 150 million, for delivery in, say, three months' time.

The alternative is to sell forward to match the maturity of the bond, but this is much less attractive. Hedging a 10-year bond with a 10-year forward would be difficult, because the 10-year forward market is thin and illiquid. You would be conceding a substantial liquidity premium to the foreign exchange market for the privilege of executing the hedge. By the same token, unless you were willing to concede a second premium, you would be committed to holding the bond and its hedge to maturity.

If the forward sale is in US dollars, then you are in effect holding synthetic US dollar Japanese bonds. Depending on the relative slope of the yield curves (which will affect the forward exchange premium or discount) this maneuver can produce attractive results. There is an implied exposure to the shape of the yield curve, but this is generally of much lesser impact than the effect of currency movements.

However, the costs of this operation need to be properly measured. Suppose you are running the position for a year, with three-month forward contracts. You will roll the hedges four times. Suppose you are hedging yen assets and today's spot is

$1 = JPY 150. On the Reuters screen today is a three-month forward price of 129/125 meaning a seller of yen forward would sell at 150−1.25 = 148.75. Suppose rates do not change at all in the next three months. At maturity of the forward, you buy back at 150 the yen you sold at 148.75 and you extend the contract at the same rate. You crystallize a cash-flow difference (in this case a profit) and you pay the forward market spread each time you roll the contract.

Suppose the true interbank rate is 128/126: You are being charged a point each time you roll, say four points p.a. That costs $0.04/150 = 0.03\%$ p.a. or three basis points. (For other, less liquid currencies, or for amounts smaller than standard interbank size, the cost would be higher; for a diversified portfolio perhaps six or seven basis points would be a sensible average figure). More significant would be the cost of the odd cash flows thrown up by the rolling of forward contracts, particularly if losses require a sale of securities from elsewhere in the portfolio. Estimates of these costs vary but anywhere from 15 to 50 basis points, depending on size and frequency of cash flows, would be appropriate. In addition, there would be the costs of someone's time to handle the hedging program, or an outside manager's fees. Total costs would probably be a minimum of $\frac{1}{4}\%$ and could range up to $\frac{3}{4}\%$ p.a. Thought might also have to be given, in some cases, to the fact that the forward exchange gains or losses would be realized, while the gains or losses on the assets being hedged would generally be unrealized, with possible reporting/accounting implications.

NOTES

1. See *Bank of England Quarterly Bulletin*, February 1995, p. 48.
2. "The transmission mechanism of monetary policy," *Bank of England Quarterly Bulletin*, August 1994, p. 261.
3. C. Dunis and M. Feeny, *Exchange Rate Forecasting*, Woodhead-Faulkner/Simon and Schuster, 1989.
4. A.F. Perold, "The implementation shortfall: Paper versus reality," *The Journal of Portfolio Management*, Spring 1988.

9
Money and Foreign Exchange Mechanics

In this chapter, we discuss basic money market and foreign exchange calculations. For a much more detailed explanation which covers specialist technicalities such as short-date foreign exchange rates, holiday adjustments and the like, the reader is requested to consult the author's *Foreign Exchange and Money Markets Guide* (John Wiley, New York, 1992).

For the sake of simplicity, we concentrate on Euromarket calculations. This allows us to focus on the transnational aspects of the market and avoids questions of reserve requirements or other features specific to particular markets. Therefore, throughout this chapter, all comments relate (unless otherwise stated) to the Euromarket, that is, deposits traded outside the country of origin. Deposits traded in the country of origin are referred to as domestic.

9.1 CONVENTIONS

The Euromarkets use two bases for calculating interest. These are the 360-day year and the 365-day year. The 365-day year is used for sterling, the Irish pound, the Kuwaiti dinar, and the Belgian franc. All other currencies are dealt on a 360-day basis. The Belgian franc is also dealt on a 360-day basis if both parties to deal are non-Belgian. Sometimes the Canadian dollar is dealt on a 365-day basis with customers, but interbank Euro-Canadian is usually 360. Given mutual agreement, any basis can be used.

The method of calculation for 360 basis is as follows. Suppose the deal is for 91 days, the interest rate 10%, the principal amount US$1 million. Then the interest is calculated from

$$\frac{10}{100} \times \frac{91}{360} \times 1,000,000 = 25,277.78$$

Because this method uses actual days elapsed and a 360-day year, it is sometimes called a 365/360 or actual/360 basis.

The calculation method for 365-day basis is similar. We replace 91/360 by 91/365:

$$\frac{10}{100} \times \frac{91}{365} \times 1,000,000 = 24,931.51$$

Note that for the same nominal interest rate of 10%, the 365-day basis produces a lower interest amount. Thus a 10% Eurodollar rate (360-day basis) is equivalent to a 10.138 89% rate on a 365-day basis. Equally, a 9.863% Eurodollar rate, 360 basis, is equivalent to 10% on a 365-day basis. The 365-day method is sometimes called the 365/365 method, or actual/365.

Another method of calculating interest rates is used in certain European countries for domestic deposits. It can be described as the Continental, or 360/360 method, compared with the Euromarket (365/360) or the sterling (365/365) method. The two latter methods compute interest on the actual day elapsed, whereas the Continental method treats the year as consisting of twelve 30-day months. Thus, a deal running from December 5, 1990 to December 5, 1991 would be treated as a 360-day deal. A deal running from December 5, 1990 to May 12, 1991 would be treated as having 157 days ($5 \times 30 + 7$) instead of the actual 158 days. Note that the result of this method is to produce a lower effective rate, for a given nominal rate, than the 365/365-day sterling method, which in turn is lower than the 365/360 Euro- or US method.

Euromarket practice is to pay interest at the maturity of the deal, except where periods of over one year are involved. In that case, interest is paid annually on the "anniversary" of the deal. Let us look at a two-year deal done on December 5, 1990. Interest would be paid on December 5, 1991. Interest would be paid again, and the principal repaid, on December 5, 1992. A two-and-a-half year deal done on the same date would pay interest on the same dates, with a final interest payment (and repayment of principal) on June 5, 1993. If the anniversary is not a business day, the procedure adopted is the same as in the forward market: it will be rolled forward to the next business day, providing this does not take us into the next month.

The deposit market quotes two rates for a given period. The offered rate is the rate at which the dealer is prepared to lend money. The bid rate is the rate at which the dealer is prepared to borrow. Normal US practice is to quote the bid rate first. Normal London market practice is to quote the offered rate first. Hence "$7\frac{1}{4}-\frac{1}{2}$" in the United States, "$7\frac{1}{2}-\frac{1}{4}$" in London, both mean "I lend at $7\frac{1}{2}$%, borrow at $7\frac{1}{4}$%."

A large amount of Eurocurrency lending involves the London interbank offered rate (LIBOR). It can be defined in two ways: (1) the rate at which funds are offered to a first-class bank in London for the maturity period in question; (2) the rate at which a first-class bank in London offers funds to another first-class bank in London. In either case, LIBOR attempts to measure the cost to a bank of raising new funds from the market in order to on-lend. It is the basis of almost all variable-rate lending in the Euromarkets. In view of its importance, it should be stressed that the LIBOR concept is purely judgmental. For example, three-month LIBOR for US$1000 million will very likely differ from three-month LIBOR for US$5 million. We are considering the dealer's judgment of what it would cost to raise that amount for on-lending. It may well be that it is judged that it would cost more to raise the larger amount, because it will move the market against the dealer. Hence, normal practice for any given loan is to calculate LIBOR as the average of the rates quoted by several "reference banks" selected for the purpose. The rates published in the financial press reflect a consensus of often diverse views. LIBOR is usually fixed at a time specified in the original loan agreements (normally 11.00 a.m. London time). It is quoted for deposits starting from the spot date (see below) for various periods, of which the most common are three and six months.

The LIBOR convention has spawned many variations. These include SIBOR (Saudi or Singapore interbank offered rate), NIBOR or NYBOR (New York), KIBOR (Kuwait), PIBOR (Paris), FIBOR (Frankfurt), ADIBOR (Abu Dhabi), HKIBOR (Hong Kong), MIBOR (Madrid), and so on. In all cases, the concept attempts to measure a bank's funding costs for a loan, though the details vary from centre to centre. It is quite possible to apply the concept to other Eurodeposits or domestic deposits (for example, many domestic UK loans are linked to sterling LIBOR).

9.2 TYPES OF DEPOSIT

A call deposit is defined as a deposit which is repayable "at call." In practice, due to time zone considerations, and the need to transmit confirmations between countries, such deposits may be repayable at up to two days' notice, unless special arrangements have been made. The situation varies according to currency, and the ability to take call funds from a customer depends on the currency. In some currencies, there is not a well-developed call money market that makes it difficult to lay off funds.

An overnight deposit is defined as a deposit made today that is repaid (or replaced) on the next business day. Overnight deposit trading is also complicated by time zone considerations. A Hong Kong bank can deal US dollar deposits overnight without difficulty, since New York will normally be 13 hours behind, giving plenty of time for instructions to be processed in Hong Kong and acted on in New York. However, London cannot normally deal overnight deutsche mark deposits as deals have to be in the Frankfurt clearing by 8.00 a.m. Effectively this means that processing and confirmation among the placing bank, the accepting bank, the placing bank's German correspondent, and the accepting bank's German correspondent would have to be completed by 8.00 a.m. on the same day as the deal, which is not really practical.

The time zone problem is less pressing for deposits starting tomorrow and maturing in the next business day, usually referred to as "tomorrow/next" or "tom/next." (It will be noticed that tom/next deals mature on the spot date.) It is possible to deal tom/next in most currencies that have a well-developed Eurocurrency market, but because of the time zone problem the market tends to dry up very early. As in the foreign exchange market, the deposit market quotes spot/next (from spot to the next business day), spot/week, and so on.

A deposit in the Euromarket, unless otherwise stated, with begin on the spot date. This will be two business days from today. A period deposit is defined as a deal starting on the spot date and maturing on some fixed and predetermined date. The phrase "the periods" usually refer to some or all of the "standard" periods of 1, 2, 3, 6, 9, or 12 months. Value date conventions for period deposits are the same as for foreign exchange, with the exception that it would be possible (though in practice unusual) to deal for a value date in which the dealing centre was closed but the settlement centre was open. For example, suppose that New York and Frankfurt were open, but London closed, on a given day. The foreign exchange market—and London—would deal US$/DEM for settlement on that day, but London would not normally deal Eurodollars or Euromark deposits for maturity on that day.

9.3 YIELD CURVE

A yield curve is a graph which plots interest rates against time. To make it meaningful, the different interest rates should be for comparable instruments. In this chapter, that means interest rates for a deposit with a bank. In other contexts, we might plot the interest rate for Treasury bills maturing, say, in 1, 3, 6 and 12 months and talk of a Treasury bill yield curve. Because of possible capital gains on a security (or CD) and the differing taxation treatment of interest earnings and capital gains, constructing a true yield curve for securities can be quite complex. But for "clean" deposits, the question of capital gain does not arise, so the yield curve concepts are quite simple.

Suppose we have the following set of rates: 1 week, 10%; 1 month, $10\frac{1}{2}$%; 2 months, $10\frac{1}{2}$%; 3 months, $10\frac{3}{4}$%; 6 months, 11%; 9 months, $11\frac{1}{2}$%; and 12 months, 12%. Then we can draw a simple yield curve as in Figure 9.1 (line AC). We can see that it slopes upward to the right. This is called a normal upward-sloping, or positive yield curve. It is normal, because under normal circumstances a lender requires a slightly higher rate to compensate for locking away funds for a longer period. Equally, a borrower will be prepared to pay slightly more for the benefit of being insulated against interest rate movements for a longer time.

If the market thinks that rates are about to rise, the curve will rise more steeply; lenders will require extra compensation before they will lock in at today's rates. They believe that rates will soon be higher, and so they would be better off to wait until

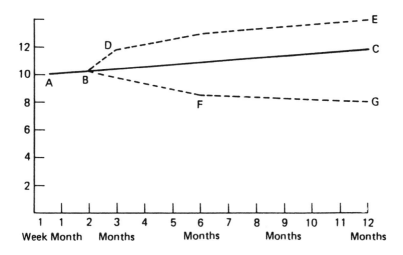

Figure 9.1 Yield Curves

the rates rise before they lend. In this situation, it might be that the 3-month rate is 12%, 12 months, 13%. We could draw a yield curve like the dotted line ABDE in Figure 9.1.

Or it might be that the market expects rates to fall. In this case, lenders will be happy to lend for longer periods at rates below today's rates. They fear that if they wait before they lend, the rates they will receive will be lower still. In this case, the 12-month rate might be only 8%, with the 6-month rate 9%, and the 2-month rate $10\frac{1}{2}$%. We could draw the dotted line ABFG in Figure 9.1.

Looking at a yield curve tells us a great deal about where the market thinks rates are going. If we look at Figure 9.1 we can see that, if today's yield curve is ABDE, the market expects rates to rise, but not for a couple of months, since AB is only sloping up gently in line with the normal pattern. If the yield curve were ABFG, the market is expecting rates to fall over a couple of months. Also, the slope of the curve suggests that between two and six months hence—BF on the curve—the market expects quite a sharp fall, which will steady off later; FG is flatter than BF. The yield curve is telling us visually about the implied forward forward rates (which are discussed later). We will come back to how the yield curve, the forward forward rates, and the implied zero-coupon rates are interlinked later in the chapter.

A technique used by many investors is called "riding the yield curve." Suppose in the shorter maturities the slope of the yield curve is positive (and is expected to remain so). This means that, say, a 6-month CD yields more than a 3-month CD. If rates do not change drastically, an investor can pick up extra yield by buying the 6-month CD and selling it in 3 months to reinvest the proceeds in the 6-month CD. In effect, the investor is collecting the premium for staying long in a market where a premium is paid for staying long. Of course, if rates have risen sharply in the meantime—as has often happened in recent years—the investor has earned less than by staying short.

9.4 MISMATCH (GAP)

This brings us to the question of mismatch (usually referred to as gap in the United States). Mismatch happens when a trader borrows or lends money for a longer or shorter period than would be needed to match the commitment. If a bank lends money for 6 months, and funds the lending initially with a 3-month deposit, it is mismatched. There are two kinds of mismatch: interest mismatch and funding mismatch (see Chapter 13). In our example, there is interest mismatch of 3 months. If after 6 months the loan is due for repayment, then the funding mismatch is also 3 months; if the 6-month loan is a rollover loan whose final agreed maturity is, say, 5 years, then the funding mismatch is 4 years and 9 months—the remaining period during which money must be raised to fund the loan.

Mismatching is the justification for a bank's existence. The origin of banking, after all, was in taking deposits, repayable at demand, and lending then out for a slightly longer period. It also carries risks; the control of these risks is discussed in Chapter 13. In proportion to the risk, it carries the chance of profits.

Suppose we have 1 month (30 days), 10–$10\frac{1}{8}$%; 3 months, $10\frac{5}{8}$–$10\frac{3}{4}$%; and 6 months (180 days, $10\frac{5}{8}$–$10\frac{3}{4}$%. The market expects a rise in rates in the next 3 months, followed by a leveling out. Suppose a customer borrows $10 million for 6 months from the bank, and the bank thinks the market has got it wrong, and rates will fall. Then it will fund itself, say, for 1 month at $10\frac{1}{8}\%$. It earns

$$10,000,000 \times 10.75/100 \times 180/360 = \$537,500$$

for the 6-month loan, paying

$$10,000,000 \times 10.125/100 \times 30/360 = \$84,375$$

for the 1-month funds. Suppose in a month's time the rate for 5-month money (150 days) has fallen to 10%, paying

$$10,000,000 \times 10/100 \times 150/360 = \$416,666.67$$

(ignoring interest on interest). Its total costs are $501,041.67 and its total earnings $537,500, leaving a profit of $36,458.33.

This compares with the $\frac{1}{8}\%$ that the bank would have earned if it had immediately been able to fund itself for 6 months at $10\frac{5}{8}\%$, which would have shown a profit of only $6250.00 if it had not run a deliberate mismatch. Of course, the $30,000 odd extra profit from this mismatch could just as easily have been a loss if the bank had misjudged rate movements. A number of the world's largest banks have lost tens of millions of dollars on mismatch positions; hence the need for tight controls.

9.5 FORWARD FORWARD RATES

We turn now to the mechanics of calculating a forward forward rate (a rate for a deposit or a borrowing starting at a future rate). Until the development of the forward rate agreement (FRA) and swaps markets (see below) the forward forward market was an important arena for interest rate trading by banks. Although this might seem a rather specialized exercise, the forward forward rate is vital in at least two important areas: FRAs (see below) and arbitrage between the deposit market and the financial futures market (see Chapter 10). For example, the rate on the three-month Eurodollar futures contract is nothing but an implied forward forward rate. (Conversely, the deposit forward forward rates are often driven by the rates in the futures market.)

The simplest approach is to consider a specific case. A bank is lending for 60 days at 20% against a deposit for which it has paid 10% for 30 days. What is the break-even rate on the second period—that is, how much can it afford to pay for a deposit starting on day 31 and maturing on day 60? We assume the deposit and loan are for US$1 million and interest is paid on a 360-day basis. Then, the bank pays interest in first period of

$$\frac{10}{100} \times \frac{30}{360} \times 1,000,000 = \$8333.33$$

The bank earns interest over the lifetime of the loan of

$$\frac{20}{100} \times \frac{60}{360} \times 1,000,000 = \$33,333.33$$

However, in accordance with Euromarket convention, interest earned on the 2-month loan is not paid to the bank until the end of the 2 months, whereas the bank must pay away interest on the 1-month deposit at maturity. So for the second period it not only has to fund its $1 million principal amount but also the US$8 333.33 which it has paid away in interest. So the amount to be funded in the second period is $1,008,333.33.

Now we know that the bank has earnings of $33,333.33 over two months and costs (so far) of $8333.33. So there is a net $25,000 which is available to pay the interest on our new principal of $1,008,333.33. So to calculate our forward forward interest rate we work the $25,000 as a percentage of the principal and annualize up from our 30-day period to a 360-day period:

$$\text{Forward rate} = 100 \times \frac{360}{30} \times \frac{25,000}{1,008,333.33} = 1200 \times 0.024,7933 = 29.751\ 96\%$$

In order to reduce this to a formula, we set up some definitions. The formula is set up in terms of middle market rates for simplicity.

R_1 = rate for shorter, first period
R_2 = rate for second period
N_1 = number of days in first period
N_2 = number of days in total second period, that is, including first
B = interest basis (usually 360)
P = principal amount
I_1 = interest due in first period
I_2: = interest due in second period
I_3: = interest residual

Interest paid in the first period is

$$I_1 = \frac{R_1}{100} \times \frac{N_1}{B} \times P$$

Interest earned in total period is

$$I_2 = \frac{R_2}{100} \times \frac{N_2}{B} \times P$$

Hence interest available for the second period, I_3 is

$$I_3 = I_2 - I_1 = R_2 \times \frac{N_2}{100} \times \frac{P}{B} - \frac{R_1}{100} \times \frac{N_1}{B} \times P = \frac{P(R_2 \times N_2 - R_1 \times N_1)}{100 \times B}$$

Our forward forward interest is calculated by working I_3 back into an annual percentage of the principal (notice that the principal is now $P + I_1$):

$$\text{Forward forward rate} = \frac{100 \times B \times I_3}{(N_2 - N_1)(P + I_1)} = \frac{P(R_2 \times N_2 - R_1 \times N_1)}{(N_2 - N_1)(P + I_1)}$$

If we set the principal amount equal to $1, or unity, the formula simplifies to

$$\text{Forward forward rate} = \frac{R_2 \times N_2 - R_1 \times N_1}{(N_2 - N_1)\left[1 + \frac{R_1 \times N_1}{100 \times B}\right]}$$

Putting that in words:

$$\text{Forward} = \frac{\left(\begin{array}{c}\text{Long period rate} \times \\ \text{Days in long period}\end{array}\right) - \left(\begin{array}{c}\text{Short period rate} \times \\ \text{Days in short period}\end{array}\right)}{\begin{array}{c}\text{Days left in} \\ \text{long period}\end{array} \times \left(1 + \dfrac{\text{Short period rate} \times \text{Days in short period}}{100 \times \text{interest basis (i.e. 360 or 365)}}\right)}$$

Although we have worked throughout in terms of mid-market rates, the formula can be applied using actual bid and offer rates chosen appropriately. If we want the rate for forward forward lending, R_2 will be the offered rate for the long period, R_1 the bid rate for the short period. Conversely for the forward forward borrowing rate.

To show the application of the forward forward formula, consider the case of a corporate borrower who knows that in 3-months' time there will be a need to borrow $10 million for 3 months. Because the treasurer of the company is conservative, she wishes to lock in the rate at which the borrowing is done now, and also to arrange the actual commitment of the loan. (In practice, the deal would probably be done through the FRA market, but dealing in the forward forward market does pre-commit the funding.) The treasurer approaches the bank and asks for a quotation on this basis.

Suppose the 3-month period has 90 days and the bid rate is 11%; the 6-month period is 182 days and the offered rate is 9%. In that case, the bank can raise funds for the longer period at 9%, laying them off temporarily at 11%, and so the forward forward rate is

$$\frac{(9 \times 182) - (11 \times 90)}{92(1 + 11 \times 90)/36\,000} = \frac{1638 - 990}{92 \times 1.0275} = \frac{648}{94.53} = 6.855\%$$

and this is the rate at which the bank would be prepared to commit to lend to the company. (In practice, this would tie up both sides of the bank's balance sheet unnecessarily and the deal would be fixed through the FRA market.)

9.6 THE CONCEPT OF PRESENT VALUE

The concept of present value is fundamental to money and bond markets. The present value of a sum of money X due at some future date D is that sum of money which, if it were invested at the interest rate prevailing for deposits from today to D, would accumulate to X.

Let us take an example. You offer to buy my car, but you do not have enough money to pay me today. You offer to pay me $10,000 in one week's time. Since I need the car to go to work, I will have to replace the car today. If you do not pay me today, I will have to put up my own money to pay for the replacement car today. Since I have implicit faith in your ability to pay and in your trustworthiness, the only question in my mind is whether the present value of what you will pay me is more or less than what I will have to pay today for the replacement car.

Suppose I know that I can invest my money for one week at 8%. Then I know that if I invest $9984.47 for 7 days on a 360-day basis I will have

$$9984.47 \times (1 + [8/100 \times 7/360]) = \$10,000.$$

Putting that another way round, I know that the present value of $10,000 in 7 days' time is $9984.47 using a discount rate of 8%. In fact,

$$\$9984.47 = \$10,000/(1 + [8/100 \times 7/360]).$$

The formula we just defined is fine for what we were doing, namely discounting a single sum of money for a period of less than a year. To get the more general formula, it helps to start at the other end: a sum of money invested today. A sum with a present value of 100 invested today at an annual interest rate of $r\%$ will yield us $100(1 + r)$ at the end of year 1. (Note that r is a decimal $10\% = 0.10$.) At the end of year 2 we will have $100(1 + r)^2$ and at the end of year n we will have $100(1 + r)^n$. So we can say, future value in year n = present value × $(1 + r)^n$. Therefore, turning the formula round:

$$\text{Present value} = \frac{\text{Future value in year } n}{(1 + r)^n}$$

Another way of saying this is that the present value is the future value discounted back to today at a rate of r. It is very important to realize that once we have discounted a sum of money back to today, it is valued in today's money. A sum of money, say $150, due in one year's time, discounted back to today, to produce say $135, is valued in today's money. Another sum, say $2000, due in five years' time, discounted back to today, to produce say $1750, is also valued in today's money. Because the two sums are valued in the same money, we can add them together.

Therefore, provided we discount each cash flow properly, we can discount every single cash flow in a stream of multiple cash flows back into a single sum of money. This is what happens when a bond dealer works out the price of a bond. Each coupon payment on the bond is discounted back to today. The present value of each coupon, together with the present value of the bond's repayment amount, are added together. The total is the present value of all the cash flows of the bond. That total is what that stream of cash flows is worth today. Therefore, it will be the price that the dealer will be willing to bid for the bond.

Consider a stream of cash due at the end of each of the next five years: year 1: $110; year 2: $121; year 3: $133.10; year 4: $146.41; year 5: $161.05. Suppose we want to find the present value of this stream of cash flows. We can invest money for the five years at 10%, so that is the rate of discount we consider appropriate. What is the present value of the stream of flows? We take our formula

$$\text{Present value} = \frac{\text{Future value in year } n}{(1 + r)^n}$$

and we apply it. The sum due at the end of year 1 is to be discounted by $(1 + r)1$, that is, 1.10; so $110 in a year's time is worth $100 today. Similarly, the sum due at the end of Year 2 is to be discounted by $(1 + r)^2$: that is, we work out $\$121/(1.10)^2$, which also turns out to be $100. Likewise, $\$133.1/(1.10)^3$ is worth $100; and if you check the others you will see they also are worth $100 today. So although the cash total of that stream of cash is $671.56, the total net present value of the stream of cash is $500. We can write:

$$\begin{array}{c} \text{Present value} \\ \text{of a stream} \\ \text{of cash flows} \end{array} = \frac{\text{Future value}}{\text{in year 1}} + \frac{\text{Future value}}{\text{in year 2}} + \dots + \frac{\text{Future value}}{\text{in year } n} \\ \frac{}{(1 + r)^1} \qquad \frac{}{(1 + r)^2} \qquad \frac{}{(1 + r)^n}$$

9.7 YIELD CURVES, FORWARD RATES, ZERO-COUPON CURVES, AND MEDIUM-TERM FORWARD FORWARD RATES

Now that we have sorted out how to do present value calculations we can come back to the basic yield curve concept that we talked about earlier and dig a little deeper. The yield curve contains a lot of information embedded in it. First, the implied forward forward rates are indicated by the slope of the yield curve. If the slope between any two points is upward, the forward forward rate for the period between these points is above the current rates; if it is downward, it is below. So, embedded in the yield curve, is a second curve, of the forward forward rates. And there is also a third set of rates: the "zero-coupon" curve.

The zero-coupon rate for any given maturity is what the market would be prepared to pay on a deposit or bond which pays no interim interest payments, but only a lump sum at maturity. (Some people refer to the zero-coupon curve as the spot rate curve.) Although the zero-coupon curve may seem obscure, it can be important to interest rate swap dealers (see Chapter 11), because they can, if they choose, treat their interest rate positions as individual cash flows, which should be valued at the zero-coupon rate for that maturity.

We cannot observe the implied zero-coupon curve directly (except in the US Treasury bond zero coupon market), and it has to be worked out step by step. A convenient way to do this is as follows. Let us look at the one-to-five year yield curve for Eurodollar deposits. Since interest payments, in line with Euromarket practice, are on an annual basis, the one-year deposit rate is in fact a zero-coupon rate: there are no interim interest payments. The two-year deposit rate is not, because there would normally be a payment of interest at the end of year 1.

Suppose we are contemplating investing $1000 dollars. Suppose we have the following interest rates:

1 year	8%
2 years	9%
3 years	10%
4 years	11%
5 years	12%

Suppose we are interested in finding out what the two-year zero-coupon rate implied by these rates is. Suppose we deposit $1000 for two years at 9%. We know we will get two cash flows: a payment of $90 at the end of year 1, and $1090 at the end of year 2. We will also receive a year's interest on the $90 coupon payment, but we do not know what that will be worth.

One way round this uncertainty is to take the following approach. I know the one-year zero-coupon rate is 8%. So I know that the present value today of that $90 is $83.33 (ignoring day-count questions and discounting on an annual basis). I would

Table 9.1

	Deposit Yield Curve	Zero coupon Yield Curve
1 year	8	8.00
2 years	9	9.05
3 years	10	10.14
4 years	11	11.30
5 years	12	12.56

be indifferent between receiving $90 in a year's time and receiving $83.33 today by, say, selling my right to the coupon to someone else. Suppose I do that. Then I now have a two-year zero-coupon deposit. I place $1000 − $83.33 = $916.67 today, and in two years I will receive $1090.

Now it is quite simple to work out the two-year zero-coupon rate: it is 9.045%. We can apply this technique step by step. The three-year deposit gives me cash flows of $100, $100, and $1100. I sell off the first two cash flows for $92.59 and $84.10, respectively. That makes my net investment today $823.31 which returns $1100 in three years' time, for an implied zero-coupon rate of 10.14%. At the end of this process, I have the yield curves shown in Table 9.1.

9.8   FORWARD RATE AGREEMENTS

Forward forward rates are dealt through an active market in London and in certain other centres for forward rate agreements (FRAs). These are contracts between banks and their customers, or other banks, that allow for the forward hedging of interest rate movements: they are the money-market equivalent of forward foreign exchange contracts. Another way of looking at them is to say they are single-period interest rate swaps.

They provide a very useful way to hedge against future movements in interest rates. Their prime advantage is that they allow this to be done without tying up large parts of the balance sheet. Until the FRA market was developed in the early 1980s, banks would trade their view of interest rates through the forward forward market (see above). But this meant taking and placing deposits for the periods in question, which meant inflating both the asset and liability sides of the balance sheet. FRAs are a much more efficient method of handling the interest rate hedging required.

Let us define some terms. A forward rate agreement is one where a notional borrower agrees with a notional lender the rate of interest which will be applied to a notional loan for some period in the future. Note the use of the word notional: there is no actual borrowing or lending involved. When the time comes to settle up, all that happens is an exchange of cash equal to the difference between the actual rate on the day and the rate agreed in the FRA.

The buyer of the FRA is the notional borrower—the party seeking protection against a rise in rates. The seller is the notional lender—the party seeking protection against a fall in rates. The contract amount (CA) is the notional sum on which the FRA is based. The contract rate (CR) is the rate of interest being hedged, usually LIBOR.

The contract period (CP) is the term from settlement date to maturity date, that is, the term of the notional deposit/loan. The settlement date is the date on which the settlement sum is payable. The maturity date is the date on which the notional loan/ deposit matures. The settlement rate (SR) is the rate fixed on the fixing date as being that applicable to the settlement on the FRA. The fixing date is the date on which the settlement rate is fixed; for LIBOR that would normally be two business days ahead.

The settlement sum is the sum paid in settlement of the FRA. If paid at maturity it would be (SR-CR) × CP/360 × CA/100, assuming the currency in question is dealt on a 360-day year basis. However, in practice the custom in the FRA market is to pay the settlement sum on the settlement date. (The practical benefit is that this clears the deal off the books straight away and cuts down the credit exposure that would arise if one had to wait until the notional maturity date to be paid.)

Thus the settlement sum has to be discounted back from that which would be payable at maturity to its present value today. For this, we use the present value formula developed in the last section. Thus, for a sum paid on settlement date, the value would be

$$[(SR\text{-}CR) \times CP/360 \times CA/100]/(1 + SR \times CP/36{,}000)$$

Note that the numerator is the same as before; the denominator is the discount factor to bring the value back to today. The formula can be simplified to

$$(CR\text{-}SR) \times CP \times CA/(36{,}000 + (SR \times CP)).$$

Let us look at an example. I buy a 3 × 6 FRA for a contract amount (CA) of $10 million. The rate (CR) is 10.5%. The contract period (CP) is 90 days. When the contract comes to settle, the settlement rate (SR) is 12.25%. Then the settlement value of the FRA is

$$[(12.25 - 10.5) \times 90/360 \times 10{,}000{,}000/100]/(1 + [12.25 \times 90/36{,}000]).$$

This gives us $43,750/1.030 625 = $42,449.97. Had we been prepared to wait for settlement until the end of the contract period the sum payable would have been $43,750; the discount factor we apply to this to find its present value on the settlement date is 1.030,625.

The way in which FRAs are priced is simple: if there is a financial futures market for a comparable instrument, pricing is taken from the futures market. If not, it is taken from the cash deposit yield curve. Forward forward rates for the period in question are worked out and applied to FRAs. Thus, if I wanted to find the correct price for the 3 × 6 sterling FRA I could either look at the LIFFE 3-month sterling deposit future contract, or else look at the yield curve for 3-month and 6-month sterling deposits. From these I would work out the forward forward rate for 3 months against 6 months and this would give me the rate applicable for the FRA. Because the forward forward, FRA and futures markets are all closely integrated, arbitrage will keep the three markets in line.

9.9 NEGATIVE INTEREST RATES

Many people raise their eyebrows at the idea of negative interest rates. But they do occur, and they can be highly profitable. It is very pleasant to be paid to borrow money. Negative rates generally happen in one of two ways: either there is intense upward pressure on a currency, or there is intense downward pressure which is expected to be only temporary.

Negative interest rates can be thrown up in the forward forward markets if a currency is under sufficiently intense pressure. During the spring of 1981, the French franc was extraordinarily weak, and the Banque de France was determined to support it by squeezing money market rates in the then thinly traded Euro-French franc deposit market. Overnight Euro-French francs at one point were lent out at over 5000% and one-week money was running at over 300%. Applying our forward forward formula above we can see that the forward rate for the remaining six days was –424%: by lending out at 5000% for a night, funded with one-week money, we could afford to lend for the remainder of the week at rates as low as –400% and still make money. Although this kind of situation can fairly be called an extreme case, fluctuations on this scale do occur in narrow money markets and can be very profitable.

A good example of the effects of the opposite situation, currency inflows, is the Swiss franc in 1977/78. The inflow of hot money into Swiss francs was so great that the Swiss authorities imposed a commission on deposits with banks such that a foreign depositor in a Swiss bank account was paying 40% p.a. for the privilege—a commission of 10% per quarter. Some people held on to their deposits, though, and watched the Swiss franc appreciate by 50%. A negative interest rate can be worthwhile if the currency is rising faster than the negative rate eats away your capital. Another example of this occurred in the late 1980s during a period of upward pressure on the Hong Kong dollar.

9.10 MONEY MARKET SECURITIES: CERTIFICATES OF DEPOSIT

There are two main differences between time deposit calculations and money-market securities trades. First, money-market paper can be, and often is, sold before maturity—there is secondary market trading. This is not normally the case with a time deposit, which is typically held to maturity. In looking at money-market paper, there is the possibility of a change in price of the instrument—the possibility of a capital gain or loss. Second, most deposits are dealt on an interest-bearing basis—I place $100 with you and get back, say, $105. But some money-market paper is dealt on a discount basis: I invest $92.75 with you and get back $100. That is, the face amount of the deal is the amount at maturity, not the amount at the start of the deal, as it is with interest-bearing deposits or interest-bearing instruments.

Some years after the birth of the Eurodollar market, the concept of the certificate of deposit (CD) was introduced. The CD has since become an important source of funds for banks. The CD was first issued in the US domestic market in 1961 and in the Euromarket in 1966. Essentially, a CD is an instrument (normally negotiable) evidencing a time deposit made with a bank at a fixed rate of interest for a fixed period. CDs bear interest and CD rates are in general quoted on an interest-bearing (rather than a discount) basis. Normally, interest on a US dollar CD is calculated for actual days on a 360-day basis and paid at maturity. But for CDs issued with a maturity over one year, interest is normally paid semiannually. Sterling CDs are dealt on a basis comparable to that of US dollar CDs except that interest is calculated on a 365-day basis. Interest is paid annually on the anniversary of issue of CDs of maturity over one year.

Since its introduction, the concept of a CD has been introduced to most of the major money markets. The speed at which this has happened has varied in accordance with the attitude of the domestic authorities of the currency concerned. For example, until 1986 the Bundesbank did not permit the issuance of deutsche mark CDs. This was because, having suffered the effects on its currency of massive inflows from abroad during the 1970s, the Bundesbank was not anxious to encourage the growth of a money-market instrument that would allow foreigners to move into and out of the deutsche mark market more easily.

CDs are available in various types as well as various currencies. The first variation was the floating rate CD (FRCD). These were introduced in 1977. They have maturities, usually, of three to five years. Interest on FRCDs is normally payable semiannually and is usually linked to six-month LIBOR. Other FRCDs have been issued at different margins or at the "mean of bid and offer."

Another variant is the discount CD. This was introduced early in 1981 in the US domestic market and subsequently in London. Here the CD does not pay a stated rate of interest. Instead, the certificate bears a wording along the following lines: "XYZ Bank certifies that a sum has been deposited with this bank which together with interest solely in respect of the period to the maturity date will on the maturity date equal US$ X." The advantage of a discount CD is that its price can immediately be compared with other discount instruments such a Treasury bills. The disadvantage is that it cannot easily be compared with other CDs.

9.11 DISCOUNT SECURITIES

Treasury bills, commercial paper, bankers' acceptances, and various other instruments are dealt on a discount basis; and from time to time this applies also to CDs. In cases where local exchange control forbids forwards exchange cover on interest payable, it may also be convenient to deal clean deposits on a discount basis. We will set out the calculations as for a bill; they can of course be applied to the other instruments mentioned. We will look at the calculation for price given discount rate; discount rate given price; conversion of interest rate to discount and vice versa.

Suppose we have a bill for $1 million which is being discounted at 10% for 90 days using a 360-day year. Then the discount amount is

$$10/100 \times 90/360 \times 1,000,000 = \$25,000$$

Or

$$\text{Discount amount} = \text{Discount rate}/100 \times \text{Discount period}/360 \times \text{Face value}$$

The price today is the face value less the discount amount, \$975 000 or

$$\text{Price} = \text{Face value } [1 - \text{Discount rate}/100 \times \text{Discount period}/360]$$

To find the discount rate given the price or the discount amount, we manipulate this formula. If the discount amount is given we turn the first formula around to get

$$\text{Discount rate} = \frac{\text{Discount amount}}{\text{Face value}} \times \frac{360}{\text{Discount period}}$$

Conversely, if we are given the price, we turn the second formula around to get

$$\text{Discount rate} = [1 - \frac{\text{Price}}{\text{Face value}} \times \frac{360}{\text{Discount period}}$$

We have been using a discount rate rather than an interest rate. The difference is that a discount rate is applied to the principal at the far end of the deal (the face value); an interest rate is applied to the principal at the near end. In our example, the face value is \$1,000,000 and the principal at the near end is \$975,000; so if we express the discount amount as a percentage of the near end we see that it is not 10% but 10.2564%. The formula for converting a discount rate to an interest rate is

$$\text{Interest rate} = \frac{360 \times \text{Discount rate}/100}{360 - \text{Discount rate}/100 \times \text{Discount period}}$$

where the interest rate is on a 360-day basis. To make it a 365-day basis we put 365 in the top line. Conversely, to get the discount rate from the interest rate we turn this formula around to get

$$\text{Discount rate} = \frac{360 \times \text{Interest rate}/100}{360 + \text{Discount rate}/100 \times \text{Discount period}}$$

Eurocommercial paper (ECP) is issued on both a yield-bearing and a discount basis, though the latter is more common. The basis of ECP calculations is simply the standard discounting (or, if the ECP is interest-bearing, yield calculations) applicable to other short-term instruments.

9.12 FOREIGN EXCHANGE CALCULATIONS: SPOT

This section sets out the basics of a spot deal: where the settlement is made, when it is made, what the quotations mean, and how cross spot rates are worked out.

A foreign exchange deal is an exchange of two currencies. When the deal has been agreed upon, the parties to the deal arrange settlement. This takes place in the two countries whose currencies are being used. For example, a deal exchanging US dollars for deutsche marks is settled by a payment of US dollars in the United States against a payment of deutsche marks in Germany. In this book, the term settlement country will refer to the country where the actual transfer of funds is made.

Where the deal is made—the dealing centre—need not be in one of the settlement countries. For example, it is possible to trade French francs against deutsche marks in London. A company making a FRF/DEM deal with a bank in London may think that its francs and deutsche marks are being transferred in London. This will seem especially plausible if the bank is running accounts for the company in London denominated in the two currencies. But the bank's own currency holdings which correspond to these accounts actually will be held in the settlement countries. Therefore, the rules applying to such transactions—for instance, with respect to settlement dates—will be the same as for deals conducted in the normal way.

A spot foreign exchange deal is one made for settlement in two working days' time. Thus under normal circumstances a spot deal done Monday is settled on Wednesday. A working day is normally defined as one in which both banks are open for business in both settlement countries. Settlement of both sides of a foreign exchange deal should be made on the same working day. Because of time zone differences, settlement on any given working day will take place earlier in the Far East, later in Europe, and later still in the United States. This implies a risk. A bank selling deutsche marks may deliver them in Frankfurt before receiving the dollars in New York. If the recipient in Germany goes bankrupt before delivering the dollars (as happened in the case of Herstatt Bank), losses may arise.

The term "quoted currency" means the currency that is variable in an exchange rate quotation; the term "base currency" means the currency that is fixed. Thus if £1 = US$1.6050, sterling is the base currency and the US dollar the quoted currency. For convenience, I shall write exchange rates as base/quoted (in this case £/US$).

Direct quotation takes the form of variable amounts of domestic currency against a fixed amount of foreign currency. The foreign currency is the base currency. A Swiss bank quoting CHF 85.5 per DEM 100 would be quoting direct; a variable amount of Swiss francs against a fixed deutsche mark amount. Many people say "normal" for direct currencies. Indirect quotation, conversely, takes the form of fixed amounts of domestic currency against varying amounts of foreign currency. A British bank quoting £1 = DEM 4.1325 is quoting indirect. Many people in the market say "reciprocal" for indirect quotations.

In the United States, both types of quotations are used: for domestic business, US terms are often used, that is, normal direct quotation (DEM 1 = US$0.5525). For international business and increasingly for domestic business also, US banks use European terms or reciprocal indirect quotation (US$1 = DEM 1.81). The reason for this is the international market's habit of dealing against the US dollar, using direct terms. US banks have fallen into line with international market practice.

9.13 SELLING AND BUYING RATES

Where the currency's exchange control regulations permit, a bank will normally quote a "two way price" in the currency. So a bank might quote the exchange rate as US$1 = DEM 1.6550/60. This conventional way of writing the rate shows that the bank will sell DEM 1.6550 in exchange for US$1; it will buy deutsche marks at 1.6560. The lower rate is the selling rate for deutsche marks; the maxim is "sell low, buy high."

The reason for this apparent perversity is that the bank's "income" from a sale is fixed at $1; it tries to sell as few deutsche marks as possible in exchange for the $1. To test the maxim, suppose the bank sells DEM 1.650 million, receiving US$1 million. It then uses the US$1 million to buy DEM 1.6560 million, netting a final profit of DEM 1000. The narrower the spread between the selling and buying rates, the less the bank's profit.

The conventional quotation needs explaining when the "big figure" (of 1.65 in our example) is being straddled. Say we have a selling rate of 1.6495 and the buying rate is 1.6505. Normal market convention is to write this as 1.6495/05. The "big figure" on the left is 1.644; on the right side it is understood as being the next "big figure" up, 1.65.

9.14 CROSS-RATES

A cross-rate may be defined as an exchange rate that is calculated from two other rates. For example, the DEM/CHF rate can be derived as a cross-rate from the US$/CHF rate.

The practice in the world foreign exchange market at present is that currencies are mainly dealt against the US dollar (although for some European currencies the main activity will be against the deutsche mark). If bank A asks bank B for its deutsche mark rate, that rate will be quoted against the US dollar unless otherwise specified. Since the vast bulk of dealings are done against the US dollar, it follows that the "market rate" for a currency at any moment is most accurately reflected in its exchange rate against the US dollar. Thus a bank asked to quote £/DEM would normally calculate this rate from the £ /US$ and US$/DEM rates, if an exact market rate is required.

I will use the rule that an exchange rate between two currencies, neither of which is the US dollar, will be referred to as a cross-rate. The term "exchange rate" will normally refer to the rate for a currency against the US dollar, unless otherwise specified.

There are three cases to consider; both exchange rates quoted direct or normal, both indirect or reciprocal, and the case where one is direct and the other indirect. Let us look first at the case where both are normal. For example, US$1 = DEM 1.8110/20 and US$1 = CHF 1.6230/40. The US dollar is the base currency in both cases. We want to find the selling and buying rates for Swiss francs in terms of deutsche marks (the deutsche mark will be our base currency).

If we are selling Swiss francs, we must be buying deutsche marks. So we take the US$/CHF selling rate, 1.6230, and divide it by the buying rate for deutsche marks, 1.8120. (We divide by the currency that is to be the base, in this case the deutsche mark.) The selling cross-rate therefore is CHF 89.56 per DEM 100 after rounding in the bank's favour. Similarly, the buying rate is found by taking the CHF buying rate, 1.6240, and the DEM selling rate, 1.8110, to give 89.68.

A parallel procedure is followed when both currencies are reciprocal: the US dollar is the quoted currency in both cases. For example, we have £1 = US$2.2530/40 and CAD 1 = US$0.8950/53. We want the cross-rates, using sterling as the base currency. The rate at which we sell US dollars against sterling (we buy sterling) is 2.2530. We buy US$ against CAD (we sell Canadian dollars) at 0.8953. Because we are dealing indirect currencies, we divide by the quoted currency. So we sell Canadian dollars against sterling at 2.5164.

When one rate is normal and the other reciprocal, the procedure is the same but we multiply (alternatively we may convert the reciprocal currency to normal by taking reciprocals and then dividing by the base currency). Suppose we have

Table 9.2 Calculating cross rates

	Both normal	Both Reciprocal	One Normal, One Reciprocal
Currency we want to show in the cross-rate as: Quoted	US$1 = CHF 1.6230/40	CA$1 = US$0.8950/53	£stg 1 = US$2.2530/40
	divide by	divide into	multiply by
Base	US$ 1 = DEM 1.8110/20	£stg 1 = US$2.2530/40	US$1 = DEM 1.8110/20

£1 = US$2.2530/40 and US$ = DEM1.8110/20. The rate at which we sell DEM against US$ is 1.8110; the rate at which we buy sterling against US dollars (sell US dollars against sterling) is 2.2530. Multiplying these gives selling rate for deutsche marks against £ sterling of 4.0801, and a buying rate of 4.0843. The calculations are summarized in Table 9.2.

9.15 FORWARD FOREIGN EXCHANGE CALCULATIONS: PREMIUM AND DISCOUNT

A forward exchange contract is an agreement between a bank and another party to exchange one currency for another at some future date. The rate at which the exchange is to be made, the delivery date, and the amounts involved are fixed at the time of agreement.

Such a contract is to be distinguished from a foreign exchange futures contract. These are discussed in more detail in Chapter 10. However, for comparison, a futures foreign exchange contract is a contract between two parties for the exchange of a certain amount of foreign currency at a future date. The amount and the date are normally standard. For instance, in the case of the International Monetary Market of Chicago's sterling contract, the contract is for £62,500. Delivery is normally the third Wednesday of the contract month (March, June, September, or December). A futures contract need not involve a bank as counterparty. A forward contract is normally completed by delivery of all or part of the sum involved. This is unusual in the case of a futures contract which is usually closed by trading in the reverse direction before the maturity of the original futures contract.

Suppose a quoted currency is more expensive in the future than it is now in terms of the base currency. Then the quoted currency is said to stand at a premium in the forward market, relative to the base currency. Conversely, the base currency may be said to stand at a discount relative to the quoted currency.

Take the US dollar as the base currency and the deutsche mark as the quoted currency. We may have a spot rate of US$1 = DEM 2.2500. The rate quoted by a bank today for delivery in one year's time (today's one year forward rate) may be

US$1 = DEM 2.2150. In this example, the dollar buys fewer deutsche marks in a year's time than it does today. The dollar stands at a discount relative to the deutsche mark. Putting it in converse terms, the deutsche mark stands at a premium relative to the dollar.

The size of the dollar discount or deutsche mark premium is the difference between 2.2500 and 2.2150, that is, $3\frac{1}{2}$ pfennigs. It would normally be quoted as 350 points. To arrive at the forward price, the deutsche mark premium or dollar discount must be subtracted from the spot. Conversely, a deutsche mark discount or dollar premium is added.

As in the spot market, banks in the forward market will normally quote a selling and a buying rate. The convention is that the selling rate for the quoted currency (the buying rate for the base currency) is quoted first. In our example, the spot rate might be quoted at 2.2500/10 and the one-year forward discount for US (or deutsche mark premium) at 350/340. In other words, if the dealer is buying US dollars forward he will charge a discount of 350 points, but if he is selling, he will give away only 340 points discount. In European terms, he will sell deutsche marks at a premium of 350, but only buy at a premium of 340.

There is an apparent inconsistency in the quotation. The spot is quoted at 2.2500/10, that is, low/high, and the deutsche mark premium/dollar discount at 350/340, that is, high/low. In both cases, the same convention is followed; that is, the selling rate for the quoted currency is given first. The apparent inconsistency flows simply from the fact that the deutsche mark premium/dollar discount is to be subtracted from the spot rate. So the selling price for delivery in three months' time (often referred to as the outright three month price) is 2.2500 less 350 points, that is, 2.2150. Now the buying price is 2.2510 less 340 points, that is, 2.2170. So we can quote the three-month outright as 2.2150/70 which matches the way in which the spot is quoted.

A price of 350/340 indicates a premium for the quoted currency in the forward market and a discount for the base currency; conversely, a price of 340/350 would indicate a discount for the quoted and a premium for the base. This can be summed up (see Figure 9.2) as

High/Low = Subtract
Low/High = Add

In premium/discount terms in the United States:

High/Low = Discount for the dollar
Low/High = Premium for the dollar

Elsewhere the tag is reversed as the market there looks at rates in currency terms:

High/Low: Premium
Low/High: Discount

9.16 HEDGING COSTS

We often need to work out a percentage cost per annum of a forward contract. This varies according to whether our calculations are based on the spot price or the outright forward price. Views differ on this; my own view is that the choice should

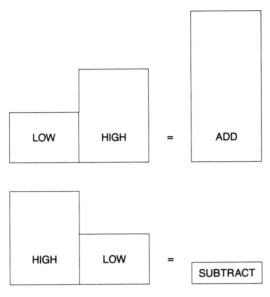

Figure 9.2 Treatment of Forward Margin

vary according to the underlying deal. If one is hedging a forward commitment, then the outright rate should be used. Thus a firm needing to buy forward DEM 1 million against US dollars for the purchase of machinery should use the outright rate. This is the important rate for its business; it determines the amount of dollars required. In other cases it may be more appropriate to use the spot rate. If we are considering an investment, we would probably want to express the hedging cost or profit as a percentage of our original investment, so we would probably use the spot rate. It is like the money-market difference between a discount rate and an ordinary interest rate.

Suppose again that we have a spot rate of 2.2500/10 and a 3-months' forward rate of 350/340. Then, working on middle rates of 2.2505 and 345, we can calculate that the approximate hedging cost for 3 months is 0.0345 divided by 2.2505 or 0.0153. (We might prefer to use the market's selling rates of 2.2500 and 350.) Multiplying by 100 to express this in percentage terms, we find this 1.53% for 3 months. We multiply this by four to gross it up to annual terms of 6.13%. (This is slightly inaccurate. If we really needed to be exact to six places of decimals or so, we would gross it up by compounding.) The formula, therefore, is:

$$\text{Hedging cost} = \frac{\text{Forward premium}}{\text{Outright or spot}} \times \frac{12}{n} = \frac{F}{O} \times \frac{12}{n} \quad \text{or} \quad \frac{S}{O} \times \frac{12}{n}$$

where n = number of months in the forward contract.

9.17 FOREIGN EXCHANGE CALCULATIONS: SWAPS

In the context of short-term foreign exchange markets, a swap is an exchange of one currency for another on one day, matched by a reverse exchange on a later day. A typical swap trade might be the sale of £1 million against US$2.2 million for spot value, coupled with the purchase of £1 million for delivery in three months against US$2.17 million. We swapped £1 million into dollars: we sold £1 million and bought it back three months forward. The swap rate is the difference between the rates of exchange used in the two trades. In our example, where the spot trade is done at 1.6000 and the forward at 1.5700, the swap rate is 0.03 or 300 points.

In most swap deals, the two exchanges are made at the same time with the same counterparty. But this need not be the case. One could buy spot from one counterparty and sell outright forward to another. Such a trade may be called an "engineered" swap to distinguish it from the more usual or "pure" swap. In the pure swap, the spot rate used is not very important. What matters is the swap rate: the premium or discount received for the forward sale of dollars which are bought spot. The market tends to use a spot rate that is close to the current market rate, but chosen so as to make calculation easy.

Swaps have two basic uses: (1) to switch a deal from one currency to another, and back again, on a hedged basis; and (2) to move a given currency deal forward or backward in time. An example of the first kind of swap could be if a bank had to lend Euro-forints. Because of Hungarian exchange controls and other problems, the "natural" market for Euro-forints is very thin. So to provide Euro-forints, a bank will normally borrow US dollars, buy lire in the spot market, and sell them back in the forward market. It "manufactures" Euro-forints from Eurodollars.

An example of the second type of deal is when a customer makes an outright forward sale of, say, DEM 5 million six months forward to a bank. The bank will

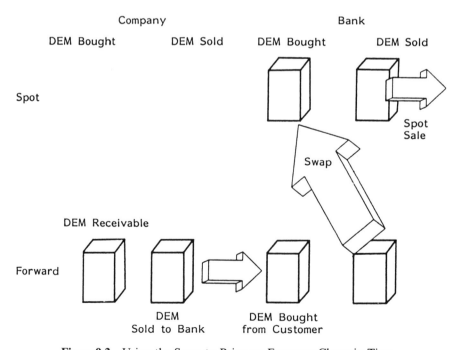

Figure 9.3 Using the Swap to Bring an Exposure Closer in Time

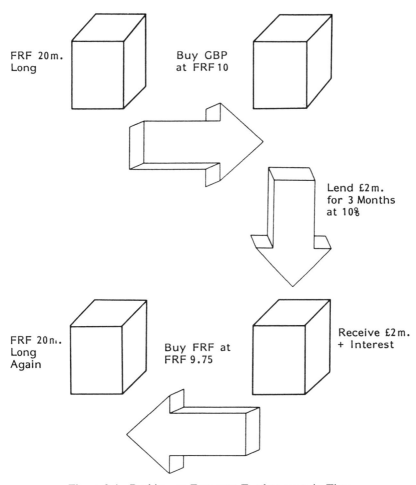

Figure 9.4   Pushing an Exposure Further away in Time

hedge this by a spot sale and a forward swap, rather than an outright deal. Inter-bank outright deals are very rare because they are regarded as too risky. It may be difficult to find a counterparty willing to take such a risk. So the bank will sell the DEM 5 million in the spot market. It will then do a swap, buying DEM 5 million spot and selling them forward. (The steps are set out in Figure 9.3.) The swap carries no exchange risk, and it is much easier to find a counterparty. So the swap market helps to bring a forward exposure nearer, so that it can be closed out more easily. Equally, it can be used to push an exposure away in time.

Suppose I am an exporter with a steady stream of French francs coming in. Suppose the franc is very weak, so that I am not inclined to sell my francs now, because I expect the currency to recover. Then I could, if the exchange control system in my country permits it, swap my francs for three or six months, let us say into sterling if I am based in the UK. I am still long of francs, but instead of switching out of francs I am effectively lending them and borrowing sterling against them.

When the deal unwinds I receive my francs back again and can—I hope—sell them at a better rate. Figure 9.4 shows this in simple terms. Equally, a bank might want to run a basic long position in francs without showing it in the spot book. To do this it would swap the position out into the forward book. (We saw in Chapter 4 how a dealer would look at the foreign exchange and money market route to solve this problem.)

Another important use for swaps is as a straight trading operation. Swaps let us take a view on interest rates. Remember the rule of Chapter 4—if the interest differential moves in a currency's favour, the forward margin moves against it. So let us look at a situation where one-year US dollar and £ sterling are both 10%. The forward margin will be near zero (if you are not sure why, read over Chapter 4). So a US investor pays no premium for forward sterling. Suppose this investor thinks that in 1 month the 11-month rate for sterling will be below the 11-month US dollar rate. That means that forward sterling will be at a premium. So it makes sense to buy forward sterling. And to do this without incurring an exchange risk, the deal is done in the swap market. That is, the investor sells sterling spot and buys it 12 months forward, believing that in 1 month the sterling can be sold at a premium.

9.18 FINDING INTEREST RATES FROM SWAP RATES

We need the calculation of the swap yield if we must compare interest rates between currencies. Suppose we want to find the cheapest way to borrow Eurodeutsche marks. We can either borrow DEM directly or borrow another currency (typically Eurodollars) and swap into DEM. We have to find the cheapest rate at which a bank could lend DEM.

The quickest, crudest measure of the cost of the deal is like this. We take the Eurodollar interest rate and subtract the swap yield (be it positive or negative). Suppose we have a middle US$/DEM spot of 1.80 and that dollars are at a three-month discount (deutsche marks are at a premium) of 300 (middle). Suppose it cost us 10% to borrow three-month Eurodollars. We need the swap yield. As we saw above if F is the margin, S the spot and O the outright, the swap yield is F/S or F/O depending on circumstances. (When we work out the exact formula, we will see that the yield works out as F/S for normal or indirect currencies such as the deutsche mark and F/O for reciprocal or indirect currencies such as sterling.)

We take the swap yield here as $0.03/1.80 = 0.01667$. This is 0.0667 if we multiply by four to put it out on an annual basis. Putting it in percentage terms, we have 6.67%. This is the swap profit. Because the bank is buying its forward dollars at a discount (receiving a premium on the forward deutsche marks it is selling), the swap yield is positive. The profit on the swap can be used to offset its Eurodollar costs. So the "manufactured" deutsche marks cost 10% less 6.67%, or 3.33%. We then compare this with the cost of raising Eurodeutsche marks directly (Figures 9.5 and 9.6). If the currency being produced is at a discount in the forward market, F will be negative. Then $R2$ will be greater than $R1$. If the currency is at a premium, so F is positive, $R2$ will be less than $R1$. Effectively, $R1$ is the direct interest cost and F/S is the swap yield adjustment.

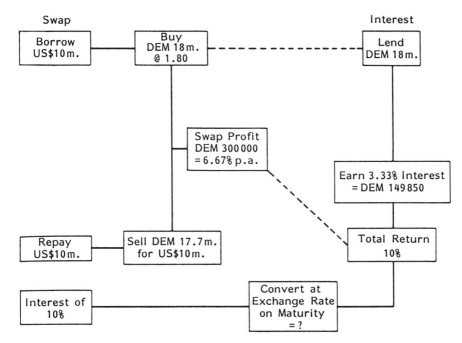

Swap Interest

| Borrow US$10m. | Buy DEM 18m. @ 1.80 | - - - - - - - - - | Lend DEM 18m. |

Swap Profit
DEM 300 000
= 6.67% p.a.

Earn 3.33% Interest
= DEM 149 850

| Repay US$10m. | Sell DEM 17.7m. for US$10m. | | Total Return 10% |

| Interest of 10% | Convert at Exchange Rate on Maturity = ? |

Figure 9.5 Arbitrage: Interest Unhedged

$$R2 = R1 - \left(\frac{F}{S} \times \frac{360}{N} \times 100 \right)$$

where R1 = interest rate on currency borrowed
R2 = interest rate on currency lent
F = forward margin in points (treated as negative if the quoted currency is at a discount—so that then R2 > R1)
S = spot rate in points
N = number of days

In words:

$$\frac{\text{Second currency}}{\text{interest rate}} = \frac{\text{First currency}}{\text{interest rate}} - \left(\frac{\text{Swap}}{\text{Spot}} \times \frac{360}{\text{days}} \times 100 \right)$$

For an investor looking at the differential between the two currencies we would write:

$$\text{Interest differential} = \frac{\text{Swap}}{\text{Spot}} \times \frac{360}{\text{days}} \times 100$$

If the actual differential is bigger than the amount implied by the swap calculation, the switch is worth making.

Figure 9.6 Crude Arbitrage Formula

This formula ignores the foreign exchange exposure on the interest payable on the deal. If there is a large swing in rates during the life of the deal, this could wipe out any profit. A more exact calculation allowing for this is set out in *Foreign Exchange and Money Market Guide*.

9.19 FINDING SWAP RATES FROM INTEREST RATES

We have seen that the swap rate and the interest rate differential between two currencies are closely linked. In our examples so far, we have taken the swap rate as given and used it to derive interest rates. We now reverse the process and derive swap rates from interest rates.

The term "interest rate" glosses over a number of problems (see above). In this chapter, interest rate is taken to mean interest rate available to participants in the international market, adjusted for special factors such as reserve asset costs and withholding taxes—in other words, to borrow a phrase, "net accessible interest rates."

We begin with the simplest formula, ignoring spreads and the hedging of interest. We have: $S = 2.0950$; $R1 = 10.875\%$; $R2 = 15\%$; $N = 92$; $B1 = 360$; $B2 = 365$ where S = middle spot rate: $R1$ = interest rate on dollars; $R2$ = interest rate on sterling; N = number of days in the deal; $B1$ = number of days in dollar interest basis: and $B2$ = number of days in sterling interest basis.

Suppose we have £1 million to invest in either sterling or dollars: we want to know the forward margin which would make the two deals equivalent. We start by putting the interest rates at common basis. For the sake of convenience, we shall put them on the 365-day basis, which means multiplying R1 by 365/360 to produce, say, 11%. Now, if we swap into dollars, there is an interest loss of 4% for 92 days on $2 095 000, which must be compensated for by a profit on the swap. The exact loss is:

$$\frac{2\,095\,000 \times 4 \times 92}{360 \times 100} = \$21\,415.55$$

We must therefore make at least $21 415.55 on our swap, so £1 million sold spot for $2 095 000 must cost only $2 095 000 − $21 415.55 = $2 073 584.45. Hence our break-even outright forward rate is 2.073 584, say, 2.0736, making the break-even margin 214 points. Notice that if our principal had been only £1, we would have had

$$\frac{2.0950 \times 4 \times 92}{360 \times 100} = 0.0214$$

from which we can deduce a formula

$$\text{Forward margin} = \frac{\text{Interest difference} \times \text{spot} \times \text{days}}{\text{Interest basis} \times 100}$$

$$F = \frac{S \times (R_2 - R_1) \times N}{B \times 100}$$

where we have S = spot in points; F = forward margin in points; N = number of days; and B = common interest basis.

This crude formula is convenient for quick calculations. A more exact formula is to be found in *Foreign Exchange and Money Markets Guide*.

──10──
Financial Futures

In this chapter, we start to look at the derivative markets. Derivatives is a term which is usually applied to futures, options, and interest rate and currency swaps. These are markets that were "derived" from other markets: the first financial futures contracts were derived from the foreign exchange market, interest rate swaps were derived from the bond market, and so on. In general, the derivatives markets have shown very rapid growth during the 1980s. For example, in 1980 the annual trading volume of interest rate futures contracts was 12 million. By 1993, the top 10 contracts worldwide traded 318 million contracts, with 79 million in US Treasury bond futures alone. In 1980, the share of futures activity accounted for by the United States was 100%: by 1993, the figure had fallen below 50%, as the market had begun to move to a global footing. Interest rate and currency swaps also grew during the 1980s, from a volume of perhaps $1 to $2 billion of currency swaps outstanding in 1980 (when interest rate swaps did not exist) to over $4,000 billion in 1993. Options, particularly options traded over the counter (OTC) (that is, outside organized exchanges) also grew strongly and by 1989 the BIS estimated daily foreign exchange option trading at $22 billion, of which 80% was OTC; during that year, as a whole, 40 million contracts for interest rate options or options on interest rate futures were traded on organized exchanges.

10.1 THE MARKETS

Of these markets, the first to develop was that for financial futures, which now make up a very important segment of the worldwide financial markets. Futures contracts are standardized agreements to buy or sell a specific commodity at a specific time and place in the future, at a price established through open outcry in a central, regulated marketplace. The two key components of a futures contract are that the agreement is standardized and that price is the only variable. The origins of such contracts go back to Chicago in the nineteenth century, when futures contracts on grain were first developed. (Some would argue they go back to the Dutch tulip mania of 1634.)

A financial futures contract is a contract to deliver, or take delivery of, a financial instrument at a future date. For example, a Treasury bill futures contract is a contract to deliver, or take delivery of, a Treasury bill on a specified date. In some cases, where delivery is difficult, the contract may be settled by a cash payment, for example, Eurodollar futures contracts.

Let us take a simple example. I want to invest $100,000 in a US Treasury bond for delivery in June. I can wait until June—taking the risk that the price might move against me—or I can buy a futures contract. I go to the futures market and see that the price for June 15 delivery is 92: if I were to settle today, I would have to pay $92,000. I buy one contract. I do not pay for the bonds today. Instead, I put up a margin deposit.

The amount of this margin is fixed by the exchange at $4500 per contract. So I put up $4500 on deposit with my futures broker. The deposit is evidence of my good faith that I will fulfill my obligation to take delivery of the bonds in June. As bond prices vary, the value of my futures contract varies. I have a profit or loss on my purchase. If losses erode the value of my margin, my broker will call on me to put up extra margin. Conversely, if I earn profits, I will get back some margin. The aim is to keep the margin stable in line with the value of my obligation.

When the contract comes to settlement, suppose I decide to take delivery of the bonds. A settlement price for the bonds is fixed. Say that price is 105. Then I must pay $105,000 for my bonds; but on that settlement day, my futures contract is also worth $105,000. So I have a $13,000 profit on the futures contract which offsets the rise in price of the bonds. The futures contract has served to fix my bond purchase price.

The main attraction of futures in risk management is their leverage, or gearing in UK terminology. Suppose a trader deliberately takes a position, either as a straight-forward speculation, or as an arbitrage. The simplest case are traders who want to back their judgment on the outlook for interest rates or currencies. The essential difference between doing this in the futures market and doing it in the "cash market" is that in the futures market, one can trade on margin. This gives a high degree of leverage. This leverage lets the speculator make large profits compared with the amount of margin money committed.

Suppose on December 1,1991, a trader thinks interest rates will rise in the next few months, causing bond prices to fall. The trader deposits the required margin (say, $4000 per contract) with a broker, and sells two Treasury bond futures contracts at 67-00. Two weeks later, interest rates have risen. Prices for Treasury bond futures contracts have dropped to 66-08. The trader closes the position by buying two bond futures contracts, making a profit of $750 on each contract. The $1500 profit on the $8000 margin is a return of over 18% during the two weeks, before deducting commission and exchange fees. Leverage has increased the returns.

This leverage works both ways, making it possible to lose more money than originally invested. Because of this, prices are marked to market on a daily basis by the exchanges. Settlement is made daily through the clearing corporation. Thus, if prices move against an investor, his account is debited.

If the debits reduce the money in the margin account below the prescribed "maintenance" level, additional margin must be posted to bring it back up to the initial margin level. Hence the investor quickly feels the effect of any weakening in position, through margin calls. It is this margin call system which has generally protected the exchanges and their member firms from losses via investor default: although investors are highly leveraged, the margin maintenance system quickly brings to light any potential problems.

Another attractive feature for those who wish to trade in the major futures markets for its own sake is that they are very liquid. Average daily trading volume on the Chicago Board of Trade Treasury bond futures contract in 1993 was over 320,000 contracts for a face value of $32 billion. One could shift a significant volume in this market without making a major impact. In other instruments, this is less true. Many futures contracts have not proved successful, and daily volume is negligible. In this case, if one wishes to trade in a particular instrument which is not readily available, one is reduced to trading in a proxy instrument, and making allowances by means of appropriate weighting factors, considered next.

Table 10.1 gives the date of introduction of major contracts, Table 10.2 shows the main activity in 1994. As will be seen, the development of financial futures is recent. The International Monetary Market (IMM) in Chicago opened futures trading in seven foreign currencies in May 1972. The first interest rate futures contract was introduced in October 1975, but the first really successful interest rates futures

Table 10.1   Date of Introduction of Some of the Major Futures Contracts

1972	IMM	Foreign exchange
1974	IMM, Comex	Gold
1975	CBOT	GNMA
1976	IMM	Treasury bill
1977	CBOT	Treasury bond
	CBOT	90-day commercial paper
1978	Sydney	Gold futures
1979	Sydney	Bank bill futures
	CBOT	US treasury 10-year notes
1980	IMM	CD
	Sydney	A$ futures
1981	IMM	Eurodollar
1982	LIFFE	£, DM, SFR, yen
	LIFFE	Euro$, long gilt, 3-month sterling deposits
	CME	S&P 500
1983	Sydney	All Ordinaries Share Price Index
1984	LIFFE	FTSE 100, UST-bonds
	Sydney	Australian Treasury bonds
1985	Tokyo SE	JGB futures
1986	MATIF	French government bonds
	SIMEX	Nikkei-DJ futures
1988	Tokyo SE	TOPIX futures
	Osaka SE	Nikkei-225 futures
	LIFFE	Bund future
	CBOT	5-year Treasury note futures
1989	TIFFE	Euro-yen, yen/$
	LIFFE	Euro-DM LIBOR future
1990	DTB	Bund future, DAX future
	CBOT	2-year Treasury note futures
1991	LIFFE	Italian government bond futures
	DTB	BOBL future
1994	Osaka	Nikkei 300 futures

Table 10.2 Top Futures Contracts 1994

	Million Contracts Traded	Exchange
Euro$	104.8	CME
US T-Bond	99.9	CBOT
Notionnel	50.1	MATIF
Real (Brazil)	39.2	BM&F
Euro-yen	37.4	TIFFE
Bund	37.3	LIFFE
Euromark	29.3	LIFFE
Interest rate (Brazil)	28.5	BM&F
Ibex35	27.0	MEFF
10-year T-Note	24.1	CBOT
Long gilt	19.0	LIFFE
S&P500	18.7	CME
3 month sterling	16.6	LIFFE
DEM	10.9	CME
Ibovespa	10.6	BM&F

Top Futures Exchanges 1994 (m. contracts)

CBOT	219
CME	205
LIFFE	153
BM&F	110
MATIF	93
DTB	59
NYMEX	58
TIFFE	38

Source: *Futures & Options World*, February 1995.

contract was the 91-day Treasury bill contract introduced by the IMM in January 1976, followed in August 1977 by the Chicago Board of Trade (CBOT) futures contracts on US Treasury bonds.

In September 1982, the London International Financial Futures Exchange (LIFFE) opened for business. It started with two contracts, for Eurodollars and the pound sterling, but by early December the initial complement of seven contracts had all been introduced: short sterling interest rates; long gilt-edged government securities; Swiss franc, Japanese yen, and deutsche mark futures. More recently LIFFE has introduced a successful futures contract based on German government bonds (Bunds), following this up in April 1989 with a future based on DM LIBOR and an option on the Bund future. Table 10.3 shows LIFFE's turnover by product for 1993: of the average daily turnover of $136 billion, $85 billion, or 63%, was nonsterling based, showing just how internationally oriented LIFFE is.

The Tokyo futures market was established in October 1985. But in an astonishing explosion of trading, volume in the Japanese government bond futures contract on the Tokyo Futures Exchange after only 10 months exceeded that in the US Treasury bond contract. Daily trading in the Japanese contract reached an average of $32.8

Table 10.3

	1993 $bn
Short £	35.8
Short £ option	7.9
Euromark	45.1
Euromark option	6.9
Eurolira	3.6
Euroswiss	4.9
Euroswiss option	0.09
Euro ECU	3.28
Euro$	0.96
Euro $ option	0.03
£ gilt future	3.47
£ gilt option	0.61
Bund future	12.1
Bund option	2.61
BOBL future	0.86
BTP	3.11
JGB	1.59
FTSE	1.37
FTSE (Am) option	0.46
FTSE (Euro) option	0.14
Equity options	0.65

billion in August 1986, compared with $19.7 billion in US bond contracts. The market is housed in the Tokyo Stock Exchange building and is open from 9 to 11 a.m. and from 1 to 3 p.m. As always, Japan is unique. There is no pit on the floor of an exchange, no crowd of jostling traders. Most of the people in the room are seated at computer terminals. The Futures Exchange at its foundation had to blend with the existing methods of the Tokyo market. This meant that there must be a continuing role for *Saitori* (brown-jacket men). The *Saitori* match buy and sell orders. They do not take positions themselves. Thus, futures brokers placing orders, or wishing to trade their own book, must telephone the *Saitori* allotted to them to place the order via the terminal, and wait word of execution from the *Saitori*.

In September 1988, the Tokyo Stock Exchange introduced futures based on its TOPIX equity index, and its Osaka counterpart introduced a contract on the Nikkei-225 equity index. In June 1989, the Tokyo International Financial Futures Exchange (TIFFE) opened for business, trading Euro-yen and Eurodollar deposit contracts as well as a yen/dollar contract. The former has been successful—trading 23.3 million contracts in 1993—but the yen/dollar future failed. Japanese futures markets, particularly the Nikkei-225, suffered from some official disapproval in the early 1990s. The collapse of the Japanese "bubble" was blamed in part on derivatives, and the authorities took steps to discourage stock market derivatives. They also encouraged the creation of the Nikkei-300 index future on the grounds that the Nikkei-300, as a capitalization-weighted index, was less open to manipulation than the Nikkei-225 which is a price-weighted index.

The next important financial futures exchange to open after Tokyo was in France,

Table 10.4

	MATIF turnover 1993 '000 contracts	Globex share
10% notional bond future	36 804	1911
Notional bond options	11 573	218
PIBOR futures	11 863	801
PIBOR options	4830	288
CAC40 futures	5908	196
ECU bond futures	873	38

Source: *MATIF Annual Report*, 1993.

where in February 1986 the Marché à Terme des Instruments Financiers (MATIF) was opened (Table 10.4). The MATIF has gone on to establish itself as a serious challenger to LIFFE as a centre for derivatives trading in Europe, though it has suffered the odd problem, such as the FFR 250 million lost by the state-owned nuclear fuels company, Cogema, on the MATIF and in related options trading. A contract on French Treasury bills was introduced in 1986, which developed poorly, owing to the lack of liquidity in the secondary cash market, but in September 1988 the MATIF successfully introduced a contract on PIBOR (Paris interbank offered rate).

In 1989 the MATIF, CME, CBOT, and Reuters signed a contract for a system called Globex. Globex was developed by Reuters as a worldwide automated dealing network for trading outside official exchange hours. Tensions between the CME and CBOT prevented its early success, but the MATIF's participation in 1993 gave the system a substantial boost. MATIF contributed 80% of Globex's 1993 volume.

Another key development for the MATIF was the signature in December 1993 of a cooperation agreeement with DTB, the German futures exchange. By the end of 1994, DTB screens had been installed in Paris, but the MATIF's members had not yet decided which contracts to make available to this joint venture.

The DTB, which opened in 1990, has been particularly successful in equity options—by 1993 the DAX option was the second most widely traded option contract in the world after the S&P100—but has had more of a struggle in fixed income, given that LIFFE already had deutsche marks interest rate contracts. However, the DTB BOBL contract (on five-year German government bonds) defeated the LIFFE BOBL contract in 1993. A key feature of the DTB is that it was the first fully electronic futures exchange (partly because regional jealousies in Germany militated against establishing a single floor in Frankfurt).

Other important financial futures exchanges operate in Toronto, Singapore, Hong Kong, and Sydney. A futures and options exchange in Denmark opened in September 1988. Global expansion of the futures and options markets seems likely to continue. Futures and options markets have spread as far afield as Brazil and also Chile where a futures contract on the peso has been put in place. (For countries with limited foreign exchange reserves, a futures contract on the currency which can be cash-settled in domestic currency provides a useful method of hedging exchange rate risk without draining foreign exchange reserves.)

A key issue is the battle between traditional "open outcry" (whereby prices are set by an auction in a "pit" where traders shout bids and offers) and the new technology. The latter is represented by Globex, by the DTB screen system and by LIFFE's screen-based trading system. This is the automated pit trading system (APT), which aims to emulate the features of open outcry pit trading.

Originally developed for use outside the exchange's normal working hours, the APT system is also being used during trading hours for the relaunched LIFFE contract on Japanese government bonds (JGBs). The APT system has been successful, trading 2.4 million contracts in 1993.

10.2 ORGANIZATION OF THE MARKETS

Before discussing the financial futures contracts in more detail, let us review the organization of the markets. Since the major markets today are generally floor-traded rather than computer-traded, the discussion will tend to concentrate on the traditional style of futures market.

The following description, in outline, applies to the CBOT, the IMM, and other similar institutions. Essentially, the membership of the market can be divided into two categories: brokers and locals. Brokers trade for nonmember customers and for other members. Locals trade for themselves. The locals are essential for the liquidity of the market. They are usually involved in three types of trading.

1. *Position traders.* They will take a position, sometimes very large, and keep it until something causes them to change their mind. Position traders are relatively long-term traders, particularly compared to scalpers.
2. *Scalpers.* These are floor traders who are constantly buying and selling. Often, scalpers keep positions for only a matter of minutes or seconds. Their contribution to the market is continuous moment-by-moment liquidity.
3. *Spreaders.* They concern themselves with the relative value of one contract month against another. They are arbitraging one period against another. Their contribution to the market is to give liquidity to the more distant periods.

The other main source of liquidity is the very large number of small, individual speculators who trade on the exchange through the brokers. Although each may trade only one or two contracts, there are many thousands trading on the exchange, who again contribute to liquidity.

Trading takes place in the pits during specific hours. There is a separate trading area for each contract, so there is a bond pit, a Eurodollar pit, and so on. Orders are received on the trading floor by telephone or telex, and passed to the broker in the pit. Traders shout out the quantity and the price at which they want to buy or sell. They also use standard hand signals, especially when trading is noisy. The process is shown in Figure 10.1.

At the close of each day's trading, every member submits a trade confirmation record for every deal done on behalf of the firm or its customers. Every one of these trades must be "cleared," that is, verified and guaranteed, by the clearinghouse. The clearinghouse settles the account of each member firm at the end of the trading day. It matches each of the day's purchases and sales. It collects all losses and pays all

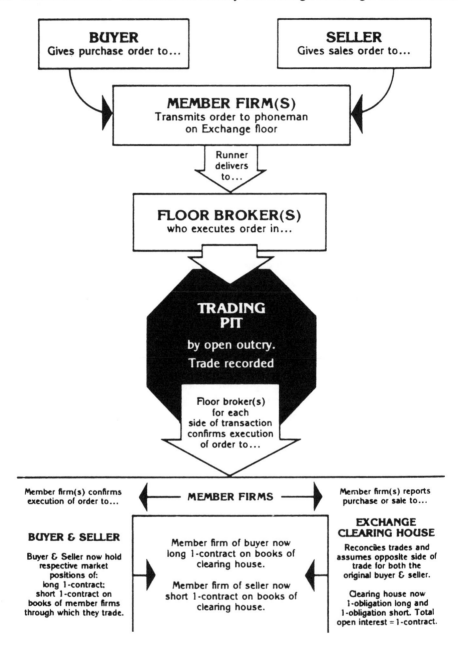

Figure 10.1 Order Execution Process (Adapted from *Trading in Tomorrows*, IMM, Chicago, p. 11)

profits. Its contribution to the safety of the market is to be the buyer from every seller and the seller to every buyer. A sale of Treasury bill contracts by A to B becomes a sale (by A) to the clearinghouse and a purchase (by B) from the clearinghouse.

This is a key safeguard for users of the exchanges. There is no need to worry who has taken the other side of the trade. The exchange clearinghouse itself guarantees the performance of every trade because it is the exchange itself which takes the opposite side to every contract. However, the exchange will not deal directly with public customers, but only with its clearing members.

In effect, the exchange does business only with its clearing members and the clearing members do business with all others. For example, the exchange sets margins for its clearing members and its clearing members in turn set margins for their customers. Thus, customer margins flow directly to the clearing member who, in turn, must settle with the exchange at the close of business each day. Each day the exchange requires a cash settlement from the clearing member based on the day's market positions and activity. This is regardless of the status of the member's customer margin money. A clearing member might let a customer be short of margin for a period of time, but this would have to be funded at its own expense. The clearinghouse would not allow a clearing member to be undermargined overnight. Also, the exchange will supervise the financial status of its clearing members. So far, these arrangements appear to have been successful in preventing major problems; both the CBOT and the IMM state that there has never been a financial loss due to default on a futures contract on their exchanges.

With the growth of electronic trading, it may be useful to compare the traditional trading system described above with the electronic markets. A floor-traded market is a pure auction from the open to the close. Trades take place when the highest bid meets the lowest offer. In theory, when two orders at the same price come to market, the first order to reach the pit gets priority. But in practice, the human element sometimes takes priority. Say a mild-mannered trader comes into the pit 10 seconds before an aggressive one with the same order. Although the quiet trader has priority, the noisy, aggressive one will probably have the order filled first. The human element also produces "out-trades"—disputed trades where traders disagree whether they bought or sold, or the amount done. In a screen system, all buy and sell orders are displayed on the screen along with their quantities. Orders can be placed at a limit above or below the market, at the bid or offer, or at the market. However, buyers and sellers remain anonymous. This puts all market participants on an equal footing, unlike the Chicago market.

On the other hand, electronic systems also have weaknesses. For example, in the Japanese equity index futures market, only members of the Osaka Securities Exchange have access to the terminals for trading Nikkei futures. It costs millions of dollars to join the exchange and it will not rent terminals to nonmembers. Thus the private individual is excluded from being a "local." This is not true of a floor trading exchange such as Chicago, which in that sense is more "democratic."

A special feature of the Japanese market is the role of the *Saitori*, mentioned earlier. Their role is to keep an orderly market by maintaining an "indication price" which is their best estimate of the "right" price for the market. Usually, this is the last traded price. But if the *Saitori* feels that the price has moved since the last trade, the indication price will be raised or lowered.

This is important when there is an imbalance in the market. Imbalances often occur in Tokyo because all market orders must clear for a trade to take place. If there are 1000 buy contracts and 500 sell contracts, all to be done "at market," no trade will take place. This rule also applies to market openings and closings. For this reason, it can take as much as an hour or more to open the futures market if there is an imbalance. The *Saitori* tries to remedy order imbalances by moving the indication price. However, the indication price can only be changed by a limited amount at a time. And the *Saitori* must wait a defined period before making another change. This is intended to "slow down the market." But if the real market price is moving faster than the *Saitori* can move, no trades can ever take place until the market reaches "limit up" or "limit down."

The German system, on the DTB, is different because it does not have any human intervention. Price limits do not exist and imbalances do not lock the market—orders can be partially filled. The first order entered into the system is filled, then, the next, until all possible trades are completed. Thus market continuity should be better than in Japan.

A useful comparison of the Japanese electronic and US "human" systems under stress came in August 1990 when Iraq invaded Kuwait. A calculation by Goldman Sachs of the average daily time that the Nikkei and S&P futures contracts were not available for trading during August was 2.7 minutes for the S&P and 60.2 for the Nikkei. That is, during the month, the Nikkei was locked and untradeable for an average of an hour a day. Furthermore, the S&P averaged 2500 trades per day in an average amount of 19 contracts for a daily trading volume of 45,500 contracts. The Nikkei averaged 374 trades per day for 161 contracts for an average volume of 60,400. That is, the Nikkei traded more sporadically but in larger size. Trading was concentrated into shorter intervals. And the median tick move—the change in market level—was twice as large for the Nikkei than the S&P 500.

A one-month test under very unusual circumstances is by no means conclusive. But the results do suggest that the Japanese system, which excludes individual locals and locks out imbalanced markets, provided a less continuous market than the free-for-all S&P 500. However, it is not a true test of electronic trading vs floor trading, since the DTB and LIFFE systems operated differently. Neither, however, was trading a major contract electronically during this period so it is not possible to compare them. Electronic systems do have many advantages: fairer order priority, anonymity, fewer errors, and faster dissemination of information. Provided they do not exclude individual "local" traders as the Japanese system does, good electronic systems may in the long run prove the better system, assuming they are allowed to operate continuously by partially filling orders.

It is because of these problems that LIFFE's APT system has tried to create "electronic open outcry." The key difference is that APT is not an order matching system under which bids and offers are stored until they can be filled. APT bids and offers, as in the pits on the trading floor, are only valid "for as long as the breath is warm." To achieve this, there is a price: the APT terminal has to be a high-powered work-station capable of 12 million calculations per second.

10.3 EURODOLLAR FUTURES

There is now a wide range of instruments traded in the financial futures markets, from the simplest (the Eurodollar or Treasury bill contract) to the more complex

(Treasury bonds, stock index futures) to the exotic (DIFFS—contracts developed in Chicago for trading on interest rate differentials between two currencies). An exhaustive survey would probably also exhaust the reader's patience, since the differences between many of these, for example, a contract on three-month US dollar deposits and a contract on three-month sterling deposits, are relatively minor and confined to clearing and settlement issues rather than any major differences in concept. Therefore this chapter discusses only three kinds of contract: a short-term interest rate contract, a short-term discount rate contract (Treasury bills), and a foreign exchange contract. With variations applicable to local clearing and settlement conditions, the principles explained should be applicable to futures markets on foreign exchange and money markets worldwide.

We will start with what is perhaps the simplest futures contract, the Eurodollar future. It is also probably the most important short-term interest rate futures contract on a worldwide basis. To give an idea of the scale of the IMM's liquidity in this contract, in normal times 500 lots and often 1000 lots can change hands without changing the price. That is, up to $1 billion can be done in a single trade.

The Eurodollar contract is traded in substantially similar form in Chicago, on the IMM, in London, on LIFFE, and in Singapore on SIMEX. SIMEX and the IMM have a "mutual offset" arrangement whereby positions taken in Singapore can be closed in Chicago and vice versa.

The IMM contract is for a $1 million face value Eurodollar time deposit with three-months' maturity. Last trading day is the second London business day before the third Wednesday of the delivery month. Delivery months are March, June, September, December, and the spot (current) month. A specific feature of this contract is that it is cash-settled. That is, unlike the Treasury bill or Treasury bond contracts, physical delivery of the underlying instrument does not take place. The primary reason for this is that there would be an implied credit risk on the bank whose Eurodollar deposit was delivered. Since the Eurodollar futures market now stretches out almost to four years in maturity, predicting the credit quality risk would be difficult.

The cash settlement has been an important element in the success of the contract. By contrast, the domestic US CD contract (which settled by actual delivery of CDs) was introduced in 1981. The Mexican crisis of 1982 and Continental Illinois' collapse in 1984 quickly meant that the traditional CD "run" (whereby the top 10 US banks' paper was traded interchangeably) disintegrated. Traders delivered the weakest CDs into the futures contract; buyers of CD futures found themselves "wearing" weak paper. This process destroyed the contract. Cash settlement means there is no risk of this happening.

The size of the Eurodollar contract is $1 million face amount. The price is quoted in terms of the IMM index, that is, the difference between the deposit rate and 100. Thus, a Eurodollar deposit rate of 9% is quoted in index form as 91.00. Prices are quoted in multiples of 0.01 (thus the minimum possible change in the value of the contract—the tick value—is US$25: $0.01/100 \times 90/360 \times \$1,000,000$).

The settlement mechanics are that on the last trading day the IMM clearinghouse contacts 12 major London "reference" banks for their perception of the LIBOR rate at which prime banks can raise three-month deposits, both at the end of trading and at a random time in the last 90 minutes of trading. After eliminating the two highest and the two lowest quotes, the average of the remaining eight is taken as the LIBOR rate. Suppose this works out at 8.5%. Then the "settlement price" which is used to work out the payments due to and due from holders of outstanding futures contracts will be 100 − 8.5 = 91.5. That is: on the settlement date, the interest rate implied by the futures contract must be equal to the cash three-month deposit rate prevailing at that time. So in fact looking at futures prices gives a quick forecast of where the market sees the three-month Eurodollar rate going.

Suppose today is June 13, 1991. The September Eurodollar futures contract is trading at 93.5. That means that the market is saying that in September Eurodollar rates will be at 6.5%. (Remember the contract prices as 100 −Eurodollar rate). I believe that by the time we get to September 15, the rate will have risen sharply to 9%. That would imply that on its settlement date the Eurodollar future will trade at 91. The market expects rates to fall, I expect rates to rise. I sell 50 September Eurodollar contracts at 93.5. If I am right, then in September, the futures contract will settle at 91. I sold at 93.5; I close out the position by buying back at 91. I will make a profit of 2.5, or 250 ticks. Since we know the value of a tick is $25, that means my profit will be $6250 per contract, or $312 500 in total.

Here I simply traded on my view of rates. But another way of looking at this is to argue that by dealing today at 93.5 I have effectively "locked in" a deposit rate of 6.5% in September. That ability to lock in future rates is what makes the Eurodollar futures market so attractive to banks, since it allows them not only to trade speculative interest rate views but also to offer hedges to their corporate customers who are borrowing (see the section on hedging below) and also to arbitrage against other markets, notably the rate for forward rate agreements (see Chapter 9) and interest rate swaps (see Chapter 11).

10.4 TREASURY BILL FUTURES

The IMM Treasury bill future was the first successful interest rate futures contract and, though it has lost ground to the Eurodollar contract, it remains an important instrument in its own right as well as being used in "TED spread" trading (see next). The main reasons for its decline are firstly that the Euro contract, introduced in 1982, was soon traded on other exchanges worldwide, while a position in the IMM Treasury bills contract can only be traded during Chicago hours. Secondly, trading in the secondary Treasury bill market can be affected by the amount of paper locked away. In the spring of 1989, for example, of $7 billion of three-month bills auctioned, $4.4 billion were bought by "noncompetitive" buyers intending to hold the bills as investments to maturity. Thus of that bill only $2.6 billion was available; an aggressive investment bank, working perhaps with one or two other institutions, could easily establish a sizable enough position in the cash market to squeeze the futures market. A few squeezes of this type were enough to discourage some trading in the futures market, which in turn made the market easier to squeeze.

The standard contract is for 13-week US Treasury bills having a face value at maturity of US$1 million. The delivery unit on the IMM is Treasury bills maturing 90 days hence. At the seller's option, 91- or 92-day maturity bills can be delivered. (In point of fact, the vast majority of deliveries are made in 91-day bills.) The price is quoted in terms of the IMM index, that is, the difference between the actual yield and 100. (It should be borne in mind that Treasury bill rates are quoted on a discount basis and not a yield basis, see Chapter 9.) Prices are quoted in multiples of 0.01 (thus the tick value is US$25, as for the Eurodollar contract).

Contracts for the 90-day Treasury bill are traded for March, June, September, and December. Trading in the contract normally ends on the second business day after the 13-week Treasury bill auction of the third week of the delivery month (that is, usually the Wednesday following the third Monday of the month). Delivery takes place the following day (the Thursday).

Unlike the Eurodollar contract, the Treasury bill contract settles by delivery of a Treasury bill. So the pricing of the Treasury bill future is primarily driven by its relationship to the cash market for Treasury bills. The link between the two markets is called the implied repo rate. The basic idea behind the implied repo rate can be explained as follows. Suppose I buy a Treasury bill which is deliverable into the futures contract. At the same time I sell a Treasury bill future, with the intent of delivering the cash bill as settlement of my futures position. This position will have a revenue and a cost. The revenue will be the profit (if any) on the sale price of the future in excess of the cost of the cash bill. The cost will be the cost of financing my holding of the cash bill until I deliver it in the futures settlement. The implied repo rate is the rate that I can afford to pay as a cost of finance, and still break even.

The implied repo rate measures the interest expense saved by a leveraged buyer who chooses a futures contract instead of a cash settlement purchase. It measures the time value of money for the time period between cash and futures settlement dates. If the implied repo rate is above the actual financing rate for the period, futures are expensive relative to the underlying instrument. We should buy cash and sell futures. Conversely, if the implied repo rate is below the actual rate, futures are cheap relative to the instrument. We should buy futures and sell cash.

In practice, of course, these rules cannot be automatically followed because of the fact that the trader is uncertain about the amount of variation margin that will have to be paid or received in the interval from now to maturity, nor is it always possible to arrange finance for the period from now to maturity at a single fixed rate.

10.5 FOREIGN EXCHANGE FUTURES

Foreign exchange futures are not so important in their own right as interest rate futures contracts, since the liquid interbank forward foreign exchange market has always provided tough competition for the futures. But there is an important market for arbitraging between the futures and forward markets and so it is important to understand the mechanics.

We will take as an example the Chicago Mercantile Exchange contract for sterling. This is for an amount of £62 500, with contracts for March, June, September, and December. Delivery date is the third Wednesday of the contract month, and delivery is made by payment of sterling against dollars paid by the buyer of the contract.

The operation of the market is very simple. Today is January 11, 1993. The March futures contract settles on the third Wednesday in March 17, 1993. The future is trading at $1.9217. I know that in the interbank forward market the $/GBP rate for that date is $1.9212. I buy interbank forward £625,000 and sell the futures contract to make a five-point profit. Because this type of arbitrage is so easy, many banks specialize in "trading the IMM dates." Therefore, the futures market price is in practice fixed by the cash market price for that day, which is worked out in the usual manner (see Chapter 9).

There are two complications to this simplicity. The first is that traditionally US foreign exchange quotations were reciprocal, that is, DEM 1 = 0.6579 rather than US$1 = DEM 1.5200. Thus in comparing with the normal interbank forward quotations, one has to invert the futures price.

The second complication applies when dealing crosses. It flows from the fact that the standard amounts of the contracts are expressed in the foreign currency. Thus the yen contract is for JPY 12,500,000; the DEM contract is for DEM 125,000. Unless the JPY/DEM cross is at 100, one of these two contracts will be "heavier" than the other. Suppose the actual JPY/DEM cross is DEM 1 = JPY 90. Then the yen contract is worth DEM 138,888.89 while the deutsche mark contract is worth DEM 125 000. Therefore in trading the crosses on the futures market one would need to weight the size of one's position. The weight is the current cross rate as a proportion of the cross-rate implied by the contracts. In this case the number of yen contracts would be 90% of the number of deutsche mark contracts, for example, one might sell 180 yen contracts and buy 200 deutsche mark ones.

10.6 HEDGING

To hedge is to reduce risk. When an investor faces the risk of a change in interest or exchange rates which the former does not want to bear, financial futures may be used to offset the risk. If the risk is of a fall in interest rates, futures are bought and if the risk is of a rise, futures are sold. To be precise, one may say that in such circumstances a hedger transfers risk by temporarily offsetting a position in a cash market with a related position in a futures market.

Let us look first at a short hedge. Suppose that a company has agreed to borrow Eurodollars on a three-month rollover basis. It fears that interest rates are about to rise. It wants to lock in current interest rate levels on its borrowings. It will then sell Eurodollar futures contracts to the amount required. This is a "short" hedge. The mechanics are as follows.

Suppose today is March 14, 1992. Three-month Eurodollar LIBOR is 8%. Three-month Eurodollar futures for delivery June 16 are 92 (8%) but the firm fears that by June three-month LIBOR on its $10 million borrowing could be 10%. That would mean that the spot contract in June would be 90. So the firm sells 10 June contracts at 92. If its fears are correct, and the June contracts do go to 90, it buys back the contracts on June 14 (last trading day for the contract) at 90 and makes a profit of 2.00 per contract, that is, 200 basis points. Each basis point on a $1 million contract is worth $25, so its profit is $25 \times 200 \times 10 = \$50,000$.

It now borrows for three months (say 90 days) at 10%, costing:

$$10/100 \times 10 \text{ million} \times 90/360 = 250,000.$$

From this can be deducted the profit on the futures, making a total cost of $200,000, producing an effective rate of 8% which the borrower has locked in today for three months hence. In other words, it has locked in today's futures rate for its borrowing.

What would have happened if the interest rate had gone the other way, say, to 6%? Then the Euro contracts would have traded at around 94. Closing them out would have cost 2.00 per contract, so the loss would be $50,000. The cost of the cash borrowing would now be $6/100 \times 10$ million $\times 90/360 = \$150,000$, and the all-in cost would again be $200,000. In other words, the cost is insensitive to interest rate movements.

What we have just said is broadly true. But the hedge will not actually be perfect for several reasons. First, there would be an impact from changes in the pattern of variation margin during the interval to the futures delivery date. In practice, we are hedging a future cash flow with an instrument where profits and losses hit our books today. A related point is whether one should hedge not the nominal amount of the borrowing, but today's present value of that amount. This is often referred to as "tailing the hedge" and is customary if the deal is large.

Second, there will be basis risk: the futures market may not move exactly in line with the cash market. Particularly if rates turn out to be fairly stable, there can be a bigger profit and loss impact from basis risk than from interest rate movements.

10.7 FUTURES AND FRAS

Eurodollar futures are closely linked to the market for FRAs (see Chapter 9) and—since FRAs are a kind of single-period swap—the interest rate swap market. Suppose today is March 13, 1992, and the three- and six-month Eurodollar deposits, value March 15, are trading at 8.25 and 8.5%, respectively. Suppose the days in each period are 90 and 180, respectively. We know from our forward forward formula (see above) that the FRA rate should be

$$(8.5 \times 180 - 8.25 \times 90)/([180-90] \times [1 + \{8.25 \times 90/36000\}]) = (1,530 - 742.50)/$$
$$(90 \times 1.020\,625) = 787.5/91.856\,25 = 8.57\%.$$

That would imply a futures price for June (the price for a 90-day Eurodollar deposit running from June 15 to September 15) of 91.43. Suppose in fact that the future were trading at 91.25, implying a forward rate of 8.75. Then it would be possible to buy the future (hedging against a fall in rates) and also to buy the FRA (hedging against a rise in rates). The future would lock in a lending rate of 8.75% and the FRA would lock in a borrowing rate of 8.57% for a spread of 18 basis points. In other words if the FRA rate is below the rate given by the future, buy the future and buy the FRA. Conversely, if the FRA rate is above the future, sell the FRA and sell the future.

The hedge will not be quite so perfect as it looks, because of the time value of money on the variation margin. Consider a company with a $10 million floating rate loan linked to six-month LIBOR. It fears rates will rise, and so buys a 6×12 FRA from its bank. Suppose we have the following conditions: value March 19, 1991 we have:

LIBOR		FUTURE	
3 months	8.50%	Jun.	91.28
6 months	8.70%	Sep.	91.17
9 months	8.88%	Dec.	91.02
1 year	9.05%		

For convenience we take the year as having 360 days and 6 months as having 180. Thus the forward rate is

$$(9.05 \times 360 - 8.7 \times 180)/(180 \times [1 + (8.7 \times 180/36,000)]) = 9.01\%.$$

Suppose the bank loads its quote to 9.10%. Having done the deal it wants to hedge using the futures market. It sells 10 September contracts (at an implied rate of 8.83%) and 10 December contracts at an implied rate of 8.98%.

The implied total cost over the six-month period that is locked in by the futures contracts is worked out by compounding the near contract (at 8.83%) up over the second period at the second rate of 8.98%:

$$(1 + 8.83 \times 90/3600) \times (1 + 8.98 \times 90/36\,000) = 1.022\,075 \times 1.022\,45 =$$
$$1.045\,020\,584 = 4.502\%$$

per six months which equates to just over 9% annually.

It looks as if the bank has locked a 10 basis point profit over six months on $10 million—say $5000. But now suppose, the day after the deal is done, that cash Eurodollar rates fall 1% and stay fixed at that level until the September futures date. We would have the following rates:

LIBOR		FUTURE	
3 months	7.50%		
6 months	7.70%	Sep.	92.07
9 months	7.88%	Dec.	91.92
1 year	8.05%		

Suppose the September futures contract we sold has risen by 90 ticks, and the December by 90 ticks. Bearing in mind that the tick on this contract (see above) is worth $25 and we did 10 contracts in each maturity, our loss totals $2 \times 10 \times 90 \times 25 = \$45,000$. Since we have assumed that rates now remain rigidly fixed to the September delivery date, there are no further changes in our position and no variation margin movements; we have to fund this loss till delivery date. Say we do this at the six-month rate of 7.7%, then our funding cost is $1,732.50 ($45,000 at 7.7% for half a year)—one-third of our apparent profit disappears.

The problem is that the value of a future settlement amount under the FRA is being hedged with an instrument which throws up changes in value today. One way round this would be to hedge not the settlement amount but the present value of the settlement amount (i.e. we would "tail the hedge"). With the passage of time, that present value rises, so that one would gradually increase the size of the hedge as we get closer to the settlement date, if we want to be perfectly hedged. (But by that time, we might be more confident about the trend in rates and happy to leave the balance of the position open.)

10.8 OPEN INTEREST AND VOLUME

Any trader in the futures markets needs to know the liquidity and depth of the markets. The two most general measurements of liquidity and depth for any futures market are trading volume and open interest. Trading volume is the number of contracts traded during a period of time; open interest is the number of open contract units at a point in time.

Futures trading volume is reported as one side only. In other words, a daily volume of 12,000 means 12,000 contracts bought and 12,000 contracts sold. Buys and sells are not added together. The number of contracts bought always equals the number sold since there must be a buyer for every seller. A large volume of trading is a good indication of a liquid market. Liquidity can be gauged by the ability of market participants to execute commercial-size orders quickly at a price close to the price of the last transaction.

Open interest is the number of contracts recorded with the exchange at the close of business each day as transactions that have not been offset by an opposite trade or settled by delivery. Open interest, like trading volume, counts one side only—an open interest of 5000 is 5000 bought positions and 5000 sold positions. A relatively large open interest tends to indicate commercial hedging, because hedgers are more likely than speculators to hold positions as prices fluctuate.

Both volume and open interest are frequently watched as technical indicators of the state of the market. For example, a gradual increase in volume during a downtrend often indicates a continuation and acceleration of the price decline. Gradually increasing volume during an uptrend suggests a further rise in prices. Equally, a rising price trend with a gradual increase in open interest means that new long hedgers or speculators are entering the market. They are paying higher prices to persuade new short hedgers or speculators to sell. If this process continues for several days, the new long speculators will be accumulating profits and additional buying power (because they have extra margin). The new speculative sellers will have losses and will be feeling financial pressure (because they have to put up extra margin). Such a market is technically strong, particularly if volume is increasing along with open interest.

11
Interest Rate and
Currency Swaps

As the chapter title suggests, the swaps discussed in this chapter are different from those discussed earlier in the context of the forward exchange market. Like those deals, they involve the exchange of one thing for another, hence the common name. But these deals are generally longer term (though there is a thriving one-year interest rate swap market). They will involve more than one exchange. Often they are conducted by the capital markets arm of a bank, rather than the money and foreign exchange trading operations. On the other hand, many banks group all these activities together, on the grounds that all these markets are interlinked, which is the reason for including them in this book.

In this context, we will define an interest rate swap as a contract to exchange one type of interest payment for another set of interest payments. A currency swap is a contract to exchange a series of payments in one currency for a series of payments in another currency.

11.1 ORIGINS OF THE SWAP MARKET

Swaps, as defined above, took off during the 1980s. From perhaps $2 billion outstanding in 1980 the interest rate and currency swap market has now grown to the point where an estimated $4000 billion of contracts are now outstanding. The first swaps to emerge were currency swaps, which began in the mid-1960s. But the market remained a fairly small one during the 1970s. The emergence of the interest rate swap, in 1980/81, together with the decision by the World Bank to embark on an ambitious currency swap program, transformed the situation.

The market now has a huge range of counterparties, using swaps for a range of different reasons. Banks use swaps for asset and liability management; companies use them for similar purposes and also to raise finance through the bond market, notably the Eurobond market, at rates which are better than those their bankers can offer. This flexibility has led to a huge growth in the market. In 1980, the market size for currency swaps was perhaps $2 billion; interest rate swaps did not exist. The

Table 11.1   Swap Market Volume, 1989/93 (US$ bn)

	Interest Rate Swaps		Currency Swaps	
	1989	1993	1989	1993
US$	994	2457	354	640
JPY	128	1247	201	318
GBP	100	437	33	88
DEM	85	629	53	139
AU$	68	131	61	93
FFR	42	456	8	46
CA$	29	126	32	71
CHF	28	182	64	147
XEU	18	133	39	74
NLG	6	52	10	20
HK$	2	10	1	4
BEF	1	31	3	14

Source: ISDA, reported in *International Banking and Financial Market Developments*, BIS, November 1990, February 1995.

International Swap Dealers' Association (which covers a large part, but by no means all, of the market) has published figures for market volume for some years. Table 11.1 compares 1993 with 1989:

Figure 11.1 shows the volume of new swaps dealt in some of the key market sectors during 1990–93, and their maturity structure is shown in Figure 11.2.

Swaps have had a great impact on the international bond market. Earlier issuers of new Eurobonds were relatively tied down. If they issued, say, a deutsche mark bond, the extent to which they could hedge the long-term exchange risk of the bond

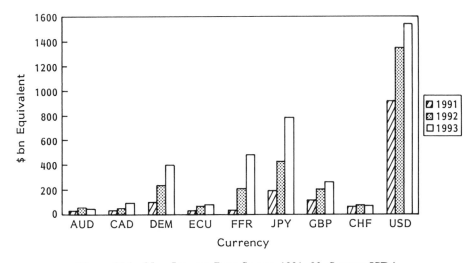

Figure 11.1   New Interest Rate Swaps, 1991–93. Source: ISDA

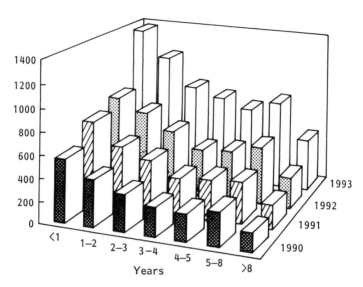

Figure 11.2 Maturity Structure of Interest Rate Swaps, 1991–93. Source: ISDA, reported by BIS

was rather limited. The growth of the currency swap market meant that for the first time, issuers could tap the currency market where they could raise the cheapest funds. A company such as BMW could issue a bond denominated in New Zealand dollars and then do a currency swap to transform its liability into deutsche marks. Equally, the growth of the interest rate swap market meant a similar liberation in the choice between fixed and floating rate bonds. As Figure 11.3 shows, the currency swap market is more important for those countries where the capital market is an important international source of funds, for example Switzerland, whereas the interest rate swap market tends to be more active in those currencies where domestic financial markets are relatively active.

Once the swap technique had been invented, of course, people found many other ways of using it. The market has even been used by governments: the governments of France and Canada have both done interest rate swaps. In the longer run it is conceivable that the market may be used by central banks for yield curve management, just as in the past they have used forward exchange markets.

Interest rate swaps have been used to switch from floating rate to fixed, from fixed to floating, from fixed rate to zero coupon, from zero coupon to floating, from zero coupon to semiannual fixed, and so on. Essentially, the combination of interest rate and currency swaps now means that any stream of cash flows can be transformed into virtually any other stream: annual ISMA basis Japanese yen payments can be transformed into quarterly US dollar, amortizing lease type payments, if desired, at a price.

Despite early worries about the credit risk implied in swaps, an International Swaps Dealers' Association survey showed total write-offs of US$33 million on portfolios aggregating over $250 billion, a default rate of 0.01%—considerably better than traditional banking default rates. (Although a government veto on swap

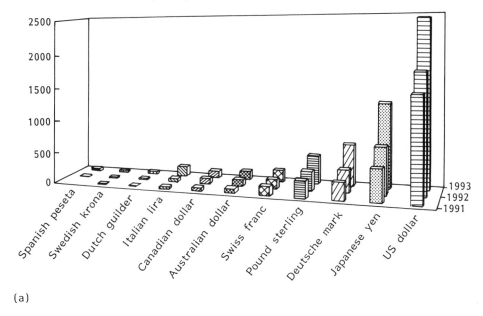

(a)

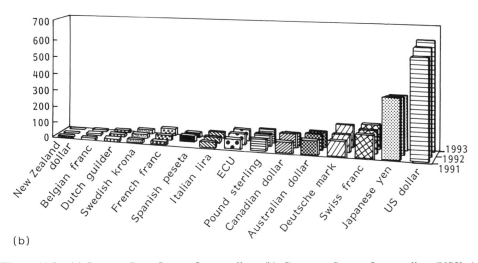

(b)

Figure 11.3 (a) Interest Rate Swaps Outstanding; (b) Currency Swaps Outstanding (US$bn). Source: ISDA, via BIS

payments due from the London borough of Hammersmith and Fulham caused problems: partly for political reasons the municipality had used swaps and options to generate revenue from speculative transactions. The legal ability of the municipality to undertake such activity was later overturned by the House of Lords, on the grounds that they were *ultra vires*.)

11.2 INTEREST RATE SWAPS

An interest rate swap lets an institution manage its liabilities: whether they be fixed rate, or floating rate. Many people find the concept confusing. It may help to think of a fixed–floating interest rate swap as issuing a fixed rate bond to refinance a floating rate note, or vice versa. The only difference is that in the swap there is no actual borrowing or lending (this is where the market differs from that for currency swaps, where the principal amounts of the swap are actually exchanged under normal circumstances, at least at maturity). Another analogy is with the foreign exchange market: an interest rate swap is a forward contract to exchange interest payments. An example may help.

Suppose it is December 1, 1993; you are the corporate treasurer of XYZ Ltd. You have borrowed floating rate money from a syndicate of banks, for five years at six-month US dollar LIBOR $\frac{1}{2}$%, in an amount of $10 million. Your company does not have the financial strength to access the public bond markets. So it is hard for you to raise five-year money at a fixed rate. However, you fear that interest rates will rise. You decide to enter into a swap with a bank to fix for five years the cost of your interest rate liabilities, which would otherwise rise as LIBOR rises.

Suppose the bank quotes you a fixed rate of 9.5%, payable semiannually on a 30/360 basis against six-month LIBOR. Payment on both sides is in arrears. Then you are committed to the cash flows shown in Table 11.2. On the other side will be the floating rate income. The bank pays you six-month LIBOR. Consider two possibilities: LIBOR rises by $\frac{1}{4}$% every six months over the period from a starting level of 8%, and LIBOR falls by $\frac{1}{4}$%. Then we will have (assuming for simplicity the LIBOR is paid also on a 30/360 basis—normally it is on actual/360 for US dollar swaps) the swap flows shown in Table 11.3.

The payments by the bank to you will exactly match your LIBOR payments to your banking syndicate, except for the latter's $\frac{1}{2}$% margin. So the LIBOR payments always net to zero, and your cost is fixed at the $9\frac{1}{2}$% swap rate plus the $\frac{1}{2}$% syndicate margin, for an all-in cost of 10%.

The origins of the interest rate swap technique were in the Eurobond market where fixed rate issuers who wish to raise floating rate money. A typical example in the early days would be a Japanese bank. Because most banks typically lend money on a floating rate basis, Japanese banks were not in the habit of issuing fixed rate

Table 11.2 Interest Rate Swap Cash Flows

1 Jun. 1994	$475 000
1 Dec.	$475 000
1 Jun. 1995	$475 000
1 Dec.	$475 000
1 Jun. 1996	$475 000
1 Dec.	$475 000
1 Jun. 1997	$475 000
1 Dec.	$475 000
1 Jun. 1998	$475 000
1 Dec.	$475 000

Table 11.3 Swap Flows if Rates Rise/Fall

		Income	
	Fixed Payment	Case I LIBOR Rises	Case II LIBOR Falls
1 Jun. 1994	$475,000	$400,000	$400,000
1 Dec.	$475,000	$412,500	$387,500
1 Jun. 1995	$475,000	$425,000	$375,000
1 Dec.	$475,000	£437,500	$362,500
1 Jun. 1996	$475,000	$450,000	$350,000
1 Dec.	$475,000	$462,500	$337,500
1 Jun. 1997	$475,000	$475,000	$325,000
1 Dec.	$475,000	$487,500	$312,500
1 Jun. 1998	$475,000	$500,000	$300,000
1 Dec.	$475,000	$512,500	$287,500

Eurobonds. They did not need fixed rate funds. Therefore, their paper was relatively scarce in the fixed rate bond market, and commanded attractive premiums. Thus, they were able to issue cheaply and then to swap into floating rate funds.

An example would be as follows: a strong borrower, AAA, would pay LIBOR + $\frac{1}{8}$% for a seven-year revolving credit from its banks, if it chose to arrange one. For a seven-year bond issue, it would pay 11%. Conversely, a weaker borrower, BBB, must pay 12% for a seven-year bond issue or LIBOR + $\frac{1}{2}$% for seven year money from the bank.

The difference between the two borrowers in the bank credit market is only $\frac{3}{8}$%; in the bond market it is 1%: a "credit differential" of $\frac{5}{8}$%. The first swaps used this differential to arbitrage. AAA issued a bond and entered into a swap with BBB. Both borrowers were able to save money: here, the $\frac{5}{8}$% is split as to $\frac{3}{8}$% for AAA and $\frac{1}{4}$% for BBB.

There has been a tendency in the academic literature to explain swaps in terms of relative comparative advantage. While this explains why the technique was developed, I believe a better way to think of the interest rate swap market today is as an arena for the trading of LIBOR for forward delivery. Just as there is a market for the forward delivery of deutsche marks against US dollars, so there is a market for the forward sale or purchase of LIBOR. A firm entering into a swap under which it pays 10% p.a. on $100 million against six-month US dollar LIBOR for five years is contracting to pay a fixed sum to ensure forward deliveries of six-month US dollar LIBOR on $100 million. We can say that 10% p.a. is the price of forward deliveries of US dollar six-month LIBOR for five years.

Hence, the interest rate swap market has become an arena for transferring interest rate risk which sits alongside the interest rate futures market and the FRA market. In all these markets, those who anticipate rising rates trade with those who either expect a fall in rates or else have a requirement to switch their exposure to a floating rate basis (e.g. banks which have borrowed fixed-rate funds which they now plan to lend on a floating rate basis).

11.3 PRICING AN INTEREST RATE SWAP

Suppose today is March 3, 1991. You are pricing a swap for your company which is interested in swapping out of six-month US dollar LIBOR and paying a fixed US dollar rate. On consulting a Reuters swap screen (such as SWAP or HIRS) you see the following:

Treasury	Swap Spread	Swap Cost
2 year	7.64 T + 47/54	8.11/18
3 year	7.75 T + 65/70	8.40/45
4 year	7.78 T + 68/76	8.46/54
5 year	7.90 T + 70/78	8.60/68

To interpret this data, one needs to know that swap rates are priced off the corresponding US Treasury bond. Thus, if the company were to pay fixed for two years, the swap cost would be the Treasury rate, 7.64%, plus the swap spread of 54 basis points, for an all-in total of 8.18%, plus the credit spread (if any) being charged by the intermediary bank for providing the swap. If the company wanted to deal in the opposite direction, i.e. receive a fixed rate, the spread would be 47 basis points for an all-in cost of 8.11%, which is what it would be paid by the market, less any credit spread charged by the bank.

It is important to be aware that the rate is quoted on a "Treasury bond basis," that is, a semiannual actual/365 rate. To convert this to a 360-day rate we multiply by 360/365 to convert 8.18 to 8.07% (note the 11 basis point difference). To convert this to an annual rate (to make it comparable to, say, a Eurodollar money market rate) we need to use the following formula:

$$r = (1 + i/n)^n$$

where r = annual rate; i = semi-annual rate; and n = number of periods per annum (2 in this case). In this case we have

$$r = (1 + 0.0807/2)^2 = 8.23\%$$

In summary, to convert a Treasury bond rate to an annual money market rate: (a) multiply by 360/365—reducing the nominal rate (by 11 points in this case) and (b) compound up to annual—raising the nominal rate (by 16 points in this case). If the company borrows on a Eurodollar money market basis but is charged interest semi-annually rather than annually then the current swap rate for comparison purposes would be 8.07%.

11.4 WHAT DETERMINES SWAP SPREADS?

The answer to this question depends on which segment of the market we are discussing. The short end of the US dollar interest rate swap curve, for example tends to be much more volatile, because it is much more influenced by the futures market, against which arbitrages tend to be run for short swaps. The supply and demand factors in the US dollar interest rate swap market overall include:

1. Volume of bond issues available to be swapped, that is, the condition of the US dollar bond market, both Euro and domestic; the former being heavily influenced also by currency considerations and the number of issuers requiring floating rather than fixed; which is influenced also by expectations about the course of rates.
2. Volume of other fixed rate instruments being placed and available to be swapped out of; for example, deals are often driven by medium-term deposits and certainly there are swaps out of CD issues. Similarly, the domestic US private placement market is often a source of supply. When US insurance companies have excess cash flow they often give attractive fixed rate loans which are then swapped into floating.
3. At the shorter end of the market, swappers are often hedging the other side with futures contracts or FRAs, so if the futures are trading rich against the cash markets, it can be profitable to be a fixed rate receiver on a swap and sell a strip of futures contracts.
4. A technical point is that swap market-makers will often hold their positions hedged against Treasury bonds. Normally, if they are payers, say, in the three-year swap, they will be long of three-year Treasuries as a hedge. The Treasuries will be financed in the "repo" market. If the repo rate rises above the Treasury rate, there will be a cost of carry and they will want to sell off the position, driving down the swap spread.
5. A further technical point is that when a new Treasury bond issue in a given maturity appears, swaps start to price against the "when-issued" Treasury, which generally yields a little less; swap spreads tend to kick up to compensate around the time of the changeover. This factor should wash out over time but often does not for a while.

Demand factors include:

1. The major influence is the corporate sector's general view of rates. If there is a consensus that rates will fall, swap spreads tend to fall, and vice versa. However, if the Treasury bond market traders are more bullish than the corporate sector, spreads tend to widen (as Treasuries fall faster than the swap rates) and vice versa.
2. When swap rates are below those on domestic US private placements, medium-term borrowers switch into the swap market.
3. When swap rates are above those available on the bond market for comparable issuers, demand switches to the public bond market.
4. At times banks—particularly domestic US banks—are willing to make unmatched fixed rate loans, especially when rates are falling. This tends to push swap spreads down by reducing demand for swaps by fixed rate borrowers. Conversely, a pullout by banks switches corporate demand to the swap market.

Other influences include the fact that the swap market is dominated by banking counterparties: corporate to corporate deals are less common than when the market started. So when there is concern about the banking system, spreads rise against Treasuries. At the time of the Continental Illinois crisis in 1984, spreads at the shorter end—two and three years—jumped around 40 to 50 basis points very quickly. Seasonal factors are also relevant: the market is relatively young to show a true seasonal pattern but certainly towards the end of the tax year it is quite common to see a clearing-out of positions, sometimes on the basis of up-front cash payments in exchange for off-market coupons.

11.5   ASSET SWAPS

An important investment application for swaps is in the so-called "asset swap" market. Asset swaps are a way to shift paper from one market to another. Bonds have been issued consisting of floating rate notes swapped into fixed rates. An example would be the BECS issue in 1985, in which $100 million of UK government US dollar floating rate notes were swapped into fixed rate dollar bonds, producing "synthetic US dollar gilt edged bonds." More often, a fixed rate bond coupled with an interest rate (and perhaps a currency) swap, to produce a synthetic floating rate note.

It was not long before investment banks realized the value of the asset swap technique. Put bluntly, a failed fixed rate bond could be transformed into a floating rate note and placed with banks, who are well accustomed to buying floating rate instruments. A particularly widespread use of the technique has been in the Japanese equity warrant bond market.

At its height, bonds in this market were being issued with coupons as low as 1 or 2%. This was because the attractions of the warrant were so great, that the bond to which the warrant was attached could be relatively lowly valued. Thus, immediately after the bond was issued, and the warrants were stripped away from it, the straight bond would fall to a sharp discount: a price of $70 or even $60 per $100 nominal. Traditionally, many investors are not interested in buying deep discount, low coupon bonds, for accounting and other reasons. Thus, while the warrant was a roaring success, the bonds would languish.

It was not long before the asset swappers perceived the opportunity. They would move in to buy the unwanted bonds, couple them with an interest rate swap, and sell them to the banks. These bonds, however, were operationally a great deal more complex to swap, because of the deep discount nature of the cash flows.

Asset swap activity has had both positive and negative effects. On the positive side, for every new issue, there is now generally a floor point below which the bond cannot fall. At some point it becomes "swappable": the bond's spread over Treasuries is above the spread which the swap market requires to swap into floating rate. At that point, the bond can be redistributed into the floating rate market. This provides a natural floor price for the bond in the fixed rate market. On the negative side, the asset swapped bonds tend to be firmly held to maturity, which tends to reduce liquidity for the remaining bonds (by reducing the total "float"—tradeable bonds—down to a level where it is not worth market-makers' time to quote prices on the bond).

11.6 CURRENCY SWAPS

The currency swap market is thought to have begun in the UK during the 1960s. The reason was the existence of UK exchange controls at that time which prevented UK firms wishing to invest abroad from simply selling sterling to buy foreign currency. The Bank of England wanted to prevent outflows of sterling, and so required British firms to borrow overseas to finance overseas investments. This had the drawback that their overseas subsidiaries were often quite weak credits compared with the UK parent; yet the UK parent often could not guarantee the overseas subsidiary because of exchange controls. So bankers came up with the idea of a swap between the UK parent and an overseas counterparty. The use of the swap meant that the Bank of England could be sure that an outflow of sterling today would be offset by an inflow at a later date when the swap unwound.

It may be helpful to start with a brief outline of how a currency swap works. Suppose that ICI needs US dollars for its operations in the United States, and DuPont needs sterling for its UK operations. A solution to their need is for ICI to sell its sterling to Du Pont for dollars. To cut out the risk of exchange rate movements, they contract to reverse the deal in, say, five years. Say ICI sells £10 million to DuPont in exchange for $18 million.

Effectively, ICI is lending sterling to DuPont, who are lending dollars to ICI. (Though the legal structure does not involve any assets on the balance sheet nor is the deal documented as a loan: it is an exchange of currencies.) So during the life of the deal, ICI pay the rate for five-year dollar loans—say 7%—and DuPont pay the rate for five-year sterling loans—say 9%. At the end of the deal, ICI and DuPont re-exchange. (In some countries, such as the UK, it is desirable to interpose a bank between the two parties, because tax law would otherwise require the interest payments to be made net of tax. Interposing a bank also has the advantage of insulating the two parties from the credit risk of the other.)

The cash flows are set out in Table 11.4 from ICI's point of view, assuming that ICI borrowed the £10 million to lend to DuPont, also at 9%. At the start of the deal there is an inflow of £10 million from the original funding. This is paid across to DuPont at the start of the swap. In exchange, there is an inflow of $18 million from DuPont. The net effect is an inflow of $18 million.

Table 11.4 Currency Swap Cash Flows

	Swap cashflows		Original Funding	Net
	$	£		
Year 0	$18m.	(£10m.)	£10 m.	$18m.
Year 1	($1.3m.)	£0.9m.	(£0.9m.)	($1.3m.)
Year 2	($1.3m.)	£0.9m.	(£0.9m.)	($1.3m.)
Year 3	($1.3m.)	£0.9m.	(£0.9m.)	($1.3m.)
Year 4	($1.3m.)	£0.9m.	(£0.9m.)	($1.3m.)
Year 5	($19.3m.)	£10.9m.	(£10.9m.)	($19.3m.)

For each of the next five years, ICI pays its lending bankers £0.9 million in interest on the original funding, and receives a corresponding payment from DuPont of £0.9 million, while paying out $1.3 million to DuPont. (Where practical, these payments are netted off.) The last payment includes redemption of the principal amounts. The net result is that a sterling stream of cash flows is transformed into a dollar stream.

Let us look at an issuer who wants to raise five-year money in US dollars. Suppose his advisers tell him that the cheapest course would be to raise five-year deutsche marks, and swap them into US dollars. How will this work?

Suppose the rate (ignoring fees) for five-year deutsche mark Eurobonds is 7% and the bond is issued at par for DEM 200 million. Suppose today's spot US$/DEM rate is $1 = DEM 2.00. Suppose that an American company wants five-year deutsche mark financing at a rate of 8%, in exchange for being paid 10% on the US dollar equivalent financing it will provide. We assume that the deal can be structured so that all interim flows, and the principal being re-exchanged at maturity, can be exchanged at a rate of $1 = DEM 2.00.

Here the issuer's bond cost is 7%, but 8% is earned on the swap, so there is a net additional 1% saving, making a total US dollar cost of 9% p.a. What has happened is that the issuer, perhaps because it is a better known credit in the Euromarket, is able to raise five-year money cheaper than its swap counterpart: in exchange for passing on the cheap deutsche mark, it is able to borrow cheap dollars.

Notice that the final cash flow includes exchange of principal amounts, unlike the interest rate swap deal; thus, the credit exposure (see below) on a currency swap will usually be much larger than under an interest rate swap. (In fact, in a currency swap, it is theoretically possible to lose more than 100% of the principal amount.) It is theoretically possible to do a currency swap without exchanging principal at the end of the deal (it is quite common to do so without the initial exchange, which can be done in the spot market) but in that case the terms would normally include a "floating principal amount" which is recalculated for each interest payment date.

11.7 THE IBM/WORLD BANK SWAP

A more detailed real-life example may be of interest. In 1981 IBM and the World Bank entered into a currency swap: the World Bank, which had issued comparatively little US dollar paper, could raise funds at an attractive rate in the US market. It wanted Swiss francs and deutsche marks, but had issued a lot of bonds in Switzerland and Germany. IBM wanted to crystallize its foreign exchange gains on some existing Swiss franc and deutsche mark bonds outstanding. The solution benefiting both was for the World Bank to issue a US dollar bond and swap the proceeds with IBM. Details of the transaction have never been published in full; the following outline draws on D. R. Bock's description (*Swap Finance*, B. Antl (Ed.), Euromoney Publications, London, 1986, pp. 218—223).

The bond issue was launched on August 11, 1981, settling August 25, which became the settlement date for the swap. The first annual exchange under the swap, however, was to be on March 30, the next coupon date on IBM's bonds—215 days (rather than 360 days) from the start date. The first step was to calculate the value of the Swiss franc and deutsche mark flows which were (say) at 8 and 11% p.a. respec-

Table 11.5 IBM/World Bank Swap Cash Flows

Exchange Date	CHF Flows	CHF Discount Factor	DEM Flows	DEM Discount Factor
3/30/82	12,375,000	0.955,077,46	30,000,000	0.939,576,44
3/30/83	12,375,000	0.884,330,99	30,000,000	0.846,465,26
3/30/84	12,375,000	0.818,824,99	30,000,000	0.762,581,32
3/30/85	12,375,000	0.758,181,28	30,000,000	0.687,010,20
3/30/86	212,375,000	0.702,010,45	330,000,000	0.618,928,11
Net present value	CHF191,367,478		DEM301,315,273	

tively. The initial 215-day period meant that the discount factors were $215/360 = 0.597\,222$, $1.597\,222$, $2.597\,222$ and so on. Applying the Swiss franc rate of 8%, then, the discount factors were

$$1/(1.08)0.597\,222) = 0.955\,077\,46 \quad 1/(1.08)1.597\,222) = 0.884\,330\,99, \text{ etc.}$$

The final terms of the swap were agreed on August 11, two weeks before the settlement date. So the World Bank bought the Swiss franc and deutsche mark net present value amounts worked out above, using two-week forward foreign exchange contracts. Supposing that these contracts were at CHF 2.18 and DEM 2.56 per US dollar, the dollar amounts needed by the World Bank were $87,783,247 to buy the Swiss francs and $117,701,753 for the deutsche marks, totaling $205,485,000.

It was then necessary to work out the dollar amount of the bond to be issued. Supposing the issue to be at a coupon of 16% with fees of 2.15% (i.e. net proceeds of 97.85%) the dollar amount of the bond issue had to be

$$\$205,485,000/0.9785 = \$210,000,000.$$

So the final results of the deal are as shown in Table 11.5.

11.8 SWAP CREDIT RISK

An important aspect of swaps is the question of credit risk. The credit risk on an interest rate swap falls into two parts. first, the risk that the counterparty fails; second, the risk that interest rates have moved in the wrong direction. Thus, if interest rates move in the wrong direction but the counterparty does not fail, there is no loss: equally, if the counterparty fails but interest rates have moved favorably, the bank doing the original swap may find that the bankruptcy of its counterpart crystallizes a profit, rather than a loss. It should be noted, therefore, that the credit risk here is in fact two-way: the bank has a credit risk on its counterparty, but if rates move the other way, the counterparty will have a credit risk on it.

To illustrate the credit risk, let us suppose that a bank enters into a swap deal with a company which agrees to pay 14% for five years against six-month LIBOR. Interest rates fall sharply, but after two years, the company goes bankrupt. There are three years remaining in the life of the swap, and at this time, the three-year rate is

10%. Accordingly, the bank undertakes a new swap with another counterparty, which agrees to pay the bank 10% for the next three years. Assuming that the bank had covered its original contract, let us say with another bank, its original obligation to pay 14% to the other bank is still in force for the next three years.

Hence, on the one hand, it is receiving 10% and, on the other, paying 14%, and it has crystallized a loss for three years. In the converse case, in the event that rates had risen sharply after the contract was concluded, the bank would crystallize a profit: on the other hand, it is quite probable that the trustee in bankruptcy would elect to continue the contract, since it is favorable to the firm, rather than default. The whole subject of credit risk for swaps and other off-balance sheet instruments is dealt with more fully in Chapter 13.

11.9 SWAPS VALUATION AND ACCOUNTING

The subject of valuing and accounting for swaps has been bedevilled by debates between proponents of various views and by the fact that swaps are applied in so many different financial contexts. The key debate has been between accrual accounting and mark-to-market. Proponents of accrual accounting argue that the value of the swap should not be fully taken to income until it has expired because until maturity there remains a credit risk, which means there is a risk that the income is not in fact earned. The parallel is with the interest earned on a loan.

Proponents of mark-to-market point out that the net present value of the income stream from a swap will vary in line with market rates of interest. For example, take the case of a firm which has entered into an asset swap whereby they hold a bond and an interest rate swap as a combined package. The bond must be marked to market under existing accounting rules: if the interest rate swap is not, there will not be a true picture of the value of the position.

On the other hand, where a swap has been booked against a bank loan, perhaps to make it into a fixed rate, since the loan is not marked to market, it would be inconsistent to mark the swap to market. The difficulty arises from the fact that swaps are used both by operations who customarily mark to market—bond traders for example—and those who do not—e.g. bank lending departments.

Essentially the appropriate treatment must depend on (a) the treatment given to the asset or liability which the swap is hedging; (b) the intent of the original swap—was it taken on as a trading position or to hedge an exposure? (c) local applicable regulations.

11.10 COMMODITY SWAPS

An important extension of the swap technique has been to the commodity markets—an interesting example of history moving full circle, since it was the commodity markets which developed futures, without which swaps would not have grown to the scale they have done. The most widely used commodity swap market is that for oil and related products, but the technique has been used in gold and copper markets also and in principle could be applied to the market for any commodity where there is a standardized, traded commodity—though preferably one where there are futures contracts which allow for laying off short-term risk.

An example of how the commodity swap technique can fit into the wider framework of international finance was a deal done with a Mexican copper firm. This deal opened the way to voluntary new bank lending to a Mexican borrower at a time when the country was not seen as a good risk. The Mexican firm borrowed about $200 million from a banking syndicate, with repayments coming from the sale of copper to a Belgian company. The sale price is fixed at the average market price at time of delivery—so clearly the Mexican firm would be exposed to a fall in the copper price over the three-year term of the loan. The solution was a three-year copper swap with a French bank, under which the bank contracted to pay a fixed price for the Mexican firm's copper, in exchange for receiving the floating, market price. To eliminate its risk, it is understood, the French bank entered into a matching, opposite swap with a copper user which wished to hedge against a rise in copper prices.

These applications are part of a wider trend of integrating commodity and financial markets. For example, the gold market has developed significant activity in gold borrowing and lending; gold loans have been made to gold producers, and the banks involved in the loans are active borrowers of gold from gold holders, so that there is now a gold LIBOR just as there is a dollar LIBOR or a yen LIBOR. Another related move has been the introduction of FRAs (see Chapter 9) on gold. These allow gold borrowers and lenders to hedge short-term movements in the gold LIBOR rate.

Clearly, the whole financial markets technology—swaps, options, caps, floors, collars and so on—can in principle be applied to any commodity. However, the practical restrictions are that there has to be a sufficiently widely traded benchmark and preferably a decent futures market for hedging. In fact, the question of liquidity in these markets becomes of key importance for bank intermediaries because of the question of counterparty risk.

If a swap counterparty fails, banks will normally seek to find another counterparty to step into the swap so that the bank's position is still matched. But whereas it is fairly straightforward to assess the counterparty risk on a five-year interest rate swap against three month LIBOR—there will always be someone who is prepared to replace a defaulted swap at a price because so many firms are exposed to LIBOR—this does not apply to, say, a five-year copper swap.

In the copper swap discussed above, the French bank faces two risks: (a) the copper price movement—which could be positive or negative; (b) the risk that they are left with an open swap position which cannot be closed out at any price. As these markets develop they will raise interesting questions for the regulators regarding the capital adequacy rules that have been put in place for swaps. (See Chapter 13 on Risk.)

12
Options

An option is a contract which conveys the right, but not the obligation, to buy or sell a financial instrument. Options are a very useful tool in money and foreign exchange markets. They allow us the luxury of a one-way bet. We can bet that a rate will go up and make a profit from that; but if it comes down, we do not lose. They are particularly useful for hedging cash flows when we feel rather uncertain about the future. They have a second use: they can be used to take leveraged, or geared, positions. These attractions have led to very rapid growth in the options markets in recent years. There are options on "cash" markets for foreign exchange, deposits, bonds, bills, equities, and commodities; there are options on swaps, and on equity indices; and there are options on a range of futures contracts.

12.1 THE ROLE OF OPTIONS

People think options are complex. This is only partly true. The basic fact about an option is that it is a one-way bet. You pay a price for the privilege of the one-way bet. Deciding on whether that price is worth it to you is very simple. It has very little to do with the market's calculation of fair value—where all the complexity lies. The golden rule is to use your common sense and assess the value to you. It is like buying a house. The vendor may tell you how much he or she spent on the plumbing and wiring, how many years they have spent redecorating. But your only decision is: either the house is worth it to you at that price or it is not.

A long time ago, Adam Smith drew this same distinction between price in the market and value to the owner: "Nothing is more useful than water: but it will purchase scarce anything; scarce anything can be had in exchange for it. A diamond, on the contrary, has scarce any value in use; but a very great quantity of other goods may frequently be had in exchange for it." It is the same with buying an option. Either the option meets your business or investment needs at a price that you think is worth it, or not. If you are buying an option, the value to you may be much more—or much less—than the market is charging. Conversely, if you are selling (or writing) an option, no matter what you think the fair value of the option is, its price will be what the market will pay for it. All those elaborate computer models mean nothing if no one wants to buy the option. Although there are some quite complicated theories of options pricing, the final decision is the same as any other financial decision: is the value of this thing, to me, more or less than the price in the market? Having said all that, we still need to know how the market values options. That is what we look at in this chapter. We start by looking at the role of options in the marketplace today.

Options serve the needs of a number of users—investors, hedgers, and speculators. For the investor, and for the hedger, the main attraction of options is that they give him or her a one-way bet. A pension fund may own shares in IBM; the option allows them to protect themselves (insure themselves) against the risk of a fall in the stock while allowing them to gain from a rise. Or take a company borrowing at six-month LIBOR. Financial markets have been volatile; the treasurer is very uncertain about the direction of the next move in rates, but the company is heavily borrowed and can ill afford a sharp rise in rates. By buying an interest rate cap (a type of option) the treasurer can protect the company against a rise in rates while leaving the company positioned to benefit from any possible fall.

The cost of the option needs to be factored into the calculation. Sometimes, if uncertainty in the financial markets is very widespread, the cost of the option will be excessive in relation to the company's risk. Often, however, this is not the case. Historically, it has quite often been possible to buy interest rate insurance at relatively low cost (as Chemical Bank proved in 1989 when its profit and loss figures were hit by a revaluation of its interest rate options book: they had been priced too cheaply).

For the speculator, one of the main attractions of options is that they give the speculator a great deal of gearing or leverage. One can make large percentage profits from only a small change in the price of the underlying currency. And the risk is limited to a fixed dollar amount—the price originally paid for the option. Suppose for example we have sterling trading at $2.00 and a six-month option to buy sterling at $2.20 costs us $0.025, that is 2.5 cents. Suppose sterling jumps now to $2.10. For reasons we will explain below, the option's price would not move exactly in proportion, so the option's price may rise from $0.025 to $0.035. Sterling rose by 5%: but the price of the option rose by 40%.

Options are also important because they bring an extra dimension to financial instruments. First, the development of options markets has meant it is possible to trade volatility. That is, one can take a view not on the direction of a price change, but on how volatile it will be. An example would be the "straddle" trade discussed next. The trader takes no view on the direction of the market but bets that it will be more volatile than today. Secondly, many of the new financial instruments, particularly those seen in the bond markets (see J. K. Walmsley, *The New Financial Instruments*, John Wiley, New York, 2nd edn forthcoming) have "embedded" in them a form of option: either an interest rate option, or a currency option. Thus, analysis of these instruments depends on option pricing.

12.2 THE OPTIONS MARKET

Though they have only recently taken off in volume worldwide, options have been around a long time. "Traditional" options on equities (effectively an over-the-counter

(OTC) option written by a market-maker) developed on the London stock market in the nineteenth century. But until 1973, it was possible to buy an option, but it was not really possible to trade it. Exchange-traded options were introduced in 1973 by the Chicago Board Options Exchange (CBOE). The single most important CBOE innovation was to set up standard option prices and expiry dates. This allowed development of a secondary market. That brought liquidity into options trading.

Both the options and futures industry have been experiencing a period of world-wide growth. The OTC market has grown explosively, but its growth is difficult to measure in the absence of reliable statistics. The growth of exchange-listed options has been rapid. The CBOE was followed by the American Stock Exchange, the Philadelphia Stock Exchange, the Midwest Stock Exchange, and the Pacific Stock Exchange. Until 1982, growth in the United States was held back by the struggles between the various regulatory bodies. From 1982 to 1985, the dominant feature was the explosion of new contracts in the United States as the various exchanges struggled for successful market products. This spread of futures and options abroad was first seen in 1985/86.

Early players were the European Options Exchange in Amsterdam and the London Stock Exchange, and the London International Financial Futures Exchange (LIFFE, set up in 1982, merged with the Stock Exchange's London Traded Options Market in 1990 to form the London Derivatives Exchange). In Sweden, the Options-maklarna (OM) has become an international player, setting up its operations in London and other centres also. In France, the Monep is active and the Deutsche Terminbörse has options on equities. Table 12.1 shows the major contracts world-wide.

The debate on OTC versus exchange-traded options has been ongoing. The merits of exchange trading are transparency—the last price at which the contract traded is always known—and (usually) liquidity—a traded option that we have bought can be sold again. This is not so easy for an OTC option. Proponents of OTC options point to their flexibility—an option can be tailored to suit the user's needs and in parti-cular can be written for a longer term; most exchange-traded options have a maximum maturity of one year and the vast bulk are for three or six months. Liquidity in certain options markets—notably currency and some interest rate

Table 12.1 The Top 10 Financial Options Contracts (million Contracts) 1994

S&P 100	CBOE	81.8
Eurodollar	CME	28.1
Treasury bond	CBOT	28.1
S&P500	CBOE	28.0
DAX	DTB	23.5
IBEX 35	MEFF	7.5
SMI	SOFFEX	6.6
Swedish OMX	OM	5.8
FTSE 100	LIFFE	4.7
Nikkei 225	Osaka	4.2

Source: *Futures & Options World*, February 1995.

options—is also sometimes better in the OTC market than on the exchanges. In stock market options, the reverse is generally true, at least for options on individual stocks, although a number of market-makers in London and elsewhere will write OTC options in size on equity indexes.

Another issue that arises in comparing OTC versus exchange-traded options is the legal and tax position. In many cases, the tax treatment of an option varies depending on whether or not it is traded on a recognized exchange. Likewise the legal position regarding OTC options can be tricky (as in the case in the UK where the local authority, Hammersmith and Fulham, was found not to have the legal power to write OTC option contracts).

By contrast, when dealing on an exchange, one's counterparty is the clearinghouse. For practical purposes, in normal circumstances, the question of credit risk does not arise. The Options Clearing Corporation in the United States, which is owned by its members, has substantial protection in place against possible default; in London, options contracts clear through the London Clearing House (formerly International Commodities Clearing House (ICCH)) which is owned by several major banks (Barclays, Lloyds, National Westminster, Midland, Royal Bank of Scotland, and Standard Chartered Bank), who between them represent an extremely strong credit.

Traded options on debt instruments were introduced later than on stocks. The first was in October 1982, when the CBOT introduced an options contract on Treasury bond futures. In subsequent years, they have become quite widely spread. There is an option on the Treasury note future (CBOT), an option on Eurodollar futures (IMM), options on specific Treasury bonds (CBOE) and Treasury notes (CBOE), together with options on 10-year Treasury notes (AMEX), and options on 13-week Treasury bills (AMEX). In addition, in Montreal, options on government of Canada long-term bonds are traded, while in Europe, the London Stock Exchange offers options on gilt-edged (as do LIFFE) and the European Options Exchange offers options on Dutch state loans. In addition, many banks will write OTC options on specific interest rates or securities. One of the most widely used is the area of caps and floors which is dealt with below.

The OTC market in currency options began to develop in the early 1980s, but the first listed currency options were those on the Philadelphia Stock Exchange, which were introduced in December 1982. Options are also traded on the IMM, which introduced an option on the deutsche mark in 1983, and the CBOE, which has options on deutsche marks, Swiss francs, French francs, Canadian dollars, sterling, and Japanese yen. Options have also been introduced on the London Stock Exchange on sterling and deutsche marks and on the LIFFE. In general, exchange-traded options extend up to nine months only, though the OTC market offers longer-term options. It is also possible to indirectly buy long-term currency options by buying securities with embedded currency options.

Options on futures are also widely available. An option on a futures contract differs from the more traditional options in only one essential way: the underlying security is not a spot security, but a futures contract on the security. So if an option buyer exercises the call, a long position is acquired in futures instead of a long position in the cash security. The resulting long and short futures positions are like any other future positions and are subject to daily marking to market.

Although an option on a futures contract may seem complicated, in many ways it is simpler to analyze and trade than an option on a cash instrument. This is because the impact of the cash flows of the security is already taken into account in the price of the futures contract. Hence, it need not be considered in pricing the option. Futures do not pay coupons. As a result, the highest volume of trading in debt options on the exchanges has been in options on futures contracts. These contracts include options on Treasury bond futures, options on Treasury note futures, and options on Eurodollar time deposit rate futures.

The mechanics of taking delivery are that the futures position is established at the strike price, then immediately marked to market. The difference between the strike price and the current futures price is paid to the call option holder, if the mark to market shows up a loss.

Finally we should mention warrants, a kind of sister market to the options market. A warrant is an option; the basic difference is that a warrant is usually listed on a stock exchange rather than traded on an options exchange. Also, a warrant usually has a longer life—warrants exist with maturities of 10 or 15 years. A number of banks have issued currency and interest rate warrants (see J. K. Walmsley, *New Financial Instruments*, John Wiley, New York, 2nd edn forthcoming), and there is a large market for equity warrants (particularly of Japanese stocks).

12.3   BASICS OF AN OPTION CONTRACT

An option is an agreement between two parties. One party grants the other the right to buy or sell an instrument under certain conditions. The instrument may be a stock, bond, futures contract, interest rate, or foreign currency. The counterparty pays a premium for the privilege of being able to buy or sell the instrument, without committing to do so. There are two basic types of options: puts and calls. A call option gives the buyer the right to buy or "call away" a specified amount of the underlying instrument at the specified price, during a specified period. The price at which the instrument may be bought is the exercise price or the strike price. The last date on which the option may be exercised is called the expiry date, or the maturity date. A put option gives the buyer the right to sell or put to the writer a specified amount of the underlying instrument at the strike price until the expiry date.

The period during which the option can be exercised depends on its type—American or European. Under an American option, the holder of the option has the right to exercise at any time before maturity. Under a European option, the holder may only exercise it at the time of expiration, or for a short period beforehand.

A call option is best described by a simple example. Suppose Bank A sells us a three-month European call option on the deutsche mark at a strike of DEM 2.00, in an amount of DEM 10 000 000. This means that we have the right, in three months, to pay $5 million to buy DEM 10 million. Clearly, if the deutsche mark strengthens to, say, DEM 1.90 per dollar (so that it would cost us $5 263 157 to buy DEM 10 000 000 in the market) the option will have substantial value to us. Conversely, if, at the maturity of the option, the spot rate is DEM 2.20, the option will have no value.

Let us put together some basic building blocks for analyzing options. Let us look at an option on sterling at $2.00 per £1: a call option, American style. Let us see how the option would behave on the last day of its life. When spot sterling is trading in the market at say $2.20, it would be possible to buy the option, exercise it at $2.00, and sell at $2.20. So the option will be worth at least $0.20—the difference between $2.00 and $2.20. If the option costs less, one could buy, exercise, and sell for a net profit. And it will be worth no more than $0.20—if it were worth more, anyone buying the option would take a loss (assuming we are trading in the final few minutes of the option's life). Conversely, if sterling were trading at $2.10 at this time, the option would be worth $0.10. If the pound were below $2.00, the option would be worthless—you could buy sterling cheaper directly in the market than by exercising the right to buy at $2.00.

We said that if sterling were trading at $2.10 at the maturity of the option it would be worth $0.10. This difference between the currency price and the exercise price of the call option is often called its intrinsic value. Thus, when sterling is at $2.10, the option has an intrinsic value of $0.10: at $2.30, an intrinsic value of $0.30. The only thing that affects intrinsic value is the gap between price of the underlying instrument (in this case sterling) and the strike price. Any excess premium over the intrinsic value of the option is called the time value, which is discussed more fully below.

If the sterling is above the strike price, then the option will have intrinsic value, and is said to be "in the money." If the sterling's value equals the strike price, then the intrinsic value is zero. The option is said to be "at the money." If sterling is trading below the strike price, then the option is said to be "out of the money."

12.4 OPTION PAY-OFF DIAGRAMS

It is possible to draw a diagram showing the outcomes for different exchange rates at maturity—an option payoff diagram. Table 12.2 and Figure 12.1 show the results. This is the basic payoff profile of a call option, to which we will often return. At this stage, the key point to note is that there is unlimited profit potential as the pound rises, and limited loss as it falls. (There will be a loss, not shown in the table: the loss is the amount of premium spent in buying an option which turned out to be worthless at expiry.)

Table 12.2 Call Option Payoff Profile—Strike $2.00

Market Rate at Maturity	Intrinsic Value of the Option
$2.40	0.40
2.30	0.30
2.20	0.20
2.10	0.10
2.00	0
1.90	0
1.80	0
1.70	0
1.60	0

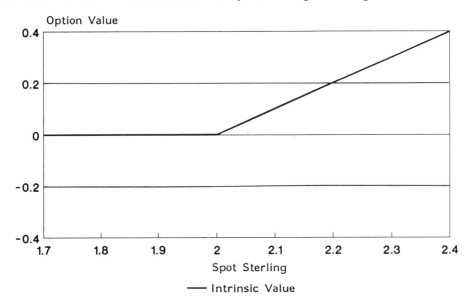

Figure 12.1 Call Option Profile

Table 12.3 Put Option Payoff Profile— Strike $2.00

Market Rate	Intrinsic Value
$2.40	0
2.30	0
2.20	0
2.10	0
2.00	0
1.90	0.10
1.80	0.20
1.70	0.30
1.60	0.40

We can do the same exercise for a put on the pound at $2.00, (see Table 12.3). Again, we can draw the profile of the put in the last few minutes of its life (Figure 12.2). There is unlimited profit potential, this time as sterling falls, and limited risk of loss—the maximum loss will be the premium paid out.

Let us look at the position that would arise if instead of buying a call we had sold, or written, a call. When we bought a call, we had the right but not the obligation, to buy sterling at $2.00. But now we have sold the call. We have the obligation, but not the right, to sell the pound at $2.00. If sterling rises above $2.00, we must sell it to the party who bought the option, instead of selling in the marketplace. So we will make a loss. The loss is unlimited: for example, if sterling rises to $3.00 our loss will be $1.00 per pound. If sterling, at the expiry of the option, closes below $2.00, we will make a profit. Our profit will be the premium we charged for selling the option. Our profit is limited to the premium. So the writer of a call has unlimited risk, with a limited profit potential. We can see this in the diagram (Figure 12.3). The same applies if we were to write a put (Figure 12.4). Why would anyone be crazy enough to write options, then? Well, writing an open (or "naked") options position can be

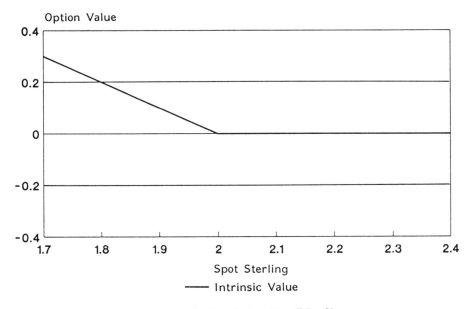

Figure 12.2 Put Option Payoff Profile

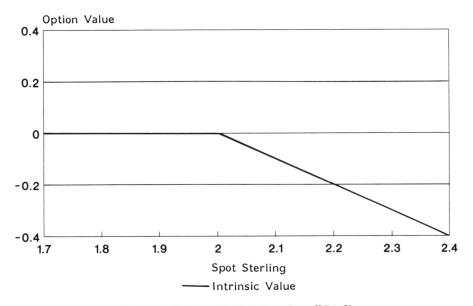

Figure 12.3 Short Call Option: Payoff Profile

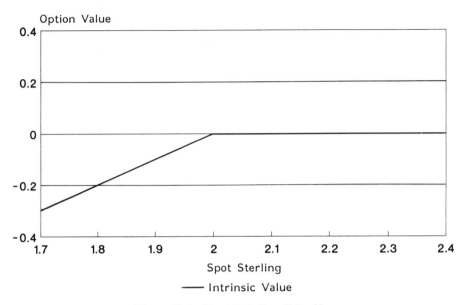

Figure 12.4 Short Put: Payoff Profile

very risky: but it can be well rewarded, in the shape of a substantial premium. After all, that is how insurance companies make money. They take risks in exchange for premium income. The option writer is in the same business, of selling insurance. Also, there are hedging techniques which can reduce the risk.

Finally, because we will be needing to combine positions later, it will be helpful if show a similar payoff diagram for the straightforward long and short positions. Figure 12.5 shows the payoff if we are long sterling at, say, $2.00—our profit rises as sterling rises, as sterling falls we start to make a loss. Likewise we can draw the payoff from being short.

12.5 COMBINED POSITIONS

More complex options strategies can be employed. The first one we will introduce is a very important one because it shows the relationship of puts and calls to the underlying asset. If you look at the diagram for being long an asset, you will see a line sloping up from left to right. If you look at the diagram for being long a call, you will see a line sloping up from left to right in the top right corner of the diagram. If you look at the diagram for being short on a put, you will see a diagram sloping up from left to right again, but this time in the bottom left corner. This suggests that being short a put, and long a call at the same strike, will produce the same payoff profile as being long the asset. This is in fact right: it will always be true that, for any given strike level for a put and call, we can write

$$+ \text{ asset } = + \text{ call} - \text{put}$$

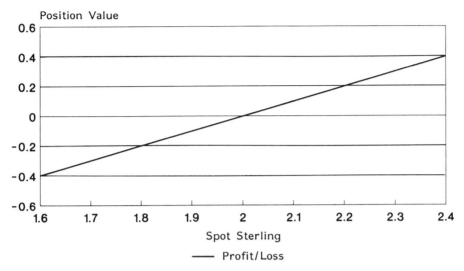

Figure 12.5   Long Asset Position Payoff Profile

where + means we are long, – means we are short. Thus being long of a call and short a put on a given asset is equivalent in profit terms to being long of the asset. Conversely, to be short the asset is the same as being long a put and short the call. More formally, we could write C for the price of the call, P for the price of the put, A for the price of the asset and S for the strike price:

$$A - S = C - P$$

That is, the intrinsic value of the option (the difference between asset price and the strike of the option) will be equal to the difference between the price of the call and the price of the put. This is known in the jargon as "put–call parity."

Note that the above statement of put–call parity is strictly true only for American options—those allowing exercise at any time. If the two options involved were European options allowing only for exercise at maturity, we would have to allow for the time value of money:

$$\text{PV}(A - S) = C - P$$

where PV means the present value. Also, we can rearrange the original equation. We could write, for example, + asset + put = + call or + asset – call = –put. So if we owned the asset and a put on the asset, it would be the same as owning a call on the asset; if we owned the asset and had sold a call on it, it would be the same as being short a put on the asset. This put–call parity is often useful when we want to construct a synthetic position—either to create a put, for example, if we cannot buy a put directly in the market, or even to create the asset from the put and the call—a synthetic asset.

The next two basic combinations of option positions are the straddle and the strangle. The straddle is when we buy a put and a call at the same strike price. Although we pay out two lots of premium, we will make money if the market

Table 12.4 Option Straddle

Market Rate	Put Option Strike $2.00 Put Intrinsic Value	Call Option Strike $2.00 Call Intrinsic Value	Combined Intrinsic Value
$1.60	0.4	0	0.4
1.70	0.3	0	0.3
1.80	0.2	0	0.2
1.90	0.1	0	0.1
2.00	0.0	0	0
2.10	0	0.1	0.1
2.20	0	0.2	0.2
2.30	0	0.3	0.3
2.40	0	0.4	0.4

Table 12.5 Option Strangle

Market Rate	Strike $2.00 Put Intrinsic Value	Strike $2.10 Call Intrinsic Value	Combined Intrinsic Value
$1.60	0.4	0	0.4
1.70	0.3	0	0.3
1.80	0.2	0	0.2
1.90	0.1	0	0.1
2.00	0.0	0	0
2.10	0	0	0
2.20	0	0.1	0.1
2.30	0	0.2	0.2
2.40	0	0.3	0.3

becomes volatile. Either the put or the call will pay off. We lose out if the market stays stable. Let us combine the put and call on sterling at $2.00 that we looked at. We would get the payoff pattern as shown in Table 12.4.

The strangle is a similar strategy, but the put and call have different exercise prices. Normally one or both of the options bought are out of the money, so that the cost of the strangle is less than the straddle. The price paid is that the strangle needs a larger market move to pay off than the straddle. Suppose we do the same as before but with a call strike price of $2.10 (Table 12.5).

12.6 OPTION VALUATION

We come now to the theory of how to value options. Once again, it should be stressed that this is a black art. It is not a science. A classic example of this came when the large American bank, Bankers Trust, was forced by the Federal Reserve to take an $80 million charge to earnings because the Fed felt that Bankers Trust had not properly valued their option book. As we shall see, there will always be room for doubt about the value of an individual option. This is because its value depends on an estimate of the future volatility of the underlying instrument.

The first, and most important, model used in options pricing was that developed by Fisher Black and Myron Scholes in 1973. We will discuss some of the variants to this model below. The Black-Scholes model made several critical assumptions:

1. Prices may change rapidly but cannot "jump." One can trade continuously in the market.
2. There is a risk-free rate of interest for borrowing and lending from the current period until the expiration of the option.
3. Transactions costs and taxes are ignored.
4. The continuously compounded rate of return of the asset has a normal distribution—that is, the asset price is log-normally distributed.

Given these assumptions, Black and Scholes showed that the price of the option would be determined by:

1. The current price of the underlying instrument.
2. The exercise price of the option.
3. The remaining life of the option.
4. The level of interest rates.
5. The projected volatility of the underlying instrument.

Of these, all but (5) are known at the time the option is priced: thus volatility is the key to options pricing.

In looking at the option's value, the first two factors are primary. This is clear if we look at the option on the day that it expires. On that day, only the currency price and the striking price of the option determine the option's value. The other factors have no bearing. Look at our earlier example of a $2.00 call on sterling. We said that if sterling were trading at $2.10 at the maturity of the option it would be worth $0.10. When sterling is at $2.10, the option has an intrinsic value of $0.10: at $2.30, an intrinsic value of $0.30. The only thing that affects intrinsic value is the gap between price of the underlying instrument (in this case sterling) and the strike price.

But in the period before the expiry of the option, there is another element in its price, in addition to its intrinsic value. This is referred to as the time value premium. In general, the time value premium is found by the following formula for an in-the-money call option on an asset (sterling in our example above):

Call time value premium = Call option price + Strike price − Asset price

For example, sterling is trading at $2.05, and the sterling October $2.00 call is priced at $0.08. The in-the-money amount (the intrinsic value) is 5 cents ($2.05 − $2.00) and so the time value (price less intrinsic value) is 3 (8−5).

The intrinsic value of the option is easy to calculate. The "fair value" of the time value premium is not so simple. It depends only partly on the time to maturity. It also depends on the volatility of the underlying asset and on interest rates. It will vary, too, according to how far in- or out-of-the-money the call option is.

If the call is out of the money, then the premium and the time value premium are the same. Let us say sterling is at $2.05 and a sterling October $2.10 call sells at $0.04. The call has no intrinsic value by itself when the currency (at $2.05) is below the striking price ($2.10). So both the premium and the time value premium of the call are 4 points.

The option's time value premium decays much more rapidly in the last few weeks of its life than it does in the first few weeks. In fact, for reasons we will see later, the rate of decay is related to the square root of the time remaining. To illustrate this we can draw a graph of the effect of time on an option's premium. The chart (Figure 12.6) shows the effect of holding everything else constant. As the option comes closer to expiry, it loses value more and more quickly.

Another important point about time value is that it is always greatest for an option which is at-the-money. If the option is deep in or out of the money its time value is very low. We can see why this is if we think of the deal from the point of view of the option writer. Suppose we are quoting to write an option to sell sterling at $2.10. Once the option is written, then as we get closer to expiry, if sterling is near $2.10, we will need to be thinking about buying some sterling. We need to buy to cover our commitment to deliver sterling at $2.10. Now suppose there are 30 days to go on this option and sterling is now at $1.80. Then the risk of our having to deliver on this option is quite small—sterling is not very likely to rise 30 cents in 30 days. Equally, as one day passes and there are now 29 days to run, our risk will decline, but not by very much, since the risk was already small. So the fall in the premium we will charge will not be large. The effect of time value on the premium is small in these circumstances.

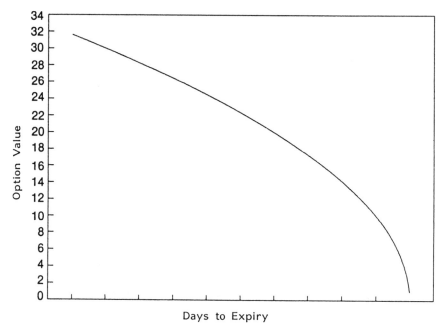

Figure 12.6 Option Value over Time

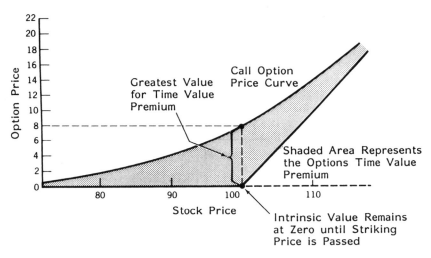

Figure 12.7 Time Value out-, at- and in-the-money

Conversely, suppose we are quoting the same option and sterling is trading today at $2.40. The option is virtually certain to be exercised. We will buy sterling now to cover our position since we will almost certainly have to deliver. Again, if the maturity of the option which we are quoting were to be shortened by a day, our risk will not be much less. So the premium we charge will not fall much. Time value of a deep in-the-money option is low.

It is when the option is at the money that our uncertainty is greatest. If we are quoting a $2.10 option for sterling and sterling is trading at $2.10 then the market could go either way from now till maturity. In these circumstances, an extra day's life on the option really does have an effect on our risk. Time value is at its greatest when the option is at the money. We can illustrate this (Figure 12.7). The figure shows the value of the option premium at maturity and 30 days before maturity. The shaded area between the two lines is the time value of the option and as can be seen the gap between the two lines is at its widest when the option is at the money.

12.7 VOLATILITY

A key factor in option pricing is volatility. The more volatile an instrument, the higher the associated option price. Volatility is a measure of how the price of the underlying instrument varies. It is defined as the standard deviation in price returns of the instrument underlying the option.

What is the standard deviation? To find the standard deviation of a series of numbers we work as follows. Suppose we measure an overnight interest rate over two weeks, giving us 10 observations. We want to measure how variable, or volatile, the interest rate is. Suppose we observe the following interest rates, in percent: 6, 12, 11, 14, 7, 9, 11, 3, 12, 8. The first step is to work out the average or mean interest rate over the period: this is 9.30%. Then we measure how much each rate varies from the mean. We want to average that variation, allowing for negative variations as well as positive. The easiest way to do this is to calculate the differences: 14 − 9.30—and square them. Thus in this case we have −4.7^2 = 22.09. This makes sure we have positive numbers. We add up the squared totals and average them (strictly speaking we divide by $n-1$, where n is the number of observations). The result is called the variance. In this case, it is 11.12 (working to two decimal places). But because the variance is the result of squaring the percentage rates it is more meaningful to take the square root, which in this case is 3.33. The square root of the variance is called the standard deviation. We have a series of interest rates with an average, or mean, of 9.30% and a standard deviation of 3.33%. The standard deviation gives us a measure of how likely the interest rate is to stray away from its mean. Of course, this is a historical number: next month's standard deviation could be quite different. Volatility itself can be volatile.

Measuring the volatility of an instrument in terms of its standard deviation gives us an idea of its likely trading range, all other things being equal. For example, if a currency priced at $1.00 has an annualized volatility of 20%, then the most likely range of prices (i.e. within one standard deviation) by the end of the year is $0.85 and $1.20 ($1.00 divided by 1.2 and multiplied by 1.2, respectively). To be precise, the definition of annual historic volatility normally used in the options markets is

$$\text{Volatility} = \sqrt{\text{Variance } [\log (P_t/P_{t-1})] \times 250}$$

where $t = 1 \ldots n$; n is the number of trading days over which volatility is measured (we assume 250 trading days p.a.).

Let us take a call option on sterling with a strike price of $2.10, when the currency is at $2.00. If the expected volatility of sterling is 20%, there is a greater chance that the price will be above $2.10 at the expiry of the option than if expected volatility is only 10%. The fact that there is a higher probability of large price falls is of no concern to the holder of a call option because loss is limited to the premium paid. So the holder will be prepared to pay more for an option on a currency which has an expected volatility of 20%, than for an option on a currency with an expected volatility of 10%. Equally, the writer of the call option faces a greater risk on the more volatile currency, and therefore will charge a higher premium to write it.

Estimating the future volatility of the underlying instrument is perhaps the hardest task in pricing an option. It is the only variable affecting the option premium that is not directly observable in the market when the option is priced. All we know at that point is what its volatility has been in the past. Conversely, once the option is priced (for example, an exchange-trade option where we can see the price at which the option last traded) we can work out what volatility is implied in the price, assuming we know the options pricing formula that was used.

12.8 THE BINOMIAL MODEL

Different writers of options in the market will price their options differently because they have differing views on future volatility. It is this that makes option pricing a bit of a black art. To add to the confusion, there are a number of different options pricing models. The most widely known is that of Black and Scholes. The Black model is a variant of Black–Scholes suitable for options on futures. Other popular models are the Garman–Kohlhagen modification of Black–Scholes (widely used for currency options) and the Cox–Ross–Rubinstein model, or binomial model, which overcomes the problems the Black–Scholes model has in handling dividend payments on underlying equities. The binomial and Black Scholes models converge when trading is assumed to be continuous. In practice, bigger errors are likely to result from wrong forecasts of volatility than minor variations in the underlying theoretical models. Of the models mentioned, the binomial is one of the most commonly used. It is also rather easier to explain intuitively, so we will start with it before moving on to the Black–Scholes model.

Let us start with an American call on sterling at $2.00. Spot sterling today is trading at $2.05. We shall call the exercise price of $2.00 E, and the spot price S. Then $S - E$ = $0.05. That is, if we buy the option and exercise today, the option will pay us 5 cents. So the call will be worth at least $0.05 and probably more if there is any time to expiry. If we write the value of the call as C we know we must have $C \geqslant S - E$. Also, since we know we can choose to walk away from the option, its value can never be negative: we can never be harmed by owning it. So we know the value of a call will always be $C \geqslant 0$. In fact, we can write $C \geqslant$ [Maximum of 0, $S - E$].

Can we make this more exact? One way to proceed is to start with the concept of a riskless hedge: a hedge that eliminates all risk. The assumptions behind most riskless hedge valuation models are as follows:

1. Prices may change rapidly but cannot "jump."
2. There is a risk-free rate of interest for borrowing and lending from the current period until the expiration of the option.
3. Transactions costs and taxes are ignored.

What we will do is set out a "binomial tree" showing the possible outcomes of the movement in sterling over time. At any point, sterling can move up or down. At each point along the branches of the tree we will work out the fair price of an option on sterling, working back from the future to today. The approach was initiated by William Sharpe and developed further by Cox, Ross, and Rubinstein.

We assume a starting price for sterling of $2.00. Then we assume the price of sterling in each period can rise or fall by $0.01: it is equally likely to rise or fall. A three-period example is shown in Figure 12.8. At the start of the first period, we want to value a European call option. It has a strike of $1.99. It expires after two periods, i.e. at the start of the third period. How do we set about this? To start with, we know the value of the option at expiry. On expiry, sterling can be either $1.98, $2.00, or $2.02. And the option will be worth $0.03 if sterling's price is $2.02, $0.01 if it is $2.00, and nothing if it is $1.98. Next, to get back from period 3 to period 2, we use the riskless hedge.

Let us assume sterling's price is $2.01 at the start of period 2. We want to find the option price. We do this by imagining a portfolio. It is long one pound sterling, and short one call option on sterling with a strike of $1.99. At the start of the next period (period 3), the price of sterling could rise from $2.01 to $2.02 or fall to $2.00. The option writer must deliver sterling at the strike price of $1.99. So, at $2.02, he will lose $0.03. Likewise, if sterling falls to $2.00, he will lose $0.01.

Period   Period   Period

1   2   3

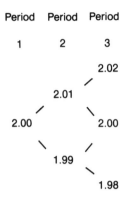

Figure 12.8   Sterling Binomial Tree

So at the start of period 3, whether the price moves up or down, the value of the portfolio will be \$1.99 (\$2.02 − \$0.03 or \$2.00 − \$0.01). So there is no risk in this portfolio. It can earn no more than the risk-free rate. (If it did, arbitragers would borrow to invest in it and would drive down the return.) Likewise, it cannot earn less (there would be arbitrage in the opposite direction). So the rate of return on the risk-free portfolio must equal the risk-free rate. Let us assume that the risk-free rate is 0.02% per period. (If our periods were days, that would compound up to about 7.5% on a 360-day year.) Then the return on the portfolio will also be 0.02% per period.

We can now find a price for the option at the start of the second period, given the sterling price of \$2.01 we assumed above. We know the portfolio earns the risk-free rate. And we know it ends up worth \$1.99. So the starting value, or cost, of the portfolio must be \$1.99 discounted back over one period. That is, \$1.99/1.0002 or \$1.9896. But we also know that the cost of buying the portfolio is \$2.01 (the price of the underlying sterling) less any premium earned on the option written. Therefore, the option must earn \$2.01 − \$1.9896 = \$0.0204. If it did not, the portfolio would not be worth exactly \$1.9801. Any other option cost would mean the risk-free portfolio does not earn the risk-free rate. So, if the price of sterling at the start of period 2 is \$2.01, then the value of the option must be \$0.0204.

We can now use the same method to solve for a different price. What is the option price, if the price of sterling at the start of period 2 is \$1.99? In this case, we set up another portfolio. It has one pound sterling, plus, now, two short calls. We choose the number of calls to be two by asking: how many calls are needed to make the portfolio riskless (that is, the same value whatever happens to sterling's price, whether it rises from \$1.99 to \$2.00 or falls to \$1.98)? To find this, say K is the number of \$1.99 calls written. We know that if the price rises to \$2.00, we must deliver at \$1.99, and so each call will lose \$0.01. If the price falls to \$1.98, there is no loss. So we want K such that

$$\$2.00 - K \times \$.01 = \$1.98 - K \times \$0.$$

So

$$\$2.00 - \$1.98 = K \times \$.01 - K \times \$0 = K \times \$.01$$

and so $\$.02 = K \times \$0.01$. Solving for K shows that we need two short calls to make the portfolio riskless. (Before, we had $\$2.02 - K \times \$0.03 = \$2.00 - K \times \$0.01$ and so $\$0.02 = \$0.02 \times K$- and hence $K = 1$.)

Now the price at the start of period 3 can go from our assumed $\$1.99$ to either $\$2.00$ or $\$1.98$. At $\$2.00$, the option has a $\$0.01$ loss for a total loss of $\$0.02$ on the two options. At $\$1.98$, the option expires worthless. Thus, the portfolio next period will be worth $\$1.98$, regardless of whether the price goes up to $\$2.00$ or down to $\$1.98$ ($\$2.00 - \$0.02$ or $\$1.98 - \$0$). So its initial cost must be $\$1.98/1.0002$, that is, $\$1.9796$. Sterling costs $\$1.99$. The two options, then, must earn $\$1.99 - 1.9796 = \$0.0104$, by the same reasoning as before. So, each option must be worth $\$0.0052$. We now know the option's value for the two possible prices of period 2 (Figure 12.9).

There is one last step. We must work back to today. Suppose we set up a portfolio that is long one pound sterling, and short 1.32 call options. (To find that number we use the same approach as before. We say we must have

$$\$2.01 - \$0.0204K = \$1.99 - \$0.0052K$$

so

$$\$.02 = (\$0.0204 - \$0.0052)K$$

so $K = \$.02/\$.0152 = 1.32$.) In Table 12.6, we show that if the price of sterling goes up to $\$2.01$, the value of the portfolio will be $\$1.9831$. It will still be worth that if the price of sterling falls to $\$1.99$. Therefore, the cost of the portfolio today must be $\$1.9831/1.0002$, or $\$1.9827$. But that cost must also equal $\$2.00$, the value of our holding of sterling today, minus the revenue from selling 1.32 calls. So each call must sell for $(\$2.00-1.9827)/1.32 = \$0.0131$.

We have at last worked back to answer our question. We have found the fair price for the option today if sterling is selling for $\$2.00$. Given the risk-free rate of interest and the set of possible future prices, $\$0.0131$ is the only possible answer. To solve for the fair value of longer term options, all we need is a bigger set of possible prices. Then we can use the same method to find the current fair price of the option.

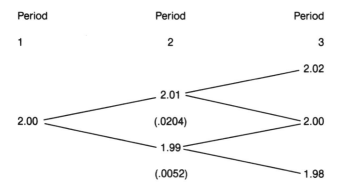

Figure 12.9 Sterling Binomial Tree: Period 2 Prices

Table 12.6 Portfolio Values (Portfolio = 1 Pound Sterling (Long) + 1.32 Calls (Short)

Case	Price of £	Short Call Position Value	Portfolio Value
Price rises to $2.01	2.01	1.32 × 0.0204	2.01 − 0.0269 = 1.9831
Price falls to $1.99	1.99	1.32 × 0.0052	$1.99 − 0.0069 = 1.9831

All this may seem far from the real world. After all, prices move all the time, not just once per period. Even worse, they can move to any one of many new values, not just two, as we have assumed. But if readers are willing to accept our basic assumptions, their objections can be overcome by suitably changing the binomial model.

Our model worked over three periods. If we divide these into infinitely short periods, we move toward continuous price changes. Now we have a very large number of observations. In these circumstances, we can generalize the model to become the Black–Scholes model. But before we do that we will look at the normal distribution.

12.9 NORMAL DISTRIBUTION

The normal distribution is well known in statistical theory: it is bell-shaped (Figure 12.10). The normal distribution is important because it is quite a realistic representation of the distribution of a number of common occurrences. The reason for this is the central limit theorem—once described as "one of the most remarkable in all mathematics." It says that no matter what the nature of the underlying distribution, provided it has a finite variance, it will approximate to the normal distribution for large samples. Since most statistical distributions that are likely to apply in the real

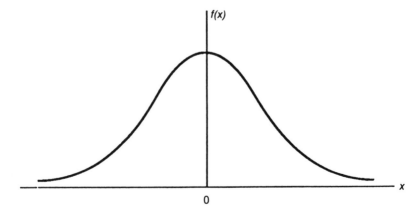

Figure 12.10 Normal Distribution

world have finite variances, that means that we can argue that for sufficiently large samples we are justified in assuming that the underlying distribution of changes in the exchange rate (or whatever else we are writing an option on) is normal. More exactly, the standardized, continuously compounded rate of return of the asset (sterling in our example) tends to approximate a normal distribution. Hence, the relative change in price (S^*/S) has a normal distribution, where S^* is the new price and S the old. (So in fact the exchange rate itself will have what is called a "log-normal" distribution: its logarithm is normally distributed.)

Suppose we write an option on a currency whose price is 100. We know the price movements of the exchange rate over the last six months. These suggest its probability distribution is quite like a normal distribution. Over the last six months the currency price's mean, or average, is 100. Its standard deviation, or variability, is 12.

How do we find the probability that the currency's price on maturity of the option is a given distance from the mean? We use the area underneath the curve between the mean and the price at maturity. How do we measure this area? The easiest way is by looking up a table for the "standardized normal" distribution. (That is, the distribution of a normal variable with mean 0 and standard deviation of 1.)

So the "standardized normal" distribution has to be applied to our currency. We do this by taking all the possible exchange rates. We subtract from them the mean of 100, and then divide the result by 12, the standard deviation. We have now "standardized" our exchange rate distribution. In mathematicians' terms, we apply the transformation (x minus mean/standard deviation). An example will illustrate this.

Let us take the probability of the exchange rate being, say, 0 to 3% higher than the original price. That is, between 100 and 103. We take $x = 100$ and $x = 103$ and write (x-mean)/standard deviation, or $(100 - 100)/12 = 0$ and $(103 - 100)/12 = 0.25$. We then find the probability that x is between 0 and 0.25 in the standard normal distribution, by looking it up in the statistical tables for the normal distribution. Here it is shown by the area under the curve marked with the letter A in Figure 12.11. The area A is roughly 10% of the total area under the distribution curve. So the chance of the price being between 100 and 103 at maturity is 10%. The cost to the option seller of this event will average $1\frac{1}{2}$% (the average difference between 100 and 103).

Suppose we repeat this for each slice of 3 percentage points above the strike price. Then we will get a whole series of probabilities for each event. And each event has a cost, half way between the percentage points, as in Table 12.7. So the total expected cost to the option seller of price movements is 4.802%. So given this cost, option sellers will then decide how uncertain they feel about this estimated cost, and if necessary add some loading to protect themselves, and then price the option accordingly. In fact, what we have done here is add up the cumulative area under the normal curve: the technical term for this is the cumulative normal density.

12.10 BLACK–SCHOLES FORMULA

We have seen, in a general way, how the binomial model works, and how it can be argued that, for large numbers of independent observations over time, the logarithm of changes in price, $\log(S^*/S)$, has a normal distribution (that is, the price has a

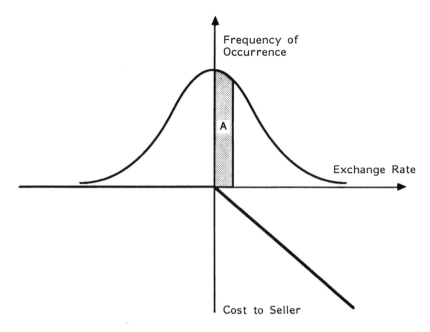

Figure 12.11   Possible Prices at Maturity-Standardized Normal Distribution

Table 12.7   Exchange Rate Charges: Normal Curve

Percentage Range above Strike Price	Average Value of Range (A)	Probability of Occurrence (the Area Under the Normal Distribution Curve) (B)	Expected Cost to Option Seller (A × B)
0–3	1.5	0.0987	0.1480
3–6	4.5	0.0928	0.4176
6–9	7.5	0.0823	0.6172
9–12	10.5	0.0675	0.7087
12–15	13.5	0.0531	0.7168
15–18	16.5	0.0388	0.6402
18–21	19.5	0.0267	0.5206
21–24	22.5	0.0173	0.3892
24–27	25.5	0.0106	0.2703
27–30	28.5	0.0060	0.1710
30–33	31.5	0.0032	0.1008
33–36	34.5	0.0016	0.0552
36–39	37.5	0.0008	0.0300
39–42	40.5	0.0004	0.0162
TOTALS		0.5	4.8018

"log-normal distribution"). The assumption of normality does agree with common sense: it says that small relative changes, either up or down, are very common, but large changes become proportionately less common. The normal distribution has a mean, μ, and variance, σ^2. If we consider the behaviour of $\log(S^*/S)$ over T periods we will find that over that time it has a mean μ and variance $\sigma^2 T$.

Now we can move on from the binomial model to the Black–Scholes model. Black–Scholes assumes that the price is log-normal, which as we have seen is usually reasonable—though not for bonds, which we discuss below—and this assumption gets us away from specifying a binomial-type path for prices. Instead we can set up a (fairly) simple formula. We can write the Black–Scholes formula like this:

$$C = N(\text{d}1)S - e^{-rT} N(\text{d}2)E$$

where $N(.)$ refers to the cumulative normal density. (We saw how to use $N(.)$ earlier when we explained the normal density.)

What this formula says is that the value of the call is equal to the expected value of what we will get from the call, minus the expected cost. We can say that $N(\text{d}1)S$ is the expected value of the asset we will acquire under the call: we will get an asset with a value of S. That asset is weighted by a probability: $N(\text{d}1)$ is the probability we will exercise. (We will see later that $N(\text{d}1)$ is also the "delta" of the option.) And $e^{-rT} N(\text{d}2)E$ is the expected cost, in present value terms, of having to exercise the option. And the call is worth the net difference between what we expect to get and what we expect to have to pay for it.

Given its assumptions, the Black–Scholes method is powerful and consistent, but the assumptions are heroic. The biggest leap of faith is when we assume the distribution of price changes is normal. As we said, this is fine, provided we have a large number of observations from a stable underlying distribution. If there is structural change going on, or if central bank intervention or monetary policies change, we do not necessarily satisfy that condition. Over the very long run, it may be true that there is a normal distribution at work: but it may be around an underlying trend. If you had been short sterling from 1948 to 1976 you would have made a ton of money because sterling went from \$4.80 to \$1.50: there was a trend in the UK's external position. The exchange rate itself did not have a stable mean, which is a precondition for a normal distribution to exist. A related point is the fat tails argument: the "tails" are the extreme left- and right-hand portions of the bell-shaped curve of the normal distribution. There is some empirical evidence to suggest that in practice these tails are "fatter" than predicted by the normal distribution. In other words, we seem to get extreme swings in rates more often than would be predicted by the normal distribution. Argument continues on this point.

The second great leap of faith is when we assume that future price behavior can be predicted from past prices. We assume the standard deviation of the stock's price movements will remain the same. In other words, that volatility will remain stable. Another problem is that we must assume the market in the underlying instrument is continuous and perfect. As traders well know, particularly in options-related markets, this is by no means the case.

There are also some specific technical problems with the Black–Scholes model: interest rate options have to be looked at separately because it will not always be true that the price of the asset is independent of the risk-free rate of interest. The model needs to be modified to handle assets deliverable in the future (for example, for options on futures contracts): this variation gives the Black model. The Black–Scholes model is not well adapted for situations where dividends or other cash flows are earned on the underlying asset: there is the possibility of early exercise (see next section). In these situations, the binomial model discussed earlier would normally be used.

12.11 MEASURES OF OPTION RISK AND SENSITIVITY

In managing an options book, dealers pay attention to a number of risk measures. The most important are referred to as delta, gamma, kappa (or vega), and theta. Other measures sometimes referred to are rho and lambda. (The phrase, "It's all Greek to me" takes on a new meaning in the world of options.)

The delta of an option is the change in the price of the option that results from a change of one dollar in the price of the underlying asset. Delta varies between 0 and 1 (or 0% and 100% depending how you want to express it). Figure 12.12 shows how delta rises from very low values when the option is out of the money to 1 when the option is deep in the money. At that point the option is certain to be exercised, has no time value, and behaves like the asset itself.

We defined delta as the change in the option price for a change in asset price. That means that delta can be defined as the slope of the tangent to the option's price curve. It measures the sensitivity of the option's price to the underlying asset. The more in the money the option is, the more sensitive its price is to that of the asset. Conversely, for a deep out-of-the-money option, even quite a large change in the

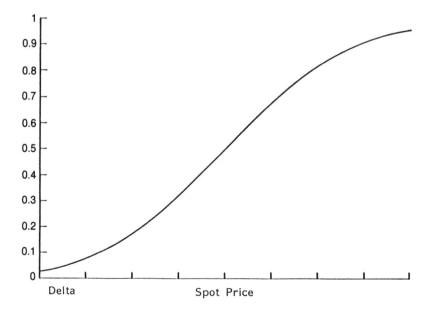

Figure 12.12 Delta Curve Rises with Spot Price

asset price will have no effect. The question is sometimes asked: why does delta change if volatility changes? The answer is: because a change in volatility changes the shape of the premium/asset price curve, hence the slope of the curve (delta) changes.

Another way of looking at delta is to say that it measures the probability that the option will be exercised. When the option is deep out of the money, there is little chance that it will be exercised, and delta is zero. When the option is deep in the money, the option is almost 100% certain to be exercised, and delta will be one. When the option is at the money, the chances are 50/50 and delta will be around 0.5. The implication of this is that delta can be used as a measure of the exposure implied by an option position. Suppose we have written a call on $100 million Euro-dollar futures at 90.5 (an implied interest rate of 9.5%). Suppose the delta of the position is currently 0.25: that is, a 25% chance the option can be exercised against us. On a probability-weighted basis, therefore, our exposure is equivalent to being short $25 million worth of Eurodollar futures at 90.5. Therefore, to hedge our position, we could buy $25 million of futures. This is the concept of delta-weighted hedging.

The next important measure of option sensitivity is gamma. This measures the sensitivity of delta to changes in the asset price. Thus gamma is a measure of the stability of delta. The higher gamma is, the more rapidly delta changes as the price of the asset changes. If we look again at Figure 12.12, we can see that delta does not change much as the asset price changes if the option is deep out of the money. Thus gamma is low. Nor does delta respond much to changes in asset price when the option is deep in the money. Again, gamma is low. Gamma is highest when the option is at the money. It is then that delta is moving most quickly. For the delta-weighted hedger, it is important to measure gamma. A high gamma means the hedge must be adjusted much more often: delta hedging a high-gamma position tends to be much more expensive. Gamma is highest when the option is at the money and when it is short-dated. It is lowest for long-dated out-of-the-money options.

Another way of looking at gamma is to say that it measures the curviness of the option premium curve. Just as the delta measures the slope of the tangent to the curve at today's price, so gamma measures the curviness of the curve at that point. (In the language of calculus, delta is the first derivative and gamma the second derivative.) You might say that delta is the speed of change, and gamma is the acceleration. Figure 12.13 shows gamma for different price levels and days to maturity. Offsets to gamma—ways of hedging our gamma exposure—would be to sell short-dated at-the-money options if we are long, and buy if we are short; we can avoid building up exposure to gamma by dealing in out-of-the-money far-dated options.

The next measure we must look at is called kappa (or vega or zeta or epsilon). This measures the impact on the option's premium of a 1% change in volatility. We said earlier that the more volatile the underlying asset, the more valuable the option on the asset will be. There will be a greater chance the option could move in our favor during its lifetime. Kappa particularly affects longer-dated options pricing.

Kappa is at its largest for at-the-money long-dated options. If an option is deep in or out of the money a change in volatility will not mean very much, whereas it could have a significant effect if the option is at the money. Likewise, kappa is more

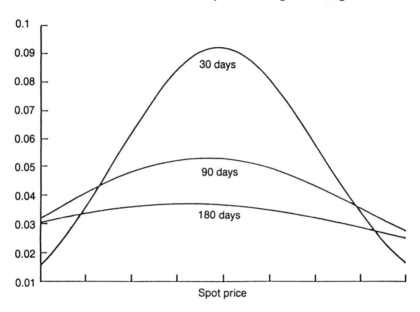

Figure 12.13   Gamma: 30, 90, 180 Days to Expiry

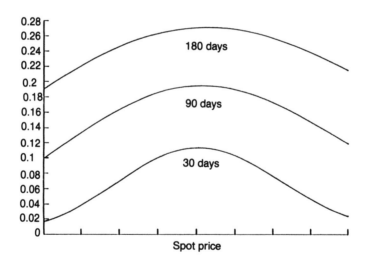

Figure 12.14   Kappa: 30, 90, 180 Days to Expiry

important for a long-dated option since the longer time allows a greater chance for the option to move in the buyer's favor. Figure 12.14 shows the effect of kappa for different asset price levels and days to maturity. Offsets to kappa are to write options if we are long of kappa, buy options if short; and if we do not want to build up kappa we should tend to deal in out-of-the-money options.

The fourth important measure of options sensitivity is theta. Theta measures the

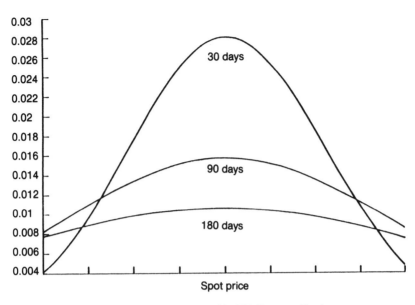

Figure 12.15 Theta: 30, 90, 180 Days to Expiry

impact of time on an option's fair value. More exactly, it measures the effect of a shortening of one day in the option's life to maturity on the option premium. We said earlier that early in an option's life the effect of time decay is not very large. It increases as the option's life shortens, and the reason for this is fairly clear. The percentage impact on the option's value of a 1-day shortening in its life is small if the option has 90 days to run, but much larger if it has only 1 day left. Also, theta has a bigger impact on at-the-money options. We saw earlier that time value for deep in/out-of-the-money options is small. Figure 12.15 shows how theta behaves for different periods to maturity and asset price levels. Figure 12.16 shows the effect of theta on an at-the-money option compared with in/out-of-the-money options.

Finally, two other measures which are sometimes used are rho and lambda. Rho measures the sensitivity of the option's price to interest rates. It can be defined as the dollar change in the option's price for a 1% change in the rate of interest. Rho can be divided into two effects. The first is the effect of interest rate changes on the price of the asset, which will be important if the option is on a bond or on a currency for forward delivery. The second reflects the fact that an option is a geared, or leveraged, instrument. The option gives the holder a claim on the asset, without having to finance its purchase. For example, I could buy an option on 1000 IBM shares, whose worth is $100,000; if the option costs me $2500, I have obtained effective control of $100,000 of assets for $2500. My alternative would have been to borrow the remaining $97,500 to finance outright purchase of the underlying shares. Lambda is the percentage change in option price for a percentage change in stock price; effectively, it is the delta restated into percentage terms. (Economists would say that lambda is the elasticity of the option price with respect to asset price.)

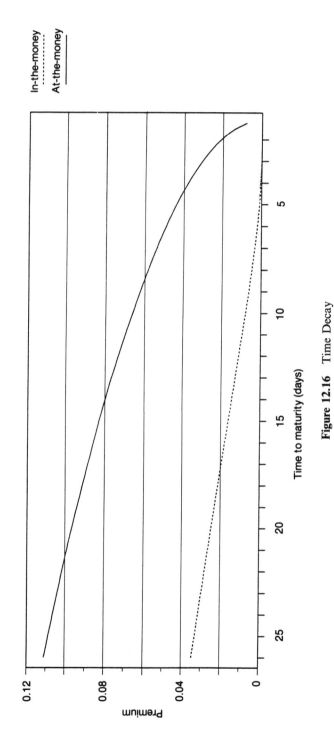

Figure 12.16 Time Decay

12.12   AMERICAN VS EUROPEAN OPTIONS

We have said that an American option is one that can be exercised at any time until maturity. A European option is one that can only be exercised at maturity. Common sense tells us that the American option must always be worth at least as much as the European: it conveys more rights and so must be worth more.

The question is how much more. The answer depends on the nature of the underlying asset. For instance, if the asset underlying the option is an equity which pays dividends, there can be circumstances in which it is optimal to exercise early. Likewise, for a currency option on a high interest rate currency—sterling—if the option is deep in the money, it may be worth exercising in order to get the high yield. This will normally only be true if the option's price does not itself reflect the value of the dividend due on the equity or the interest rate payable on the currency: that is, the market is not pricing efficiently. It can be shown that the right of early exercise is not in itself normally worth a great deal. It will almost always be better to sell an American option in the marketplace than to exercise it. The reason is that until it expires the American option will have some time value. In an efficient market, someone will always be willing to pay something for that time value. There are three exceptions to this rule: (1) for an American option on an instrument which is about to pay a cash flow: under certain conditions early exercise may be worthwhile; (2) when dealing costs in the options market are high; and (3) when the option is so deep in the money that time value is negligible.

If dealing costs in the options market are high, then it may be cheaper to exercise the option than to incur the dealing cost by selling the option. Likewise, we saw earlier that when an option is deep in the money it will have almost no time value, and in this case exercise may be the best choice. Suppose spot sterling is $1.50; we own a three-month $1.40 call worth $0.10, that is, the call has no time value. Suppose three-month forward sterling is trading at $1.45. Then we can exercise the option at $1.40, and sell in the spot market at $1.50, for a profit of $0.10. If we still need sterling, we can buy forward at $1.45. Alternatively, we can sell the option for $0.10, and buy forward at $1.45. In either case the net cost of forward sterling to us is $1.35.

12.13   CURRENCY OPTIONS

We come now to currency options. One simple point should be made at the outset: up to now it has been quite clear when we talk about an option, what it is the option is on. But now we have scope for confusion. Is a DEM/US$ call a call on the DEM and a put on the US$, or a call on the US$ and a put on the DEM? For exchange-traded options, this is not generally a real problem but when quoting OTC options it is very important for all parties to be clear precisely what is meant. Consider the following example:

1.   Buy a June 15 DEM call struck at DEM 1.50 for 2%.
2.   Buy a June 15 DEM call struck at DEM 1.50 for $0.0133.
3.   Buy a June 15 DEM call struck at $0.67 for $0.0133.
4.   Buy a June 15 US$ put struck at DEM 1.50 for DEM 0.026.

All of these are quotations for precisely the same deal. The method used in (1) or (2) might be used in the OTC market in London or New York; method (4) might be used by a Continental bank in the OTC market; method (3) is that used in the exchange-traded market. It is a question first of which is the base currency and which the quoted; second whether the currency is quoted in indirect or direct terms (that is, DEM 1.50 per dollar or $0.67 per deutsche mark); and third whether the premium is quoted as an amount of currency or, as is common in the wholesale interbank market, as a percentage.

To get around some of these problems, the British Bankers' Association (BBA) in 1985 introduced the so-called LICOM terms: This stipulates the following definitions (amongst others):

Call: An option by which the grantor grants the purchaser the right to buy the underlying currency.

Counter Currency: The currency to be exchanged for the underlying currency being (1) in respect of US$ related options, the US$ with the non-US$ currency as the underlying currency and (2) in respect of non-US$ related options, the currency stipulated at the time of quotation with the underlying currency also stipulated at the same time.

Settlement price: The exchange rate between the underlying currency and the counter currency ruling at 1500 hours London time on the exercise date, determined [by an information vendor—Telerate—who will take the eight most recent currency prices for the currency available within its system and average the middle four of these prices] as published by the information vendor for the time being designated by the BBA.

Underlying currency: The currency in which the option is granted which means (1) in respect of US$ related options, the non-US$ currency with the US$ as the counter currency and (2) in respect of non-US$ related options, the currency stipulated at the time of quotation with the counter currency also stipulated at the same time.

Note, incidentally, that the LICOM terms provide for net cash settlement for options. (That is, a cash difference is paid rather than there being a commitment to do a spot foreign exchange deal at the time of settlement. This reduces counterparty credit risk considerably.)

Options pricing for currency options follows the same basic principle as for other options pricing. But there are several differences, of which the most important arise from the fact that we now have two sets of interest rates to consider, one in each currency. We know, therefore, that the forward exchange rate will be different from the spot rate. There are two sets of effects to consider:

1. The effect of the interest differential.
2. The effect of changes in the interest differential.

Let us look first at a situation where spot sterling is trading at $2.00 and three-month forward sterling is trading at $1.95. Let us look at a three-month American call on sterling with a strike of $1.95: the option is in the money, because I can exercise at $1.95 and sell at $2.00. So the American call is worth at least its intrinsic value of $0.05. But suppose the option were a European option: I can only exercise at expiry. The value, S, of the optioned asset is not the spot price but the forward price. In other words, the American call includes the forward points; the European call does not. To allow for this, the following conventions tend to be used:

Higher interest rate currency (e.g. ITL, GBP):
  At-the-money calls struck at spot rate
  At-the-money puts struck at forward rate
Low interest rate currency (e.g. JPY, CHF):
  At-the-money calls struck at forward rate
  At-the-money puts struck at spot rate

12.14 GARMAN–KOHLHAGEN CURRENCY OPTIONS MODEL

In discussing the Black–Scholes model earlier, we glossed over an important fact: in a foreign currency option, there are two rates of interest involved, the domestic and the foreign rate of interest. In 1983, Garman and Kohlhagen modified the Black–Scholes model to handle foreign currency options by allowing for this. Using the same notation that we had before, the Garman–Kohlhagen model for a European call is

$$C = e^{-r_f T} SN(\text{d1}) - E\, e^{-r_d T} N(\text{d2})$$

where r_f is the foreign interest rate and r_d the domestic interest rate to the expiry date of the option. The first term reflects the fact that the spot rate is not the true price of the asset because we are dealing with a European call: the spot has to be converted into the equivalent of a forward rate. The definitions of the other terms are as before, except that d1 is rewritten:

$$\text{d1} = \frac{\ln(S/E) + (r_d - r_f + \sigma^2/2)T}{\sigma\sqrt{T}}$$

By comparison, the original Black–Scholes formula was:

$$C = SN(\text{d1}) - E\, e^{-rT} N(\text{d2})$$

We can if we choose rewrite the Garman–Kohlhagen formula in terms of forwards:

$$C = [FN(\text{d1}) - EN(\text{d2})]e^{-r_d T}$$

where

$$\text{d1} = \frac{\ln(F/E) + (\sigma^2/2)T}{\sigma\sqrt{T}}$$

and

$$\text{d2} = \text{d1} - \sigma\sqrt{T}$$

Using this, rather simpler notation, we can also write the formula for a European put as follows:

$$P = [F[N(\text{d1}) - 1] - E[N(\text{d2}) - 1]]e^{-r_d T}$$

An alternative approach is to modify the binomial model to allow for two rates of interest. As with the single currency binomial, in the limit the binomial model tends towards the Black-Scholes/Garman-Kohlhagen model.

12.15 CAPS AND FLOORS

The market for caps and floors is an extension of the OTC market in fixed-income options, discussed earlier. The interest rate cap sets a maximum level, or cap, on a short-term rate index. The buyer of the cap is compensated if the index goes above the strike level. Similarly, a floor provides a minimum rate on some index. The cap can be thought of as a series of single-period options. For example, a cap on three-month LIBOR for four years can be looked at as 12 options of differing maturities on LIBOR. Thus the pricing is handled by the methods outlined earlier. Once we have priced the cap or floor, there is a question of whether anyone would want to buy it. Our pricing arrives at a value that is consistent with a theoretical model. But in the real world, the borrower or investor has the alternative of borrowing or lending at a fixed rate. They will analyze the cap or floor in that context.

Before doing the analysis, we will explore the nature of caps and floors in more detail. A cap or floor contract is specified by the following:

1. *Underlying index*. Caps and floors can be created on many indices. For example, caps can be bought on one-, three-, or six-month LIBOR. Caps and floors have been set on the following indices: LIBOR, commercial paper, prime, Treasury bills, certificates of deposit, and on certain tax-exempt rates in the US market.
2. *Maturity*. This has ranged from 3 months to 12 years.
3. *Frequency*. This covers the reset dates, on which the level of rates is compared with the strike level to find what payment needs to be made—monthly, quarterly, and semiannual are most common. Similarly, frequency refers to the payment dates.
4. *Strike level*. Usually, one fixed level applies to the entire program, although the level can change over time in a predetermined way.
5. *Notional principal amount*. Like the strike level, the amount underlying the contract can be constant or it can change over time.

A typical cap agreement could have the following terms:

Underlying index: three-month LIBOR (as per Reuters LIBO screen)
Term of cap: 3 years
Rate fixing: quarterly
Strike level: 8%
Payment: quarterly, in arrears (actual/360 calculation basis)
Notional amount: $30 million
Up-front fee: 1.12% of par ($336 000)

In this agreement, the writer of the cap would pay the owner of the cap in any quarter when three-month LIBOR was over the 8% cap level on the fixing date. If LIBOR were quoted at 9% on the fixing date, the payment would be

9% over 360 × 92 × $30 million − 8% over 360 × 92 × $30 million = $76,666.67.

In this case, the writer would pay the holder of the interest rate cap $76,666.67. On the other hand, if LIBOR were at or below 8%, no payment would be made.

When considering whether to buy a cap, a corporate treasurer may well consider its cost over the life of the cap deal, given a particular interest rate outlook. Table 12.8 shows one such analysis, of a quarterly cap on three-month LIBOR. Here we have a $100 million borrowing at LIBOR repaid after three years, plus a cap with a strike rate of 8.5%, costing 1.12%, for three years, on an amount of $100 million. The alternative is fixed rate funding for three years at 8%. Our first step is to amortize the cost of the cap over the deal's life. At 8%, this amortized cap cost comes to 0.11% per quarter. That is, if we borrowed at 8% enough to pay to the cost of the cap, and repaid it quarterly, principal and interest payments on the loan would equate to 0.11% per quarter.

Suppose that for the first period, three-month LIBOR is fixed at 6%. Then our borrowing cost is $1.52 million, and there is no payment under the cap. Hence our all-in cost for the period is $1.63 million. Now suppose that LIBOR jumps to 10%, and remains there for the life of the deal. Our borrowing cost jumps to $2.53 million per quarter, and we receive a payoff from the writer of the cap of $0.38 million, making our net cost $2.15 million plus the amortized cost of the cap, or $2.26 million.

We can price the true cost of funds under this outlook as the internal rate of return of the column headed "Net Cash Flow": this comes to 8.9% on a semiannual bond basis. Therefore, we would have been better off to have fixed in the first place

Table 12.8 Sample Cap Deal Structure

Cap strike rate	8.50%	Payments p.a.	4
Cap fee	1.12%	Amortized cap cost	0.11
Fixed funding	8.00%	IRR (semi-annual bond eqvt)	8.90%
Term in years	3		

Quarter	LIBOR Rate	Liability Cash Flow	Cap Payoff	Capped Cash Flow at 8%	Cap Cost Amortized	Net Cash Flow
0		−100				−100
1	6.00%	1.520	−0	1.52	0.11	1.63
2	10.00%	2.53	−0.38	2.15	0.11	2.26
3	10.00%	2.53	−0.38	2.15	0.11	2.26
4	10.00%	2.53	−0.38	2.15	0.11	2.26
5	10.00%	2.53	−0.38	2.15	0.11	2.26
6	10.00%	2.53	−0.38	2.15	0.11	2.26
7	10.00%	2.53	−0.38	2.15	0.11	2.26
8	10.00%	2.53	−0.38	2.15	0.11	2.26
9	10.00%	2.53	−0.38	2.15	0.11	2.26
10	10.00%	2.53	−0.38	2.15	0.11	2.26
11	10.00%	2.53	−0.38	2.15	0.11	2.26
12	10.00%	102.53	−0.38	102.15	0.11	102.26

Table 12.9 Cap Break-Even Analysis

Cap strike rate	8.50%	Payments p.a.	4
Cap fee	1.12%	Amort. cap cost	0.11
Fixed funding	8.00%	IRR (s/a bond eqvt)	7.99%
Term in years	3		

Quarter	LIBOR Rate	Liability Cash Flow	Cap Payoff	Capped Cash Flow at 8%	Cap Cost Amortized	Net Cash Flow
0		−100		−100		
1	6.00%	1.52	0	1.52	0.11	1.63
2	6.00%	1.52	0.00	1.52	0.11	1.63
3	6.00%	1.52	0.00	1.52	0.11	1.63
4	6.00%	1.52	0.00	1.52	0.11	1.63
5	6.00%	1.52	0.00	1.52	0.11	1.63
6	10.00%	2.53	−0.38	2.15	0.11	2.26
7	10.00%	2.53	−0.38	2.15	0.11	2.26
8	10.00%	2.53	−0.38	2.15	0.11	2.26
9	10.00%	2.53	−0.38	2.15	0.11	2.26
10	10.00%	2.53	−0.38	2.15	0.11	2.26
11	10.00%	2.53	−0.38	2.15	0.11	2.26
12	10.00%	102.53	−0.38	102.15	0.11	102.26

at 8% than to pay the cap premium, because rates did not remain low for long enough to allow us to pay off the cost of the cap.

Table 12.9 shows that in this situation, LIBOR would have to remain at 6% for five quarters, 15 months, for the cap to be a better alternative. Table 12.10 highlights a point that may not be immediately obvious: as far as the borrower is concerned, it does not matter how high rates go, once they go through the cap strike level. If, instead of going to 10%, they go to only 8.75%, his smaller payoff is balanced by a smaller borrowing cost, so that the IRR of the entire deal is still 7.99%. All that matters is that LIBOR should go through the strike level; after that, it does not matter how high rates go. This is due to the cap being an option, and thus a one-way bet. The converse is true for the writer of the cap.

Another way of looking at the break-even is to ask the question: given that the LIBOR for the first period is fixed at 6%, what rate can be reached in period 2 and remain thereafter, so that we break even. As Table 12.11 shows, the answer is 7.49%. If rates go above 7.49%, and remain there, then we would have been better off taking fixed rate funding. A quick and dirty approximation to this break-even rate can be found by taking the annual cap cost (0.44%) and deducting it from the fixed funding rate of 8%. The resulting figure is 7.56%, not far from the true rate.

By the same token, one might ask what the break-even rate would be for the writer of a cap. Given the same initial rate as in Table 12.11, Table 12.12 shows that thereafter the rate must rise to 8.96% for the writer of the cap to break even. In this context, cap earnings are defined as the initial cap fee of 1.12%, less the net present value—at the fixed funding rate of 8%—of the stream of cap payoffs of 0.12 per period.

Table 12.10 Cap Analysis: Small Rise in LIBOR

Cap strike rate	8.50%	Payments p.a.	4
Cap fee	1.12%	Amort. cap cost	0.11
Fixed funding	8.00%	IRR (s/a bond eqvt)	7.99%
Term in years	3		

Quarter	LIBOR Rate	Liability Cash Flow	Cap Payoff	Capped Cash Flow at 8%	Cap Cost Amortized	Net Cash Flow
0		−100		−100		
1	6.00%	1.52	0	1.52	0.11	1.63
2	6.00%	1.52	0.00	1.52	0.11	1.63
3	6.00%	1.52	0.00	1.52	0.11	1.63
4	6.00%	1.52	0.00	1.52	0.11	1.63
5	6.00%	1.52	0.00	1.52	0.11	1.63
6	8.75%	2.22	−0.06	2.15	0.11	2.26
7	8.75%	2.22	−0.06	2.15	0.11	2.26
8	8.75%	2.22	−0.06	2.15	0.11	2.26
9	8.75%	2.22	−0.06	2.15	0.11	2.26
10	8.75%	2.22	−0.06	2.15	0.11	2.26
11	8.75%	2.22	−0.06	2.15	0.11	2.26
12	8.75%	102.22	−0.06	102.15	0.11	102.26

Table 12.11 Cap Analysis: Break-Even Rate

Cap strike rate	8.50%	Payments p.a.	4
Cap fee	1.12%	Amort. cap cost	0.11
Fixed funding	8.00%	IRR (s/a bond eqvt)	8.00%
Term in years	3		

Quarter	LIBOR Rate	Liability Cash Flow	Cap Payoff	Capped Cash Flow at 8%	Cap Cost Amortized	Net Cash Flow
0		−100		−100		
1	6.50%	1.65	0	1.52	0.11	1.63
2	7.49%	1.90	0.00	1.52	0.11	1.63
3	7.49%	1.90	0.00	1.52	0.11	1.63
4	7.49%	1.90	0.00	1.52	0.11	1.63
5	7.49%	1.90	0.00	1.52	0.11	1.63
6	7.49%	1.90	−0.06	2.15	0.11	2.26
7	7.49%	1.90	−0.06	2.15	0.11	2.26
8	7.49%	1.90	−0.06	2.15	0.11	2.26
9	7.49%	1.90	−0.06	2.15	0.11	2.26
10	7.49%	1.90	−0.06	2.15	0.11	2.26
11	7.49%	1.90	−0.06	2.15	0.11	2.26
12	7.49%	101.90	−0.06	102.15	0.11	102.26

Table 12.12 Cap Analysis: Break-Even for Writer

Cap strike rate	8.50%	Payments p.a.	4
Cap fee	1.12%	Amort. cap cost	0.11
Fixed funding	8.00%	IRR (s/a bond eqvt)	8.95%
Term in years	3	Net cap earnings	.00%

Quarter	LIBOR Rate	Liability Cash Flow	Cap Payoff	Capped Cash Flow at 8%	Cap Cost Amortized	Net Cash Flow
0		−100		−100		
1	6.50%	1.65	0	1.65	0.11	1.76
2	8.96%	2.27	0.12	2.15	0.11	2.26
3	8.96%	2.27	0.12	2.15	0.11	2.26
4	8.96%	2.27	0.12	2.15	0.11	2.26
5	8.96%	2.27	0.12	2.15	0.11	2.26
6	8.96%	2.27	0.12	2.15	0.11	2.26
7	8.96%	2.27	0.12	2.15	0.11	2.26
8	8.96%	2.27	0.12	2.15	0.11	2.26
9	8.96%	2.27	0.12	2.15	0.11	2.26
10	8.96%	2.27	0.12	2.15	0.11	2.26
11	8.96%	2.27	0.12	2.15	0.11	2.26
12	8.96%	102.27	0.12	102.15	0.11	102.26

Looking at it another way, the writer of the cap must pay away 0.12 per period, which is more or less offset by the amortized cap earnings of 0.11 per period. We can also look at the borrower's break-even cost in this way. Here the break-even rate against which we are comparing is not the cap strike rate of 8.5%, but the alternative rate for the borrower, the fixed funding rate of 8%.

Our first step is to express this as a quarterly rate, to make it comparable with the amortized cost of the cap of 0.11 per period; 8% semiannually equates to 8.16 p.a., which equates to 1.98% per period. From this we deduct the 0.11% per period cost of the cap amortized, plus one basis point to allow for the fact that the initial 0.11% was essentially thrown away, to arrive at a net rate per period of 1.86%. This compounds up to 7.65% p.a., or 7.51% semiannually, about the same as our break-even calculation.

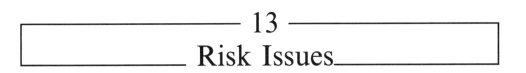

13

Risk Issues

13.1 GENERAL CONTROL OF RISK

All foreign exchange and money market activity, in one way or another, is about taking risk to earn a return. But, as the collapse of Barings in February 1995 proved yet again, uncontrolled risk can be disastrous. There are many possible ways to classify risk. One way is to split risk into name, liquidity, credit, control, and market. Market risk can be subdivided into forced sale risk, interest risk, exchange risk, basis risk, volatility risk, and risk of change in shape of the yield curve.

An important general point needs to be made at the start. Traditional risk controls consisted largely of fixed limits. For example, a forward exchange dealer might be told "You must not have an exposure greater than $15 m. in the one-year maturity and $10 million in the two-year maturity." The introduction of the BIS controls, (see below) means that, increasingly, exposures are being "marked to market" as part of the risk control process. A second general trend is that firms are harnessing the power of the computer to provide a sensitivity analysis of positions: "What if rates move by 5%?" At the extreme, some banks are using Monte Carlo simulation techniques to generate literally millions of "what-if" scenarios. In any event, the trend is towards measuring "value at risk" under some specified assumptions such as "95% confidence intervals" (see below).

But before getting into the details, we start by pointing out that a very large part of risk control has nothing to do with systems or procedures but with basic common sense. This means looking through the procedures to think about the real world, and recognizing that that world has imperfections.

Sophisticated tools are useless unless the basics are right. The golden rule is that rigid rules are no substitute for a good relationship with the dealing and backup teams. But there are obvious basics, such as separation between the dealing room and the back office. This should prevent unauthorized dealing from being concealed by inadequate back office procedures. Independent, random checks on trading activity can also serve a useful function. It was, indeed, failure to observe this elementary procedure which brought Barings to its knees.

13.2 NAME RISK

Because so many things can go wrong, outsiders when they assess another institution think first in a general way about that institution's standing and reputation: the "quality of the name." Risk to the firm's name is the most important, though the most nebulous, risk. Any institution that hopes to do business must have a good reputation. Once that is lost, confidence of counterparties will no longer be available, and it will find it impossible to deal in the markets.

We can break down the risk further: moral hazard, and over-exposure. If an institution's employees engage in criminal or immoral activities, the reputation of the institution will be at risk. An isolated instance of such conduct, however, can be a great deal less damaging than the other type of main risk, namely over-exposure in the market. If an institution is thought to be over trading, counterparties will become much more careful about the degree of credit they are willing to grant it. Thus, most banks and other companies active in financial markets will normally have controls on the extent of trading activity that are expressed not merely in terms of position risk but also of total transaction volume or "name in the market."

In the foreign exchange market, for example, a limit on the total foreign exchange book is normally set. It is necessary to have some control on the volume of activity to prevent over trading and to keep total exposure under reasonable control. Normally the aggregate book would be defined as all outstanding foreign currency contracts (purchases plus sales, spots plus forwards) with customers, banks, branches, and subsidiaries. Interest arbitrage spot and forward contracts with counterparties should be included, but if interest arbitrage transactions are generated internally within a dealing room (say, between subsections of the room), these ought to be excluded. They do not put the bank at risk in the outside world. A similar limit would apply to the total outstanding volume of the Eurocurrency and domestic currency book. At the same time, these limits cannot be too small: a bank will need a certain reputation in the market place. If the firm has not dealt in the market for the last seven years, it cannot expect an instant response from the market when it telephones for a price.

13.3 LIQUIDITY RISK

Liquidity risk flows from the basic fact that any business may be profitable, but can still go bankrupt because it does not have enough cash on hand to pay its immediate bills. Most banks which collapse do so because of liquidity problems, rather than solvency problems. The collapse of Continental Illinois in 1984, for example, followed revelations of severe losses on its energy lending portfolio. But that in itself was not enough to push the bank into difficulties. What really caused the problems was that news about the losses caused counterparty banks in the Eurodollar market (Continental's prime funding source) to cut back on their interbank lines of credit. It was the drying up of liquidity, rather than the solvency problem, which caused Continental to get into difficulties. The two are often related: but an instructive comparison can be made with Bank of America, which also experienced heavy losses during the 1980s. Unlike Continental, it also had a very large retail deposit base which was much more stable than the international wholesale market on which Continental depended for its funding. Thus, it remained liquid throughout its crisis, and was able to survive.

Banks will normally control liquidity risk by monitoring their "funding ladders" which track the maturity of liabilities against maturity of assets. Corporate treasurers similarly seek to ensure that they have at a minimum sufficient committed lines of credit from their banks for sufficient maturity to overcome any short-term funding pressures.

13.4 CREDIT RISK

Credit risk is an obvious and fundamental risk for any bank. Lending will mostly be controlled by a set of counterparty limits fixed in relation to the counterparty's perceived credit worthiness. But other activities—notably forward commitments such as forward foreign exchange, forward rate agreements and swaps—also imply credit exposure. There is a need to assess the overall picture.

Extensive discussions in this area led up to the issue in December 1987 of a proposal by the Basle Committee of Central Banks representing the first initiative aimed at regulating bank capital adequacy on a global basis. The BIS proposal is focused primarily on credit risk. It laid down a two-tiered capital standard measured against risk-weighted assets. The risk weightings were defined in terms of credit risk equivalent.

The agreement was left to be implemented by national authorities. In the United States, the Federal Reserve in cooperation with the Controller of the Currency and the Federal Deposit Insurance Corporation developed capital adequacy guidelines, and similar guidelines were implemented by the Bank of Japan. The European Community in December 1989 published a solvency ratio directive, laying down general principles which are then implemented by the national central banks. There are differences between the implementations in detail, for example, the treatment of holdings of subordinated debt in Japan and the United States is less restrictive than that applied by the Bank of England, and the Japanese definition of Tier Two includes elements of unrealized gains on equity holdings. The broad outlines of the principles are consistent.

There is a fundamental point to be made: Strong ratios need not mean strong banks. The collapse of the British bank, Johnson Matthey, was a case in point. The bank, to quote the British Bankers Association: "like many of the fringe banks before it, boasted ample capital ratios and would have passed the statistical test of most prescriptive systems with flying colours. Its problems stemmed from loan concentration, poor loan quality and gravely inadequate management systems." The US thrift industry provides a raft of similar examples.

In the foreign exchange and money market area, a number of subsidiary questions arise in that the credit risk on some of these instruments is not always clear. Credit risks in foreign exchange occur in two areas. The first type of risk is on outstanding forward contracts. Suppose a customer went bankrupt after doing a forward sale of deutsche marks to a bank. The bank would have to buy forward deutsche marks to replace those it would have been receiving from the customer. It is at risk because the rates might have moved against it. The risk is marginal rather than total. The amount at risk is determined by the possible exchange rate movement. This type of risk is controlled by an aggregate limit on outstanding forwards. The second area of risk is often called the settlement risk, or credit risk. It is best seen in the failure of Herstatt Bank, referred to earlier. Banks which had delivered DEM to Herstatt against US$ found that they did not receive the US$ although they had paid for DMK to Herstatt. So banks will normally set a limit on the total value they will allow for settlement on any one day. A refinement would be to include in this amount a part of outstanding forwards, say over one year.

The trend in the market-place today is to move beyond setting a fixed cash limit exposure, and towards recognizing that on any given day the exposure will vary in line with market conditions. This trend has been explicitly recognized by the Basle Committee risk weightings (see below), which require a deal with a customer to be "marked to market" on a regular basis and an allowance made for future exposure. Capital weightings are then applied to the resulting exposure.

A typical example might be that Bank A will set a limit for Company X in the following terms: maximum settlement risk, $20 million; maximum exposure up to 1 year, $10 million; maximum aggregate exposure on "Basle formula basis" $40 million.

As well as these limits, a bank will set credit limits on the money market side. First, there will be limits on its total lendings to any single counterparty. These will be set just like any other lending limit. A refinement would be to set sub-limits, smaller in size, for medium-term lending. A less obvious credit risk is incurred when taking deposits. First, when accepting an overnight deposit in a currency in a distant centre (for example, a London bank taking overnight Eurodollars), a bank can find itself repaying the deposit before it is sent the initial confirmation that the deposit was made. It may be repaying a nonexistent deposit. Second, a bank which takes a very large amount of deposits from a single customer may become vulnerable to sudden withdrawals. This latter risk is not so much a credit risk as a liquidity risk.

Measuring the bank's true exposure in some of these markets—particularly options markets—is extremely difficult. There is no magic formula which can be simply applied. The Basle formula is essentially arbitrary, although it reflects the best judgment of a group of experienced central bankers. The measurement of risk in these areas has a large element of judgment. Indeed, some banks have resorted to Monte Carlo simulation techniques to estimate their risks: by throwing the dice often enough you try to see the pattern of risk.

13.5 CONTROL RISKS

The next set of risks can be called control risks. They can be broadly subdivided into systems risks and settlement risks. Systems risks are best illustrated by the plight of the Bank of New York in 1985. The bank is one of the largest clearing banks for trading in US Treasury bonds. In the process of installing a sophisticated new system, it failed to test the system adequately in advance. The result was that the system broke down during its early operations. The bank thus acquired the unfortunate distinction of having to arrange probably the largest single overnight borrowing facility in history: $24 billion from the Federal Reserve. It goes without saying that such an occasion can be both expensive and embarrassing. The same occasion high-lights the potential possible scale of risk arising from a snarl-up in settlements.

Another example of the problem, from a related market, was the settlements problem that emerged in the London securities markets during and immediately after the reforms of 1986—the so-called "Big Bang." What began as small problems accu-mulated owing to the rising volume of trading and the shortage of experienced settlement staff in the London market. The main trading firms found themselves funding a massive back-log of unsettled transactions. Bills of several million pounds to finance unsettled trades, were common. Other settlement risks can be even more painful: the attempted fraud on Hill Samuel, under which the criminals had success-fully penetrated the EUCLID system for transferring Eurobonds, but were for-tunately detected before completing their transfer, is an illustration of the risks that can arise from the settlements process.

13.6 MARKET RISK

There are four basic components of market exposure:

1. the level of rates;
2. the shape of the yield curve (or in forward foreign exchange, the relative shape of two yield curves);
3. volatility exposure, for options; and
4. basis risk between different markets.

Measurement of the scale of risk varies from institution to institution. Some institutions run "scenario analysis" showing what happens to them under various market assumptions. Others break down risk into predefined categories and allocate risk limits to each category which then remain fixed.

The Bank of England, in its risk assessment of London institutions, includes a separate category of market risk: "forced-sale risk." This aims to assess the extra risk arising from being a forced seller when seeking to close a position and will depend on the degree of market liquidity.

The derivatives markets pose their own special set of risks. Some of these are tra-ditional risks transferred to another context: for example, the leverage effect of futures. Once the exposure is correctly identified as being not merely the margin, but the amount of underlying assets controlled through the futures market, the measure-ment of risk is fairly straightforward. It is like the risk on the underlying instrument on which the futures contract is based. Similarly, the risks in the interest rate and currency swap markets are generally similar to those in the underlying interest rate and foreign exchange markets.

Risks in the options market, however, are somewhat more complex. The first and primary risk is the difficulty of valuing the contracts properly. In general, this is fairly limited for exchange-traded options, since the current price in the market can be generally taken as a good guide. (Although this need not apply if the market is not very liquid.)

It is for the over-the-counter (OTC) options markets that the real difficulty arises. The complexity of the valuation models can be such that only a very few people in the institution understand them. There can be room for argument about the assumptions applied. The classic example was the disclosure some years ago that Bankers Trust was forced by the Federal Reserve to take a charge to its fourth-quarter earnings of $80m. This arose out of a disagreement between the Federal Reserve and the bank over the proper valuation of Bankers Trust's options book. If two institutions of the experience and standing of Bankers Trust and the Federal Reserve cannot agree about valuation of the options book, then clearly there is considerable scope for distortion of true positions.

A related issue is that even if the position has been correctly valued, the complexity of some of these markets means that the number of institutions involved is extremely small. Therefore, the forced-sale risk is much greater. That is, if there are only four or five institutions in the whole world who understand the transaction, your ability to trade out of it in times of serious difficult is greatly reduced compared with your ability to trade out of a spot foreign exchange position.

13.7 VOLATILITY AND BASIS RISK

Volatility risk is exposure to changes in volatility levels. The risk arises mainly in the case of options. There are at least two levels of risk. First is the straightforward risk that the options book—be it in interest rates, foreign exchange, or any other market—has been wrongly priced. That is, the assumed volatility built into the pricing has been incorrectly estimated. Chemical Bank some years ago reported a substantial hit to its quarterly earnings from its mispriced interest rate cap book: volatility had been systematically underestimated. Some people refer to this as "the black box" risk: members of staff may rely blindly on some computer program which does not in fact properly price a specific risk.

A more subtle type of volatility risk is gamma risk in a delta-weighted hedging operation (see Chapter 12). If gamma is high, then small changes in underlying prices will produce large changes in delta, and therefore will mean large rebalancing of hedges, crystallizing large hedging losses and incurring high transactions costs.

Basis risk raises the whole question of the efficacy or otherwise of hedging. A cautionary tale in this regard is that of Franklin Savings. This was a US savings and loan institution, but it was not run into the ground by irresponsible or obviously fraudulent management as were so many other US thrifts. Its demise came about because of a dispute between itself and the US regulators over the effectiveness or otherwise of its hedging program.

At the root of the dispute was FAS80, the US financial accounting standard covering hedge accounting. Briefly, FAS80 laid down that gains and losses from a hedging program could be deferred if the firm could demonstrate two factors: correlation and offset. Correlation means that hedges and the underlying liabilities or assets must have some connexion. Offset simply means that hedges and things being hedged should move in opposite directions and not the same way. But FAS80 did not define these terms precisely.

Franklin's policy was to test for correlation at the start of the hedge and then again after six months, arguing that the hedge needed time to stabilize. The US authorities argued for the net-offset approach, which essentially tests hedges on a cumulative basis over a rolling 12-month period. Franklin argued that this approach was flawed when interest rates were volatile: hedges that passed on a month-to-month basis failed when tested cumulatively. When the matter went to court, the evidence of expert witnesses conflicted; and in 1989 the FASB taskforce tried to reach a consensus on correlation testing and failed. The matter was dropped without resolution. The outcome, therefore, was that the US authorities in effect threw up their hands and said "We do not really know what constitutes a hedge."

Enough has been said to indicate that evaluating the effectiveness of a hedging program is by no means simple. The degree of basis risk can vary according to differing market conditions, and when measured over different periods of time. As a final general observation on market risk it is worth repeating the comment of RGL Liesching: "Losses migrate into portfolios that are not marked to market (corporate liabilities, investment portfolios, pension funds, and so on). Similarly, the losses which occur in risk management come from those areas of the management process which are not focused on—which are not marked to market."

13.8   CONTROL BY THE AUTHORITIES

A major problem in the control of risk by the authorities is that each country typically imposed its own regime. Of late there has been some convergence, led by the Basle Committee, which comprises the world's major central banks. They collectively have tended to seek to manage the risk-taking propensity of financial institutions by imposing capital requirements on them.

Capital requirements may, broadly speaking, take three forms. These are

1. the formula approach;
2. the building-block approach; and
3. the portfolio approach.

The formula approach was adopted by the Basle Accord in 1988 in respect of banks' capital requirements in relation to credit risk: broadly, a formula using a flat 8% requirement.

By contrast the building block approach typically bases the capital requirement partly on the gross value of positions and partly on the net value (after allowing for hedges). In other words the position risk requirement (PRR) is defined as:

$$\text{PRR} = x + y\Sigma p_i$$

where p_i = position as a percentage of the gross book
x = capital requirement on the gross book
y = capital requirement on net positions

Until 1988 the UK system in respect of securities position risk was a building-block approach with $x = 7.5\%$ and $y = 2.5\%$. Subsequently the UK adopted a portfolio approach under which for a firm whose trading book consists of a portfolio of the most liquid category of UK equities the position risk requirement was, crudely speaking, defined as twice the weekly standard deviation of returns of the portfolio. If necessary, adjustments were then made for less liquid securities, and for books diversified across national markets.

The regulatory scene is currently (March 1966) in some flux. The Capital Adequacy Directive (CAD) is in process of implementation, with most countries having finalised their regulations, although the German legislation implementing it is not expected to be in place until late 1996. After the CAD was finalised, the Basle Committee adopted proposals on market risk measurement which gave banks more flexibility in the use of internal models, but at a significant price. Banks adopting its proposals will calculate the capital required by using their internal models and are then required to multiply this by three.

The CAD allows much less scope for the use of models. However, in an attempt to bridge the gap between the CAD and Basle, the so-called Amsterdam Accord was negotiated. Unfortunately, it has been of little help. The SFA's interpretation of this was published in Board Notice 254 and appears in line with other supervisors' interpretation. BN254 permits firms to get round the need to do a frequent calculation of capital requirements under CAD, by using their own internal models. But the capital held must be at least that which would be required by the CAD.

The mechanics are that firms are required to "benchmark" their internal models against the CAD to get a scaling factor. Suppose the CAD rules would require capital of £125 million and the firm's internal models suggest a capital requirement of £100 million. Then the benchmark scaling factor is 1.25. The firm may use its internal model routinely but must hold 1.25 times as much capital; and the SFA can check at random intervals to ensure that the scaling factor remains realistic.

13.9 VALUE AT RISK

One of the fundamental concepts in modern financial risk management today is that of "value at risk". This concept seeks to measure the possible losses from a position or portfolio under "normal" circumstances. Clearly, the definition of "normal" is critical. The answer to this question is in essence a statistical one. A common approach as exemplified in the RiskMetrics(tm) approach adopted by JP Morgan (see Appendix 2) is to assume that changes in prices and yields of financial instruments are normally distributed. Given this assumption, volatility can be expressed in terms of the distribution of changes' standard deviation from the mean. The Risk-Metrics approach has been to use 1.65 standard deviations at its measure of risk which encompasses 95% of occurrences (since risk only measures a negative outcome, one side of the distribution is excluded). (See Box for a brief explanation of the concept of confidence intervals.)

Suppose that we have an estimate, $\bar{x}$, of the average of a given statistical population, where the true mean of the population is μ. Suppose that we believe that on average $\bar{x}$ is an unbiased estimator of μ. Although this means that on average $\bar{x}$ is accurate, the specific sample mean that we observe will almost certainly be above or below the true level. Accordingly, if we want to be reasonably confident that our inference is correct, we cannot claim that μ is precisely equal to the observed $\bar{x}$. Instead, we must construct an interval estimate or confidence interval of the form

$$\mu = \bar{x} \pm \text{sampling error}$$

The crucial question is: how wide must this confidence interval be? The answer, of course, will depend on how much $\bar{x}$ fluctuates. The first step is to establish how stringent our requirements are. Suppose that we decide that we want to be 95% confident that

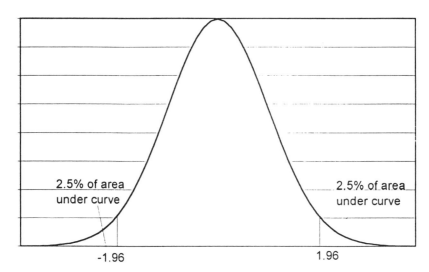

2.5% of area
under curve

2.5% of area
under curve

-1.96   1.96

our estimate is accurate. Suppose, also, that we believe that the elements of the population are normally distributed. In that case, we would expect that the population would be distributed along the lines portrayed in the following chart:

A well-known feature of the normal distribution is that 2.5% of the outcomes of a normally distributed process can be expected to fall more than 1.96 standard deviations from the mean. Clearly, therefore, 95% of the outcomes can be expected to fall within +/- 1.96 standard deviations. That is to say, there is a 95% chance that the random variable $\bar{x}$ will fall between $\mu - 1.96$ standard deviations and $\mu + 1.96$ standard deviations. This would be referred to as a "two-sided" confidence interval. It measures the probability of a move upwards or downwards by the random variable outside the limits we would normally expect.

A case can be made, however, that we should only consider a one-sided test if we are concerned with the risk of loss: a move upward into profit is of less concern. It is well known that 5% of the outcomes of a normally distributed process can be expected to fall more than 1.65 standard deviations from the mean. This would be referred to as a one-sided confidence interval.

Putting that in less scientific language, suppose that we have a position in sterling: we are long of sterling at $1.70. We believe that $1.70 represents the mean sterling's distribution; we believe that the sterling exchange rate has an annual standard deviation of 17 cents (10% volatility). In that case, if we wish to have a 95% confidence interval for sterling, we will set the interval at 1.65 times 17 cents (assuming a one-sided confidence interval). That is, an interval of 28.05 cents. In other words, we are 95% confident that sterling will remain above $1.3695 during the next year.

Alternatively, if we were to set a two-sided confidence interval, we would use an interval of 1.96 times 17 cents—an interval of 33.32 cents. In this case, we would expect with 95% confidence that sterling would remain in the range $1.3668 to $2.0332.

Clearly, an annual standard deviation of 17 cents will translate into a smaller daily movement: in fact, to convert from annual to daily we must divide the annual rate by $1/\sqrt{250}$. The denominator of 250 arises from the assumed number of 250 working days in the year. We use the square root to conform with the definition of the normal distribution. Thus the daily standard deviation is 17/15.811 = 1.07517 cents.

Hence, on a daily basis, using a one-sided confidence interval, we would be 95% confident that sterling would not fall by more than $1.65 \times 1.07517 = 1.77404$ cents. That is, we would be 95% confident that sterling would remain above $1.6822. Using a two-sided confidence interval we would be 95% confident that sterling would remain within the range $1.70 +/-(1.96 \times 1.07517) = \$1.6789 - \$1.7211$.

The RiskMetrics(tm) approach's assumptions imply two key consequences:
(a) by setting a confidence level of 95%, we say that we are prepared to accept a 5% chance that the market will move beyond our parameters. That is, on one day in 20, sterling will fall by more than 1.77404 cents (using a one-sided confidence interval).
(b) we accept the risk that in reality the exchange rate moves in a non-normal manner; as mentioned elsewhere, there is a good deal of evidence that many rates evidence "fat tails", implying that the number and size of large changes is higher than forecast by a normal distribution. On the other hand, there is not yet sufficient evidence to suggest that this discrepancy is large enough to justify abandoning the assumption of normal distribution.

The RiskMetrics(tm) approach defines market risk firstly in terms of absolute market risk: the estimate of total loss expressed in currency terms (e.g. dollars at risk). Alternatively, we may define risk in terms of relative market risk. This concept, more relevant to the investment management community, measures the risk of underperformance against a benchmark index.

Secondly, it defines risk in terms of time horizon. Daily Earnings at Risk (DEaR) is defined as the expected loss over a one-day horizon. Value at Risk measures the potential loss over a longer horizon, such as one month.

The methodology used is to base estimates of volatility and correlations on historical data. This is a methodological choice. There are various alternative approaches to estimating future volatility. Subjective forecasts can be used; alternatively, implied volatilities from exchange-traded instruments can be used. On the other hand, many instruments are not exchange-traded; nor is the forecasting power of implied volatility necessarily greater than historical volatility. The RiskMetrics(tm) approach therefore has been to use exponentially-weighted moving averages of historical rate movements. This ensures that the volatility estimates respond quickly to market shocks, but also that they gradually revert back to more "normal" levels.

13.10   THE EUROPEAN CAPITAL ADEQUACY DIRECTIVE

In March, 1993, the Council of the European Union adopted Directive 93/6/EEC on the Capital Adequacy of Investment Firms and Credit Institutions, which sets out minimum standards in this area. The object of the Directive was to create a so-called "level playing field" between commercial and investment banks. As will all European Union Directives, the actual implementation depends enormously on the individual approach adopted by member states, since it is they who frame the national legislation which gives the directives legal force. Because London is such an important centre for financial markets, the approach adopted by the Bank of England is probably of general interest. The following material is drawn from the Consultative Document entitled "Implementation of the CAD for UK incorporated institutions authorised under the Banking Act 1987", published in December 1994. The details are highly complex, and what follows is a simplified summary.

The CAD introduces the concept of a "trading book". The CAD prescribes the minimum capital requirements for the trading book encompassing not only market related risks but also noted risk in the trading book. By default, everything that is not in the trading book is in the banking book and subject to the existing credit-risk-based regime. The key point is that the trading book receives, in some respects, a more favorable treatment. As a result, the composition of the trading book reflects the outcome of an argument between the German banking authorities and the more liberal British approach. The German authorities were anxious to prevent instruments such as repos being used as substitutes for bank loans. Hence a number of restrictions were imposed on some of these activities: repos, for example, many only be included in the trading book if "the transaction in question is an inter-professional one".

The trading book definition is based upon three broad criteria:

(a) is the instrument a "financial instrument"? and
(b) is the "financial instrument" held for trading purposes? or
(c) is the position hedging an exposure in the trading book?

The definition of a financial instrument is derived from the Investment Services Directive, which becomes operational on 1 January 1996 (as does the CAD). They include:

1. (a) transferable securities
   (b) units in collective investment undertakings
2. money-market instruments
3. financial futures contracts, including equivalent cash settled instruments
4. forward rate agreements
5. interest rate, currency and equity swaps
6. options to acquire or dispose of any instruments listed above

The trading book is defined as:

(a) ... proprietary positions in financial instruments which are held for resale and/or which are taken on by the institution with the intention of benefiting in the short term from actual and/or expected differences between their buying and selling prices ... or positions taken in order to hedge other elements of the trading book.
(b) the exposures due to the unsettled transactions, free deliveries and over-the-counter (OTC) derivative instruments ... exposures due to repurchase agreements and securities lending...
(c) those exposures in the form of fees, commission, interest, dividends, and margin on exchange-traded derivatives...."

The Bank of England considers that positions are held with a trading intent if:

(a) they are marked-to-market daily as part of the internal risk management process;
(b) the position takers have autonomy in entering into transactions within pre-determined limits; or
(c) they satisfy any other criteria which the bank applies to the composition of its trading book on a consistent basis.

Foreign exchange risk is to be calculated as follows: the net spot position plus the net forward position plus irrevocable guarantees which are certain to be called plus net future income/expenses fully hedged plus the net delta equivalent of the options book (if the model used has been accepted by the Bank) plus certain minor items are added to calculate the net open position.

The basic method for calculating the capital required is to apply an 8% capital requirement to the net open position. Alternatively, with the agreement of the Bank, a back-testing method may be used as follows:

1. (a) the five-year method: we calculate the losses which would have occurred over the last five years if every day we opened a new position and held it for ten days. We work out the largest loss we could expect to see 95% of the time. That is, we calculate the "95% loss quantile". If the observation period covers 1300 valuations, then this will correspond to the 65th largest loss (i.e. we exclude the largest five percent of losses).

   (b) the three-year method: we proceed as before, but calculate the 99% loss quantile: i.e. we exclude the largest one percent of losses. If the observation period covers 780 valuations, then this will correspond to the eighth largest loss.

2. the capital requirement is the higher of two percent of the overall net foreign exchange position and the result arrived at in 1 (a) or 1 (b) above.

(Special treatment may be applied to currencies subject to binding inter-governmental agreements, such as the Belgian and Luxembourg francs, and short-term options—"carved-out options").

13.11 INTEREST RATE POSITION RISK

For the first time, as a result of the CAD, the Bank of England proposes to require capital to be held against interest rate position risk. The Bank of England proposals cover the following instruments:

(a) bonds, loan stocks, debentures etc.,
(b) non-convertible preference securities;
(c) convertible securities;
(d) mortgage backed securities and other securitized assets;
(e) certificates of deposit;
(f) Treasury bills, bank bills (bankers acceptances), local authority bills;
(g) commercial paper;
(h) Euronotes, medium term notes, etc.;
(i) foreign exchange forward positions;
(k) derivatives based upon the above instruments and interest rates;
(l) interest rate exposure embedded in other financial instruments.

The proposal states

"Advice must be sought from supervisors on the treatment of instrument types that deviate from these structures, or may be considered complex. In some circumstances the treatment of an instrument may be uncertain, for example bonds whose coupon payments are linked to equity indices. Where possible the position risk of such instruments should be broken down into its components and allocated appropriately between the equity, interest rate and foreign exchange risks countries."

Some sources of interest rate exposure will attract specific and general risk requirements, others may attract counterparty credit requirements as well as general risk requirements, and, where the interest rate exposure is derived from other products there may in some cases be general interest rate exposure requirements only, as the counterparty and specific risk requirements will be determined by the foreign exchange and equity position risk rules.

The division into specific and general risk recognizes that individual instruments may experience changes in value for reasons other than market movements. Specific risk attempts to account for this. The general risk requirement allows for the impact of parallel and non-parallel shifts in the yield curve.

Broadly speaking the specific risk requirements are parallel to those laid down for general counterparty credit risk. For example, debt instruments will be given a 0% specific risk weighting if they are issued by, or fully guaranteed by, Zone A central governments and central banks.

Two methods of calculating general interest rate risk are permitted. Method 1 is a relatively simple approach, in which fixed rate instruments are allotted to certain bands according to whether their coupon is above or below 3%, and according to maturity. Method 2 uses the concept of duration. (see box)

Under this approach, the yield to maturity on each instrument is calculated at the current market price of the investment. The modified duration of each instrument is then calculated. Individual net positions are allocated to one of the three zones specified in Table 13.1, according to the modified duration. The next step is to multiply the current market value by the modified duration and the assumed change in rates to form the unmatched weighted positions. (Long and short positions within a zone may be offset. The net remaining balance is referred to as the unmatched weighted position.)

Unmatched weighted positions for a zone may be offset against positions in other zones as follows:

1. the unmatched weighted long (short) position for zone 1 may offset the unmatched weighted short (long) position in zone 2. The extent to which the unmatched weighed positions in zones 1 and 2 are offset is described as the matched weighted position between zones 1 and 2.
2. after (1), any residual unmatched weighted long (short) positions in zone 2 may then be matched by the unmatched weighted short (long) positions in zone 3.

Table 13.1

Zone	Modified duration	Assumed move in rates (p.a.)	By zone Matched	Unmatched	Between zones Matched
1	$\leq$ 1 year	1%	$\times$ 2%		i&2 $\times$ 40%
2	1–3.6 years	0.85%	$\times$ 2%		
3	>3.6 years	0.7%	$\times$ 2%		2&3 $\times$ 40%
					1&3 $\times$ 150%

The extent to which the unmatched positions in zones 2 and 3 are offset is described as the matched weighted position between zones 2 and 3.

(3) finally, any residual unmatched weighted long (short) positions in zone 1 may then be matched by offset unmatched weighted short (long) positions in zone 3. The extent to which the unmatched positions in zones 1 and 3 are offset is described as the matched weighted position between zone 1 and 3.

Any residual unmatched weighted positions will be totaled. They will then be added to the other components of general interest rate risk capital requirements which are found from the total of:

Matched weighted positions in all zones × 2%
Matched weighted positions between zones 1 and 2 × 40%
Matched weighted positions between zones 2 and 3 × 40%
Matched weighted positions between zones 1 and 3 × 150%

An important innovation in the CAD is that the Bank of England will recognize the models used by certain institutions and will allow them to use these models in calculating their capital requirements. There is a simple approach for banks without recognized models and a more complex approach for institutions with recognized models—which will normally result in lower capital requirements for a given quantity of position or foreign exchange risk. Banks are therefore given an incentive to take a more sophisticated view of the risks in options business and to use model based risk management systems if they are engaged in interest rate derivatives business. However, at the time of writing (March 1995) the CAD only permitted a limited use of these models since it ignored any allowance for diversification of risk.

The Bank recognizes that in many respects the model is one of the less important risks:

"The model review process is likely to focus at least as much on the use of the model in the context of the firm's business as on the mathematics—for instance, whether the revaluation rates fed into the model are independently verified, the part played by senior management in control over the use of models, and whether the model is applied to products which stretch it beyond its capability.
"The review will encompass both the model and its operating environment and so it is not the case that a commercially produced model which has been recognised for one bank will automatically be recognised at another. In the case of banks where there are multiple models for one product, the model that is used for risk management and/or determining profit and loss is the model the Bank will be most interested in, although it may be necessary to look at both front and back office models. It is not our concern to examine subtle modifications to models made by traders for quoting prices."

Institutions which mark to market and manage the interest rate risk on derivative instruments on a discounted cash flow basis may use sensitivity models to calculate positions for inclusion in the duration based ladder approach. Instruments which qualify for this treatment are the following:

(a) interest rate futures
(b) forward rate agreements
(c) forward commitments to buy or sell debt instruments
(d) options on interest rates, debt instruments, equities, equity indices, financial futures, swaps and foreign currencies

(e) warrants
(f) swaps
(g) amortizing bonds

Note that the CAD does not allow non-amortizing bonds to be included. This is a very puzzling approach, which has yet to be adequately explained.

More complex instruments and swap pricing models will be examined separately by the Bank. In most cases the model review process is likely to take the form of a dialogue above matters (if any) which should be addressed before recognition is granted. It is expected that the Bank will look at several products in a single visit and that once systems and controls have been examined in some detail in a given bank there will be less these two spend a lot of time approving each individual model.

13.12 COUNTERPARTY RISK

The CAD will provide, as was the case under the previous BIS regime and the EC Solvency Directive, for capital to be held against the counterparty credit risk entailed by financial transactions. The precise details are complex, but in essence counter-parties are divided into:

Central Governments and Central Banks
Regional Governments and Local Authorities
Credit Institutions
Investment Firms
Recognized Clearing Houses and Exchanges
Multilateral Development Banks
Other Counterparties

The capital weighting applied varies by counterparty type. Claims (other than tradable securities) on central governments and central banks in Zone A (in essence, OECD countries and certain others) are weighted at 0%. Claims on Zone A banks are weighted at 20%. Claims on investment firms in the banking book are treated as if they were claims on Other counterparties: that is, they attract a weighting of 100%. On the other hand, claims reported in the trading book on investment firms that are subject to the CAD are weighted at 20%. Similarly, claims on recognized clearing houses and exchanges reported in the trading book are weighted at 20%; these would include initial cash margins and surplus variation margin at futures exchanges or clearing houses. Banking claims on such entities would attract the Other weighting of 100%.

Off-balance sheet risk is subject to a similar regime, but before applying the capital weighting as above, "credit conversion factors" are applied. These adjust the exposure to reflect the fact that off-balance sheet exposures are typically "replace-ment" exposures—that is, for a loss to arise, two things must happen: the counter-party must go bankrupt, and the market must have moved adversely. As an example, a bank which has contracted to buy forward £10 million at $1.50 is expecting to pay $15 million for the sterling. If the counterparty goes bankrupt and sterling is at

$1.40, it would only have to pay $14 million for its sterling, and could in principle have made a profit. (In fact, this would be unlikely, since the liquidator would probably choose to continue the contract.)

Two approaches to credit equivalents are permitted: the original exposure method, which is permitted to institutions which are not very active in the market, and the replacement cost method. For the original exposure method, the notional principal amount is multiplied by the following conversion factors to obtain the future credit exposure for interest rate contracts: 0.5% for contracts with remaining maturity of one year or less; 1.0% per annum for each remaining year. Thus, for example, a $100 million five-year interest rate swap would show a measured credit exposure of $5 million. For exchange rate contracts, the conversion factors are 2% for the first year, 5% for the second year, and 3% for each subsequent year.

The replacement cost method consists of two steps:

1. mark the contract to market
2. add on an amount for potential future credit exposure which reflects the remaining maturity of the contract, calculated as follows: interest rate contracts for less than 1 year remaining—0%, over 1 year remaining 0.5% per annum; exchange rate contracts with less than 1 year remaining—1%; over 1 year, 5% per annum.

In July 1994 the Basic Committee On Banking Supervision published proposals to amend the Capital Accord of July 1988. Under this amendment, an expanded matrix will be applied, as follows:

Table 13.2

Residual Maturity	Interest Rate	FX and gold	Equity	Precious Metals*	Other commodities
<1 year	9	1	6	7	12
1–5 yrs	0.5	5	8	7	12
>5 yrs	1.5	7.5	10	8	15

The proposed factors were developed using Monte Carlo simulations of matched pairs of representative transactions and are intended to provide reasonable prudential coverage for a high proportion of potential exposures.

At the same time, the committee announced that it now saw merit in recognizing netting effects on potential future exposure. It proposed that the add-on for netted transactions (A_{net}) would equal the average of the add-on as presently calculated (A_{gross}), reduced by the ratio of net current replacement cost to gross current replacement cost (NGR), and the add-on as presently calculated:

$$A_{net} = 0.5* A_{gross}* (1 + NGR)$$

where NGR = the level of net replacement cost/level of gross replacement cost.

In this context the NGR can be seen as somewhat of a proxy for the impact of netting on potential future exposure: the advantage of the formula from a supervisory perspective is that it uses bank-specific information (i.e. the NGR) but imposes greater stability over time and across banks than a formula giving full weight to the NGR.

13.13 DIVERSIFICATION AND RISK REDUCTION

A key issue which has been the subject of extensive debate between regulators and practitioners has been the extent to which allowance should be made for the risk reduction benefits of a diversified set of exposures, in comparison with an undiversified set. The CAD, unlike the Basle Committee, uses simple additive techniques and presumes that financial instruments are perfectly correlated. That is, a portfolio of 5 different $5 million exposures is treated as having $25 million of exposure. As we saw in Chapter 8, portfolio diversification will always reduce aggregate risk unless correlation is unity. Thus, the approach of the regulators is extremely conservative. Certainly, for day-to-day management purposes, most practitioners will allow for the benefits of diversification. The approach followed by the regulators is only suitable in respect of worst-case outcomes. It must be admitted that in the worst case, many financial assets do display a high degree of correlation. The classic example is the Crash of 1987, when equity markets around the world displayed a much higher degree of correlation than normal.

In practice, however, a diversified portfolio of risks will almost invariably be less risky than the additive approach would suggest. However, we still have the problem of accurately estimating the correlation between our different exposures. The approach adopted, for example, by JP Morgan in its RiskMetrics model is to calculate exponentially weighted averages of daily correlations.

13.14 NETTING SYSTEMS

The Basle ratios permit, where recognized by the relevant supervisory authority, the netting of interbank positions. The legal status of netting will vary from country to country. Accordingly, what is said here can only be general in nature.

Movement towards netting on a cross-border basis and multi-currency netting systems has been encouraged by the Bank for International Settlements. In February 1989, the BIS produced a Report on Netting Schemes (sometimes referred to as the Angell Report). In November 1990, this was followed up by the Report of the Committee on Interbank Netting Schemes. The report recommended further pursuit of multilateral netting schemes, on the grounds that

> "by reducing the number and overall value of payments between financial institutions, netting can enhance the efficiency of domestic payment systems and reduce the settlement costs associated with the growing volume of foreign exchange market activity. Netting can also reduce the size of credit and liquidity exposures incurred by market participants and thereby contribute to the containment of systemic risk."

The report laid down perceived minimum standards for multilateral netting schemes, principally that they should have a well-founded legal basis under all relevant jurisdictions, clearly defined procedures for the management of credit and liquidity risks, fair and open access to admission, and operational reliability of technical systems and back-up facilities. The committee suggested a presumption that the "host country" central bank in whose market the netting system is located or operating will undertake supervision.

A potential problem is that the application of technology has made possible the geographic dispersion of the functions of netting or clearing, on the one hand, and the ultimate settlements in a given currency, on the other. Although multilateral netting systems directly link the credit and liquidity risks and risk management of banks in different countries, there is no one central bank or supervisory authority in a natural position to consider the overall soundness and prudential adequacy of these systems.

Bilateral netting arrangements are in place between a number of participants in the foreign exchange markets. More recently, attempts have been made to develop a multi-lateral netting system. As an example, the ECHO netting project (for Exchange Clearing House Organization) aims to set up a common Clearing House which becomes the common counterparty for all deals arranged among the members. The principles are, of course, precisely the same as those for a domestic clearing house, such as that which handles the settlement of bank checks. Thus, a bank which does 3000 deals a day, involving 24 currencies, with its main interbank counterparties will have to make 3000 payments and receive 3000 payments, a total of 6000 entries over its nostro account. If all the counterparties were members of the clearing house, then the bank would make or receive a maximum of only 24 items in total. The reduction in cost and risk are very significant.

The issue does not apply only to the foreign exchange market, for the International Swap Dealers Association has also been actively seeking to promote world-wide swap neeting agreements. It successfully lobbied for a change to the US bankruptcy law to allow for netting out of swaps to prevent "cherry-picking" (the practice whereby a liquidator of a firm would acknowledge only those contracts that were favorable and dispute the rest).

13.15 REAL-TIME GROSS SETTLEMENT

In some countries there remains inherent uncertainty over the legal soundness of netting. Given the scale of funds currently moving through money-transfer systems—CHIPS alone handles a daily volume in excess of $3,000,000,000,000—central banks have become increasingly concerned to move payments systems onto a real-time basis. (A real-time computer system handles money transfers instantaneously instead of the payments being "batched" for later processing). In addition, they are seeking to have money transfers handled gross—i.e. without netting. There are two reasons for this: firstly, the legal doubts in some countries referred to earlier, and secondly the fact that in a netting system we cannot have "payment finality." In a netting system it is always theoretically possible that a payment might be cancelled, at any time until the net settlement is made. With a real-time gross settlement system, true payment finality can be achieved.

Appendix A
EMS and Currency Baskets

The parity grid is simple in bilateral terms. If currency A is at its limit against B, the two central banks must intervene. But the presence of other currencies in the grid means that the apparent 2.25% fluctuation margins are actually less than they seem. Suppose we have three currencies in our system. They declare the following central rates against the ECU.

$$\text{ECU } 1 = \text{DEM } 2.5 = \text{FRF } 6 = \text{BEF } 40$$

This implies the following parity grid:

	BEF	DEM	FRF
BEF	1	15.6440 16 16.3640	6.5184 6.6667 6.8184
DEM	0.06111 0.0625 0.06392	1	0.4074 0.41667 0.4261
FRF	0.1467 0.15 0.1534	2.3466 2.4 2.4546	1

Note that the upper and lower limits calculated here are not exactly 2¼% above or below the parity. The factors are +2.2753% and –2.2247% or, to put it another way, the central parity is multiplied not by 1.0225 and 0.9775 but by 1.022753 and 0.977753. The latter number is the reciprocal of the first, and 0.045 less (that is, the total difference is twice 2¼%, as it would be if 1.0225 and 0.9775 were used). Hence, the DEM/BEF lower limit of 16.3640 multiplied by the BEF/DEM upper limit of 0.06111 produces 1, just as the central rates do when multiplied.

Given the grid, the only way that the deutsche mark can move its full theoretical 4½% range from the bottom of the EMS to the top is if both other currencies were exactly at their central rate, that is, FRF/BEF 6.6667. In that case, the DEM/BEF rate can move freely between 15.6440 and 16.3640. But suppose the French franc is at its lower limit against the Belgian franc, that is, FRF/BEF 6.5184. Then the DEM/BEF range is cut in half since long before the deutsche mark has got to its upper limit against the Belgian franc it has reached its upper limit against the French franc. To be exact, the DEM/BEF range is 4½% less the spread between the French franc and Belgian franc; if that spread is at its limit of 2¼%, then the most that DEM/BEF can move is 2¼%.

As a practical point, we should add that if the deutsche mark rose to its upper limit against the French franc, intervention would probably start to pull the French franc up with the deutsche mark, so that it could move more against the Belgian franc. But this applies less in the case of thinly traded currencies. For example, if instead of the deutsche mark, the Danish krona was moving, the volume of DKK/FRF business would be smaller and less likely to pull the French franc up against the Belgian franc.

Another factor which could give greater freedom to "heavy" or important currencies such as the deutsche mark compared with the Danish krona is the technical construction of the ECU. A currency that is pegged against a basket containing the currency has more freedom than if the basket does not contain the currency. To see why, let's look first at a currency that is pegged against a basket not containing itself, let's call it the Home. The Home is pegged against the SDR, say, at SDR 1 = HOME 4. The SDR consists of US$0.54 + DEM0.46 + £STG0.071 + FRF0.74 + Y34. Suppose we have US$/DEM = 2.30, £STG/US$ = 1.80, US$/FRF = 6.0, US$/Y = 220. Then SDR 1 = US$ 1.1456 (see Chapter 13) and the HOME rate will be US$1 = HOME 3.4916. Now suppose that the deutsche mark strengthens by 10% to US$/DEM = 2.07. If all other rates are unchanged, SDR 1 = US$1.679 and US$ 1 = HOME 3.4249. In other words, the deutsche mark's strength against the US dollar pulls up the SDR against the US dollar. This in turn pulls up the HOME against the dollar. The percentage change in the HOME against the dollar is the same as the change in the SDR, that is, 2% (which is the 10th deutsche mark change weighted by the share of the deutsche mark in the SDR, which is about 20%).

Now let's look at what happens when a currency is pegged against a basket that includes itself. In this case, if the currency moved 10% as before, and the currency's weight were 20% as before its movement against the basket would be *less than* 10%, because it would pull the basket up with it. Let's look at the deutsche mark in the EMS. Currently, the ECU/DEM parity is ECU 1 = DEM 2.05586. The ECU is defined as DEM0.6242 + GBP0.08784 + FRF1.332 + ITL151.80 + NLG0.2198 + BEF3.301 + LFR0.13 + DKK0.1976 + IEP0.00855 + GRD1.44 + ESP6.885 + PTE1.393. Suppose we have the following rates against the US dollar: US$/DEM = 1.4925, £ = 1.9465, FRF = 5.0700, ITL = 1124.00, NLG = 1.6820, BEF = 30.80, LFR = 30.80, DKK = 5.7500, IEP = 1.7870, GRD = 301.95, ESP = 94.85, PTE = 133.40. These rates give us ECU 1 = US$1.3665 which implies ECU1 = DEM2.0395. Suppose as before the DEM strengthens by 10% against the US$ to 1.3433. This pulls up the ECU to ECU 1 = US$1.4130 which implies ECU1 = DEM1.8980 a swing of 7% instead of 10%.

This technical factor is relevant to the divergence indicator. The divergence indicator is the movement of a currency from its ECU central rate. The EMS allows a 2¼% movement; within this, there is a "threshold of divergence" at 75% of the permitted movement. As we have seen, a rise in the deutsche mark of 10% against the US dollar would be a rise of only 6½% against the ECU. For the rising value of its deutsche mark component is pulling the ECU up against the US dollar. But if we assume the same initial rates, and look at a 10% rise of the Danish krona, to DKK 5.175 per US$, we find that the ECU rises only to $1.4373 from $1.3849, instead of rising to $1.4335 as it did when the deutsche mark rose 10%. The reason is that the DKK's weight in the ECU is less: only about 3% compared with more than 30% for the deutsche mark. It follows that a 2¼ move of the deutsche mark against the ECU will allow the deutsche mark to move further against the dollar than would be allowed for the Danish krona, because the deutsche mark would pull the ECU further up than the Danish krona would. To compensate for this, the EC calculates an "adjusted divergence" indicator, which is given by ADI = DI × (1 − w) where ADI = adjusted divergence indicator, DI = divergence indicator, and w is the official weight for the currency. In the case of the deutsche mark, w = 0.301 (that is, 30.1%), whereas for the Danish krona w = 0.0245. Hence for the deutsche mark ADI = 0.689 × DI whereas for the Danish krona, ADI = 0.975 × DI.

There is still one more calculation to be made before we have the finally adjusted divergence indicator. This is to take account of currencies (like sterling and the peseta) which have a wider band than 2¼%, and of currencies (like the drachma) that have no band at all. The problem is that if, say, sterling rises by 6% against the US dollar, pulling the ECU up with it, other currencies would be forced to move up against the dollar to keep their divergence indicator within the threshold. The EC solution is to pretend that sterling, the peseta, and the drachma stay within a 2¼% band. That is, the divergence indicator is adjusted to strip out the effects of movements in sterling, the peseta, and the drachma that exceed 2¼%.

Table A.1. EMS European Currency Unit Rates

	XEU Central Rates	Currency Amounts against XEU Feb. 13	% Change from Central Rate	% Spread vs. Weakest Currency	Divergence Indicator
Spanish peseta	133.631	128.294	−3.99	5.41	70
Belgian franc	42.4032	42.1267	−0.65	1.87	38
Deutsche mark	2.05586	2.04647	−0.46	1.67	37
Dutch guilder	2.31643	2.30603	−0.45	1.66	28
Italian lira	1538.24	1540.12	0.12	1.08	0
Irish punt	0.767417	0.768956	0.20	1.00	−3
Danish krone	7.84195	7.87615	0.44	0.76	−14
French franc	6.89509	6.97512	1.16	0.04	−57
Sterling	0.696904	0.705285	1.20	0.00	−24

ECU central rates set by the European Commission. Currencies are in descending relative strength. Percentage changes are for ECU; a positive change denotes a weak currency. Divergence shows the ratio between two spread: the percentage difference between the actual market and ECU central rates for a currency, and the maximum permitted percentage deviation of the currency's market rate from its ECU central rate. Adjustment calculated by Financial Times.
Source: Financial Times, 14th February 1991.

To do this, we start by finding the weakest currency in the EMS. Then we see if it has moved more than 2¼% against sterling. If it has, we calculate an adjustment. This is the percentage change in the currency against sterling from the base date, less 2¼%, multiplied by sterling's weight in the ECU. A parallel factor is calculated for the peseta and the drachma. The three factors are added together to produce a combined adjustment. This is then deducted from the divergence to get the fully adjusted divergence indicator. The results of these calculations are published daily in the *Financial Times* of London and elsewhere. Continuous updates are shown on Reuters Monitor page EMSA. A sample (from the *Financial Times*) is shown in Table A.1.

A final technicality arises in the calculation of new central rates. In the snake, parities were declared against the European Monetary Unit of Account. This was fixed in terms of gold. Its value did not change as exchange rates changed. So if it was agreed to revalue the deutshe mark by 10%, all that was needed was to change the DEM/EMUA rate by 10%. But a deutsche mark revaluation against the ECU pulls up the ECU. Suppose the deutsche mark revalues 10%; it will pull the ECU up by about 3% (as its weight is about 30% of the ECU). So the net deutsche mark movement against the ECU is only 7%, and the deutsche mark and all other currencies will be below their ECU parities, so all EMS currencies would look weak at once. To prevent this, the deutsche mark revaluation has to be combined with devaluations by other countries. A 10% deutsche mark revaluation needs to be achieved by combining a 3% devaluation of all other currencies with a 7% deutsche mark revaluation.

A technical point arises in ECU trading when there is a change in the composition of the unit. (If current discussions on "hardening" the ECU eliminate changes in the ECU this point will no longer matter.) Changes in weight—either because of the entry of new currencies in the system, or because of changes in the relative economic importance of different countries—will change the interest rate payable on the ECU. (They will not change the external value of the ECU on the day of the change, because the recomposition of the ECU is constructed so as to have no net exchange rate effect.)

As an example, on June 19, 1989, the EC announced that the Spanish peseta and Portuguese escudo would become part of the basket, with effect from September 20, 1989. As just mentioned, those dealing forward ECU for the value date of the change were unaffected because the exchange value of the ECU did not alter. But holders of bonds and ECU deposits were affected because the weighted average ECU rate would reflect the inclusions of two relatively weak, high-interest-rate currencies. The theoretical impact was of the order of 50 basis points; on the day of the announcement, however, the impact was only 4 to 5 basis points because yields were already priced to reflect much of the expected revision. The market started pricing the change in from February.

For those who prefer symbols, the following is a brief summary of the above. We define $W(i)$ as the fixed currency amounts in the ECU; for instance, if the deutsche mark is currency number one, we have $W(1) = 0.6242$. We define $A(i)$ as the current central rates of each currency against the ECU (e.g., $A(1) = 2.05586$ for the deutsche mark), $C(i)$ as the present market exchange rate against the US dollar for each currency. Note that sterling and the Irish punt have to be inverted to make them consistent. We define $G(i)$ as the current percentage weight of each currency in the basket. Then the value of the ECU is give by:

$$ECU = \sum_{i=1}^{12} \frac{W(i)}{C(i)} = E$$

$$\text{Clearly, } G(i) = \frac{W(i)}{A(i)} = \frac{0.6242}{2.05586} = 30.1\% \text{ for the deutsche mark}$$

To calculate the divergence indicator $D(i)$ we first find the current exchange rate for each currency against the ECU, $E \times C(i)$. Then we define:

$$D(i) = 100 - \frac{100 \times E \times C(i)}{A(i)}$$

To allow for the effects of sterling, the peseta, and the escudo we find the weakest currency. K, and calculate (assume sterling is currency two, the peseta currency three, the escudo currency five, and the drachma currency seven):

$$Q(2) = \left[\left(\frac{C(K)}{C(2)} \times \frac{A(2)}{A(K)} \times 100 \right) -2.25 - 100 \right] \times G(2)$$

$$Q(3) = \left[\left(\frac{C(K)}{C(3)} \times \frac{A(3)}{A(K)} \times 100 \right) -2.25 - 100 \right] \times G(3)$$

$$Q(5) = \left[\left(\frac{C(K)}{C(5)} \times \frac{A(5)}{A(K)} \times 100 \right) -2.25 - 100 \right] \times G(5)$$

$$Q(7) = \left[\left(\frac{C(K)}{C(7)} \times \frac{A(7)}{A(K)} \times 100 \right) -2.25 - 100 \right] \times G(7)$$

The final adjustment $Q = Q(2) + Q(3) + Q(5) + Q(7)$. We then compare $D(I) + Q$ with the permitted threshold.

Appendix B
Swift and ISO Currency Codes

An alphabetical list of codes for the representation of currencies and funds based on international standard ISO 4217 follows:

Code	Currency	Country
AED	UAE Dirham	United Arab Emirates
AFA	Afghani	Afghanistan
ALL	Lek	Albania
ANG	Netherlands Antillian Guilder	Netherlands Antilles
AOK	Kwanza Angola	Angola
ARS	Peso Argentina	Argentina
ATS	Schilling	Austria
AUD	Australian Dollar	Australia
		Christmas Island
		Cocos (Keeling) Islands
		Gilbert Islands
		Heard and Mcdonald Islands
		Kiribati
		Nauru
		Norfolk Island
		Tuvalu
AWG	Aruban Guilder	Aruba
BBD	Barbados Dollar	Barbados
BDT	Taka	Bangladesh
BEF	Common Belgian Franc	Belgium
BEC	Convertible Belgian Franc	Luxembourg
BGL	Lev	Bulgaria
BHD	Bahraini dinar	Bahrain
BIF	Burundi Franc	Burundi
BMD	Bermudan Dollar	Bermuda
BND	Brunei Dollar	Brunei
BOB	Boliviano	Bolivia
BRE	Cruzeiro	Brazil
BSD	Bahamian Dollar	Bahamas
BTN	Ngultrum	Bhutan
BUK	Kyat	Burma
BWP	Pula	Botswana

Code	Currency	Country
BZD	Belize Dollar	Belize
CAD	Canadian Dollar	Canada
CHF	Swiss Franc	Liechtenstein
		Switzerland
CLF	Unidades de formento	Chile
CLP	Chilean Peso	Chile
CNY	Yuan Renminbi	China
COP	Colombian Peso	Colombia
CRC	Costa Rican Colon	Costa Rica
CSK	Koruna	Czechoslovakia
CUP	Cuban Peso	Cuba
CVE	Cape Verde Escudo	Cape Verde
CYP	Cyprus Pound	Cyprus
DDM	Mark der DDR	German Democratic Republic
DEM	Deutsche Mark	Germany, Federal Republic of
DJF	Djibouti Franc	Djibouti
DKK	Danish Kroner	Denmark
		Faeroe Islands
		Greenland
DOP	Dominican Peso	Dominican Republic
DZD	Algerian Dinar	Algeria
ECS	Sucre	Ecuador
EGP	Egyptian Pound	Egypt
ESP	Spanish Peseta	Andorra
		Spain
ETB	Ethiopian Birr	Ethiopia
FIM	Markka	Finland
FJD	Fiji Dollar	Fiji
FKP	Falkland Islands Pound	Falkland Islands
FRF	French Franc	Andorra
		France
		French Guiana
		French Southern Territories
		Guadeloupe
		Martinique
		Monaco
		Reunion
		St. Pierre and Miquelon
GBP	Pound Sterling	United Kingdom
GHC	Cedi	Ghana
GIP	Gibraltar Pound	Gibraltar
GMD	Dalasi	Gambia
GNF	Guinea Franc	Guinea
GRD	Drachma	Greece
GTQ	Quetzal	Guatemala
GWP	Guinea-Bissau Peso	Guinea-Bissau
GYD	Guyan Dollar	Guyana
HKD	Hong Kong Dollar	Hong Kong
HNL	Lempira	Honduras
HTG	Gourde	Haiti
HUF	Forint	Hungary
IDR	Rupiah	Indonesia
IEP	Irish Pound	Ireland
ILS	Israeli Shekel	Israel

Code	Currency	Country
INR	Indian Rupee	Bhutan
		India
IQD	Iraqi Dinar	Iraq
		Neutral Zone (between Saudi Arabia and Iraq)
IRR	Iranian Rial	Iran
ISK	Iceland Krona	Iceland
ITL	Lira	Italy
		San Marino
		Vatican City State (Holy See)
JMD	Jamaican Dollar	Jamaica
JOD	Jordanian Dinar	Jordan
JPY	Yen	Japan
KES	Kenyan Shilling	Kenya
KHR	Riel	Kampuchea, Democratic
KMF	Comoros Franc	Comoros
KPW	North Korean Won	Korea, Democratic People's Republic of
KRW	Won	Korea, Republic of
KWD	Kuwaiti Dinar	Kuwait
		Neutral Zone (between Saudi Arabia and Iraq)
KYD	Cayman Islands Dollar	Cayman Islands
LAK	Kip	Lao People's Democratic Republic
LBP	Lebanese Pound	Lebanon
LKR	Sri Lanka Rupee	Sri Lanka
LRD	Liberian Dollar	Liberia
LSL	Lotl	Lesotho
LUF	Luxembourg franc	Luxembourg
LYD	Libyan Dinar	Libyan Arab Jamahiriya
MAD	Moroccan Dirham	Morocco
		Western Sahara
MGF	Malagasy Franc	Madagascar
MMK	Kyat	Myanmar
MNT	Tugrik	Mongolia
MOP	Pataca	Macasi
MRO	Ouguiya	Mauritania
		Western Sahara
MTL	Maltese Lira	Malta
MUR	Mauritius Rupee	British Indian Ocean Territory
		Mauritius
MVR	Rufiyaa	Maldives
MWK	Malawi Kwacha	Malawi
MXP	Mexican Peso	Mexico
MYR	Malaysian Ringgit	Malaysia
MZM	Metical	Mozambique
NGN	Naira	Nigeria
NHF	New Hebrides Franc	New Hebrides
NIO	Cordoba oro	Nicaragua
NLG	Netherlands Guilder	Netherlands
NOK	Norwegian Krone	Antarctica
		Bouvet Island
		Dronning Maud Land
		Norway
		Svalbard and Jan Mayen Islands
NPR	Nepalese Rupee	Nepal
NZD	New Zealand Dollar	Cook Islands

Code	Currency	Country
		Niue Islands
		New Zealand
		Pitcairn Islands
		Tokelau
OMR	Rial Omani	Oman
PAB	Balboa	Panama
PEN	Nuevo sol	Peru
PGK	Kina	Papua New Guinea
PHP	Philippine Peso	Philippines
PKR	Pakistan Rupee	Pakistan
PLZ	Zloty	Poland
PTE	Portuguese Escudo	Portugal
PYG	Guarani	Paraguay
QAR	Qatari Rial	Qatar
ROL	Leu	Romania
RWF	Rwanda Franc	Rwanda
SAR	Saudi Riyal	Neutral Zone (between Saudi Arabia and Iraq)
		Saudi Arabia
SBD	Solomon Islands Dollar	Solomon Islands
SCR	Seychelles Rupee	British Indian Ocean Territory
		Seychelles
SDP	Sudanese Pound	Sudan
SEK	Swedish Krona	Sweden
SGD	Singapore Dollar	Singapore
SHP	St. Helena Pound	St. Helena
SLL	Leone	Sierra Leone
SOS	Somali Shilling	Somalia
SRG	Surinam Guilder	Surinam
STD	Dobra	Sao Tome and Principe
SUR	Rouble	Byelorussian SSR
		Ukrainian SSR
		Russia
SVC	El Salvador Colon	El Salvador
SYP	Syrian Pound	Syrian Arab Republic
SZL	Lilangeni	Swaziland
THB	Baht	Thailand
TND	Tunisian Dinar	Tunisia
TOP	Pa'anga	Tonga
TPE	Timor Escudo	East Timor
TRL	Turkish Lira	Turkey
TTD	Trinidad and Tobago Dollar	Trinidad and Tobago
TWD	New Taiwan Dollar	Taiwan, Province of
TZS	Tanzanian Shilling	Tanzania, United Republic of
EGX	Uganda Shilling	Uganda
USD	US Dollar common	
USN	US Dollar next day funds	United States
USD	US Dollar	American Samoa
		British Virgin Islands
		British Indian Ocean Territory
		Guam
		Haiti
		Johnston Island
		Midway Islands
		Pacific Islands (Trust Territory)

Code	Currency	Country
		Panama
		Panama Canal Zone
		Puerto Rico
		Turks and Caicos Islands
		United States Miscellaneous Pacific Islands
		United States Virgin Islands
		Wake Island
UYP	Uruguayan Peso	Uruguay
VEB	Bolivar	Venezuela
VND	Dong	Viet Nam
VUV	Vatu	Vanuatu
WST	Tala	Samoa
XAF	CFA Franc	Cameroon
		Central African Republic
		Chad
		Congo
		Equatorial Guinea
		Gabon
XCD	East Caribbean Dollar	Anguilla
		Antigua and Barbuda
		Dominica
		Grenada
		Montserrat
		St. Kitts-Nevis
		St. Lucia
		St. Vincent and the Grenadines
XEU	European Currency Unit (ECU)	
XOF	CFA Franc	Benin
		Ivory Coast
		Niger
		Senegal
		Togo
		Upper Volta
XPF	CFP Franc	French Polynesia
		New Caledonia
		Walls and Futuna Islands
YER	Yemeni rial	Yemen, Republic of
YUN	Yugoslavian dinar	Yugoslavia
ZAR	Rand	Lesotho
		Namibia
		South Africa
ZMK	Zambian Kwacha	Zambia
ZRZ	Zaire	Zaire
ZWD	Zimbabwe Dollar	Zimbabwe

Further Reading

There is of course a huge literature on the topics of interntaional money and foreign exchange markets. I attach here merely a list of some of the books I have found useful. Some of them will contain much more comprehensive bibliographies.

L.S. Copeland, "Exchange Rates and International Finance", 2nd edition, Addison-Wesley, UK, 1994

P. de Grauwe, H. Dewachter and M. Embrechts, "Exchange Rate Theory: Chaotic Models of Foreign Exchange", Blackwell, Oxford UK 1993

C. Dunis & M. Feeny. "Exchange Rate Forecasting", Woodhead-Faulkner/Simon and Schuster, 1989

G. Gemmill. "Options Pricing: An International Perspective". McGraw-Hill, UK, 1993

F. Giavazzi, S. Micossi, M. Miller (eds). "The European Monetary System", Cambridge University Press, Cambridge, 1988

B. Manson. "The Practitioner's Guide to Interest Rate Risk Management", Graham & Trotman, London 1992

M.H. Pesaran & S.M. Potter (eds). "Nonlinear dynamics, chaos and econometrics", John Wiley & Sons, Chichester, 1993

E. Peters, "Chaos and Order in the Capital Markets", John Wiley & Sons, 1991; E. Peters, "Fractal Market Analysis", John Wiley & Sons, 1994.

Index

Note: Page references in *italics* refer to Figures; those in **bold** refer to Tables

ADIBOR 140
adjustment 57
Agreement on Multilateral Monetary
    Compensation 63
allotment rates 15
AMEX 197
Andean Reserve Fund 74
Arab Monetary Fund (AMF) 63–4, 74
arbitrage 46–7, 143, *161*
artificial currency units 72–3
Attali, Jacques 21
Australian money-market 11, 18, **19**, 32
authorized dealers 11
automated pit trading (APT) system 169
automated teller machines (ATMs) 83

Bahamas 41
Bahrain 41
Baker, James 38
balance of payments policy 121–3
Banca d'Italia 11, 87
Banco de Mexico 65
bandwagon effect 97, 129
Bank for International Settlements (BIS) 19,
    28, 39–40, 60, 61–3, 74, 231, 245
    member central banks **62**
    Report on Netting Schemes (Angell
        Report) 245
Bank of America 25, 230
Bank of Canada 10–11, 18
Bank of England 12–13, 21, 28, 39, 53, 67–8,
    114, 233
    currency swap market 189
    effect of direct controls on bank lending
        115
    on interest rate position risk 240, 242–3
    intervention (1964–67) 48–9

risk control and 235–6
    on trading intent 239–40
    use of central bank swaps 65
Bank of England Act (1946) (UK) 67
Bank of England Quarterly Bulletin 123
Bank of Finland 39
Bank of Italy 39
Bank of Japan 11, 16–17, 38, 64, 71–2, 231
Bank of New York 232–3
bankers' acceptance (BA) markets 6
Bankers Trust (BT) 26, 27, 205, 234
    options book 234
Bankhaus ID Hersatt *see* Hersatt Bank
Banking Act (1979) (UK) 68
Banque Commerciale pour l'Europe du Nord
    21
Banque de France 16, 65, 69–71, 150
bar chart 124, *124*
Barclays Bank 21, 24, 25
Barclays Bank v. *Arab Bank* 26
Barings Bank 229
Basle Concordat 13, 63
BECS issue (1985) 188
Berlin Wall 38
Big Bang 12, 68, 93, 233
bills pass 10
binomial model 208–12
Black–Scholes model 205, 208–9, 212,
    213–16
Black Wednesday 39
BMW 182
Brady plan 42
Bretton Woods conference 34, 40, 58
British Bankers' Association (BBA) 222, 231
British Telecom 3
buffer stock financing facility 60
Bulis 14
Business International Corporation 97

butterfly effect 99
buying rates 153–4
BZW 107

call deposit 140
Canadian money-market 18
Canadian Payments Association 18
candle charts 125–8, *127*
caps 224–8
Carter, President 26
Cayman Islands 41
Cedel clearance system 20
certificates of deposit (Cds) 6, 14, 16, 24,
    150–1
CFA franc 73
channel 125, *125,* 128
chaos theory 98–106
chaotic attractors 100
charting 123–5
Chase Manhattan Bank, case against 26
Chemical Bank 195, 234
Chicago Board of Trade (CBOT) 168, 169,
    171,197
Chicago Board Options Exchange (CBOE)
    196, 197
Chicago Mercantile Exchange 7, 175
China 21
CHIPS 25, 26, 27, 246
Citibank 21, 25, 27
CME 168
commercial paper (CP) 6, 14, 16
Common Agricultural Policy 76
Communauté Financière Africaine 73
compensatory and contingency financing
    facility (CCFF) 60
Connally, John 35, 67
Continental Illinois 10, 173, 230
    crisis 188
contract amount (CA) 149
contract period 149
contract rate (CR) 149
Convention for the Unification of Certain
    Rules Regarding Air Transport (1929)
    73
conventions 138–40
Corporation bills 12
coupon pass 9
Cox–Ross–Rubinstein model 209
cross-over models 129–30
cross-rates 155–6, **156**
CTE (Italy) issues 20
currency baskets 72, 73
currency cocktails 73
currency codes 251–5
customer repos 9

D-loans 11
Daily Earnings at Risk (DEaR) 238
DEC 106
DECtalk 106
delta risk 216, 217
DEM receivable, financing **45**
Department of Trade (UK) 68
deposit note 6
Depression 34
derivatives 7
deterministic models 98
Deutsche Bundesbank 10, 11, 14–15, 20, 31,
    38, 42, 48, 68–9
    reserve requirements 26
    use of swaps 49, **49**
Deutsche Terminbörse 14, 168, 172, 196
    (DTB)
devaluation of a currency 121
DIFFS 173
discount markets 12
discount securities 151–2
discount window 10
disintermediation 115
divergence indicator 86
domino-style banking collapse 42
Dornbusch model 95
double top 125, *126*
Doyle, Maurice 91
Dutch tulip mania (1634) 163

East Caribbean Currency Authority 74
Eastern Caribbean Central Bank 61
ECHO netting project 246
ECU 73, 74–6, 86
ECU Banking Association 19
ECU bond 20
ECU market 19–20
effective exchange rates, calculation of 77–8
efficient market hypothesis (EMH) 95–7
efficient portfolio 134
electronic open outcry 172
Emerging Markets Trading Association 42
enhanced structural adjustment facility
    (ESAF) 60
EUCLID system 233
Euoclear clearance system 20
Eurco 73
Euro-deutsche mark 26
Eurobond market 23, 35
Eurocommercial paper (ECP) 23, 25, 43, 152
Eurocredits 23
Eurodollar market 21–4
    fixed maturity 24
    history 34–40
    legal nature of 26–7

Eurodollar market *continued*
    total assets *22*
Euroequities 23
Euromarket 13
    cross-border assets *23*
    cross-border liabilities *23*
    key role 22–3
    workings of 24–5
Euromoney 97
Euronotes 43
European Coal and Steel Community 75, 80
European Commission 20, 81–2
European Community 82, 231
European Currency Unit *see* ECU
European Economic Community (EEC) 36
    unit of account 73
European Investment Bank 75
European Monetary Agreement 63
European Monetary Cooperation Fund
    (EMCF) 19, 63, 70–1, 75, 86, 87, 90
European Monetary Institute (EMI) 63,
    86–7, 90–1
    EMI Key 91
European Monetary System (EMS) 13, 19,
    36, 40, 63, 75, 110
    bilateral central rates **88–9**
    crisis 39
    currency baskets and 247–50
    selling and buying rates **88–9**
    technical operation 86–90
European Monetary Union 39, 79–93
    benefits of 81–2
    costs of 82–3
    as a discipline 85
    optimum currency areas and 83–5
    political background 79–81
    problems of transition to 92–3
European Monetary Unit of Account 75
European Options Exchange 196, 197
European Payments Union 63, 73
European Union 39, 79, 82
    Capital Adequacy Directive 238–40
European Unit of Account (EUA) 73, 75
Exchange Rate Mechanism (ERM) 13, 40,
    85, 86, 110
    crisis (1992) 3
Exchange Stabilization Fund (ESF) 67
exponential moving average 129–30
Exxon 24, 25

F-loans 11
FECOM (Fonds Européen de Coopération
    Monétaire) 86
Federal Deposit Insurance Corporation 231
Federal (Fed) funds 4

Federal Open Market Committee (FOMC) 66
Federal Reserve 9–10, 21, 65–7, 205
    open market operations 7, 8–9
Federal Reserve Agreements **65**
Federal Reserve Bank 61, 63
    swap network 50, *51*
FIBOR 140
filter rule 128–9
filter trading rules 96
financial futures 7, 13
    contract 162–3
    dates of introduction of major contracts
        165
    foreign exchange 175–6
    FRAs and 177–9
    markets 163–9
    organization 169–72
    top contracts (1994) **166**
    trading volume 179
Financial Services Act (1986) (UK) 68
Finnish exchange rate crisis 39
fiscal policy 116–18
floating exchange rate 36
floating principal amount 190
floating rate certificate of deposit (FRCD)
    151
floating rate notes (FRNs) 14
floors 224–8
Fonds de Stabilization des Changes
    (Exchange Stabilization Fund) 70
foreign exchange exposure 44
foreign exchange intervention 47–52
    money supply and 52–6
foreign exchange market 27–33
    2-way price 31–2
    activity, April 1992 **29**
    exchange controls 28, 32
    definition 27
    growth in turnover **28**
    history 34–40
    influence on money-market flows 2–3
    size of world market 28
    workings 31
forward exchange contract 155
forward forward rates 143–5
forward rate agreements (FRAs) 7, 143,
    148–9
forward rates 123–4, 147–8
fractals 103–4
    dimension 104–6
FRACTINT 104
France 15–16
Franklin 234–5
Franklin National Bank 42
Full Employment Balanced Growth
    (Humphrey-Hawkins) Act (1978) 66, 68

funding ladders 231
funding mismatch 142
futures see financial futures

gamma risk 216, 217, 234
Garman–Kohlhagen currency options model
    209, 223–4
Gaulle, General de 35, 70
general arrangements to borrow (GAB) 60
gensaki 17
Germany
    money-markets 14–15, 48
    reunification 115
gilt repo facility 13
gilt-edged bonds 13, 75
Gilt-Edged Market Makers (GEMMs) 12, 13
Globex 168, 169
go-around 7
gold–dollar link 35
gold franc 72, 73
Government National Mortgage Association
    (GNMA) 6
green currencies 76–7
Greenspan, Alan 114
Group of Seven 38
Gulf War crisis 98

head and shoulders formation 125, *126*
hedge funds 40
hedging 136, 176–7
hedging costs 156–7
Henon attractor 100, *101*, 103
Herstatt Bank 42, 153, 232
    crisis 63
Hill Samuel 42, 233
HIRS 186
HKIBOR 140

IBM 107
IBM/World Bank swap 190–1
IMM 165, 169, 171, 173, 174–5, 197
interest, calculating 138–9
interest mismatch 142
interest rate swap market 7
interest rates, negative 150
International Bank for Reconstruction and
    Development *see* World Bank
International Banking Facilities (IBF) 18, 22,
    26, 37, 41, 47
International Commodities Clearing House
    (ICCH) 197
International Development Association 74
International Fund for Agricultural

Development 74
international liquidity 57–8
International Monetary Fund (IMF) 28, 34,
    36, 58–61
    Articles of Agreement 58
    Articles of Agreement, First Amendment
        73
    Balance of Payments Manual 118
    General Resources Account 60
    oil facility 60
    Special Drawing Rights (SDR) Account
        60–1
international securitisation 42–3
International Swap Dealers' Association 181,
    182, 246
intervention 28
Intra-European Payments Agreement (1948)
    63
Iran, freezing of assets 26
Iraq, freezing of assets 26
Italy, money-market 11

Japan
    key financial changes **17**
    money-market 16–18
    open market operations 11
Japan Offshore Market (JOM) 17–18, 22, 26,
    37, 41
Japanese government bonds (JGBs) 169
Johnson Matthey 231
Johnson, President 21–2
JP Morgan 236, 245
Jurgenson Report 56

kappa (vega, zeta or epsilon) risk 216,
    217–18
Kendall, Maurice 95
Keynes, J.M. 34, 116
KIBOR 140
King, Mervyn 114
Korean War 21
Kuwait, Iraqi invasion of 26, 39, 172

lambda risk 219
Lamfalussy, Alexandre 91
Latin Monetary Union 72, 73
lender of last resort 11, 12
less developed countries (LDC) debt crisis 36
Libya, freezing of assets 26, 27
Libyan Arab Foreign Bank (LAFB) 26–7
Libyan Arab Foreign Bank v *Bankers Trust*
    26
LICOM terms 222

LIFFE (London International Financial
    Futures Exchange) 16, 167, 166, 172,
    173, 196, 197
logistic equation 103
Lombard credits 15
Lome Convention 75
London Clearing House 197
London Derivatives Exchange 196
London interbank offered rate (LIBOR)
    139–40
London International Financial Futures
    Exchange (LIFFE) 16, 167, 166, 172,
    173, 196, 197
Louvre Accord 38

Maastricht Treaty 39, 90
    convergence and 91–2
Mandelbrot, Benoit 103, 106
Marché à Terme des Instruments Financiers
    (MATIF) 16, 168
marginal reserve requirements 10
mean-reverting effect 97
mean-variance optimization 133, 136–7
medium-term financial assistance (MTFA)
    90
medium-term forward forward rates 147–8
medium term note 6
Mexico
    copper swap 193
    crisis (1982) 40, 173
    devaluation 42–3
MIBOR 140
mismatch (gap) 142–3
momentum models 131–2
Monep 196
monetarism *see* monetary policy
monetary policy 109–11
    in action 111–14
    transmission of 114–16
money-market, definition 1–2
money-market rates, effects on
    of stock market issues 3
    seasonal effects 3
    foreign exchange markets 2–3
Monnet, Jean 80, 92
Moody's 6
Morgan Guaranty Trust Co. 78
moving average method 129
Mundell–Fleming model 95

Napoleon I 69
National Bank of Hungary 21
negative interest rates 150
Netherlands, The, money-market 11

NETtalk 106
netting systems 245–6
neural networks 106–7
New Economic Policy (1979) 109
New Zealand Shipping Corporation 25
NIBOR 140
Nikkei futures 171–2
Nippon Technical Analysts Association 126
Nixon, President 35
nonlinear model 98, 99
Nordic Investment Bank 74
normal distribution 212–13, **214**
North Korea, debt 42
Norway, money-market 11
NYBOR 140

OATs 20
offshore centres 40–1
oil crises 22
    1973–75 57
    1979–80 57
oil prices 37, 38, 39, 41
OPEC 36
OPEC dollar 22
open interest 179
open market operations 7–9
open outcry 169
optimum currency areas 83–5
options
    American vs European 221
    basics of contract 198–9
    carved-out 240
    combined positions 202–4
    currency 221–2
    exchange-traded 196
    on futures 197–8
    interest rate 7
    market 195–8
    measurement of risk and sensitivity
        216–20
    over-the-counter (OTC) 163, 195–6,
        196–7, 233–4
    pay-off diagrams 199–202, **199**, *200, 201,*
        202, 203
    pricing 186
    risk in 233
    role of 194–5
    straddle 203–4, **204**
    strangle **204**
    valuation 204–7
Options Clearing Corporation 197
Options-maklarna (OM) 196
Osaka Securities Exchange 171
oscillators 131–2
overnight deposit 140

Palestine, seizure of assets 26
passive management of foreign exchange risk 132–4
period deposit 140–1
phase diagrams 100
Philadelphia Stock Exchange 196, 197
PIBOR (Paris interbank offered rate) 16, 140, 168
Plaza Agreement 67, 98
Poincare gold franc 73
portfolio theory 134
    risk and return 135–6
position traders 169
present value, concept of 145–7
privatization issues, effect on money-market rates 3
purchase and resale agreements (PRAs) 10, 18
put–call parity 203

quantity theory 110
quoted currency 153

ratio momentum index 131
rational expectations 97–8
Reagan, President 26, 37, 67
real-time gross settlement 246
rediscount quotas 15
relative strength index (RSI) 130, 132
repurchase agreement 10, 11
repurchases (repos) 4, 7, 13
    aggregate size of US market 5
    use in Germany 10
reserve asset, choice of 57–8
Reserve Bank of Australia (RBA) 11, 18
Reserve Bank of New Zealand 11
reserve ratios 7
reserve tranch 59
Reuters screen 12, 20, 33, 75, 168
    swap screen 186
RGL Lieschling 235
rho risk 219
riding the yield curve 142
risk
    basis 229, 234–5
    black box 234
    of change in shape of the yield curve 229
    control 232–3
    control by the authorities 235–6
    counterparty 243–4
    credit 231–2
    definition 134
    diversification and risk reduction 245
    exchange 229
    forced sale 229, 233

general control 229
    interest 229
    interest rate position 240–3
    liquidity 230–1
    market 233–4
    name 230
    in the options market 233
    volatility 229, 234
RiskMetric(tm) approach 236–8, 245
Roosa bonds 67
round-trip trades 49

SACOR 73
Saitori 167, 171, 172
sale and repurchase agreements (SRAs) 11, 18
Salomon Brothers high grade Corporate Bond Index 134
SATURNE system 16
scalpers 169
scenario analysis 233
securities repurcase agreements (repos) 14
selling rates 153–4
settlement rate (SR) 149
Seven-day War 35
SFTE (Société Financière pour les Télécommunications et l'Electronique) 20
Sharpe, William 209
shell companies 41
short term, definition 2
short-term monetary support facility (STMS) 87, 90
SIBOR 140
SIMEX 173
Singapore 41
Smith, Adam 194
Smithsonian agreement 35
SNB 74
Soviet Union 21
Spain, money-market 11, 20
special drawing rights (SDRs) 35–6, 73–4
special purchase and resale agreements (SPRAs) 18
Spécialistes en Valeurs du Trésor 16
spot foreign exchange deal 152–3
spreaders 169
Standard & Poor 6
standard basket 73
standardized units 72–3
stochastic models 98
Stock Exchange money brokers (SEMB) 12
stock market crash 38
strange (chaotic) attractors 100–3
structural adjustment facility (SAF) 60
submarkets 4
Sveriges Riksbank 67

SWAP 186
swaps 157–60
    arrangements 64–5
    asset 2, 188
    calculating interest rates from 160–2
    commodity 192–3
    credit risk 191–2
    currency *183*, 189–90
    ECA 20
    finding, from interest rates 162
    foreign exchange 11, 48
    IBM/World Bank 190–1
    interest rate 7, 180, 181–2, *183*, 184–5
    market volume (1989–93) **181**
    maturity structure of interest (1991–93)
        182
    new interest rate (1991–93) *181*
    origins of market 180–3
    valuation and accounting 192
    what determines spread 186–8
Sweden, money-market 11
Swiss National Bank 18, 64, 72, 115
Switzerland
    gold francs 73
    impact of foreign currency inflows 52–3,
        115, 150
    international demand for Franc 3
    money-market 11, 18
    Swiss Franc liability and Sterling asset **45**
system repos 9
systemic transformation facility 60

tailing the hedge 177
taxes
    interest equalization 35
    interest withholding 47
    turnover (Germany) 14
TED spread trading 174
Telecommunication Convention (1932) 73
Telerate screen 20, 33, 75
Tequila effect 40, 42
term Feds 5
term repos 5
Thatcher, Mrs 110
theta risk 216, 218–19
Tienanmen Square 38
time value premium 205, 206
time zone problem 140
Tokyo Futures Exchange 166–7
Tokyo International Financial Futures
    Exchange (TIFFE) 167
tomorrow/next (tom/next) 140
trade policy 122
trade-weighted exchange weights (effective
    exchange rates), calculation of 77–8

trading book definition 239
tranches 58, 59
Treasury bill futures 174–5
Treasury bills 5, 6
Treaty of Rome 74
Treaty on European Union *see* Maastricht
    Treaty
trend line 124

underwritten note facilties 26
Union Bank of Switzerland 42
United California Bank 42
United Kingdom 12–13
    history of broad money targets 110
    impact of foreign exchange intervention
        52
    interest rates 13
units of account 72, 73
*Unverzinsliche-Schatzanweisungen (U-
    Schätze)* 14
US money-market 1–3
    balance of payments (1992–93) 119–20,
        120
US National Bank of San Diego 42
US primary dealers 4, **5**
US Regulation Q 35

value at risk 236–8
Value Line Fund 128
velocity 110
very short-term financing facility (VSTF) 86,
    87
Vietnam War 22, 35
volatility 207–8
Volcker, Paul 36, 66, 109, 112

Warburg, Siegmund 21
Wells Fargo 27
Wells Fargo Asia Ltd. v. *Citibank* 27
Westdeutsche Landesbank 42
when issued (wi) market 6
World Bank 58, 74, 180
    IBM/World Bank swap 190–1
World Foreign Exchange Reserves 29, *30*

yield curve 141–2, 147–8
Yom Kippur War 36
Young Plan 61

zero-coupon curves 147–8

Compiled by Annette Musker